DIETRICH BONHOEFFER WORKS, VOLUME 7

Fiction from Tegel Prison

This series is a translation of
DIETRICH BONHOEFFER WERKE
Edited by
Eberhard Bethge, Ernst Feil,
Christian Gremmels, Wolfgang Huber,
Hans Pfeifer, Albrecht Schönherr,
Heinz Eduard Tödt†, Ilse Tödt

This volume has been made possible through the generous support of the Aid Association for Lutherans, the Lilly Endowment, Inc., the Stiftung Bonhoeffer Lehrstuhl, the Bowen H. and Janice Arthur McCoy Charitable Foundation, the Trull Foundation, the Lusk-Damen Charitable Gift Fund, the New England Synod of the Evangelical Lutheran Church in America, and numerous members and friends of the International Bonhoeffer Society.

DIETRICH BONHOEFFER WORKS

General Editor
Wayne Whitson Floyd, Jr.

DIETRICH BONHOEFFER

Fiction from Tegel Prison

Translated from the German Edition
Edited by
RENATE BETHGE AND ILSE TÖDT

English Edition
Edited by
CLIFFORD J. GREEN

Translated by
NANCY LUKENS

FORTRESS PRESS   MINNEAPOLIS

DIETRICH BONHOEFFER WORKS, Volume 7

Originally published in German as *Dietrich Bonhoeffer Werke,* edited by Eberhard Bethge et al., by Chr. Kaiser Verlag in 1994; *Band* 7 edited by Renate Bethge and Ilse Tödt. First English-language edition of *Dietrich Bonhoeffer Works, Volume 7,* published by Fortress Press in 1999.

Fragmente aus Tegel: Drama und Roman first published in German by Christian Kaiser Verlag in 1978. Original English-language edition, titled *Fiction from Prison,* published in 1981 by Fortress Press. New English-language translation of *Fiction from Tegel Prison* with supplementary material first published in 2000 by Fortress Press as part of *Dietrich Bonhoeffer Works.*

Translation of this work was generously supported by the Inter Nationes Agency, Bonn.

Jacket design: Cheryl Watson
Cover photo: Dietrich Bonhoeffer. © Chr. Kaiser/Gütersloher Verlagshaus, Gütersloh.
Internal design: The HK Scriptorium, Inc.

The paper used in this publication meets the minimum requirements of American National Standard for Information Sciences—Permanence of Paper for Printed Library Materials, ANSI Z329.48-1984.

Manufactured in the U.S.A.   AF 1–8307

| 04 | 03 | 02 | 01 | 00 | 1 | 2 | 3 | 4 | 5 | 6 | 7 | 8 | 9 | 10 |

CONTENTS

General Editor's Foreword
to Dietrich Bonhoeffer Works

SINCE THE TIME that the writings of Dietrich Bonhoeffer (1906–45) first began to be available in English after World War II, they have been eagerly read both by scholars and by a wide general audience. The story of his life is compelling, set in the midst of historic events that shaped a century.

Bonhoeffer's leadership in the anti-Nazi Confessing Church and his participation in the *Abwehr* resistance circle make his works a unique source for understanding the interaction of religion, politics, and culture among those few Christians who actively opposed National Socialism. His writings provide not only an example of intellectual preparation for the reconstruction of German culture after the war but also a rare insight into the vanishing world of the old social and academic elites. Because of his participation in the resistance against the Nazi regime, Dietrich Bonhoeffer was hanged in the concentration camp at Flossenbürg on April 9, 1945.

Yet Bonhoeffer's enduring contribution is not just his moral example but his theology as well. As a student in Tübingen, Berlin, and at Union Theological Seminary in New York—where he also was associated for a time with the Abyssinian Baptist Church in Harlem—and as a participant in the European ecumenical movement, Bonhoeffer became known as one of the few figures of the 1930s with a comprehensive and nuanced grasp of both German- and English-language theology. His thought resonates with a prescience, subtlety, and maturity that continually belie the youth of the thinker.

In 1986 the Chr. Kaiser Verlag, now part of Gütersloher Verlagshaus, marked the eightieth anniversary of Bonhoeffer's birth by issuing the first of the sixteen volumes of the definitive German edition of his writings, the *Dietrich Bonhoeffer Werke (DBW)*. The final volume of this monumental critical edition appeared in Berlin in the spring of 1998.

Preliminary discussions about an English-language edition *(DBWE)* began even as the German series was beginning to emerge. As a consequence, the International Bonhoeffer Society, English Language Section, formed an editorial board, initially chaired by Robin Lovin, assisted by Mark Brocker, to undertake this project. Since 1993 the *Dietrich Bonhoeffer Works* translation project has been located in the Krauth Memorial Library of the Lutheran Theological Seminary at Philadelphia, under the leadership of its general editor and project director—Wayne Whitson Floyd, Jr., who directs the seminary's Dietrich Bonhoeffer Center—and its executive director—Clifford J. Green of Hartford Seminary.

The *Dietrich Bonhoeffer Works* provides the English-speaking world with an entirely new, complete, and unabridged translation of the written legacy of one of the twentieth century's most notable theologians. The success of this edition is based foremost upon the gifts and dedication of the translators producing this new edition, upon which all the other contributions of this series depend.

The *DBWE* includes a large amount of material appearing in English for the first time. Key terms are now translated consistently throughout the corpus, with special attention being paid to accepted English equivalents of technical theological and philosophical concepts.

This authoritative English edition strives, above all, to be true to the language, the style, and—most importantly—the theology of Bonhoeffer's writings. Translators have sought, nonetheless, to present Bonhoeffer's words in a manner that is sensitive to issues of gender in the language it employs. Consequently, accurate translation has removed sexist formulations that had been introduced inadvertently or unnecessarily into earlier English versions of his works. In addition, translators and editors generally have employed gender-inclusive language, insofar as this was possible without distorting Bonhoeffer's meaning or dissociating him from his own time.

At times Bonhoeffer's theology sounds fresh and modern, not because the translators have made it so, but because his language still speaks with a hardy contemporaneity even after more than half a century. In other instances, Bonhoeffer sounds more remote, a product of another era, not due to any lack of facility by the translators and editors, but because his concerns and rhetoric are in certain ways bound inextricably to a time that is past.

Volumes include introductions written by the editor(s) of each volume of the English edition, footnotes provided by Bonhoeffer, editorial notes added by the German and English editors, and afterwords composed by the editor(s) of the German edition. In addition, volumes provide tables of abbreviations used in the editorial apparatus, as well as bibliographies which list sources used by Bonhoeffer, literature consulted by the editors, and other works related to each particular volume. Finally, volumes contain pertinent chronologies, charts, appendices, and indexes of scriptural references, names, and subjects.

The layout of the English edition has retained Bonhoeffer's manner of dividing works into chapters and sections, as well as his original paragraphing (exceptions are noted by a ¶-symbol to indicate any paragraph break added by the editors of the English edition or by conventions explained in the introductions written by the editor[s] of specific volumes). The pagination of the *DBW* German critical edition is indicated in the outer margins of the pages of the translated text. At times, for the sake of precision and clarity of translation, a word or phrase that has been translated is provided in its original language, set within square brackets at the appropriate point in the text. Biblical citations come from the New Revised Standard Version (NRSV), unless otherwise noted. Where versification of the Bible used by Bonhoeffer differs from the NRSV, the verse number in the latter is noted in the text in square brackets.

Bonhoeffer's own footnotes, which are indicated in the body of the text by plain, superscripted numbers, are reproduced in precisely the same numerical sequence as they appear in the German critical edition, complete with his idiosyncrasies of documentation. In these, as in the accompanying editorial notes, existing English translations of books and articles have been substituted for their counterparts in other languages whenever available. The edition of a work that was consulted by Bonhoeffer himself can be ascertained by consulting the bibliography at the end of each volume. When a work in the bibliography has no published English translation, an English equivalent of its title is provided there in parentheses; if a non-English work appears only within a footnote or editorial note, an English equivalent of its title appears at that point in the note.

The editorial notes, which are indicated in the body of the text by superscripted numbers in square brackets—except *DBWE* volume five where they are indicated by plain, superscripted numbers—provide information on the intellectual, ecclesiastical, social, and political context of Bonhoeffer's pursuits during the first half of the twentieth century. These are based on the scholarship of the German critical edition; they have been supplemented by the contributions of the editors and translators of the English edition. Where the editors or translators of the English edition have substantially augmented or revised a German editor's note, the initials of the person making the change(s) appear at the note's conclusion, and editorial material that has been added in the English edition is surrounded by square brackets. When any previously translated material is quoted within an editorial note in altered form—indicated by the notation [trans. altered]—such changes should be assumed to be the responsibility of the translator(s).

Bibliographies at the end of each volume provide the complete information for each written source that Bonhoeffer or the various editors have mentioned in the current volume. References to the archives, collections, and personal library of materials that had belonged to Bonhoeffer and that survived the war—as cataloged in the *Nachlaß Dietrich Bonhoeffer* and collected in the Staatsbibliothek in Berlin—are indicated within the *Dietrich Bonhoeffer Works* by the abbreviation *NL* followed by the corresponding reference code within that published index.

The production of any individual volume of the *Dietrich Bonhoeffer Works* requires the financial assistance of numerous individuals and organizations, whose support is duly noted on the verso of the half-title page. In addition, the editor's introduction of each volume acknowledges those persons who have assisted in a particular way with the production of the English edition of that text. A special note of gratitude, however, is owed to all those prior translators, editors, and publishers of various portions of Bonhoeffer's literary legacy who heretofore have made available to the English-speaking world the writings of this remarkable theologian.

The English edition depends especially upon the careful scholarship of all those who labored to produce the critical German edition, completed in April 1998, from which these translations have been made. Their work has been overseen by a board of general editors—responsible for both the concept and the content of the German edition—composed of Eberhard Bethge, Ernst Feil, Christian Gremmels, Wolfgang Huber (chair), Hans Pfeifer (ongoing liaison between the German and English editorial boards), Albrecht Schönherr, Heinz Eduard Tödt†, and Ilse Tödt.

The present English edition would be impossible without the creativity and unflagging dedication of the members of the editorial board of the Dietrich Bonhoeffer Works: Victoria Barnett, Mark Brocker, James H. Burtness, Keith W. Clements, Wayne Whitson Floyd, Barbara Green, Clifford J. Green, John W. de Gruchy, Barry A. Harvey, James Patrick Kelley, Geffrey B. Kelly, Reinhard Krauss, Robin W. Lovin, Michael Lukens, Nancy Lukens, Paul Matheny, Mary Nebelsick, and H. Martin Rumscheidt.

The deepest thanks for their support of this undertaking is owed, as well, to all the various members, friends, and benefactors of the International Bonhoeffer Society; to the National Endowment for the Humanities, which supported this project during its inception; to the Lutheran Theological Seminary at Philadelphia and its former Auxiliary who established and still help to support the Dietrich Bonhoeffer Center on its campus, specifically for the purpose of facilitating these publications; and to our publisher, Fortress Press, as represented with uncommon patience and *Gemütlichkeit* by Henry French, Michael West, Rachel Riensche, Joe Bonyata, and Ann Delgehausen. A special word of appreciation is due to Pam McClanahan and Debbie Brandt, whose tenures at Fortress Press ended in 1998 and 1999, respectively. The privilege of collaboration with professionals such as these is fitting testimony to the spirit of Dietrich Bonhoeffer, who was himself always so attentive to the creative mystery of community—and that ever deepening collegiality that is engendered by our social nature as human beings.

Wayne Whitson Floyd, Jr., General Editor and Project Director
January 27, 1995
The Fiftieth Anniversary of the Liberation of Auschwitz
Third revision on August 28, 1999
The Ninetieth Birthday of Eberhard Bethge

ABBREVIATIONS

CD	*The Cost of Discipleship* (Simon & Schuster, 1995 edition)
CF (*DBWE* 3)	*Creation and Fall* (*DBWE*, English edition)
DB-ER	*Dietrich Bonhoeffer: A Biography* (Fortress Press, 1999 revised edition)
DBLP	*Dietrich Bonhoeffer: A Life in Pictures*
DBW	*Dietrich Bonhoeffer Werke*, German edition
DBWE	*Dietrich Bonhoeffer Works*, English edition
E	*Ethics* (Simon & Schuster, 1995 edition)
GS	*Gesammelte Schriften* (Collected works)
LL	*Love Letters from Cell 92*
LPP	*Letters and Papers from Prison* (The Enlarged Edition, Macmillan, 1972; Simon & Schuster, 1997)
NL	*Nachlaß Dietrich Bonhoeffer*
NRSV	New Revised Standard Version
SC (*DBWE* 1)	*Sanctorum Communio* (*DBWE*, English edition)
ZE	*Zettelnotizen für eine "Ethik"*

C L I F F O R D   J .   G R E E N

EDITOR'S INTRODUCTION TO THE ENGLISH EDITION

AFTER TWO AND A HALF YEARS working for the resistance movement to overthrow the Hitler regime, and writing his *Ethics* at the same time, Dietrich Bonhoeffer was arrested on April 5, 1943. While the Nazi investigators pored over the part of the *Ethics* manuscript they had confiscated from his desk, Bonhoeffer endured his first cold and uncomfortable night in the Tegel military interrogation prison, Berlin. There he was to spend the next eighteen months until he was moved to the Gestapo prison on Prinz-Albrecht-Strasse in October, 1944. Four months later he was moved south from Berlin, first to Buchenwald, and eventually to Flossenbürg, where he was executed on April 9, 1945.

Dietrich Bonhoeffer was a writer—the sixteen volumes of his collected writings, a notable output for one who died before reaching forty, testify to that. In prison, when he was not working at misleading his interrogators, he spent his time reading and writing. These writings covered a wide range of forms and served a number of purposes. Letters, both official letters that passed under the eyes of the censor and others that were smuggled out by a friendly guard, make up a large part of his prison writing. Some were written to the interrogator, Dr. Roeder, to strengthen the case Bonhoeffer was making while under questioning. Many letters were written to his parents, and a great number were written to his friend Eberhard Bethge, later his biographer and literary executor. It was these letters, published as *Letters and Papers from Prison,* and especially the theological discussion in them about a "nonreligious Christianity," that initially caused intense interest in Bonhoeffer's

1

theology in the 1960s.[1] Often taken out of context and frequently mis-understood, these theological letters can now be read in relation to Bon-hoeffer's whole corpus and theological development. In the present volume there are many editorial notes which show how the fiction illu-minates the prison letters and how the latter illuminate the fiction.

So engaged was Bonhoeffer with the theological issues that revolved around his phrases the "coming of age of humanity," the "decay of reli-gion," and "nonreligious interpretation of biblical and theological con-cepts" that he set to work on a new book. This book was to develop these ideas in three chapters beginning with "A Stocktaking of Chris-tianity," followed by "The Real Meaning of Christianity," and conclud-ing with implications for the church and Christian life. A considerable amount of the book was written, but unfortunately did not survive; a detailed outline remains.[2]

There are at least two major ways in which this new book project in prison connects to the present volume. First, there are connections between the ideas of "unconscious Christianity" in the prison fiction and "nonreligious Christianity" in *Letters and Papers from Prison,* even though the two ideas are not identical. Second, Bonhoeffer's theologi-cal reflection on these subjects was primarily stimulated by his experi-ence of the people he worked with in the resistance movement, not least his own brother Klaus and his brothers-in-law Hans von Dohnanyi and Rüdiger Schleicher. These were the sort of people he had in mind when he wrote the section in his *Ethics* on "Christ and Good People," a pas-sage that reveals that the resistance movement was the *Sitz im Leben* of his theological reflections in Tegel prison.[3] They were also the people he had in mind when he wrote of "religionless people" in a "world come of age."

Other prison writings include essays and reports. It is not surprising that a prisoner would write on "The Feeling of Time." It "originated mainly in the need to bring before me my own past in a situation that could so easily seem 'empty' and 'wasted'," he explained to Eberhard

---

[1.] These letters have been published in several editions. A new translation is in prepa-ration for the *Dietrich Bonhoeffer Works,* English edition. For now, see *LPP,* especially the theological letters beginning April 30, 1944.

[2.] *LPP* 380–83.

[3.] See *E* 61–65; this subheading does not appear in *DBW* 6.

Bethge.[4] Unfortunately this essay is lost, but notes for it and references to it survive.[5] Nor is it in the least surprising that a theologian and ethicist, vigorously defending his resistance colleagues and their plans for a coup d'état by deceiving his interrogators, should work on an incomplete essay entitled "What Is Meant by 'Telling the Truth'?"[6] Two reports from Bonhoeffer's hand were designed to improve prison conditions. One was a report with recommendations based on experiences during an air raid, and the other was a report on conditions of prison life.[7]

Bonhoeffer was also a pastor in prison. He wrote a wedding sermon for Eberhard and Renate Bethge and the baptismal sermon for their son.[8] At Christmas 1943 he wrote three sets of prayers—for morning, for evening, and in times of distress—for fellow prisoners.[9] Apparently in response to a request, he wrote a brief commentary on the first three commandments of the Decalogue.[10] He also wrote a couple of meditations on the Moravian Bible readings, which were part of his daily spiritual discipline.[11]

Important among his prison writings is a group of poems, the first that he had written. They reflect intense emotion about his friends, his fiancée, his family, and his prison experience. They also express his feelings about himself and the prospect of his own death. Several of them are quite explicitly theological, particularly "Christians and Pagans" and "Stations on the Way to Freedom."[12] The first poem, written in early summer 1944, is called "The Past." Commenting on this poem he says, "This dialogue with the past, the attempt to hold on to it and recover it,

---

[4.] *LPP* 129.

[5.] See the notes, *LPP* 33–36, and other letter references, *LPP* 39, 50, and 54.

[6.] Until now this has been published as the concluding section of previous English editions of the *Ethics* (*E* 358–67), called an appendix in the German editions and quite misleadingly "Part Two" in the English editions; the *Dietrich Bonhoeffer Werke*, however, now places it in the companion volume to the prison letters, *DBW* 16 (619–29).

[7.] The first, on *LPP* 251f., appears as part of the longer report on *LPP* 248–52.

[8.] *LPP* 41–47, 294–300.

[9.] *LPP* 139–43.

[10.] See "The First Table of the Ten Commandments" in Godsey, *Preface to Bonhoeffer*, 50–67. It was written in the summer of 1944, as seen from the letters to Bethge of June 27 (*LPP* 336) and August 3 of that year (*DBW* 16:556; this part of the letter is lacking in *LPP* 379).

[11.] See *DBW* 16:651–58.

[12.] *LPP* 348f., 370f.

and above all, the fear of losing it, is the almost daily accompaniment of my life here."[13]

Before he began to write poems, however, Bonhoeffer had already tried another form of writing to help him stay rooted in his past. In his first year in prison he had ventured into another new genre, namely fiction, in the form of the incomplete drama and novel and the short story presented below.[14] If prison experience is central to Bonhoeffer's short story about Lance Corporal Berg, the framework for the drama and the setting of the novel is clearly Bonhoeffer's family. After a few weeks in prison he wrote to his parents: "I feel myself so much a part of you all that I know that we live and bear everything in common, acting and thinking for one another, even though we have to be separated."[15] This was not just nostalgia and homesickness. Bonhoeffer's family embodied for him a tradition and culture of standards, ethics, and ways of behaving that extended from household life to public responsibility. It was a conscious part of who he was, and he expressed it often in letters. To his parents he wrote of the confidence and security that came from "the consciousness of being borne up by a spiritual tradition that goes back for centuries," and said, "It's not till such times as these that we realize what it means to possess a past and a spiritual inheritance independent of changes in time and circumstances."[16]

A fuller picture of the characters, attitudes, events, and families in the background of the prison fiction depends upon another very important group of letters that belong to the Tegel writing. These have been published only recently. Shortly before his arrest, on January 17, 1943,

---

[13.] See *LPP* 319–23, beginning with the letter to Bethge dated June 5, 1944, in which he talks about beginning to write poetry.

[14.] Beginning at Christmas 1943, he also wrote what he called "another little work . . . about the meeting of two old friends after they had been separated for a long time during the war." It surely drew heavily on the friendship between himself and Eberhard Bethge, notwithstanding his promise to Bethge in a January 1944 letter that "it will *not* be a *roman à clef*" (*LPP* 199f.; cf. 178). The piece did not survive, but some brief notes for it are included below, page 236, "Fragment of a Story."

[15.] *LPP* 40.

[16.] *LPP* 165. In the same vein he wrote to his godson: "The urban middle-class culture embodied in the home of your mother's parents [i.e., Bonhoeffer's family home] has led to pride in public service, intellectual achievement and leadership, and a deep-rooted sense of duty toward a great heritage and cultural tradition. This will give you, even before you are aware of it, a way of thinking and acting which you can never lose without being untrue to yourself" (*LPP* 294f.).

Bonhoeffer had become engaged to Maria von Wedemeyer, a vivacious and intelligent young woman from an aristocratic, landed family in Pomerania whom he had met through her family's support of his theological seminary at Finkenwalde. Fifty years passed before these letters were made public.[17] Their publication documents what previously one could only infer, that a great deal of Bonhoeffer's thought, memory, feeling, concern, and writing focused on his young fiancée and the hopes and frustrations of their engagement under these exceptionally trying conditions. This situation and the letters to his fiancée are directly relevant to the present book. One of the two central families in the novel, the von Bremers, is based on the family of Maria von Wedemeyer, and their country estate is modeled on her family's home at Pätzig.

Bonhoeffer began his fiction with the drama, probably in July 1943, toward the end of the first stage of his imprisonment and its intensive interrogations. In mid-August he wrote to his parents:

> Some weeks ago I sketched the outlines of a play, but meanwhile I've realized that the material is not suitable for drama; and so I shall now try to rewrite it as a story. It's about the life of a family, and of course there's a good deal of autobiography mixed up in it.[18]

The theme of death is prominent in the drama, but not in the novel, and it appears that Bonhoeffer may have reconceived the theme of his fiction as well as its form.

The concept of the novel was clearly stated to Eberhard Bethge that November:

> Then I started on a bold enterprise that I've had in mind for a long time: I began to write the story of a contemporary middle-class family. The background for this consisted of all our innumerable conversations on the subject, and my own personal experiences; in short, it was to present afresh middle-class life as we know it in our families, and especially in the light of Christianity. It tells of two families on terms of friendship living in a small town. Their children grow up and, as they gradually enter into the responsibilities of official positions, they try to work together for the good of the community as mayor, teacher, pastor, doctor, engineer. You would

---

[17.] See *LL*, published in its German original in 1992 and translated into English in 1995.

[18.] *LPP* 94.

recognize many familiar features, and you come into it too. But I haven't yet got much further than the beginning. . . .[19]

Whereas the drama begins with Christoph—the character who most represents Bonhoeffer himself—as an adult, the novel begins with Christoph and his siblings as adolescents; likewise Renate—who resembles Bonhoeffer's fiancée—is a younger girl in the novel. What we have is only the opening chapter of a longer work of larger scope than the drama. The chapter carries Bonhoeffer's title "Sunday," and one can imagine it was completed by the ringing of the bells at the end of the day, which is where the manuscript ends. If so, the next chapter would have dealt with the meeting of the families of the two men whose dramatic schoolboy story Major von Bremer tells in the extant text. Because of the length of this opening chapter the editors have subdivided it into eight sections using phrases and themes from Bonhoeffer's text; Bonhoeffer himself did not indicate divisions for the chapter.

Bonhoeffer remarked about the obvious autobiographical features of his fiction and mentioned to his friend Eberhard Bethge that he appeared in these writings too. Indeed, the German literary historian Walther Killy wished that Bonhoeffer had written direct autobiography rather than veiling it in fiction.[20] But the choice to veil is itself typical of Bonhoeffer, who intentionally avoided self-promotion and rather practiced "reserve"; this is highlighted in a section on that subject below in the German editor's afterword.[21]

The correspondence between characters in the drama and the novel and people in Bonhoeffer's circle is striking. Readers nevertheless should be warned about jumping to simplistic conclusions. When introducing the first full publication of the drama and novel, the Bethges warned that "one should be cautious about making too simple and too direct identifications with people from his family and associates." Their reading of characters bears quoting at length.

> In every character in the two fragments quite often very different people are combined. Father and Mother of the drama and novel clearly correspond to Bonhoeffer's own parents. But the grandmother too has features

---

[19.] *LPP* 129f.

[20.] See the lengthy excerpt from Killy's report on the fiction manuscripts, which is quoted by Renate and Eberhard Bethge in their introduction to the previous English translation, *Fiction from Prison*, 3f.

[21.] See below, pages 202–205.

of his mother (plus those of his own grandmother and the grandmother of his fiancée), and the major, father of the girl in the novel whom Christoph loves, utters Bonhoeffer's own father's words.

In Franz, the oldest brother in the novel, one recognizes Bonhoeffer's oldest brother Karl-Friedrich, who returned from World War I at the age of nineteen with socialist and anti-militarist views (junking, for example, the badge that had been awarded him as a wounded soldier when he learned it had also been awarded to an officer for falling under his horse while drunk). Karl-Friedrich was the first to read Feuerbach and Zola and to discuss them with the family. But, at the same time, Franz in the novel also bears features of Dietrich's brother Klaus, who reacted passionately and often found himself in opposition to others. Distinct traces of Klaus, who despite his basically artistic temperament tended to be conservative, are also found, however, in Christoph of the Tegel fragments. But Christoph represents, above all, Dietrich Bonhoeffer himself. Conversations like those given by Bonhoeffer here in the fragments took place in the family and also, of course, with friends like Eberhard Bethge—here embodied in the figure of Ulrich—and earlier friends such as Justus Delbrück and Franz Hildebrandt. The character of Klara in the novel can be recognized, despite some differences, as Bonhoeffer's sister Ursula. Bonhoeffer himself also appears in the younger brothers Martin and Little Brother, as well as in the main character Christoph. The threads are so manifold that it is only possible with difficulty to point out the traces of all the people who are visible in Bonhoeffer's two compositions.[22]

A second warning should be added about interpreting the views expressed in the speeches of the characters. One should not simply identify the opinions of a character with their author. As Bonhoeffer in the *Ethics* could pose an issue by setting conflicting positions against each other, such as radicalism and compromise, so here with the views of different characters. Likewise it should be noted when a character's opinions are contradicted by others.

How should a reader approach the interpretation of this text? What does one want to learn about and from the author of this fiction? Eberhard Bethge's first publication of selections from the drama and novel approached them from the perspective of theology, broadly construed. They were published in conjunction with a draft chapter from the *Ethics* under the heading "work on the ethics."[23] More recently, the

---

[22.] *Fiction from Prison*, 5f.

[23.] *GS* 3:478–512. See also the introduction to *Fiction from Prison*, 1, where Renate and Eberhard Bethge underline this point.

German editors report a similar orientation from the Germanist Christoph Perels. When asked to comment about the upcoming critical edition of the fiction, he replied: "It is not the literary qualities that warrant critical attention, but the subject matter the fragments serve to articulate. And that is questions of politics and theology." He continued: "The warm light his [Bonhoeffer's] memory shed on his own experience was not able to calm the theological restlessness of this spirit."[24] This is hardly an unexpected judgment. What is surprising is not that a theologian's fiction should be theological, but rather that a theologian was writing fiction in the first place.

The theological character of the fiction, however, has not been much highlighted. Before the drama and novel were first printed in full, the publisher regarded them as "alien elements in the program of a theological publishing house."[25] And when they were published their editors asked, "What did these nostalgic meditations on family history have to do with the theology of *The Cost of Discipleship* and *Letters and Papers from Prison?*" To be sure, the editors did note a new relation between theology and the social sciences and history, but family was emphasized, not theology. Ruth Zerner's commentary, published in both the German and English editions, rightly observes that "Bonhoeffer's novel never loses sight of the pressing political and theological issues of community life, pacifist ideals, reconciliation, and sacrificial death."[26] But her emphasis is on a theory of regression in the service of creativity—that is, it points to the theology of the 1944 letters—not to the way the novel itself is deeply theological.

The editor's afterword of the present edition also puts the emphasis heavily on family and autobiography. Although the German edition lists the two editors as authors, their foreword indicates that it is primarily the work of Renate Bethge.[27] As the daughter of Bonhoeffer's sister Ursula, she is highly qualified to interpret the prison fiction from her experience as a member of the extended family. Themes addressed in the afterword of this volume have been the subject of her addresses and

---

[24.] Letter to Heinz Eduard Tödt, February 3, 1990, quoted in *DBW* 7:16, note 43.

[25.] *Fiction from Prison,* 1.

[26.] *Fiction from Prison,* 152.

[27.] In a communication to the editor of the English edition, Ilse Tödt indicated that Renate Bethge's name alone should stand above the afterword.

publications for many years.[28] Indeed, the afterword is probably the most comprehensive of her interpretations of Bonhoeffer from the family perspective. But it is not a theological interpretation. To be sure, it touches on some overtly theological themes, particularly in the concluding sections "Christianity" and "Death and Resurrection." But this still leaves unanswered the question of what Bonhoeffer's theology has to do with other themes mentioned—power, tyranny, authority, responsibility. Is the voice of Bonhoeffer the theologian to be heard in this fiction?

If the familial-autobiographical dimension of the prison fiction has been rightly but one-sidedly highlighted in recent decades, the *theological* dimension must now be brought to the fore. Bonhoeffer stated that his aim was to write a narrative of the life of middle-class families and citizens from the perspective of Christian faith. Each dimension—family and theology—must be highlighted.

One obvious place to begin an exploration of the theology in the fiction is the major's story in the novel about the rivalry of two schoolboys who were leading figures in the same class. That this is an autobiographical story[29] that in large part tells a story from Bonhoeffer's own youth does not make its content any less theological. After telling the story the major, in a patently didactic move by the author, then proceeds to interpret it to his audience. "It was," he said, "a pure power struggle."[30] Power, to be sure, is a pivotal theme in Bonhoeffer's theology.[31] He dealt with it in his theological works and in his biblical exegesis, and he had also written an autobiographical memoir about it—set in the same school context—a decade before.[32] Indeed, if the guilty conscience was the focus of Martin Luther's struggle for Christian faith, for the modern man, Dietrich Bonhoeffer, that struggle focused on power. Faith involves a liberation of the self from itself, from the demand of the ego to be the center of the world (occupying the place of God), and from its desire to dominate others. Bonhoeffer's paradigmatic phrase

---

[28.] See, for example: "'Elite' and 'Silence' in Bonhoeffer's Person and Thoughts" (1981); "Bonhoeffer's Family and Its Significance for His Theology" (1989); "Bonhoeffer's Picture of Women" (1991); and "Bonhoeffer and the Role of Women" (1995).

[29.] See below, page 151, editorial note 29.

[30.] See below, page 159.

[31.] See Green, *Bonhoeffer: A Theology of Sociality*, especially chapter 4, where this subject is treated at length.

[32.] See *DB-ER* 40ff.

for Christ and the Christian life was "existing for others." The self that is freed from itself in being freed for God is simultaneously freed for the neighbor.

The theological and spiritual concern with power had two main dimensions for Bonhoeffer. It was personal, having to do with the self in relation to others. And it was equally public and political, as seen in Bonhoeffer's commitment to social justice and peace. Both of these are found in the major's discourse. He speaks of the illusion of those who dream of being the center of the world, indulging their fantasy of the "little ego's world dominion."[33] The center for Bonhoeffer is the place of Christ, who occupies the center in the dialectical mode of giving it up.[34] Freed from the tyranny of self, people are freed to live with and for each other. The major states that what the two schoolboys learned from their rivalry and the problems it caused the class was that they were not demigods, but "human beings who must live depending on, and related to, each other, cooperating with each other side by side."[35] This is not just a happy ending to a story—rather it is almost an exact quotation of what Bonhoeffer had written in one of his early theological books.[36] It is a brief, narrative summary of his theology of community. One of the key constructs in Bonhoeffer's understanding of relations between persons is that their wills constitute "limits" for each other, and that it is precisely in responding to the resistance of another's will that one's own ethical identity and personality is constituted.

In relation to Bonhoeffer's public and political concern with power, the major argues that nations, in the same way as individuals, can act as tyrants, dominating the world.[37] Here Bonhoeffer's critique of

---

[33.] See below, page 106, and several of Bonhoeffer's books cited in editorial note 39. See also below, page 160.

[34.] In his 1933 "Christologie" lectures Bonhoeffer interpreted Christ as the center (*die Mitte*) of human existence, history, and nature. Hence the American edition of these lectures was appropriately titled *Christ the Center*. The same metaphor is found in *Life Together* and in *The Cost of Discipleship* where Christ is the mediator (*Mittler*) of all human relationships in the Christian community.

[35.] See below, page 167.

[36.] See below, page 167, editorial note 10, and page 168, editorial note 116: "The decisive thing was not what we both lost, namely our claim to live alone in the world as demigods, but what we gained, namely a humane life in community with another human being."

[37.] See below, page 169: "The same thing holds true for nations, as well, and fundamentally for all historical movements."

National Socialism flows directly from his theological critique of dominating power. In his 1933 address on "the Führer principle"[38] Bonhoeffer made a sharp distinction between *leadership* that served an office—such as teacher, parent, statesman[39]—and the *leader* (*Führer*) who made the office serve himself and thus became the vehicle for collective egotism—another name for idolatry—and all its destructive consequences. While abuse of power sank to the depth of genocide in Nazi Germany, it was not an invention of National Socialism. The character Yellowboots represents a more universal type of person who gets a little bit of power and exercises it in a self-aggrandizing and oppressive way.

The deepest theological roots of his critique of dominating and destructive power, whether personal or political, lie in Bonhoeffer's Lutheran theology of incarnation and the *theologia crucis*. Central to his *Ethics*,[40] this theology can be traced even earlier to his Christology lectures with their emphasis on the self-giving of Christ,[41] and before that to his two dissertations. In these works Bonhoeffer presents a dialectical understanding of the power of God. In his first book it is summed up in the aphorism, "God rules by serving."[42] This reveals that the critique of worldly power is not a doctrine of divine impotence but is rooted in a radical paradigm of giving rather than dominating, of grace rather than exploitation. In the second dissertation, which qualified Bonhoeffer as a university lecturer, the same idea is developed in terms of God's freedom for humanity revealed in Christ. "The freedom of God . . . finds its strongest evidence precisely in that God freely chose to be bound to historical human beings and to be placed at the disposal of human beings. God is free not from human beings, but for them."[43] This theological paradigm needs to be remembered while interpreting the different opinions of Bonhoeffer's fictional characters when they speak of subjects like authority, leadership, and a "new elite."

[38.] See "The Leader and the Individual in the Younger Generation," in Bonhoeffer, *No Rusty Swords*, 190–204, esp. 195ff. The whole address is pertinent to Bonhoeffer's treatment of power in the prison fiction.

[39.] Bonhoeffer understood "offices" like these as a call to responsibility and to the service of those they were directed to: parents to children, teachers to students, and so on. In this 1933 address, he uses the identical language of "above" and "below," *von oben nach unten* (*DBW* 12:251), as in the *Ethics* and fiction a decade later.

[40.] Cf. *E* 73ff., 82f., 130f., and 291f.

[41.] Cf. *Christ the Center*, 46ff.

[42.] *SC* (*DBWE* 1): 177.

[43.] *AB* (*DBWE* 2): 90f.

This christological paradigm of divine self-giving and freedom leads, in turn, to Bonhoeffer's exposition of freedom as *freedom for* the other. An exemplary statement of this is found in his lectures on the creation stories of Genesis. There, freedom is defined not as an ability, capacity, or attribute that a person can possess as an isolated individual, but as a *relation* between persons. "In the language of the Bible freedom is not something that people have for themselves but something they have for others. . . . Being free means 'being-free-for-the-other', because I am bound to the other. Only by being in relation with the other am I free."[44] This understanding of freedom continues right to the end of Bonhoeffer's theological writing. Its most concentrated statement is found in the theological prison letters in the phrase Jesus, "the one for others," and the description of the Christian life as "existing for others."[45] This is the understanding of freedom, human relationships, and human community and politics that informs the major's statements about people and nations living together.

This analysis, taking the major's discussion of power as a starting point, discloses the deep theological structure of the fictional narrative and dialogue. If Bonhoeffer's prison fiction is not a high literary achievement, it is certainly theology in a narrative form. Other aspects of the fiction could be explored to disclose their theological foundations. But this exposition demonstrates that theological analysis is one of the essential tools for a full understanding of Bonhoeffer's prison fiction.

The Composition of the Manuscript of the Prison Fiction

The German text translated here derives from Bonhoeffer's handwritten manuscripts of the incomplete drama and novel, and of the story, all of which have survived. These are listed in the catalog of Bonhoeffer's papers, *Nachlaß Dietrich Bonhoeffer* (*NL*). Also listed there are the extant working notes that Bonhoeffer used for the drama and those for a second short story that he nearly completed, but that has been lost.[46] The

---

[44.] *CF* (*DBWE* 3):62f.

[45.] See, for example, *LPP* 381f. [trans. altered].

[46.] See the items cataloged *NL* A 70, 3; *NL* A 70, 4(1); and *NL* A 70, 5. The extant "Drama Working Notes" are also cataloged (see *NL* A 70, 4(2); *NL* A 86, 7; *NL* A 86, 8; *NL* A 86, 10; and *NL* A 86, 11) and are included below in the appendix, pages 237–44. Note

working notes for the drama and the lost short story are printed in the appendix. However, we have no working notes for the novel or the story published in this book.[47]

The original manuscripts were re-deciphered by Ilse Tödt and the resulting transcript checked against the previously published version. Errors or omissions in the earlier transcription were corrected; words that had been omitted in error in the manuscript by Bonhoeffer were inserted in square brackets. The German edition introduces some consistencies of form that differ slightly from the manuscripts. For example, the editors observe at the beginning of the drama that Bonhoeffer at first did not underline the names of the characters, but later did it regularly. They also point out that in the manuscript direct speech, as in the novel, often does not begin with a capital letter. These usages have been made consistent with English style without noting where changes occur. Normally, the *DBWE* follows the paragraphing of Bonhoeffer's original texts or clearly marks any paragraph breaks that have been introduced by the English edition editors. Because of the unique qualities of these manuscripts as fictional writing—and in order not to repeatedly interrupt the flow of the narrative—it was decided in consultation with the German editorial board that the present volume should conform to normal English usage for these genres of writing, and that paragraph breaks that have been added in order to accomplish this would not be marked in this volume. However, editorial notes indicate line breaks in the original by inserting short, vertical lines.

When writing for himself, Bonhoeffer used German script; when writing for others, he used Latin script. The drama, novel, and story were all written in ink, the drama manuscript being forty-six pages long (three of them blank), and the novel one hundred nineteen pages long (six of them blank). The original manuscript of the story is eleven pages long, heavily corrected; consequently Bonhoeffer began to make a fair copy of it in Latin script. He got about halfway through, the fair-copy manuscript being six pages long. The German editors used the fair

---

that *NL* A 86, 6, which the catalog queries as a possible note for the drama, is not so regarded by the German editors of *DBW* 7, while *NL* A 86, 7, which the catalog does not connect to the drama, is included by them in the "Drama Working Notes." *NL* A 86, 12, which the catalog queries as a possible note for the novel, is identified by the editors of *DBW* 7 as a "Fragment of a Story"—not the "Story" of *DBW* 7, but the other short story Bonhoeffer mentioned about the reunion of two friends [see below, page 236].

[47.] For the former see *LPP* 33–35, 331–32, 343, 379–80; for the latter see *ZE*.

copy as far as it went; when working on the second half of the story they followed the first draft, taking note of all the corrections Bonhoeffer had made on the manuscript.

The first piece to be written, in German script, was the drama. The beginning of this manuscript was revised in pencil, and editorial notes refer to this by the words "pencil deletion" or "marginal note in pencil."

In their editorial notes the German editors indicate Bonhoeffer's revisions to his manuscript. The most common revisions are indicated by the word "replaces" to indicate that a word or phrase has been superseded by another, and the word "deleted" to indicate those that have simply been removed. Other notations indicate alterations, additions, and insertions. In the first half of the short story, references are given to the first draft that Bonhoeffer corrected and rewrote in a fair copy. Occasionally Bonhoeffer wrote preliminary drafts of very important material, for example, the speech of Christoph in the drama about protecting great words from abuse; in such cases the editors give the content or information about the draft in the appendix and editorial notes.[48] Bonhoeffer's marginal notes to himself are also indicated.

Quite often the German editors give information about the sizes of paper Bonhoeffer used (and other physical information about the color, porosity, watermark, and so on); this is expressed in the terms of the German Bureau of Standards, the Deutsches Institut für Normung (DIN). This information has been used to trace the process of writing and to correlate the fiction to other letters and notes that Bonhoeffer wrote in prison. It also connects to similar information in the *Nachlaß*, the catalog of the Bonhoeffer manuscripts.

Publication and Reception of the Prison Fiction

Publication came sporadically. For years Bonhoeffer's prison fiction was published in German in a piecemeal fashion.[49] In Germany the earliest publication, in 1948, was the first part of Scene 3 of the drama; it was titled "Der Nachbar," and was introduced with a passage from the *Ethics* manuscripts, which Eberhard Bethge was about to publish.[50]

[48.] See pages 238f. and 240f.

[49.] Information about the German publishing history is from the German editors' "Vorwort" to *DBW* 7 (14f.).

[50.] *Die Schöpfung*, 43–47.

Indeed Bethge's preface for the *Ethics* is dated April 9, 1948, the third anniversary of Bonhoeffer's death, and the book appeared early in 1949. In 1954 some of the dialogue from the end of the novel fragment was published under the title "Glück und Macht."[51] Next to appear, in 1955, was another part of Scene 3 of the drama, under the title "Boden unter den Füssen."[52] Then in 1960 the largest amount of the prison fiction was published in the third volume of Bonhoeffer's *Gesammelte Schriften*. The selection included two passages from Scenes 1 and 2 of the drama and the whole of Scene 3, and, from the novel, two long dialogues with the major.[53]

In terms of the reception of this fiction it is important to note that volume three of the collected works was devoted to theology, and that these selections from the fiction were published under the heading "Work on the *Ethics*, 1942–1944." They were accompanied in this section by the first version of the *Ethics* chapter, "History and Good." While there is no reason to think that Bonhoeffer ever intended the fiction to be part of the *Ethics*—he was, after all, quite clear in his purpose for the fiction—there are certainly many connections between the ideas of the *Ethics* and those in the fiction. Having worked for two and a half years on the *Ethics* up to the time of his imprisonment, and even "reproaching" himself for not having finished the book,[54] Bonhoeffer certainly had the issues that are dealt with in the *Ethics* on his mind while writing the fiction in prison. Further, much of the *Ethics* is addressing conditions in Germany that made the resistance movement necessary. This same historical and political situation was certainly in Bonhoeffer's mind as he wrote the fiction, especially the novel. So the *Ethics* and the fiction parallel each other, and the editors point out many connections in their notes.[55]

[51.] *Unterwegs* 4 (1954): 196–205. It was also published again the following year in *Dietrich Bonhoeffer: Einführung in seine Botschaft*, a publication of the press office of the Protestant Church of the Rhineland.

[52.] It appeared in the church publication *Die Kirche in Hamburg* 2 (1955): 4.

[53.] See *GS* 3:478–512.

[54.] See the first letter to Bethge after Bonhoeffer's imprisonment, written on November 18, 1943 *(LPP* 129).

[55.] The German editors of *DBW* 7 also point out that "the earlier assumption of a connection between these [literary] fragments and the *Ethics* receded into the background as their autobiographical significance came into the foreground" (14f.).

The short story was first published in 1970 in the new edition of *Widerstand und Ergebung*.[56] Finally, in 1978 the drama and novel were published in full for the first time (but the short story was not included), along with two other family-related pieces by Klaus Bonhoeffer and Emmi Bonhoeffer, a commentary by Ruth Zerner, and an introduction and notes by the editors.[57] The edition of *Fragmente aus Tegel* in the *Dietrich Bonhoeffer Werke* was published in 1994, edited by Renate Bethge and Ilse Tödt.

Publication in English followed a similar pattern. In 1955 the excerpt "Happiness and Power," which had appeared the previous year in Germany, was published in London in the magazine of the German-British Christian Fellowship, edited by Ronald Gregor Smith and Julius Rieger.[58] In 1965 a passage from the drama, Christoph's writing about protecting from abuse great words like "freedom," appeared in the English version of Hans Rothfels's little collection of Bonhoeffer excerpts.[59] The enlarged edition of *Letters and Papers from Prison* appeared in 1971 and followed its German prototype by including for the first time in English a translation of the short story "Lance Corporal Berg." The year 1973 saw the publication in English of the three excerpts from the drama and the two from the novel that had been published in the *Gesammelte Schriften*.[60] In 1981 the English version of the full German publication of the drama and novel, translated by Ursula Hoffmann, was published as *Fiction from Prison: Gathering Up the Past*.[61]

[56.] See *Widerstand und Ergebung*, new ed., 284–92, under the title "Gefreiter Berg Erzählung."

[57.] Renate and Eberhard Bethge, "Einleitung," in Bonhoeffer, *Fragmente aus Tegel: Drama und Roman.* In their introduction the editors explain that the excerpts published in *GS* 3 were chosen because they seemed "to belong especially to the context of Bonhoeffer's theological ethics . . ." (*Fiction from Prison*, 1).

[58.] *The Bridge* (April 1955): 4–15.

[59.] See Bonhoeffer, *I Loved This People*, 49–50 [*GS* 3:479–80].

[60.] See Bonhoeffer, *True Patriotism*, 197–215 and 220–35.

[61.] This publication has an "Introduction to the English Edition" by Clifford Green, pages vii–xiv.

Matters of Translation[62]

This is a new translation, the first that is based on the German critical edition. Out of respect for the work of colleagues in translation, the 1981 version by Ursula Hoffmann was consulted by the translator, of course, but the decision was made to create an entirely new translation rather than a revision. The present version tends toward a more contemporary colloquial English, particularly in the dialogue of the drama and novel. Occasional instances of similar or identical phrasing do occur, particularly where Bonhoeffer's style and sentence structure is straightforward and there is only one way to render the German phrase. The translation of the story about Lance Corporal Berg, which John Bowden first brought into English in the 1971 enlarged edition of the *Letters and Papers from Prison,* is likewise new here.

The translator has chosen to retain the German flavor of titles and forms of address in the dialogue of the novel, such as Frau Bremer, Frau Brake, Frau Direktor (wife or widow of a principal or director), and Herr Direktor, rather than rendering them with a formal English equivalent like "madam" or "sir." Likewise, the fairy tale-like flavor in the opening scene of the drama is retained by using the term "wondrous beast," and the intimate tone of the family in the drama fragment is suggested by the affectionate "Little Brother," rather than a more common English nickname such as "Junior" or "Sonny."

In German the names of characters such as *Gelbstiefel* (Yellowboots), *Warmblut* (Warmblood), and *Schönrock* (Finefrock) have a satiric effect. Since Yellowboots is the nickname given to the character actually named Kruse, the anglicized form of *Gelbstiefel* has been used throughout the novel, whereas the German original has been retained for characters' actual names such as Pastor Schönrock and Frau Warmblut. English readers should keep in mind that the characteristically North German sound of the name "Brake" is conveyed by pronouncing it to rhyme with "Brocker," rather than "cake."

Readers may be struck by certain recurring words and phrases in the prison fiction that should be understood in the cultural and linguistic context in which Bonhoeffer wrote. Perhaps the foremost example of this is the word field of *Schweigen* (silence, reserve, reticence, refraining

---

[62.] This section was largely written by Nancy Lukens.

from speaking), *Verhüllung* (veiling), *Maske* (mask), and *Geheimnis* (secret), which often involve intentionally leaving certain things unspoken, out of respect for personal boundaries and regard for the complexity of truth. Taken out of their linguistic and cultural context, and the specific situations of the fiction, the English words "silence," "veiling," "hiding," "mask," and "secrecy" do not convey the whole value system reflected in these texts. On one hand, Bonhoeffer draws upon the mid-nineteenth-century values of the German educated middle class, or *Bildungsbürgertum*, which were formative for his generation and class. Those familiar with German literature will recognize a certain *Biedermeier* flavor to this language—in the poetic realism of writers like Adalbert Stifter and Jeremias Gotthelf—which Bonhoeffer rediscovered in the enforced leisure of his prison cell. On the other hand, it would be a mistake to see Bonhoeffer's language as primarily nostalgic, prudish, inward, or apolitical. On the contrary, terms like *Schweigen*, as the German editor's afterword emphasizes, connote a deliberate attitude that includes conscious resistance to the abuse of the "great words" in the twentieth century, not only by modern society in general, but specifically by National Socialist culture.

Further translation issues arise in rendering the words *Herr* (mister, sir, gentleman, lord, master, leader), *Herrschaft* (dominion, dominance, sovereign rule, reign, lordship, power) and *Alleinherrschaft* (sole authority, exclusive reign), *Gutsherrschaft* (ownership of an estate), *Herrentum* (rulership), and *herrisch* (domineering, wanting to be in charge), which convey theological, political, and moral meanings and judgments in Bonhoeffer's texts. We hope that the various renderings convey a sense of Bonhoeffer's focus on the ethics of all relationships of power and leadership, including his critique of the abuse of power.

The texts are also replete with references to various kinds of power, from *Kräfte* (forces, resources, strength) and *Mächte* (forces, powers) to *Gewalt* (force, power, violence), *Gewalttäter* (doers of violence, tyrants), and *Vergewaltigung* (violent abuse of power, rape). Some of these words have intrinsically negative meanings; others are more complex, and can have positive or negative meanings depending on the context. When the various terms for power occur in the fiction, the theological analysis above should be kept in mind.

Careful attention is warranted when one encounters references to the authority of people such as parents, teachers, and judges in words like *oben* and *unten*—literally "above" and "below," higher and lower. The point in Bonhoeffer's use of these words is explained in an editorial note.[63] Depending on the context, various expressions have been chosen to convey consistently the sense of Bonhoeffer's discourse on the exercise of responsible authority in social and political relationships.

Readers may also be struck, and perhaps misled, by Bonhoeffer's emphasis on *neuer Adel* (new nobility), *neue Auslese* (select few, or new elite), *Oberschicht* (new, genuine, responsible upper class), or *von Natur Edle* (people who are noble by nature). This has nothing to do with social or economic class, but with the perceived need to reclaim the value of authentic leadership as Bonhoeffer understood it.

The terms *Bürgertum* (middle class), *Bürger* (member of the middle class, citizen), and *bürgerlich* (middle-class, bourgeois) warrant comment, given their shifting meanings through the twentieth century. In Bonhoeffer's usage, the bourgeois refers to the values and attitudes of the educated middle class, or *Bildungsbürgertum,* in which he grew up.[64] It might well include people of aristocratic heritage who espouse middle-class values, as well as people who are less economically privileged, but who are committed to building community and providing responsible leadership.

Another prevalent word group in these texts has to do with the personal quality of spontaneity or candor, *Unbefangenheit.* We decided against the literal translation of "uninhibitedness" and employ instead a range of more positive and similarly common expressions, such as "free," "natural," and "spontaneous." While this choice sacrifices the negative connotation of the German root participle meaning "caught, trapped, and imprisoned," it reproduces the everyday and positive tone of the original in describing an openness based on self-confidence and trust.

Finally, the rendering of Bonhoeffer's various styles in the prison fiction needs comment. While the narrative voice is more formal, perhaps

---

[63.] See below, page 35, editorial note 52.

[64.] With regard to the difficulty of translating *Bürgertum* into English, Renate Bethge has explained that Bonhoeffer family members today have different opinions about whether it should be translated "middle class" or "upper middle class," and suggested using both (letter to Clifford Green, April 21, 1999). One might observe that a family that was not only highly educated and held prominent positions of public responsibility but also had several household servants and a chauffeur would probably be called by most people today "upper middle class." [CG]

sometimes appearing stilted to the contemporary reader, the everyday speech of the characters in the drama, the story, and the novel are rendered more colloquially, as they would speak. Where Bonhoeffer cannot resist making a character's speech the vehicle for a carefully crafted essay, as in Scene 3 of the drama or in the long speeches of Major von Bremer in the novel, no attempt is made to translate that material in any more colloquial or dramatic form than it is in the original.

Bibliography and Index

The first section of the bibliography, "Literature Used by Bonhoeffer," was created by the German editors from several categories of books. We know from his letters that Bonhoeffer had some of these in his cell. Some of them are books that he had in his own library and that still survive; editorial notes frequently indicate when passages in these books have his markings. Still others are books that we know Bonhoeffer had read before he was in prison; for example, the editorial notes referring to Bonhoeffer's *Ethics* mention books he was reading in the several years before he was imprisoned. The principle for selection, then, is to include books that Bonhoeffer is known to have read, to which various clues in his writing have pointed the editors. The conclusion that he used them or had them in mind is necessarily an editorial inference by the German editors; but the section of the bibliography entitled "Literature Used by Bonhoeffer" does not contain books that Bonhoeffer simply might have read and in which the editors find similar scenes, persons, or phrases.

Books in the bibliography that were owned by Bonhoeffer and were in his library are indicated by the notation *NL* followed by numbers and letters. These refer to the book containing the index of Bonhoeffer's literary estate, *Nachlaß Dietrich Bonhoeffer*. This work contains a short introduction by Eberhard Bethge explaining the history of Bonhoeffer's library,[65] and explaining what he calls the *Restbibliothek*, that is, the remaining books of Bonhoeffer's library. Not all the books that Bonhoeffer owned remain in this library. Some were taken to London during his pastorate and left there, in exchange for books of his London successor, Julius Rieger, which Bonhoeffer collected in Berlin. Bon-

---

[65.] See *NL*, 171–75.

hoeffer also made his own library available for his students in Finkenwalde. A number of his books also found their way into private hands. Approximately one thousand volumes now comprise this "remaining library." For many years they were in the possession of Eberhard Bethge and were consulted by him and other scholars, especially those editing volumes of the *Dietrich Bonhoeffer Werke*. They are now housed, along with Bonhoeffer's papers, at the Staatsbibliothek in Berlin.

With this volume, for the first time in the *Dietrich Bonhoeffer Works*, English edition, the index includes "biograms" for people in the index of names, following the German edition. Whereas the latter, however, did not give biographical details for people whose work appeared after Bonhoeffer's death in 1945, the English edition provides that information, since the younger generation of German and other European writers is not as well known to English-language readers. The subject index to the German edition is extremely detailed and covers twenty-nine double-column pages. It contains numerous words with only a single occurrence throughout the whole book. Those who need such fine detail can consult the German text. The index in this translation builds selectively on its German antecedent; while briefer, it contains all the key theological and historical terms. It also includes a number of key German terms and refers the reader to instances where especially important uses of the term occur, or where a discussion of it is contained in an editorial note.

Acknowledgments

A number of acknowledgments that were contained in the editorial notes of the German edition are given here on behalf of the German editors. Matthias Schollmeyer pointed out parallels to Nietzsche found in several editorial notes.[66] Christoph Perels provided information in several editorial notes about Kafka, Stefan George, and Rilke.[67] Christopher Frey provided expert information about mushrooms. Christian Gremmels referred the editors to the unpublished manuscript by Gaetano Latmiral, containing information about the numerous red

---

[66.] See below, pages 27, 57, 150, 164, 172, editorial notes 7, 19, 28, 94, and 8.
[67.] See below, pages 39, 50, and 115, editorial notes 4, 38, and 26.

signs on the doors of death-row inmates who were transferred on Friday evenings to Plötzensee and executed.[68]

The editor of the English edition is pleased to acknowledge the network of collegial cooperation that created this book. Collaboration between editor and translator has been particularly close. As a scholar of German literature, Nancy Lukens brought to her translation of Bonhoeffer's fiction a familiarity with the classical and contemporary literature which played an important role in his experience, thought, and writing style. As a literary translator and student of translation theory she has extensive experience with the issues that arise in such an enterprise as the present volume. As a teacher of German literature she has brought to her work a knowledge of possible allusions in Bonhoeffer's fiction, for example, the likely reference to Kafka's "Metamorphosis" in a dream of one of the characters in the novel. As a student of the history of anti-Nazi resistance, particularly Adam von Trott, she has a sensitivity to the language and events of Bonhoeffer's time that has informed her translation. From these resources she provided interpretation of German words in many translator's notes and other information for some editorial notes, contributed a section to this introduction, and assisted with the bibliography and index.

The editor and translator reviewed every line of the translation together and numerous formulations were contributed by the editor. Ilse Tödt also read very carefully through the entire manuscript and made frequent translation suggestions. Johannes Evelein of Trinity College, Hartford, served as consultant for this volume and provided helpful advice to the editor, particularly about conveying into English the "voice" of the German original.

In several instances Ilse Tödt also supplied revised readings of Bonhoeffer's original German manuscript in his difficult handwriting. She also provided many explanations, a number of which have been incorporated into editorial notes, sometimes as an expansion of the German editors' notes and sometimes in a note added by the editor of the English edition. She also collected the biographical information for younger European scholars in the index of names.

Several other people assisted with the volume. Renate Bethge read through the translation of the "Editor's Afterword to the German

---

[68.] See below, page 190, editorial note 35.

Edition," of which she was the chief author, and made helpful suggestions on a number of points. Hans Pfeifer served as continuing liaison with the German Editorial Board and answered many queries from the editor. David Stassen promptly provided a draft translation of index material and bibliographical titles. Victoria Barnett provided assistance in translating proper names and titles related to East German theological education. Carolyn Sperl of Hartford Seminary Library brought her usual care and competence to securing volumes through interlibrary loans; and Aaron Clegg and Molly Howard assisted the translator with interlibrary loans and in checking cross references. Florence Leduc created preliminary drafts of some of the index material. Jack Ammerman solved all computer problems with dispatch. Valerie Vick of Hartford Seminary provided efficient and cheerful office support. The University of New Hampshire supported the work of the translator with a sabbatical leave, and Dean Marilyn Hoskin provided a small grant to assist manuscript revision. As General Editor, Wayne Floyd always brought a keen eye for both detail and style, made a number of translation suggestions, and provided his usual unfailing care for consistent editorial practice. The final and fundamental word of thanks must go to Renate Bethge and Ilse Tödt whose creation of the German edition made this translation possible. To all these colleagues the editor and translator wish to express their cordial thanks.

DRAMA

Cast of Characters

Grandmother (about 70 years old)

Little Brother (about 10 years old)

Mother (Anna; housewife, wife of Hans, mother of Christoph and Little Brother)

Father (Hans; physician, medical director of a military hospital, 55 years old)

Christoph (older son, student, war veteran, 24 years old)

Ulrich (close friend of Christoph)

Renate (girlfriend of Christoph)

Heinrich (war veteran, newcomer to Christoph's and Ulrich's discussion group)

The Stranger (a "sales representative of Death")

Little Annie (deceased daughter of Anna and Hans)

Scene 1

Living room in an upper-middle-class home. Evening. Grandmother and Little Brother are sitting at a table with a lamp on it. The grandmother is a woman of about seventy, simply dressed. Little Brother, about ten, is dressed appropriately for his age. He listens very attentively as his grandmother reads to him. [1]

Grandmother: (reads) ". . . For many days and weeks now the hunter had stalked the wondrous[2] beast. Several times he had it in his sights, but didn't shoot. He couldn't stop feasting his eyes on this glorious sight. Then one evening around sunset the animal happened to step out of the woods right in front of him; it looked at him with very calm eyes, and stood still, without fear. Never before had the hunter seen the animal like this. He was seized by a wild desire to have it, not to let it go, not to let it escape again.[3] He loved this animal so much that he couldn't part from it again. Very slowly he raised his rifle, eye to eye with the animal. One last, long look, one last hesitation,[4] then the shot. Afterward everything was completely still and the last rays of the evening sun shone[5] peacefully on the fallen prey and its hunter."[6] *(She shuts the book and lays it aside.)* We'll stop here for today, Little Brother. The book doesn't say how the story goes

---

[1.] The beginning of the manuscript is written with clear blue ink on light, porous double sheets (DIN A3, folded). *NL* A 70, 4(1). Bonhoeffer used this type of paper beginning in 1942, with his work on the section of the *Ethik* manuscript entitled "History and Good." See *DBW* 6:269, editorial note 76.

[2.] Replaces: "noble".

[3.] Replaces: "to own [it], to win [it], to overcome [it]."

[4.] "Long look . . . hesitation" replaces "last look of love, of reverent wonder." [Karl Bonhoeffer wrote that Dietrich's brother was a passionate hunter who became an excellent shot. On one occasion, after he had shot a circling falcon which fell dead at his feet, "he was so shaken that he burst into tears." See "Lebenserinnerungen: Geschrieben für die Familie," 91.][CG]

[5.] Later put in brackets, i.e., considered by the editors to be deleted: "(reconcilingly and)." When writing his *Ethics*, Bonhoeffer used Romano Guardini's book, *Religiöse Gestalten in Dostojewskijs Werk*, which comments that in Dostoyevsky's works the " 'slanting rays of the setting sun' symbolize an ultimate metaphysical closeness" (98; cf. 104). Cf. also page 179: "The slanting rays . . ."

[6.] Pencil marginal note: "Change? More in fairy-tale style." On November 21, 1943, Bonhoeffer wrote his fiancée Maria von Wedemeyer: "Walter, whose photo you saw, used to go out regularly with the gamekeeper and would have liked to be one himself, but I seem to remember it was a powerful experience for him when he shot his first buck at the age of fifteen or sixteen" (*LL* 97).

from there. But you can be sure it does go on. In fact this is really just the beginning.[7]

Little Brother: Yes, Grandmother, the story can't end like that at all. But why did the animal look at the hunter so calmly and not run away? Didn't it know that he would shoot it? And hadn't it any fear at all of being killed?

Grandmother: Who knows, child? Maybe it's true what people say, that animals know nothing of death—but then why do you think they're so shy by nature? Or maybe this wondrous beast knew its hunter and knew very well that it couldn't escape him. Maybe it sensed its hunter's great love, and that made it love its hunter a little, too, and look at him with such calm, fearless eyes. Maybe it knew death was near and yet wasn't afraid. Who knows, child? 23

Little Brother: Yes, Grandmother, perhaps only the animals and the dear Lord can know that. But all people know that they have to die, don't they, grandmother?

Grandmother: Yes, they all know—*(hesitating)* but in very different ways. *(She pauses for a moment to think.)* I'll try to explain it to you. You know, don't you, that you have good parents,[8] and you want to make them very happy?

Little Brother: Yes, Grandmother, I know that.

Grandmother: Yet, even though you know, you keep forgetting and do things you wouldn't do if you remembered what Father or Mother said.

Little Brother: Yes, Grandmother.

Grandmother: But sometimes, too, you feel that Father or Mother is very

---

[7.] In his sermon on Jer. 20:7 in London on January 21, 1934, Bonhoeffer had used Nietzsche's image of the hunter to describe the calling of Jeremiah: ". . . God has his prey; or, as it is also written, the arrow of the Almighty has caught his harried prey. Jeremiah is his prophet [who is struck down by the] word of the Lord's love, who desires His creature" (*DBW* 13:347 [slight revision of *GS* 5:505f.]). See Nietzsche, *Thus Spoke Zarathustra:* "Shivering with piercing icy frost-arrows, . . . / Hit / By thee, cruelest hunter, / Thou unknown *god!* . . . / No dog—only thy game am I, . . . / What wilt thou, unknown—god?" (pt. 4, "The Magician," 364ff.). Cf. *CD* 285 [*DBW* 4:283] and frequent references to 1 Cor. 15:31 ("I die every day!"). The baptismal death of Christians is the beginning of Christ's life within them. "Christ is their daily death and their daily life" (*CD* 286 [trans. altered]). Bonhoeffer's first newsletter to the Confessing Church pastors he had trained (dated September 20, 1939, just after the beginning of the war), speaks of this inner death. "We die this death daily in Jesus Christ, or we refuse it. . . . This death is grace and is the fulfillment of life" (*The Way to Freedom*, 255; cf. 254 [trans. altered]).

[8.] Replaces: "have a good mother, whom".

close to you even if you don't see them at all, and then you only do what they would want you to do, isn't that so?

Little Brother: Yes, Grandmother.

Grandmother: You see, that's exactly how people know about dying. They know they must die, but most people forget about it during most of their lifetime. Some don't forget about it; you can tell when you meet them.[9] And then there are a very few who sense when death may come to them. They see it coming. They're very different from other people.

Little Brother: Grandmother, do you want to be among those who know when death will come to them?

Grandmother: We can't and mustn't wish for that, child. That's either a gift or a punishment from God.

Little Brother: I don't understand.

Grandmother: No, of course you don't. But now it's time for bed. Surely we'll talk about this some more. Go to bed now. Father will be late getting home again. He has a lot of patients to see in town, and when he gets home he'll be very tired and will want to be alone with Mother a while. Good night, child; the Lord keep you!

Little Brother: Good night, Grandmother; the dear Lord keep you! *(Leaves, meets his mother in the doorway.)*

Mother: (embraces the child) Sleep well, my dear boy. Did Grandmother tell you a nice story?[10] Well, sweet dreams to you, my dear . . . my . . . only child.

Little Brother: But Mother, I'm not your only child! Have you forgotten all about Christoph?

Mother: (startled) No, no, my boy, you aren't my only one—no, believe me, I haven't forgotten Christoph. Now, good night, and hurry, it's late. I'll wait up for Father and Christoph.

Little Brother: (exits—from the hallway) Say hello to Christoph for me when he gets home!

Grandmother: Would you like some time alone, Anna?

Mother: No, I don't want to be alone; I'd like to talk with you until Hans gets home. *(She walks over and sits down close to Grandmother.)* Mother,

---

[9.] Cf. Ps. 90:12: "Teach us to remember that we must die, so that we may become wise." [NRSV: "So teach us to count our days that we may gain a wise heart."][CG] Bonhoeffer, even as a student, was a gifted catechist who taught children the biblical message through dialogue. Cf. the summary in the editor's afterword to *DBW* 9: 631ff.

[10.] Replaces: "read you a nice story?"

things just can't go on like this; I just don't understand anymore.[11] It's the first time in the twenty-five years of our marriage that I don't understand Hans. It's the first time he doesn't answer my questions. He's evasive. And yet he's more loving and considerate than ever. I can see how tormented he is, how he lies awake beside me at night for hours, how he's already tired when he goes to work and often stays out late at night. It's been going on for a month now, since . . . Christoph came home. Haven't you noticed how he avoids the boy? How he often stares at him in great distress without saying a word? How he doesn't even joke with the little one anymore? How he never goes near the piano anymore? Can't you feel how he often speaks as if he were far, far away, as if he didn't even see us?

Grandmother: Yes, my dear, I have felt it, from the first day Christoph   25 came back to him—to us. Since then he's been living in another world.[12]

Mother: Mother, I don't understand all this, and I don't want to.[13] Christoph just came back from the war. He left as a child; he came back a man. But he's still the same person; I'm telling you, he's still the same.[14] He hasn't become a stranger to us. He's with[15] Renate this evening; he remained faithful to her all these long years.[16] No, Christoph is still the same; I know he is. He's as close to us as ever.

Grandmother: Yes, very close, closer than ever, and yet very distant, very distant, just as distant as Hans often is these days.

Mother: Don't say such things, Mother, that people can't understand. Don't you feel how close he is to you, how much he loves to stay up late at night with you? How he loves Little Brother, plays with him, and has long talks with him? How he goes out early in the morning to enjoy the garden, the flowers and the sun?

Grandmother: Yes, grandmothers, children, and gardens . . . they're usually a distant world for a young man.[17] They're strangely close to

---

[11.] Pencil marginal note: "Fear and foreboding must be made clearer."

[12.] Pencil deletion: "And, tell me yourself, is it any wonder, when you look at Christoph?"

[13.] Ink deletion: "Isn't Christoph still the same person, despite the war?"

[14.] Pencil deletion: "He hasn't gone bad."

[15.] Ink and pencil deletion: "his [girlfriend]".

[16.] Replaces: "since he was a boy."

[17.] Replaces: "are all equally far from the young man in the prime of life [replaces: 'who (leads) an active life']. They are another world."

Christoph—I hear Hans coming in, so I'll leave you two alone. *(aside)* May God give him the courage to speak. *(exits)*

Mother (aside): O dear God, it just can't be true.

Father: (enter a man of fifty-five, dressed like a doctor; he looks worn out. Walks over to his wife without a word, kisses her and says warmly, with a note of pity) Anna, my love.

Mother: You're home so late again, Hans.

Father: There was a lot to do in town.

26   *Mother: (somewhat absently)* Yes, I suppose there's always a lot to do nowadays.

Father: The traumas of war.

Mother: (more emphatically, to herself) Yes, the traumas of war. Are you hungry? Or shall I bring you something to drink? Ulrich's[18] parents sent a few bottles of red wine just today, to thank you for taking care of him and[19] to celebrate Christoph's homecoming and recovery. It was very thoughtful of them. They love Christoph very much.

Father: (at first glad for the offer, but changing his expression completely at the mention of Christoph's name) No thanks, Anna, I don't want anything to drink now. Christoph should take the wine and have a celebration with his friends. No, really, thank you, I don't want a drink now. Has Mother retired already?

Mother: Yes, she went up when she heard you come in; she wanted to give us a chance to be alone. She thought we might have something to talk over. But . . . she might as well have stayed.

Father: Yes, of course she could have stayed. I for one have nothing, really, nothing at all to . . . By the way, did Ulrich come to see you? He wanted to stop by right after he got out of the military hospital. He's in excellent health; he is more lively and energetic than ever. *(pauses)* It's a wonder everything[20] went so well. It looked bleak at first, and I wasn't very hopeful. Yes, miracles sometimes happen. . . .

Mother: Ulrich was here briefly. He asked for Christoph and Renate. Then he went to see them. He loves Christoph more than anything, and I'm so happy for Christoph that he has him, especially now.

Father: Yes, it seems as if times are coming when people will need loyal friends.[21]

[18.] Replaces: "Renate's".

[19.] Pencil insertion: "to thank you [who did the surgery] . . . and."

[20.] Replaces in pencil: "the operation."

[21.] Pencil notation: "Disappointment, mistrust, depression."

Mother: That's not what I meant.

Father: Never mind, Anna. I saw things today . . . I'd give anything never 27
to have seen them. A wounded young soldier[22] about Christoph's
age hauls himself across the street on crutches. Behind him walk two
young men about his age, fit as a fiddle and all dressed up. I see one
of them pointing his finger at the wounded man, putting on a repulsive grin, and saying in a voice for all to hear: "That's another one of
those eternal fools; there are still too many of them around." *(Pause)*
Anna, I thought it would be better to be dead than live to hear that.

Mother: And what did you do, Hans?

Father: What could I do? I didn't have the one thing you need at times
like that: I had no weapon. Yes, Anna, I really would have fired.[23]
(More and more agitated) Anna, there is nothing more base and
unnatural,[24] there is no crime more heinous or deserving of death,
than mocking a victim. I would have fired, Anna, even though I
knew I'd be guilty of wrongdoing.[25] So what did I do? Nothing at
all—I followed the ruthless louts, grabbed them both by the collar,
shook them until they staggered. I couldn't get a word out, I was
shaking with such senseless rage myself. The wounded soldier
stopped and turned around—I knew him, he was from my hospital.
He smiled gratefully, a little embarrassed and ashamed. Meanwhile
the rabble had gathered around us and crowded in on me. A policeman came and wanted to take my name. When the policeman heard
it—after a voice I didn't know called from the crowd, "That's the 28
medical director of the military hospital"—he looked at me for a
moment in astonishment, slowly nodded his head a few times as if
something had become clear to him, and let me go. The two hooligans flagged down a car and got in, grinning. The wounded man
said goodbye and left. I stood there and said to myself, "Better dead

---

[22.] Replaces: "officer". Sabine Leibholz-Bonhoeffer tells of a cousin who lost one eye
as a result of a head wound in 1914. The sight of this war veteran in head and leg bandages,
limping around on crutches but utterly unbroken in spirit, had made an indelible impression on her (see Leibholz-Bonhoeffer, *The Bonhoeffers,* 4).

[23.] This sentence inserted in pencil in the margin.

[24.] Replaces: "nothing baser or more common."

[25.] Pencil deletion: "in the eyes of the law." Cf. *E* 235 on the "necessity of the use of
violence as the *ultima ratio. . . .*" Bonhoeffer's ethical-theological reflections applied especially to the attempted assassination of Hitler. His family, as well as the group of conspirators to which Bonhoeffer belonged, considered the killing of Hitler an unavoidable
prerequisite to abolishing the inhumane National Socialist regime.

than this!" Suddenly, there was Christoph standing next to me and saying, "Yes, Father, you're right, better dead than this!"

Mother: Hans!

Father: What is it, Anna? Does that frighten you?[26] Things like this will happen more and more, and much worse. God, what kind of a world have we brought our children into! Sometimes nowadays I think it would be better . . . if they'd never been born.

Mother: Hans! What are you talking about?

Father: *(harshly)* Anna, be quiet, you don't understand this—you can't understand it. You don't see the world as it is. You see our home— yes, *our home* . . . We've had our worries, too, when little Annie died.[27] But out there, Anna . . . Who knows how long our home . . .[28] What kind of life is it when every day, from morning till night, they bring in young people with shot-up limbs and shredded bodies, hopes destroyed, happiness denied. And if by some miracle we manage to save one, then another stands next to him, eyes staring at death.[29] What business does a young person have with death, Anna? If death struck on the battlefield, if it seized him in the midst of action, then you could still call it merciful. But a slow, creeping, yet certain death—without hope of seeing different, better times— *(highly agitated)*[30] Anna,[31] what kind of a life is that? Better to be dead, at least for us old folk, and perhaps even for the young people—for them especially.[32] *(paces back and forth, then stops, becomes very calm)* Forgive me, please forgive me—who else can I say all this to but you? *(kisses her)*

Mother: You haven't said it all yet, Hans.

29

[26.] Replaces: "Why are you so shocked?"

[27.] Marginal pencil insertion beginning "You don't see the world. . . ," followed by "to be developed further!"

[28.] Marginal pencil notation beginning "But . . .". Cf. Bonhoeffer's sermon from Tegel prison for the wedding of Eberhard and Renate Bethge on May 15, 1943: "Our times have made especially clear what a home can mean. . . . It is a place founded by God in the world where, whatever might be happening in the world, peace, calm, joy, love, purity, discipline, respect, obedience, and tradition should reside, and, amidst all these—happiness" (*LPP* 44 [trans. altered]).

[29.] Bonhoeffer's brother Walter had died on April 28, 1918, in a field hospital on the front after a second operation to remove deeply embedded shrapnel. Cf. *DB-ER* 27.

[30.] Deleted: "standing up."

[31.] Deleted: "and as a doctor to have to look on, powerless to help."

[32.] Marginal pencil notation following "Better to be dead. . . ."

Father: (after a long pause) No, I haven't said everything yet, Anna. *(pause, then reporting very calmly)* It was about a month ago, when Christoph came home, barely recovered. His appearance worried me. One morning I had him come see me at the hospital and I examined him—I couldn't do otherwise—since then I've known . . .

Mother: Yes, since then you've known.[33] But perhaps it's just as well, for him and for all of us.[34]

Father: Yes, Anna—poor, poor Anna.

Mother: (in a faraway voice) How long does Christoph have to live? So it's true . . .[35]

Father: A year at most.

Mother: You've said nothing to Christoph?

Father: Nothing.

Mother: He doesn't suspect anything?

Father: He can't suspect anything; he has no pain, and probably won't until the end.

Mother: Thank God[36]—no one else knows? No doctor? No nurse? No friend? Not Mother? Ulrich? Renate? My God, poor Renate, what will become of her?[37]

Father: No one knows but you and me.

Mother: Then no one will hear about it from us either. *(long pause)* Hans, let me tell you what will happen. We're going to have one year of indescribable happiness with Christoph. For his sake, we will not let ourselves worry. We'll only be happy for him and with him. We'll grant his wish for a trip to the mountains.[38] We will have no tears to hide from him, because our hearts will be filled with joy until the last day. The sun should set radiantly on his life.[39] Hans, let's promise each other this. There mustn't be any pain, any grief, any bitterness in us now. Christoph would sense it, and we would do him and ourselves a great wrong. Hans, let us together bear—not the pain, but our happiness with our son.

30

[33.] Replaces: "That Christoph is dying."
[34.] Pencil insertion following "But perhaps . . ."
[35.] Pencil insertion following "So . . ."
[36.] Deleted: "God's will be done."
[37.] Pencil marginal note beginning with "Not Mother? . . ."
[38.] Ink marginal insertion.
[39.] Replaces in pencil: "[on] him".

Father: Anna, what a wife, what a mother you are. *(there is a knock at the door)*

Christoph: (enters) Good evening, Mother, good evening, Father. How nice that you're still up. Where is Grandmother? How is Little Brother?

Mother: Grandmother told Little Brother the story of the hunter and the wondrous beast, then they both went to bed. Little Brother says hello. Have you been at Renate's? And did Ulrich find you both?

Christoph: Yes,[40] I was at Renate's. Later Ulrich and I went to our group. What happened this morning is already the talk of the town. How are you, Father? If only I had arrived there a moment sooner, I would have done the honors. It was horrible to see you in that rabble there. By the way, the policeman is[41] the father of one of the fellows in our group.

Father: And what were people there[42] saying about it?

Christoph: You know, Father, that we all agree on such matters. And no one would be so bold as to criticize you lightly;[43] most of them, after all, know you. There was only one man there, a new fellow, who didn't say a word. I don't know where he's from. He's badly patched up, frightfully pale, and in pain,[44] and he looks terribly bitter. He's bottling up some kind of hatred. He appears very intelligent and not a bad fellow. But he seemed to think differently from the rest of us. But how he thinks, and why, I don't know yet.[45] When I said good-bye to him, he gave me a strange look, as if he wanted something, but he didn't say anything.

Father: A few months ago I had a fellow in the hospital. He was in an almost hopeless condition when they brought him in, terribly injured, a man of high intelligence. Day and night we fought for his life. He never uttered a single word; mostly he lay in bed with his eyes closed, but his mouth had a bitter expression. When I came

31

[40.] Deleted: "we had a nice evening together [deleted: the three of us]."

[41.] Replaces in pencil: "was".

[42.] Replaces in pencil: "in your group."

[43.] Dietrich's father, Karl Bonhoeffer, was also an authority figure whom no one criticized lightly. He had used his authority to arrange for Dietrich to stay with his parents in spite of the official injunction of January 1938 banning him from Berlin. He had also managed in 1939 to get his son's military physical exam postponed for a year in view of Dietrich's planned visit to the United States.

[44.] Pencil insertion: "and in pain."

[45.] Pencil insertion: "yet."

over to his bed, sometimes he'd open his eyes briefly and give me a
look I couldn't understand. There was a hint of deadly hatred about
it, and something like the fervent pleading of a child. We couldn't do
much but patch him up, perhaps for a few more years. Even when he
got better, he wouldn't open up at all.[46] Finally he had to be
discharged, for we had done everything we could for him. I will not
forget how this young man, whose life we had saved for at least a
couple of years, came into my office to be discharged, looked at me
with blazing eyes, and said to me with passionate agitation,[47] "Why
didn't you let me die?[48] With your skill you bullied a couple of years
of my life out of God; these years will be the devil's. You alone are to
blame for what becomes of me from now on. I can't stand this life
without turning rotten." I stood there as if devastated. I've forgotten
what I did. I think I told him that I wanted to help him, that he
should come back. I haven't seen him since. Perhaps, Christoph, he's
the same one you were talking about?

Christoph: I'll talk with him, Father.[49] Anyway, our group had another
evening of heated debate. After the incident, someone started talking about the right of free speech, and eventually we found ourselves
right back in the middle of the debate about the freedom of citizens.
It was a heated exchange. Father, I argued that freedom must never
be used as a slogan for the masses, because that would lead to the
most terrible slavery. I said freedom is rightly exercised by the few,
the noble, the chosen.[50] For the others,[51] however, law and order
would represent freedom. I also said there must be higher and lower
positions[52] among people, and anyone who doesn't grasp this

32

[46.] The following passage replaces nine deleted lines.

[47.] In the deleted portion are the words, "looked penetratingly at me, as a judge looks
at the accused, and broke his long silence."

[48.] Adolf Jost's *Das Recht auf den Tod* had introduced in 1895 the expression "mercy
killing" in connection with critically injured soldiers.

[49.] The following passage, up to "justify my arguments," page 36, appeared in *True
Patriotism*, 197f. [*GS* 3:478ff.].

[50.] Cf. Santayana, *The Last Puritan*, which Bonhoeffer knew in 1940–41: "Oliver
began to perceive that liberty is something aristocratic" (372). Cf. below, page 173. On
Bonhoeffer's view of freedom and responsibility, see *E* 244: "Factually, though not chrono-
logically, responsibility presupposes freedom, and freedom can consist only in responsibility." See also *E* 245: "The free deed knows itself in the end as the deed of God."

[51.] Replaces: "For the rest of us."

[52.] On "higher and lower positions," see *E* 267f. Here in the drama Bonhoeffer uses
the spatial metaphors "above," *ein Oben*, and "below," *ein Unten*, and later the words

brings chaos to the people. And finally, I even said that there were people who are noble by nature, who are destined to rule and be free, and then there are those who are rabble by nature, who must serve. I told them that nothing is more terrible or destructive than when this order breaks down, when the rabble rules and the noble serve. However, I said, the difference between the two types of people is that the rabble only know how to live, but the noble also know how to die. Father, is that also your view? Yes, surely it's your view, or you wouldn't have said today, "Better dead than this!" They almost went for my throat for saying this, and next time they want me to justify my arguments.[53] But that's enough for now. . . .[54]

Mother: Yes, Christoph,[55] and perhaps you're all still too young to understand quite what you're saying. What does Ulrich say?

Christoph: Ulrich always stands up for me, I can depend on him.

Mother: I don't want to stand in the way of your plans, my boy. But I wanted to suggest something to you, anyway. You know, you're not quite fully recovered yet, but you do want to be well again soon. Why don't you and Ulrich, and Little Brother if you like, take a nice trip to the mountains?

Christoph: Mother . . . to the mountains!! Yes, I want to do that. Thank you both. Is it true that Ulrich's parents sent wine today? Then let's have a glass and drink a toast to this hope of mine.[56]

Father: (gets up, brings a bottle, opens it; speaks while pouring wine without looking at Christoph) It was sent to celebrate your recovery, Christoph; so let us drink to that. To your health, my boy!

Christoph: To your health, Father, Mother! *(They clink glasses. Christoph's glass breaks. There is silence for a moment.)*

'higher' and 'lower', to summarize relationships such as those between old and young, father and child, master and servant, teacher and student, judge and accused, ruler and subject, preacher and parishioner, that is, "the concrete relation between the giver and the receiver of commands." Note that such a relation of authority and responsibility is expressly contrasted by Bonhoeffer to a social order of "privileged and unprivileged classes." Relations of ethical authority and responsibility are consistent with the equal dignity of all people before the ethical and are not to be equated with "upper" and "lower" social classes (cf. *E* 268f.). [CG]

[53.] Pencil deletion: "Some said that you can't say such things anymore, and that they would throw me out of the group if I insisted on this view."

[54.] Pencil marginal insertion: "But that's enough for now." Below it is the stage direction *"Warmly!"* indicating a change of voice to a calmer and friendlier tone.

[55.] Pencil deletion: "what dangerous things you speak of there."

[56.] "Glass" replaces "bottle"; "hope" replaces "prospect."

Little Brother: (in his nightshirt) I can't sleep, I keep seeing the hunter and the wondrous beast who both[57] loved each other so much—Christoph, you're here!

Christoph: (lifts Little Brother onto his knee) Come here, Little Brother, relax—I'll tell you something nice. Soon I'm going mountain-climbing in the Alps with Ulrich and maybe, maybe, if you're good and our parents let you, you can come along with me wherever I go.[58] But when I climb a really high peak you'll stay below, and then you'll wave to me, won't you? And I'll see you down below until I'm all the way to the top.[59] Now go back to bed and dream about it and, tomorrow, ask Mother and Father to please let you come along. *(exit Little Brother)*   34

Mother: (in the meantime, unnoticed, she has brought Christoph another glass of wine) Well, once again, here's to a good trip, Christoph *(they clink glasses),* and good night. Don't stay up too late. We're tired, it's been a long day. Good night. *(Father and Mother leave quickly)*

Christoph: (alone, picks up the pieces of broken glass and slowly drops them) Thank God. . . . They don't suspect a thing![60] *(takes a photograph from his pocket and gazes at it for a long time)* Renate! *(Curtain)*

[57.] Replaces: "I keep dreaming how the hunter shot the wondrous beast because he . . ."

[58.] Replaces: "Imagine, we'll go on a nice trip to the mountains together and you'll come along with me."

[59.] Cf. the 1930 sermon fragment on Deut. 32:48-52: "God said to Moses: 'Go up unto the mountain of the Abarim and die on the mountain opposite the Promised Land'" (*DBW* 10:583; cf. 584: "Go up the mountain and die"). [Bonhoeffer summarizes the biblical verses, rather than quoting them fully. The NRSV version of the passage reads: "On that very day the Lord addressed Moses as follows: 'Ascend this mountain of the Abarim, Mount Nebo, which is in the land of Moab, across from Jericho, and view the land of Canaan, which I am giving to the Israelites for a possession; you shall die there on the mountain that you ascend and shall be gathered to your kin. . . .'" See also the Tegel poem "The Death of Moses" (*DBW* 8:590–98), partially translated by Nancy Lukens (Kelly and Nelson, *A Testament to Freedom,* 518–20) and completely translated by Edwin Robertson (*The Prison Poems of Dietrich Bonhoeffer,* 82–89.)][CG]

[60.] The following line is a later addition. Above it is the pencil marginal note: "Renate?"

Scene 2

Christoph's study, a typical student room. Books, pictures? A desk covered with lots of handwritten papers. He sits at the harpsichord, playing "Farewell to the Clavichord" by C. P. E. Bach.[1] Afternoon. Ulrich enters unnoticed as Christoph is playing, comes up quietly behind him, and suddenly puts his hands over Christoph's eyes.

Christoph: Renate!

Ulrich: (Laughs loudly)

Christoph: Oh, it's you, Ulrich. Stop that nonsense. Always up to tricks. *(Turns toward him with a friendly look.)* But it's good to see you anyway.

Ulrich: Feeling melancholy again?[2] *(Reaches for the music and reads)* " 'Farewell to My Clavichord,' by C. P. E. Bach." What's up with you? You hardly get back to your harpsichord, which you missed so terribly, and already you want to say farewell to it again? Say, have you lost your mind, or what? Come here. Sit down and talk to me about something sensible. *(Both sit down in easy chairs,[3] fill their pipes from a tobacco jar, and light them.)*

Christoph: If you really want to hear something sensible, I'll tell you. I really do lose my mind from time to time.

Ulrich: Really! Too bad! Unfortunately I just haven't noticed it yet. Just last night your mind was in pretty good shape—admit it.

Christoph: There's no way you could have noticed it at all, because I only lose my mind when I'm alone, and even then—luckily—only occasionally. For instance, what would you think of a promising young

---

[1.] C. P. E. Bach, "Farewell to My Silbermann Clavichord" (Wotquenne Verzeichnis, no. 66). After attending the Kassel Music Festival in the autumn of 1938, Dietrich Bonhoeffer and Eberhard Bethge purchased first a clavichord and soon thereafter a table spinet and music for these instruments, especially by C. P. E. Bach. Perhaps it was such purchases that Bonhoeffer had in mind when he wrote that "the human home . . . is the place where people may relish the joys of personal life amidst the comfort and security of their loved ones and their possessions" (*E* 156f. [trans. altered]).

[2.] Bonhoeffer was subject to depression at times, which in a letter to Eberhard Bethge on November 18, 1943, he called—using the traditional language of Western spirituality—his "accidie-tristitia" or spiritual lethargy-melancholy (*LPP* 129; cf. *DB-ER* 506). See also the letter to his parents on May 15, 1943: "I'm sure I never realized as clearly as I do here what the Bible and Luther mean by 'temptation' [Anfechtung]. . . . It feels like an invasion from outside, as if by evil powers trying to rob one of what is most vital" (*LPP* 39).

[3.] Replaces: "armchairs".

man of twenty-four who for the past month has caught himself, again and again, talking out loud to himself?

Ulrich: Well, hey—that's a pretty good start! It's really too bad about the promising young twenty-four-year-old!

Christoph: You can't imagine that you could ever lose your mind, Ulrich, can you?

Ulrich: Well, I don't have as much mind to lose as you—but let me think a minute—maybe if I were madly in love? But no, I think even there I've kept my wits about me pretty well—ah, now I've got it *(play-acting).* If a man in a black coat with a deadly serious expression on his face came to me today and solemnly declared: "Sir, allow me to convey to you the regrettable news: Tomorrow, unfortunately, you will be—executed."[4] If it were the day after tomorrow it would be different, then I'd probably wait till tomorrow to lose my mind. But joking aside,[5] Christoph. This reminds me of a conversation which was not at all funny that I had with the new fellow late last night on the way home. Actually this is the reason I came to see you today. You saw him too, didn't you, the fellow with black hair who sat with us all evening without saying a word. I felt like getting him to talk a little. After all, he could be an informer, and after everything you said last night, that's the last thing we need. So I went home with him. I asked him if he had enjoyed our group. At first he didn't answer at all, and then all of a sudden he said somewhat scornfully, "Who's this young aristocrat who was spouting off his wild theories tonight?"[6] I said, "We don't have any aristocrats in the group, but if you mean the tall blond fellow who was the only one saying anything sensible tonight, that's my friend. He's the son of the medical

37

[4.] Cf. the beginning of Kafka's novel, *The Trial:* "Someone must have slandered Josef K., for one morning, without having done anything truly wrong, he was arrested [by a man] wearing a fitted black jacket" (3).

[5.] A brief deletion here (". . . Renate . . ."), reappears later in the text; cf. page 43. Pencil marginal note, deleted in ink: "conversation with the new fellow." The following text is written on two inserted sheets of DIN-A4 paper with the watermark "suum cuique."

[6.] Cf. Lütgert, *Ethik der Liebe,* 85: "If humans are viewed as rational beings, then the ideal of humanity takes on a fundamentally nonmaterial [geistig], idealistic character; thus it becomes aristocratic." Cf. below, page 52, referring to Christoph as "of high ideals." On the other hand, Lütgert argues on page 84, "If humans are viewed as natural beings, then the duty of humanity is material well-being. The goal of the humanitarian effort is then the mass containing the individuals." Cf. below, page 63f., where Heinrich speaks for the masses.

director at the military hospital." At that he mumbled something to himself, but in such a way that I was supposed to hear it: "Well, well, it's getting better every minute—the son of the doctor who deprived me of my life, or, you might as well say, my well-deserved death." I was totally perplexed. Then after a considerable pause he asked, "I suppose this won't hold up much longer, either?" and pointed to his heart.

Christoph: Really, he said that?

Ulrich: Yes. I thought he might be crazy and asked, "What are you talking about, anyway?" So he says, "I thought you were his friend? And you haven't even noticed yet, have you?" You know, I'm usually not at a loss for words. But he said all this with such cold certainty and in such a tone, as if he knew some secret. It sent icy chills down my spine for a moment. For quite a while I walked alongside him without saying anything and wanted to say goodbye as soon as possible. But then suddenly he begins again. "I like you; you're honest. But your friend, he's fooling himself and the rest of you; watch out for him." I wanted to say, "What do you think you're doing? You don't know me or my friend; and here you are playing the big psychologist." But for some reason I again said nothing and was annoyed with him and with my own stupidity. Then out of the blue he asked again, "Can you take a blow?" "Speak," I answered. I shuddered again and again. But I couldn't back out now. Well, and what followed after that I can't begin to tell you in detail. A life story, a confession if you will—but he did not swear me to secrecy. On the contrary, at the end he said, "Tell this to your friend if you want, and say hello to him for me."

Christoph: Well? Go on.

Ulrich: Listen briefly to the main points at least. He didn't know his parents. His father was in prison for years for some terrible thing—he didn't say what—and died there. He grew up in his aunt's tavern, near the docks, surrounded by sailors and prostitutes.[7] When he

38

[7.] Cf. Georges Bernanos, *Diary of a Country Priest,* 124: "Such sad faces. As I squatted down, behind the bar—for I never stayed long in the dark shed where my aunt thought I was doing my homework—those faces loomed up above my head" [trans. altered]. On December 25, 1931, Bonhoeffer wrote about his confirmation students in the north end of Berlin: "That's about the wildest section of Berlin. . . . Home conditions are generally indescribable: poverty, disorder, immorality. And yet the children are still open. I am often

reached the age where he began to grasp what was going on around him—I have to use his own words: "Suddenly, there in the middle of hell, I met—God."[8] Through some coincidence he had come across a print, I guess something like Rembrandt's "The 100 Guilder Print,"[9] you know, Christ healing the poor. Underneath were two quotations: "His heart went out in pity to the poor," and "The tax collectors and whores will inherit God's kingdom sooner than you,"[10] or something like that. And then, he said, a frightful struggle began for him. He stayed in the same surroundings and gradually grew up. He tried, as he put it, to live with God in hell. To run away struck him as cowardly. He became a dockhand. At night he read books about economics, social policy, and above all the Bible.[11] When he came home from work, he'd pick up children loitering in the street, take them to his room, give them something to eat, say a few nice things to them, and send them home.[12] But the stuffy atmosphere and the misery around him were too terrible for him. He got to know a prostitute who loved him very much. He gave her money. He never slept with her, "out of pity, and out of reverence for Christ," as he expressed it in his strange way of speaking. He said he was never religious while living through all this; he never went to church.[13] "I never had the urge to speak out as a social reformer or preacher, either; all that comes to nothing anyway. But I simply couldn't forget God anymore, and I wanted to live in my hell

39

---

speechless. How is it possible for a boy in such conditions not to sink into total depravity?" (*No Rusty Swords*, 140) [trans. altered].

[8.] Cf. Nietzsche, *Thus Spoke Zarathustra*, pt. 2, "On the Pitying," 202: "Thus spoke the devil to me once: 'God too has his hell: that is his love of man.'"

[9.] Cf. Bonhoeffer's letter of August 20, 1933, from Bethel to his grandmother Julie Bonhoeffer: "Today in church I kept thinking of Rembrandt's 'The 100 Guilder Print' and the gospel accounts of that story" (*DBW* 12:117 [*GS* 2:78]). Cf. also his London sermon on Matt. 11:28-30 from late September 1934, in which Bonhoeffer says that in his "The 100 Guilder Print," Rembrandt draws "the weary and burdened" as "the poor, the wretched, the sick, the lepers, the ragged with their furrowed faces" (Kelly and Nelson, *Testament to Freedom*, 235 [*DBW* 13:374, *(GS* 5:529)]).

[10.] Cf. Matt. 9:36 and 21:31; on these passages, see *CD* 201–3 and *E* 62.

[11.] Cf. the characterization in Bonhoeffer's letter of January 29–30, 1944: "A truly educated man of working-class origin" who worked "in the place [Tegel Prison] was killed downtown by a direct hit" (*LPP* 199) [trans. altered].

[12.] Pencil marginal note: "no ambition to be influential!"

[13.] Pencil marginal note: "war, liberation, community! Again this misery with God's power as an impossible thing."

with God, out of pity."[14] He rejected all his employer's ideas and occasional suggestions that he make something more of his life, like finish high school, go to the university, and so on. He thought that would have just been an escape, and he might have forgotten about God and pity. "I always knew I wouldn't have long to live, and I was glad about that." That's how he put it, more or less.

Christoph: So that's what he said, is it?

40   *Ulrich:* Yes, and then the war came. It was a liberation for him. He had the feeling the worst was over now. He was sure he would be killed. "I know God wanted that, too," he said. It seems he distinguished himself by extraordinary valor and comradeship. He got the Iron Cross, Second Class, for carrying three wounded comrades, one after the other, from the line of fire back into the trenches. He told me about that only when I asked. Soon after that he also earned the Iron Cross, First Class. He refused all promotions. He has a letter from his captain who promised to take personal responsibility for his continued education after the war. Then he was seriously wounded. Before he fell into a coma he said to a comrade, "See that no one wakes me up. I am so glad. I have found *my* death;[15] I have arrived." Weeks later he woke up in your father's military hospital. They had done everything humanly possible to save his life. "This awakening was my end," he said. "Since then I have hated God and everybody. It was quite clear to me right away, and every breath confirmed it, that my life had only been artificially lengthened by a year or two. What good is this life to me? I can't go back to my hell where I had God; I have no strength left. Studying and whatever else they suggest and want to help me with—oh, these pitying people!—all this has no place in *my* life. And besides, I could no longer manage it. I

[14.] See the passages in *LPP* on sharing the sufferings of God in the world (362, 370). [CG]

[15.] Cf. below, pages 242f., "Drama Working Notes": "[My] own death. happy" (*NL* A 86, 90) and "The Death who seeks me is not *mine*" (*NL* A 86, 8). Cf. Rilke's *Book of Hours,* 131: "Oh Lord, give us each our own death, / the dying that proceeds / from each of our lives; / the way we loved, / the meanings we made, / our need." See also Rilke's poem in his "Requiem" cycle dedicated to Wolf Graf Kalckreuth after his suicide. The poem speaks of an artist having three "molds," namely feeling, gaze, and death, and continues that "in the third . . . a death was molded, / deepened by genuine labor, that own death / which has such need of us because we live it . . ." (*Requiem and Other Poems,* 140). See also below page 122, editorial note 61. In his letter of November 28, 1943, Bonhoeffer describes Rilke as "decidedly unhealthy" (*LPP* 148).

used up my strength before and during the war. I have none left; and because this is no life, I can't bear the thought of death either. Oh, these clever, these pitying people! How they have cheated God and 41 me. God wanted me to die; death came at the right time. The doctors[16] wanted me to live, and now I belong to the devil. Good night! Tell your friend if you like, and say hello to him from me." With that, he quickly walked around a corner and out of my sight.

Christoph: Strange, very strange.

Ulrich: Believe me, I lay awake a long time. Not until early this morning when the sun shone so gloriously into my room did I shake off last night's discussion, like a nightmare. You know, Christoph, I really dread seeing him again.

Christoph: I'll go to see him. He isn't crazy or bad, and he's certainly not stupid. He's simply very lonely. But he seems to know something. . . .

Ulrich: Christoph, please, don't go to see him; he'll only put crazy ideas into your head. You can do without those right now; and besides, he's mistrustful of you. Go to see Renate; that's better for you. And besides, you owe her a visit and an explanation for your strange behavior yesterday afternoon.

Christoph: Renate!

Ulrich: What's the matter with you, Christoph? Sometimes you are so unpredictable these days. By the way, you don't need to go to her house; I met her a little while ago in the street.[17] She was wearing that light dress you love to see her in,[18] and once again she looked so infinitely good and kind, much more than you deserve. She asked about you, how it went with the group last night, what time we went home, and when you could usually be found in your room. She seemed a bit anxious and I think she will come by to see you.

Christoph: Ulrich, that mustn't happen.

Ulrich: But Christoph, what's that supposed to mean? Really, it's getting so I don't understand you anymore. Did Renate hurt you in some 42 way, or . . . ?

[16.] The German literally says "the people," but it refers to the doctors who treated him. [CG]

[17.] End of insert. See editorial note 5 above.

[18.] On July 3, 1943, Bonhoeffer wrote to his parents asking for a picture of his fiancée taken at the wedding of Klaus von Bismarck and Ruth-Alice von Wedemeyer: ". . . It is so pretty; and the dress I find especially beautiful." Cf. the photograph in Bonhoeffer and von Wedemeyer, *Brautbriefe Zelle 92* (276, German edition only). Cf. Bethge et al., *DBLP* 147, for a photograph of another part of the wedding procession.

Christoph: (harshly) I'm telling you, Ulrich, it must not happen. *(after a pause)* You know, too, that the whole thing was a childhood friendship and that I never said a word or did anything to bind her to me.

Ulrich: (completely surprised and horrified) What? Shame on you, Christoph, I don't know you anymore.

Christoph: (passionately) Ulrich, please, come to the mountains with me tomorrow.[19] There it will all become clear. Come with me, Ulrich!

Ulrich: I wouldn't think of spending my time with someone who is such a deserter. Christoph, if you really have lost your mind, at least ask your heart what Renate has been to you all through the war and up to now! How you longed for her, how everything you thought and did belonged to her alone, how you had no thoughts and no time for anything but her. . . .

Christoph: All that was a long time ago.

Ulrich: (not letting Christoph interrupt him) The rest of us who knew her—and perhaps sighed for her secretly at times—we held no grudges. Christoph, do I have to tell you that she was sometimes . . . in my dreams and that those were difficult nights in which I left her completely to you and you alone. Do I have to tell you that I haven't looked at another girl since I first saw Renate? Christoph, through all this I have remained your friend and was able to look you in the eye with a clear conscience. . . .

Christoph: Be quiet, Ulrich. I know all that, but talk no more. You don't understand what is happening. But believe me, some day you'll understand—and you'll be glad.

Ulrich: Oh, that's what they all say. I never would have thought you could say such a thing. Even now on your desk is her . . . *(very harshly)* Christoph, where did you put her picture? Tell me!

43 *Christoph: (softly, but unrelenting)* I put it away with the music—along with the memories I am leaving behind.[20]

Ulrich: That does it, Christoph. This is madness. I'm leaving. *(Walks quickly to the door. At the same moment Renate enters.)* Renate! Forgive

---

[19.] Deleted: "My parents have offered the two of us a trip."

[20.] On the Monday after Pentecost of his second year in Tegel Prison (May 29, 1944), Dietrich Bonhoeffer wrote to Maria von Wedemeyer: "I was once in love with a girl; she became a theologian . . ." (*LL* 208). Cf. *DB-ER* 468f.: "Bonhoeffer had parted [in 1936] from a woman friend to whom he had been especially close in the late 1920s and also again after the beginning of the Church Struggle" [trans. altered]. Cf. Bonhoeffer's letter of January 27, 1936, to Elisabeth Zinn (*DBW* 14:112ff. [*GS* 6:367f.]).

me, Renate, I was just coming to tell you. Christoph doesn't feel well today. I suppose his wounds are troubling him some again. He wants to be alone. It's better if we go. *(Renate very calmly walks over to Christoph.)* No, you mustn't stay here today; it isn't good for him. He needs rest. . . .

Renate: (next to Christoph, very quietly and lovingly) Am I disturbing your rest, Christoph?

Christoph: (now standing, takes Renate's hand) Stay here, Renate. *(Ulrich exits. Renate sits down. Christoph paces the room for a while.)*[21]

Renate: I've come to ask you to forgive me.

Christoph: You . . . Me? Forgive you?

Renate: Yes. I was wrong to speak to you the way I did last night. Seeing you again after such a long time, I was so thrilled I forgot what you had been through in the meantime. It didn't occur to me how all of that must have changed you. I was just so happy to see you. So I talked as I used to talk to you. I had no right to do that. It must have hurt you. Of course you're not the same person you were four years ago. Of all people *I* should have known that.

Christoph: You're so good,[22] Renate. You haven't changed a bit. . . . So I'm not the same person as before, eh? Maybe you're right, but perhaps in a different way than you mean. Do you want me to explain that to you?

Renate: No, Christoph, no explanations. They don't help at all.[23] Let time pass and heal things. In such moments words are totally pointless. . . . *(changing the subject)*[24] What was the matter with Ulrich? He seemed upset. Forgive me for asking; it's really none of my business. You don't need to answer.

Christoph: I hurt Ulrich. I disappointed him. He was right; I was wrong. He had to leave.

Renate: I don't believe that, Christoph. You can't ever hurt Ulrich; you couldn't hurt anybody.

44

[21.] A brief insert (on a sheet of "suum cuique" paper) follows, up to the words below, *"changing the subject."*

[22.] Manuscript unclear. "Good" appears to replace *du* (the intimate form of "you"). If this reading is correct the original would have meant "You are you, Renate [that is, you are still the same], you are always the same."

[23.] Deleted: "and only hurt."

[24.] End of brief insert.

Christoph: Unfortunately you deceive yourself, Renate. You're just as wrong about me as Ulrich was.

Renate: But it's unthinkable that anything could come between you and Ulrich, or that you couldn't work things out anymore, or that you would hurt each other.

Christoph: Not each other, Renate; I hurt Ulrich.

Renate: Let's not argue, Christoph. I believe everything you say, but Ulrich breaking off his friendship with you, bearing a grudge against you—that I'll never believe![25]

Christoph: You're right. Ulrich will never do anything like that. He's much the better of the two of us. But I . . . I bitterly disappointed him. So he couldn't do anything else.

Renate: (sadly) I'm sorry, so very sorry. . . . Then I'd better go too. *(Slowly gets up)*[26]

Christoph: Yes, that's probably better. You both thought too highly of me; that was your mistake. Let me tell you, Renate, Ulrich is a hundred times better than I am.

Renate: Poor Christoph. Farewell. *(exits)*

Christoph: (paces for a while, then drops into an armchair) Yes, poor Christoph. That's what I've done—Ulrich gone, Renate gone! Just what I wanted—and now that it's happened I feel like a madman. That's what I get for wanting to lord it over people without being cut out for the job. Theatrical heroics! The stranger is quite right: "Watch out, Ulrich, he's fooling himself and others."[27] Why don't I do what he does and simply talk about it, like he did to Ulrich, whom he didn't even know. Yes, perhaps that's it—I could talk with the stranger; but with Renate, Ulrich, or our parents, that's impossible. I have to get through this by myself. Renate—my dear girl. Day or night, there wasn't a thought that didn't belong to you, no patrol I

45

[25.] "Ulrich breaking off . . . never believe" replaces "Before Ulrich breaks off . . . the world will come to an end."

[26.] Added, then later deleted and replaced with the short insert above on page 45: "I've come to ask you to forgive me. . . ." At the end of these additions which were later deleted: "It's not your fault, I swear to you. I can't accept this from you. | *Renate:* I'm leaving, Christoph."

[27.] Cf. Bonhoeffer's letter of December 15, 1943: "I often ask myself who I really am, the one . . . who appears to others (and to himself as well) as the calm, cheerful, tranquil, superior one and lets people admire him for all this (i.e., this theatrical act, or is it not an act?)" *(LPP* 162) [trans. altered]. [See also the poem "Who Am I?" *(LPP* 347f.).][CG]

didn't go on for you. Every time I was starving, freezing, in pain, it was for you I endured it. . . . There was not a single piece of bread, not a ray of sunshine, not a flowering field in which I didn't discover you, not a single note I didn't write for you. Renate, farewell! Ulrich, you faithful friend. You've never let me down. We've shared everything,[28] hours of strength and of weakness.[29] I trusted you blindly.[30] I could tell you everything, everything—except now this one thing. Ulrich, thank you, I wish you happiness. *(Jumps up.)* Damned monologues! I'm going to see the stranger. *(Exits.)*

(A short pause during which the audience can take in details of Christoph's room. There is a knock at the door. No answer. The door opens, Ulrich enters first, then Renate.)

Ulrich: He's not here. Maybe he went outside for a while. The fresh air will dispel his moodiness.

Renate: I think he's probably looking for somebody.

Ulrich: What makes you think that?

Renate: Because we both failed him today, and now he is quite alone.

Ulrich: (somewhat stunned) Well, he did talk a little while ago about wanting to look up someone. . . . I should have stopped him! *(Hits his forehead with his hand.)* And why did I run away and not stay with him?

Renate: No, Ulrich, we must let him find his own way now. He won't do anything foolish.

Ulrich: You're probably right. Christoph hardly ever does anything foolish.

Renate: Both of us simply have to be present for him now. We mustn't pry or try to persuade him. He just needs to know we're there.

Ulrich: No, Renate, I can't deal with Christoph in such an ethereal way. I want to know what's going on with him. We have never kept anything from each other till now. He knows that there is nothing that he couldn't tell me about, and that I will stand by him, whatever it is. But I refuse to play hide-and-seek with him. It doesn't suit Christoph or me. *(with some pathos)* It is also simply a betrayal of our friendship.

46

[28.] Deleted passage contains the phrase: "you lay beside me in the military hospital."

[29.] Replaces: "In my hours of weakness I held on to you" which itself had replaced "you helped me in my hours of weakness, and quietly made the greatest sacrifice for me."

[30.] Replaces: "I could count on your rock-solid support."

Renate: Even friends, yes, even husband and wife, can't always tell each other everything. Sometimes they have to give each other a long time until the right word has grown and ripened. Words have their proper time. Forced words are like broken buds. What you solemnly call a betrayal of your friendship could be just the opposite, a necessary test of your friendship. Perhaps Christoph would betray himself and you if he spoke now about something that isn't yet ripe.

Ulrich: Between friends there are no secrets. Of course you don't whisper to each other every little heartthrob like teenage girls. You just know about those feelings, period. Openness and trust rule between friends. What else is a friend for?

Renate: There are things that sometimes one must keep silent about for a while before one can talk about them, even between friends, even between husband and wife.[31] One must give the other time. Openness is something wonderful, but being open for the other, even for the other's silence, is more important. Trust is not based on knowing everything about the other person, but on one believing in the other.[32]

47

Ulrich: One can use that to excuse all kinds of secrecy, and under such a pretext much that is uncontrollable, opaque, creeps in between two people. I'm for clarity. I can't deal with leaving things imprecise. I want to see my friend as he is.

Renate: What does that mean? Do you want to see him like a photograph that records everything? Or with the respectful and loving eyes of one who only takes in and is affected by the essential picture of the other, and who lets the other's secret be? And what is clarity, when there is often so much obscurity within people themselves? Then one must wait until the storm has passed and the water has settled and cleared up again. We must have a lot of patience with one another.

Ulrich: Don't you know that if you carry a secret around with you for too long and don't dare to tell anyone it can destroy you?

Renate: Yet you can't rob anyone of their secret without destroying them. Haven't you ever sensed that it's the really good people we know

---

[31.] Bonhoeffer's comments on the "discipline of the secret," while focused, to be sure, on God's mysteries, are probably pertinent in this context also (cf. *LPP* 281, 286, and 300). [CG]

[32.] See below, page 237, "Drama Working Notes" (*NL* A 86, 10), for the first draft of this sentence.

who carry a secret within themselves that's never revealed to us, and that they themselves dare not touch? It shines through their every word, every glance. But if you tried to put it into words, the best part of it would be destroyed. Good people don't know why they are what they are, and they don't want to know. The ultimate secret of every human being is . . . God. We should allow the other to have that.[33] But it's really absurd for me to say all this to you. What would Christoph be without you? Everything you are doing is just fine, after all, and—you will go to the mountains with Christoph, won't you, if he asks you?

Ulrich: Don't press me, Renate, please. Do you think it would be easy for me to say no to Christoph? Naturally I could hardly stand letting Christoph go alone. Still—you don't know the issue between us. Nor   48 could I treat Christoph as gently and patiently as you imagine. But just wait, it will all be straightened out all right.[34]

Renate: I couldn't bear to see you two estranged. You belong together.

Ulrich: Yes, that's true, but you belong with us. *(Stands at the desk, pointing at handwritten papers lying on it.)* Do you know what these are?

Renate: No, and I don't want to know, either.

Ulrich: But I want to show you. These are Christoph's notes of the ideas he's been presenting to our group for some time. Since he came home he's worked on nothing else but this. He's totally consumed by it.[35]

Renate: Leave it alone, Ulrich, it belongs to Christoph.

Ulrich: (laughing) That's a joke! Do you think there's a sentence in there that he hasn't already read to me, and that we haven't already talked about? It belongs to both of us. *(Picks up the papers.)*

Renate: Please, put it back.

Ulrich: No, Renate, there's really nothing in this room that doesn't belong as much to me as to Christoph. There are no secrets here. So listen, because what he's writing here is going to be good. You'll like

---

[33.] Replaces: "We cannot fathom it." On the word "secret" see *CD* 112 on Matt. 5:8 and *CD* 303 on 2 Cor. 3:18 and Phil. 1:21.

[34.] Replaces five deleted lines, beginning with the sentence, "Oh, of course I'll go, Renate. That's completely obvious," and ending with "Renate, let us both, each in our own way, be present, as you put it, for Christoph."

[35.] Replaces: "Notes for a major lecture he's to give to our group; I think it will eventually be a book." From 1940 until his arrest in 1943 Bonhoeffer had been working on the manuscript of his *Ethics*.

49

it. Here's the last page he's written.[36] *(Reads.)* "I speak to you to protect from abuse the great words that have been given to humanity. They do not belong on the lips of the masses or in newspaper headlines, but in the hearts of the few who guard and protect them with their lives. It is never a good sign when what has always been the calm and firm possession and the self-evident attitude of all the country's well-meaning people is shouted loudly in the streets as the latest wisdom. Those who guard genuine values with their lives, their work, and their homes, turn away in disgust from the clanging words intoned to convert the masses into prophets. What well-meaning person today can still utter the besmirched words freedom, brotherhood, or even the word Germany? They seek genuine values in the silence of the sanctuary which only the humble and the faithful may approach. Each of us has put our life on the line for these values. Those who mouth them today find them profitable. Let us honor the highest values by silence for a while. Let us learn to do what is right without words for a while.[37] Then, around the quiet sanctuary of the highest values a new nobility will form in our time.[38] Neither

---

[36.] Bonhoeffer wrote the following passage three times, here and twice in the "Drama Working Notes" (see below, pages 238f. and 240f.), *NL* A 86, 10 (outline), and *NL* A 86, 11 (fleshing-out of the outline, incorporated almost word for word in the manuscript). This is an allusion to the perversion of "great words," especially in National Socialist Germany. Cf. Karl Jaspers, *Man in the Modern Age,* 76 (written in 1930, before the National Socialist period and used by Bonhoeffer for his *Ethics*), on language in a mass culture: "From the mouths of those who have sunk into mere complacent existence there frequently come expressions of feigned pathos, dragged up to serve the needs of the day, such as 'the sanctity of life,' 'the majesty of death,' 'the majesty of the people [Volk],' 'the will of the people is the will of God,' 'service of the people,' etc. . . . This sophistry alternates between the clever opportunism of selfish life, on the one hand, and irrational outbursts, on the other" [trans. altered]. Bonhoeffer's passage beginning "I speak to you" and continuing up to "to do what is . . . right" (page 51) was first published, with omissions, in *GS* 3:479f.

[37.] Cf. the last section of the baptism letter of May 1944, in which Bonhoeffer wrote that when "earlier words . . . lose their force" our being Christians will be "limited to two things: prayer and righteous action among human beings" (*LPP* 300) [trans. altered]. Here in the drama, the political dimension of the discipline of silence becomes clear. Cf. Bonhoeffer's remarks regarding the "discipline of the secret" in the letters of April 30, 1944 (*LPP* 281), and May 5, 1944 (*LPP* 286).

[38.] Cf. "After Ten Years," written in 1942–43: "We are witnessing the leveling down of all ranks of society, and at the same time the birth of a new sense of nobility, which is binding together a circle of people from all former social classes" (*LPP* 12f.) [trans. altered]. As early as 1913 Stefan George had coined the phrase "new nobility" in a poem very well known in its time: "New nobility you wanted / Does not hail from crown or scutcheon! / . . . Scions rare of rank intrinsic / Grow from masses, not from peerage . . ." (*Poems,* 213).

birth nor success will be the foundation of this nobility, but humility, faith, and sacrifice. There is an infallible standard to test the great and the small, the valid and the immaterial, the genuine and the fraudulent, the weighty word and frivolous gossip: that standard is death. Whoever knows that their death is near is resolute, but also reserved. *(reads slower and slower, with an expression of bewilderment, speaking more to himself than to Renate)* Without words, indeed misunderstood if need be and lonely, they do what is necessary and right, and make their sacrifice."—It stops here. Strange . . . I really didn't know this paragraph. Here's a postscript in pencil. "What kind of lofty words are these? Why am I beating around the bush? Why don't I simply say what I mean and know? Or if I don't want to do that, why don't I just remain silent? How hard it is to do what is necessary and right, quite without words, without being understood.[39] Oh Renate! Ulrich!" *(Ulrich has read these last words with increasing horror, lowers the page, very shaken.)* Christoph! Renate, do you understand this? 50

Renate: I think so, . . . yes.

Ulrich: Forgive me, Renate, I didn't know. You were right. Forgive me, Christoph! God, it isn't possible.

Renate: Stop, Ulrich, it had to happen this way. Let's go. I'll leave Christoph a note. *(Writes something on a piece of paper. Ulrich does the same. They exit silently.)*

(Behind the door, Little Brother's voice): Christoph! Christoph! Listen, it's me! *(Rushes in)* Christoph, I can go with you; I'm going to the mountains with you! *(Looks around the empty room, notices the two pieces of paper and reads the first)* "Christoph, forgive me. Renate." *(Then the other one)* "Of course I'm coming with you. Ulrich." *(Curtain)*

[39.] Replaces: "to do silently what must be done."

Scene 3

In Heinrich's room.[1] *A bed, table, chair, sofa, picture, all in the style of the cheapest rental apartment. On the table a pistol, a bottle of schnapps and a glass, some leftovers and a few papers. Heinrich walks back and forth restlessly, smoking a cigarette. The door opens quietly, without a knock. A middle-aged gentleman enters, dressed in the inconspicuous but proper dark clothing of a middle-class salesman. He wears glasses which almost totally hide his eyes. His face is expressionless, opaque, smooth, masklike.*[2]

Stranger: Good evening, young man. *(when there is no response)* You called for me.

Heinrich: You are mistaken. I don't know you at all.

Stranger: Of course you don't. That's exactly why you called me, because you wanted to meet me.

Heinrich: I'm telling you, you've got the wrong person. I'm in no condition to want to meet people—with one exception perhaps, and it's not you.

Stranger: Who is this interesting exception, if I may ask?

Heinrich: That's hardly any business of yours. Now, if you'll be so good as to . . .[3] *(walks toward the door)*

Stranger: Since you won't tell me, perhaps I might be permitted to tell you. The interesting exception is a medical student your age, tall, intelligent, of high ideals.

52 *Heinrich: (taken aback)* What do you really want from me? Who are you, anyway?

Stranger: Your neighbor, young man, who sees you going out and coming

---

[1.] This scene was first printed in 1948 in the journal *Die Schöpfung,* then in 1960 in *GS* 3:480–95. [It was first translated in *True Patriotism,* 199–215.][CG]

[2.] Jan Sperna Weiland, *Het einde van die religie,* considers this a possible allusion to the stranger in T. S. Eliot's stage play *The Rock.* It was staged in London in 1934, during the time that Bonhoeffer was there as pastor from 1933–35. On the German stage surreal figures such as the figure of Death in street clothes and the use of understatement occurred only after 1945 [for example, in Wolfgang Borchert's *The Man Outside,* in 1947][NL]. But see Romano Guardini's "Gentleman" in his 1939 adaptation of Dostoyevsky's *The Brothers Karamazov* (*Religiöse Gestalten in Dostojewskijs Werk,* 193; see pages 55f. above, editorial note 12) as well as the figure of "The Nameless One" in Ernst Toller's *Masses and Man* (113), which dates from 1920. Bonhoeffer had read stage plays by Toller in 1931 (cf. *DBW* 10:398 [*GS* 6:201f.]).

[3.] Deleted: "I still have urgent work to do this evening."

in, morning and evening, who sees the light on in your room until dawn, and who knows what goes on in this room in the lonely hours of the night.

Heinrich: I am not interested in talking with my neighbors, especially those who pry.[4]

Stranger: "Pry" might not be the right word here. I have no need at all to pry.

Heinrich: Why are you watching me, then? Why are you interested in me?

Stranger: That is part of my job, if I may say so.

Heinrich: What is your job?

Stranger: That's not so easy to say in one word. Let's say—I'm a sales representative.

Heinrich: (laughs) Ah, and so you kept an eye on me and found out that I lack certain things necessary to a good middle-class life and you want to sell them to me. In that case you'd have done better if you'd also had a closer look at my wallet. What do you represent? Persian rugs? English textiles?[5] Parisian perfumes? American cars?[6]

Stranger: You misunderstand me, young man.

Heinrich: . . . or perhaps you're selling life insurance?

Stranger: More like the opposite.

Heinrich: (laughs) That's the first interesting thing you've said. The opposite of life insurance! Would you please explain what you mean by that? Here, have a drink *(both sit down)*. Well, speak. What firm do you represent?

Stranger: The most widespread and influential business on earth.   53

Heinrich: And that would be . . . ?

Stranger: Death.

Heinrich: Man, are you mad?[7]

Stranger: Please remain calm, young man, and rest assured that I'm quite sane. I'll explain in more detail if you wish and I'm certain that you'll understand me well, young man, very well!

[4.] Replaces: "those who are indiscreet."

[5.] Replaces: "cloth".

[6.] Cf. von Oertzen's *Junker* (read by Bonhoeffer for his *Ethics*), with reference to Germany in the last pre-war period before the outbreak of World War I: "It blindly consumed an excess of unnecessary foreign goods" (378).

[7.] Deleted: "but actually you don't look mad."

Heinrich: Yes, I won't deny that in this case I'm interested in what you do. But[8] you must permit me a few questions. Yes, I am interested in your occupation—perhaps more than you imagine.

Stranger: I know that.

Heinrich: So the essential questions, I suppose, would be how you got this job, what you're paid, and who your clientele is?

Stranger: Clever questions. I can tell we'll see eye to eye. How did I get my job? Before I answer that one, allow me to ask you a question which will greatly facilitate our understanding. Have you ever been condemned to death?

Heinrich: (hesitating) No—Yes!

Stranger: No! You thought once that you were under a death sentence, when you left for the war. You sentenced yourself to death. That's something altogether different.

Heinrich: (ominously) God condemned me to death, but the doctors outwitted God.

Stranger: (winces)[9] Nonsense, utter nonsense. You got this idea into your head; you were fed up with your life, and you thought you could order Death around. You underestimated Death. Death stood you up.

54 *Heinrich:* Death comes when I want. Here! *(Picks up the pistol.)*

Stranger: Wrong, you're dangerously wrong, if you carry on like this. You can only shoot when Death lets you. Not a moment sooner. Haven't you already had the thing in your hand a few times and wanted to pull the trigger, . . . but it wouldn't work, you couldn't, something . . . you yourself didn't know what . . . held your finger back? Don't say it was cowardice, or your thirst for life. You're no coward, and you have no thirst for life. It was Death.

Heinrich: Death is an event like a war, a storm, an earthquake. These events are in the hands—of God.

Stranger: (winces again) Wrong, utterly wrong. You still have a lot to learn, young man. Death is not an event, it is a . . . being, a . . . Lord, . . . *the* Lord. Well, to get to the point. I was condemned to death—inciden-

---

[8.] Replaces: "So you see yourself as something of an agent of Death. That is certainly worth listening to."

[9.] Cf. Bonhoeffer's sermon of January 15, 1933 (*DBW* 12:441 [*GS* 4:102]) where he speaks of naming the name "of the One before whom the wicked one in us winces." [In quoting this passage, the German editors of *DBW* 7 relied on a version of Bonhoeffer's text that subsequently has been published in a slightly different form in *DBW* 12; we follow here the wording of the latter.]

tally, I was innocent of course, but that's irrelevant here. For four weeks I stared at Death,[10] at first gaping, as if into a dark night sky when it confronts you like an impenetrable black wall, then terrified, as if staring at the falling blade of a guillotine; then again with burning desire, as if looking upon a bride on the eve of the wedding; then full of admiration as for a powerful boss.[11] When I was released it was too late, I couldn't return to life. I had already come to an agreement with Death.

Heinrich: What does that mean?

Stranger: What does it mean? I'll tell you. You see my dark glasses? I wear them because people have told me that they can't stand my gaze anymore since I returned from prison, in other words since I looked Death in the eye. Since then I see everything with the eyes of Death, and you will understand that Death sees things very differently from a living person.

Heinrich: As far as I can see, you're still a living person.

Stranger: As far as you can see, yes. But you don't see much yet. I know, you already see much more than other people. You saw Death in the eyes of the young medical student, for example.

Heinrich: Don't talk about that.

Stranger: As you wish! I was speaking about my sentencing. At that time I learned that Death is not an event, as you put it. Only those who haven't really come to know Death personally, who have not been alone with him for days and nights on end, can call Death an event. One night he began to speak with me. I must tell you that his bearing and manner of speaking were very calm and quite refined. He didn't even frighten me—no hint of shaking like a skeleton, hair standing on end, or breaking out in a cold sweat! No, there was something rather reassuring about him. I'm telling you, Death is a gentleman,[12] he requires nothing inappropriate, he is considerate,

55

[10.] Cf. Bonhoeffer's untitled literary sketch on the theme of "Death" (probably from 1932): "The thought that he must actually die one day had so overpowered him that he was still staring this Unavoidable Thing in the face, paralyzed by fear" (*DBW* 11:373 [*GS* 6:233]).

[11.] "Superior" [Chef] replaces: "Lord" [Herr]. The "Drama Working Notes" contain an earlier draft of this sentence (*NL* A 86, 8; see page 243). In that version, the lines that follow are a draft of the August 3, 1943, letter from Tegel Prison about the choice of an attorney to defend Bonhoeffer (*LPP* 87f.). In the drama manuscript, the sentence is a marginal insertion.

[12.] Cf. Guardini's quote from Dostoyevsky's *The Brothers Karamazov* about an appearance of the devil, in which Ivan Karamazov's "eyes continued to look toward that one

he is reticent, and he is very cool and collected. We talked for a long time. That is when we came to an agreement.[13]

Heinrich: That's insane!

Stranger: It wasn't until I was free again that I noticed what had happened to me. People and things looked completely different to me than before. I couldn't talk with anyone without seeing Death standing behind them. Every word they said seemed hollow, every laugh empty, their rage and their joy both seemed meaningless. In their eyes I read—without meaning to or doing anything at all myself—the time and circumstances when their life's flame would expire.[14] I happened to meet my fiancée and immediately broke off our relationship. My mother took me in her arms; I withdrew, and it was the only time since that agreement with Death that I have felt anything like tears in my eyes.

Heinrich: Horrible!

Stranger: Not as horrible as you think. Otherwise everything left me cold. Nothing could excite me anymore, nothing could upset me. On the contrary, I felt as calm, as empty, as solemn, and as indifferent as if I were in a strange cemetery.[15] I really feel quite fine. No passions anymore, no throbbing of the heart, no flaming emotion—my heart beats as regularly as clockwork. No love, no friendship, no compas-

---

point, over there by the divan. . . . Suddenly someone was seated there! . . . It was some important man, or rather a Russian gentleman . . ." *(Religiöse Gestalten in Dostojewskijs Werk,* 193). Guardini continues on the following page: "The guest speaks politely, devotedly, insinuatingly . . ." (194).

[13.] Replaces a short passage which ends: ". . . a gentleman. I replied. We talked for a long time. Finally I received my assignment from him."

[14.] Replaces: "of their death."

[15.] [The German *fremd* is both the name of the visitor, the Stranger, and here an adjective denoting the contrast between a familiar cemetery where one visits the graves of one's loved ones and an unfamiliar one.][NL] In a deleted, two page long first draft, the following passage was included at this point: ". . . Only one thing surprised me; I could even say it amused me. That was the blindness of people toward their own death. I hear them talk about death, preach and philosophize and joke about it, but I see that they have no idea who death is. For death in general, the death one philosophizes and preaches and sings and writes poems about, isn't what's interesting, is it? [Deleted: not even the death of another person] Very simply, what is interesting is my death, your death with its When, How and Where. That's precisely the death they don't know. And that's why they live, every one of them, as if there were no death for them. They all deny it, without exception, philosopher and fool alike. They philosophize and joke, they eat, drink, fall in love, and marry. They work hard and wear themselves out as if it were for eternity [replaces: as if it would go on eternally] and all the time someone they don't notice is looking over their shoulder."

sion, no tears.[16] And yet I'm more interested than ever in people, since I see how Death looks over everyone's shoulder.

Heinrich: So you mean to say that you have second sight?

Stranger: Yes and no. You see, I've lost my first sight; all I have left is what you call the "second." That is why I don't suffer from it like those who have only occasional visitations and are terrified by them.[17] You see, that's what matters most, coming clean, setting things straight. "No one can serve two masters."[18]

Heinrich: A rather monotonous kind of service, the way you talk about it.

Stranger: On the contrary, young man, quite the opposite. It's very diverse and varied. It's not the result that's interesting, the result which people call death, because that's the first time they see him. What is interesting is the slow but sure work death does on people while they're still alive. Dissolution, degeneration, decadence, and decay of the living body—that's what's interesting. Dying is interesting, not being dead. Dying takes a long time and is just as varied as life.[19]

Heinrich: This conversation is beginning to disgust me.

Stranger: I can believe that, young man, and I'll tell you why, too. You go only halfway. You're wounded but not dead; you're weak. Sure, you know more than most people—that's just why I came to see you—but you're making a terrible mistake.[20] You're splitting yourself up. You do see your own death. Good, that's a beginning. But then you're suddenly so dead serious about everything that you do and think. You start fidgeting and writhing, protesting. You're insulted that Death looks quite different from the picture you had painted for yourself.[21] You reproach Death for avoiding you when you were

---

[16.] See below, page 243 (*NL* A 86, 8), "Drama Working Notes," where one finds the additional phrase "no faith."

[17.] The deletion in the first version reads here: "It has become my nature. All I see is Death, everywhere. He is my only companion, [Deleted: very versatile and interesting company, by the way, with very high expectations, but also very magnanimous.] *Heinrich: (somewhat cynically)* All the same, rather monotonous."

[18.] Matt. 6:24, which ends with the words: "You cannot serve God and wealth." Cf. *CD* 173–77.

[19.] Cf. Nietzsche, *Thus Spoke Zarathustra*, pt. 1, sec. 21, "On Free Death": "Everybody considers dying important; but as yet death is no festival" (71). Cf. Bonhoeffer's poem "Stations on the Way to Freedom," written after the failure of the July 20, 1944, assassination attempt against Hitler: "Come now, highest of feasts on the journey to freedom eternal, death . . ." (*LPP* 391 [trans. altered]).

[20.] The deleted section at this point says: ". . . the same terrible mistake that everyone else makes too; you suddenly take everything you do and think with deadly seriousness."

[21.] Addition to the deleted section: "You want to order Death around."

seeking him, and for seeking you out now that you are avoiding him. You make a great scene with the revolver, philosophize about what would make the "most honorable exit" for you. You'd like very much to have Death tickle your vanity once more. You vacillate and get nowhere. You want to serve two masters but serve neither. So you get your thrashing from both. What a pitiful state you're in! You're dishonest! In that respect your friend, this young medical student, is quite a different kind of fellow altogether. . . .

Heinrich: I'm telling you, be quiet. If you are unhappy yourself and have to make other people unhappy, then at least leave me out of it, and that other person I don't even know.

Stranger: I'm truly sorry to have to contradict you once again. I am neither unhappy myself—as I said before—nor do I make people unhappy. On the contrary, quite the contrary![22] What do people want? I'll admit there were times when they wanted to live, just live no matter what. So they made Death into a skeleton with a scythe. They blasphemed and mocked him, for they wanted to live forever. They created a social order and laws whose sole purpose was to preserve life. Whoever violated this order and these laws became a vassal of Death so that the others could live. I confess quite honestly that I have difficulty imagining myself in those times; I don't understand them. That is because I have lost my "first" sight. But today? Who wants to keep on living, anyway? A few lovebirds who are afraid the world could collapse before they reach their lovers. A few fools drunk with their own power who build monuments to themselves that will outlast the centuries. But all the rest? Who among them still blaspheme or mock Death? Shouldn't we say they blaspheme and mock life? Once, in prison, I opened the Bible and read the words, "They struggle to find death."[23] That is a wise saying. That is how people are nowadays. They don't fear Death, they don't flee from him, but seek him out, love him. "They struggle to find death." The only way you can make people happy nowadays is to help them find Death.[24]

[22.] Deleted: "Just look at people—what gives them joy?"

[23.] Wisd. of Sol. 1:16: "[But] the ungodly struggle to find death. . . . For they consider him a friend." [NRSV: "But the ungodly . . . summoned death; considering him a friend, they pined away . . ."][CG]

[24.] Cf. *CF* on Gen. 3:22 on Adam after the fall: "Adam then and today, to the extent

Heinrich: Have you ever heard it said that people these days[25] are in bet-   59
ter health and live longer than ever before?

Stranger: Quite so. But you must understand it right. Death has changed
his tactics with the times. In the past, when people loved life and
feared death, he came suddenly, abruptly, terribly; he tore infants
from their mothers and young mothers from their children,
destroyed whole villages in a few days by epidemics and all sorts of
devastations. Today, when Death is longed for, he comes sneaking
along slowly, in gradual, hardly noticeable disintegration. In the
past, people took their lives by the dagger or by hanging; today they
take sleeping pills. Then, people struggled for days as they died; now
they slip away with morphine.[26] You see, Death adapts himself. In
barbaric times, when the main issue is survival, Death is barbaric
too. In civilized times, when people have become honest and clever,
Death approaches them in a civilized way as well—with occasional
exceptions now and then! I say all this only to prove to you that I do
not make people unhappy; on the contrary, I make them happy.

Heinrich: What you are serving up here is a rare mixture of reason and
madness. Don't you see how the masses today are fighting with all
they have to enjoy life, to achieve respect, freedom? Isn't that a will
to live that throws all your theories overboard?

Stranger: See, now you have arrived at the main point. Presumably you'll
be surprised when I tell you that I, too, actively support these various efforts. In fact, this is my primary occupation. I work as a func-
tionary in numerous organizations of this kind, partly out of   60
idealism, partly for business.[27]

Heinrich: Well, you too must earn your wages somehow; I was just wondering how you actually make your living.

Stranger: Oh, don't worry about that, young man. Frankly, Death isn't a
bad business. Depending on the circumstances, I advise some to buy

---

that Adam understands Adam as Adam, does not want eternal life; instead Adam wants
death, wants to die" (143).

[25.] Deleted: "thanks to science, live longer."

[26.] In Santayana's *The Last Puritan,* Oliver's father kills himself with a carefully mixed
potion of intoxicants, without a clear reason (319). Cf. by contrast Bonhoeffer's own
thoughts about suicide in *E* 164–71.

[27.] The deleted first draft ended with the following: "Young man, I have confidence in
you, so I am going to tell you a secret. For me, Death is a business, and I came here to invite
you to become a partner in this business. I make my living from Death, so to speak. | *Hein-
rich:* I warn you, don't come too close to me. But speak!"

life insurance and others that they shouldn't. Some I encourage, some I discourage. I'm no stranger to the marriage bureaus, and I've helped more than a few to come by a nice little inheritance with no trouble at all. Now and then a bit of the occult. Just enough of each so that I have what I need. But that's only—let's say—the material . . .

Heinrich: Let's say—the dirty part of the deal.

Stranger: You judge very harshly, young man. We all earn our money according to our abilities. But let's get back to the main point—the masses' striving for freedom, equal rights,[28] enjoyment of life, and so forth. I especially welcome these efforts and promote them. I'm interested in them, as I am in every process of dissolution and decay. People finally have become sensible; they don't want anything but what awaits them anyway—their death.[29] They themselves destroy the order and laws that forced them to stay alive. Servants who want to be free from their masters, women who want to be free from their husbands, children who want to be free from their parents—everyone who trumpets this loudly in the streets works for my cause, if you'll permit me this manner of speaking.[30] Lazy, stupid people who want the same rights as the bright and conscientious also work for my cause. Those who arrange their lives so as to attain the greatest possible pleasure contribute their part to the hastening of dissolution. Back in the barbaric times when people just wanted to live, life could be upheld only by the strictest of laws and the most austere discipline.[31] Really, you can hardly think about it without smiling.

61

[28.] Replaces: "right" [to happiness, etc.].

[29.] Cf. *DBWE* 2:69 on Heidegger's idea of "resoluteness to death."

[30.] Part of National Socialist political strategy was to incite so-called "inferiors" [Unteren] against the "authorities" [Oberen]. Cf. *Ethics,* 284–86, written in early 1943; also see *Ethics,* 147, written in 1940–41: ". . . the unnatural consists essentially in organization. The natural cannot be organized but is simply there. It is possible, for example, to organize the undermining of children's respect for their parents." Cf. Gotthelf, *Zeitgeist und Berner Geist,* who says that "people who 'made political game of parents and children, masters and servants,'" have ever since been doing the pleasure of the devil, "the first promoter of political gamesmanship." Barth spoke of the novels of Gotthelf, among others, as having a "'Christian' although not theological" ethic (*Church Dogmatics* 2/2:542). Bonhoeffer had received the page proofs of this volume of Barth's *Dogmatics* in May 1942 in Switzerland. At the beginning of his time in prison Bonhoeffer read Gotthelf's books and recommended *Zeitgeist und Berner Geist* to his parents on May 15, 1943: "It is something out of the ordinary and it will certainly interest you" (*LPP* 40).

[31.] A deleted passage begins at this point in the manuscript (see below, editorial

People wanted to live. And what did this life consist of? Work, obedience, submission, renunciation, deprivation, strain, and suffering, so that they themselves called it a vale of tears. Everyone lived only for the other: parents for their children and children so that they would be parents someday, the rulers for the subjects and the subjects for the rulers, one generation for the next and that generation for the one after. But no one—it's truly insane—lived simply and honestly for themselves. Yet they loved life and called it all—God's commandment.[32] Indeed, they were happy in their way. Today, in our "civilized" times, people have outgrown this kind of happiness.[33] Today people don't care about life anymore—did they choose it? Who requires them to live? Today they know that the greater happiness, indeed the only real pleasure, consists in the dissolution of life. Marriage, family, government, order, law—these are only the remnants of the age of barbarism, which clung defiantly to

62

---

note 33). After three lines, the double sheet numbered 7 ends. This is also the end of the portion of the manuscript written on light, porous double sheets. Beginning with a sheet numbered 8, the manuscript is on graph paper with equal squares; but this has a different pattern than the paper used for the *Ethics* manuscripts of 1940, where every other line marking the squares was in bold ink.

[32.] See *E* 272: "The commandment of God . . . embraces the whole of life." See also *E* 274: *"God's commandment, which is manifested in Jesus Christ, comes to us in the church, in the family, in labor and in government [Obrigkeit]."* [Italics in the German edition.][CG] During the last period of work on the *Ethics* manuscripts just before his arrest, Bonhoeffer was planning to develop this thesis further. Here in the drama manuscript the words "and called it all—God's commandment" are inserted above the line.

[33.] Replaces: "In the 'civilized' times of today people don't want to live anymore, they want to disintegrate, to die. No laws or orders are needed for that, only a few effective slogans like Freedom, Equal Rights, Happiness, and so on, and everything just runs its necessary course, all by itself. There's never been a time like this for people like us, I'm telling you. You have to recognize it and know how to take advantage of it. Do you understand me, young man? Let the others who don't know anything philosophize, preach, and joke about death, and let the philosophers and jokers have their fun doing that. You are wiser, you don't need that anymore. You must act, you must let Death be your livelihood. That is what I wanted to tell you. *(Standing up)* And [now] I will leave you, hoping that your next visitor won't put those old ideas back in your head. Good evening. *(As he goes out the door, Christoph enters. Heinrich stands there, perplexed and confused.)* | Christoph: *(Watches the Stranger for a moment as he leaves, then, still at the door, says to Heinrich)* Who was that? | *Heinrich*: A shady character. | *Christoph*: I've seen him often before. | *Heinrich*: [deleted: "He was here for the first time"] He came into the room unannounced; I don't know him. | *Christoph*: I came in unannounced, too, but we do know each other, don't we? | *Heinrich*: Only very distantly."

life. Today people die with gusto. I love the sweet stench of decay. There's never been a time like this for the likes of us, I'm telling you. You just have to recognize it and know how to take advantage of it. Do you understand me, young man? Come and work with me. You'll be happy and make a living. *(There is a knock.)* I'm leaving, and I only hope your next visitor doesn't muddle your mind again. My respects. Good evening! *(As he goes out the door, Christoph enters.)*

Heinrich: (stands in the room, confused. Shakes himself and mutters to himself) What the devil! Disgusting!

Christoph: (remains in the doorway for a moment, watches the Stranger leave, then says to himself) Morbid character! *(Turns to Heinrich, who still stands there motionless, and speaks with awkward formality)* Good evening!

Heinrich: (equally so) Good evening!

63 *Christoph:* I didn't mean to disturb you.

Heinrich: It's all right.

Christoph: (still somewhat upset) Who was here?

Heinrich: A stranger, a phantom of the night,[34] a jailbird, a madman, a demagogue, a murderer of souls[35] and mixer of poisons—*(wildly)* a foul stench of carrion and corpses! He came unannounced. I didn't know him. He kept on talking at me, on and on. I sat there like a stupid schoolboy and couldn't think of a word to say.

Christoph: What did he talk about?

Heinrich: (looks directly and calmly at Christoph for the first time) About *our* topic. Come here, sit down and have a drink!

Christoph: You're not surprised that I came?

Heinrich: No, I knew you would. One of us had to make the first move, and since you're the aristocrat, you came first.[36]

Christoph: What's that supposed to mean?

Heinrich: Very simple. It doesn't even occur to you that you might

---

[34.] Deleted: "a man condemned to death."

[35.] Word written in pencil.

[36.] On Heinrich's characterization of Christoph as an "aristocrat," see above, page 39. Cf. also Nohl, *Die sittlichen Grunderfahrungen,* which Bonhoeffer worked through in preparation for writing the *Ethics.* There is a marginal line on pages 73–74 beside a passage on the antagonism between aristocratic and democratic ethics, which says that the latter tends to equalize everybody, while the former emphasizes what a person is born with, rather than what one acquires during a lifetime. [Note altered by Ilse Tödt subsequent to publication of the German edition of *DBW* 7.][CG]

compromise yourself by coming to me first. People like me, before we do anything, wonder a hundred times what kind of impression it will make,[37] what the effect will be, whether or not we'll be misunderstood. You have no need for that, you're much too sure of yourself for that.[38] You just appear and assume the other person will somehow put up with the interruption and, if it's misunderstood, well, that doesn't bother you at all. That's the way you aristocrats are. We others are more distrustful—and we've seen enough to know we'd rather . . .[39] After all, you and I don't know each other at all yet.

Christoph: That's precisely why I came. We needed to get to know each   64
other.[40]

Heinrich: Oh, how I envy the oblivion of people like you! You don't worry at all about what others might think of you. Maybe the other person doesn't want to know you at all, but you don't care; you can't even imagine that's possible. You don't even notice that your self-confidence amounts to an infinite contempt for people! What's more, you seem ever so modest and quiet, just to disarm us completely. How right you are—because we let you despise us whenever you like, and we're even proud of it in a way.

Christoph: What you're saying doesn't sound like you. It's the voice of a stranger.

Heinrich: Yes, strange to you, but not to me. It's the voice of the common people for whom you have such contempt. It's good for you to hear it for once.

Christoph: I spent four years in the trenches just like you. Do you really think[41] this voice is new to me? I know it well enough. But because it comes from mistrust, there is an unclear, false tone about it. That's why it's bad. I didn't come to hear this voice, which isn't yours, but to talk with you, person to person.

Heinrich: Person to person—that's what all of you say whenever you want

---

[37.] Deleted: "whether it won't seem an imposition".

[38.] Dietrich Bonhoeffer once said to his sister Susanne that the comfort of their parents' home gave them "such blatant security" (*DB-ER* 20).

[39.] Replaces: "and with good reason."

[40.] Replaces: "I had to [get to know] you."

[41.] The beginning of the following section is the revision of a first version of the manuscript, which, although not deleted in that copy, was not copied into the later version of the manuscript (one page and four lines), which began with "Do you really think this voice [replaces: 'language'] is new to me? I know it well enough [replaces: 'as well as you']."

to silence the voice of the masses, the voice of the common people that lives in us. This voice annoys you. You want to wrench us out of the community which alone makes us count for something; and you know perfectly well that once you've isolated us as individuals, you don't need to be afraid of us anymore. As individuals we're powerless in your hands, for we aren't individuals, we're the masses[42] or nothing. Person to person? Give us a chance to be human beings first, then we'll talk person to person.[43]

65

Christoph: (after a while, thoughtfully) Contempt for oneself makes a person feel despised by everyone else as well. Heinrich, let me speak frankly with you.[44] As far as I know, our lives have followed very different paths. I don't mean to say that's unimportant. I hardly know the world you grew up in. Where I'm from one basically never gets to know your world. But you don't know my world either. I come from what people call a good family, that is, from an old, distinguished, educated middle-class family [Bürgerfamilie], and I'm not one of those who are ashamed to admit it. On the contrary, I know what quiet strength you find in a good middle-class home.[45]

[42.] Cf. Ernst Toller's expressionist drama, *Man and the Masses*, in *Seven Plays: "The Nameless One:* I am the Masses! / Masses are fate. / Masses are master [Führer]! . . ." (113f.). "*The Woman:* Whoever calls for blood of men is Moloch. / So God was Moloch, / The State Moloch, / And the Masses—Moloch" (152). Cf. Bonhoeffer's discussion of modern mass movements and the French Revolution (*E* 100f.).

[43.] Deleted: "Person to person—[deleted: that sounds so good and yet it's from] that's what you all say and don't even notice how you show contempt for us with this honorable address." The first version continued: "You are very wrong. We won't get anywhere this way. You only want to exchange roles, that's all. We can only talk person to person when we can again accept the candor in word and deed of the other without suspicion." ["Candor" here translates *unbefangen.* [NL]

[44.] The following section replaces a one and one-half page deletion that began: "It is true that our backgrounds are very different . . ." Including the rejected first version of "Do you really think this voice is new to me?" (cf. page 63), Bonhoeffer wrote three different drafts of the discussion between Heinrich and Christoph about the contrasting worlds of the "common people" and the "middle-class family."

[45.] On "home" and "middle-class family" cf. the letter for the baptism of Dietrich Bethge in May 1944 (*LPP* 294–96); also see above (page 32) the reference to *"our home."* On October 10, 1942, Bonhoeffer wrote to his nephew Hans Walter Schleicher, who had been called up for military duty: "You know, perhaps partly unconsciously—but that doesn't matter here—what higher values [Gut] are like, such as a good family life, good parents, truth, justice, human goodness [Menschlichkeit], cultivation of the mind [Bildung], and tradition. . . . You also have some sense of what the Bible, the Lord's Prayer, and church music

Nobody who didn't grow up in one can know this. It's also difficult to explain.[46] But one thing you must know. We grew up with reverence both for what has developed and for what is given,[47] and thus with respect for every human being. We consider mistrust mean and base. We look to the other person for spontaneity in word and deed, and we want to accept that without suspicion. Nothing is more ruinous for life together than to mistrust the spontaneity of others and suspect their motives. To psychologize and analyze people,[48] as has become fashionable these days, is to destroy all trust, to expose everything decent to public defamation. It's the revolt of all that's vulgar against what's free and genuine.[49] People

---

mean. All these have given you an image of Germany that you can never really lose again" (*DBW* 16:364 [*GS* 2:423]).

[46.] At this point in the long deletion is found the following: "This is a world you don't know. It's not easy to get to know, either. You must live in it, slowly grow up to be part of it. That's why you really can't talk about it at all [replaces: "Actually you can't really talk about it at all, any more than you can talk about your mother."]. |66| In fact, its reality [replaces: "its essence and its power"] lies in the unspoken, natural spontaneity of being who you are. The focus of middle-class family life is not on outward but inward things. Its life follows an order which has grown naturally; it does not need written laws. Each person has a place, and there is no ill will [deleted: "no envy"] and, above all, no mistrust. One person gives the other their freedom out of trust. In our eyes the mistrustful person appears mean. Because we feel so safe in our home, because our home is like a fortress where we can always take refuge, it's easy for you to see us as proud or contemptuous people. But believe me, in a world where reverence for all that exists is so fundamental to life, trust and respect for people thrive. Of course you shouldn't expect us to be blind to the differences among people. We distinguish between what is genuine and what is not, what is noble and what is vulgar; we distinguish between decency and meanness, truth and hollow words, substance and appearance, and *(passionately)* we won't let anyone deprive us of this right." [Deleted: "That's our task."]

In regard to this passage and the remainder of the text through page 70, see below, page 237, "Drama Working Notes": "reverence for what has developed over time . . . trust" (*NL* A 86, 7).

[47.] Replaces: "and trusting in people." [Bonhoeffer was thinking of the way certain values and attitudes develop and become established in a family's life and, by extension, in society by a similar process in culture, law, and institutions.][CG]

[48.] Cf. the letter of December 15, 1943, to Eberhard Bethge: "I've had more than enough of psychology, and I'm less and less inclined to analyze the state of anybody's soul. That is why I value Stifter and Gotthelf so much. There is considerably more at stake than self-knowledge" (*LPP* 162 [trans. altered]).

[49.] Cf. the letter of July 8, 1944, to Eberhard Bethge: "An attitude of basic mistrust and suspicion toward people is the revolt of underlings" (*LPP* 345 [trans. altered]). See also Bonhoeffer's remark that "the secrets known to a man's valet—that is, to put it crudely,

don't exist to look into the abyss of each other's hearts[50]—nor can
they—but to encounter and accept each other just as they are—
67   simply, naturally, in courageous trust.[51] Do you understand what I
mean?

Heinrich: I'm trying, but it's hard. Where am I supposed to get this trust?
What should I base it on? Don't you think we'd also like to be able to
live our lives trusting people? Do you think we like being perpetually
suspicious? But that's precisely our plight, that we can't afford to
trust. Our experiences are too bitter.

Christoph: People's experiences are just like the people themselves. The
suspicious person will never experience trust. Trust is always a leap
beyond all good and bad experiences. But it may well be that this
leap is more difficult for you than for me. That's why I came to you
and didn't wait for you. By the way, you shouldn't think that we trust
blindly and throw ourselves right into everyone's arms. We leave that
to people who babble about the equality and goodness of everybody.[52] We learned to discriminate—and we will never let anyone
take this away from us—to discriminate between the authentic and
the inauthentic, truth and lies, the noble and the vulgar, decency
and meanness.

Heinrich: And what you all call authentic, true, noble, decent—for people
like you they're unquestioned, self-evident, isn't that right?

---

the range of his intimate life, from prayer to sexual life—have become the hunting ground
of modern pastoral workers. In that way they resemble . . . the dirtiest gutter journalists"
(*LPP* 344).

[50.] The first draft continued here: ["Deleted: 'or to snoop around after ulterior
motives'] they should confidently leave that to God."

[51.] The first version ended: "*Heinrich:* And what if all your experiences were to point
in the opposite direction? | *Christoph:* People's experiences are like the people themselves.
The suspicious person will never have the experience of trusting; the ungrateful person
will never experience gratitude; the dissolute [replaces: 'vulgar'] person will never experience pure integrity of heart, because they won't believe it's real. Of course there are disap-
pointments and bad experiences, but greater than all experience is faith, for only faith
builds people up. | *Heinrich:* Not everyone can afford to have faith. | *Christoph:* You should
say 'not everyone is called to build people up.' That would be better. But, on second
thought, that's only half true. Heinrich, you fought in the war like I did. We could have met
in the trenches. Now be honest, would you have talked to me like that back then? | *Hein-
rich:* No, not back then."

[52.] Cf. *CD* 238: "nor that gullible credulity which believes that there is good in all
people" [trans. altered].

Christoph: There must be some self-evident things in life, and you must   68
    have the courage to stand up for them. You can't start life all over
    every day, calling into question again everything you learned or
    gained the day before.[53] What we consider self-evident has been
    tried through many generations and has stood up to life's tests hun-
    dreds and thousands of times.

Heinrich: Yes, in your grandfathers' lives. But times change . . .

Christoph: But people don't change, at least not in their essential rela-
    tions. That's precisely what's wrong today. People act as if the world
    had only begun with them, so they question everything and thus
    never get around to laying the one small brick that's theirs to fit into
    the structure of the whole.[54]

Heinrich: Why lay bricks if the foundation is crumbling?[55]

Christoph: You're talking like a journalist, but you know better.[56] If the
    foundation were really crumbling, it would be no use trying to lay it
    again. No people [Volk] gets a second chance to lay its foundation
    over again after a thousand years of history. If the foundation crum-
    bles, it's all over. But you see, that's not how it is. The foundation is   69

[53.] Cf. *E* 279: "Before the commandment of God . . . human beings are not continually failing and beginning again. . . . On the contrary, before the commandment of God they may at last really move forward along the road and no longer stand endlessly at the cross-roads. They can now have the right decision really behind them, and not always before them[,] . . . can allow themselves to be guided, escorted, and protected on their way by God's commandment as though by a good angel" [trans. altered].

[54.] The following appears at this point in the long deleted passage: "Marriage remains marriage, friendship friendship, loyalty loyalty, betrayal betrayal. That's precisely what's wrong with the likes of you; you always act as if the world had only begun today and only with you, so you question everything, and that way you never get around to contributing a brick to the whole." Cf. below, page 237, "Drama Working Notes": "act as if everything were beginning anew, as if there weren't . . ." (*NL* A 86, 7). Also see Jaspers, *Man in the Modern Age:* "Since human beings no longer have any specific age, they are always at the beginning and at the end simultaneously" (50) [trans. altered].

[55.] Cf. Ernst Toller, *Man and the Masses,* in *Seven Plays:* "*The Nameless One:* You fools, break the foundations! / Break, / I say, break the foundations!" (130)

[56.] The long deletion contains the following: [Deleted: "The foundation has been laid and you are the people who"] "Then they do nothing but drill away at the foundation and tear it loose and then cry out in horror and outrage, 'The foundation is crumbling!' I'm telling you, the foundation of our people [Volk] and our life is deep and solid and good. [Deleted: A thousand years of history can't be]."

deep and solid and good. You just have to build on it, not beside it, on the quicksand of so-called new ideas.[57]

Heinrich: Don't think it's the new ideas that are important to us. They may be important to the writers, who profit from them. What do we care about new ideas? I can assure you we have neither the desire nor the time[58] to chase after originality at any price.[59] We want something much simpler, ground under our feet, so we can live. That's what I call the foundation. Can't you feel the difference? People like you have a foundation, you have ground under your feet, you have a place in the world. There are things you take for granted, that you stand up for, and for which you are willing to put your head on the line, because you know your roots go so deep that they'll sprout new growth again. The only thing that counts for you is to keep your feet on the ground.[60] Otherwise you'd be like the giant Antaeus, who had to keep his feet on the ground to get his strength, and who lost it in a battle when Hercules tore him away from the

70

[57.] See Matt. 7:26 at the end of the Sermon on the Mount: "And everyone who hears these words of mine and does not act on them will be like a foolish man who built his house on sand." On "laying the foundation," cf. 1 Cor. 3:11 (underlined twice in pencil in the Greek text of Bonhoeffer's *Novum Testamentum Graece et Germanice* [ed. Nestle]): "For no one can lay any foundation other than the one that has been laid; that foundation is Jesus Christ."

[58.] In the long deletion followed: ". . . to want to be original at all costs like this riffraff. What do we care whether the ideas are old or new? We want a life that's worth living—that's all."

[59.] Deleted: "We want to live—and we can't."

[60.] In a congregational lecture in Barcelona in the winter of 1928, alluding to the uncertainty of life since World War I, Bonhoeffer said: "The ground has been ruthlessly pulled out from under our feet—or rather, let's say the middle-class parquet flooring has been ripped out from under us—and we have got to find for ourselves the little spot of earth each one wants to stand on" (*DBW* 10:285f. [*GS* 5:117]). In his May 1944 baptismal letter, "Thoughts on the Baptism of Dietrich Bethge," we read that despite the increasing urbanization of rural life, "it will be an advantage in these changing times to have a bit of ground under one's feet from which to draw the strength needed for a day's work and an evening's leisure that are new, natural, unpretentious, and filled with contentment" (*LPP* 296, [trans. altered]). Von Oertzen speaks of "ground" or "earth" under one's feet. In the East Elbian provinces, he says, the "landed gentry who were faithful to the land struggled with terrific persistence to regain 'ground under their feet,' that is to return their families and households to the countryside" (*Junker* 386f.; see also 378, 381, 383). Also, in von Oertzen's words, "After the defeat [of 1918] they returned to the land [Boden] they had come from. This is where they found the source of their strength" (384). However, cf. also page 180: "as if I had to walk on water."

earth.[61] To be sure, you do have some stupid people among you who choose to leave behind the ground they grew up on, whether out of curiosity or vanity or[62] because they foolishly think they can win us over[63]—chaff driven by the wind. If you want to live, you need ground under your feet—and we don't have this ground.[64] That's why we're scattered around whichever way the storm winds are blowing. That's why we have nothing for which we can or want to put our heads on the block. That's why we hate to give up our pathetic little life, not because we love it, but because it's all we have. And then if Death is lodged in your chest in the form of shrapnel, and it grins at you every day, and you don't know what you're still living for or what you're dying for—it's a miracle if you don't go mad, torn between despair and the urge to live, torn between hatred for everything alive and craving for wild pleasure.[65] Give me ground under my feet—give me the Archimedean point to stand on—and everything   71 would be different.[66]

[61.] Bonhoeffer referred to Antaeus in a sermon and a lecture to the congregation in Barcelona on September 23, 1928, and February 8, 1929 (*DBW* 10:516, 344f. [*GS* 5:467f., 179]). Cf. Wendel, *Studien zur Homiletik* (45f., note 180), according to which Luther mentions the Antaeus motif in his *Lectures on Romans* (*Luther's Works*, vol. 25:300 [*Werke* 56:313, 12]). Wendel refers to "a considerable number of writings with the title of *Antaeus* in the first two decades of the twentieth century," especially Freyer's *Antäus* published in 1918. [Bonhoeffer cited Freyer's *Theorie des objectiven Geistes* several times in *Sanctorum Communio.*][CG]

[62.] Deleted: "out of so-called idealism".

[63.] Replaces: "to get closer to us," which in turn replaced "to do us a favor."

[64.] The Bonhoeffer family had been very impressed by something reportedly said by one of Karl-Friedrich's comrades in World War I: "What do you mean, fatherland? My father has no land!"

[65.] Cf. *E* 107: "With the loss of past and future, life fluctuates between the crudest enjoyment of the moment and an adventurous game of chance." See *ZE* 82; *NL* A 86, 3: "Decay . . . nothingness . . . no great, quiet convictions . . . no trust." The detailed working note [Zettel] from which these words come forms the basis for a passage in the *Ethics* chapter entitled "Inheritance and Decay" (*E* 89–110) written in 1941. Cf. below, page 243 (*NL* A 86, 8), on "sensual pleasure" [Sinnenlust]. Charles West says of the drama fragment: "It is, curiously, an almost Stoic-Epicurean debate with hardly a suggestion of the message of the New Testament . . ." ("Ground under Our Feet," in Peck, *New Studies in Bonhoeffer's Ethics*, 252, note 37). The Stoic attitude is one which is seen in the statement that one can "put your head on the line" (Heinrich to Christoph, page 68), and the Epicurean is apparent in the phrase "craving for wild pleasure."

[66.] On the "Archimedean point," cf. the letter of March 27, 1944: Overcoming death through Christ's resurrection "is the answer to the δὸς μοὶ ποῦ στῶ καὶ κινήσω τὴν γῆν" ["Give me somewhere to stand, and I will move the earth" (Archimedes)] (*LPP* 240).

Christoph: (has become very thoughtful) Ground under your feet—I've never understood it like that—I think you're right—I understand—Ground under your feet—in order to be able to live, and in order to be able to die. . . .

Heinrich: Last night you spoke haughty[67] words about the rabble, and I agree with you. There is a rabble and this rabble must be kept down. But how can you blame those who've been shoved out into the world without being given ground to stand on? Can you walk past them and talk past them without being moved to compassion?[68]

[67.] Replaces: "hard". Cf. Gotthelf's story, "Elsi, die seltsame Magd": ". . . the girl who was proud of her native revulsion against everything base or intellectually backward" (115).

[68.] Cf. *CD* where Bonhoeffer cites Matt. 9:36, making his own translation, which reads that when Jesus "saw the multitudes, he was moved to compassion for them, because they were distressed and scattered, as sheep not having a shepherd" (201). In a letter of August 17, 1943, Bonhoeffer reports that he has given up writing the drama: ". . . Meanwhile, I've realized that the material really isn't dramatic, so now I'm going to try to rework it in narrative form" (*LPP* 94 [trans. altered]). The outline for the novel is partially described in a letter of November 18, 1943: "The children [of two lifelong friends] grow up, and as they gradually enter into the responsibilities of work and public office in a small town, they try to work together to build up the community . . ." (*LPP* 130 [trans. altered]). Cf. above, page 67: ". . . laying the one small brick . . ." In the autumn of 1940 Bonhoeffer had sketched his plan to develop his ideas on the "building of a future world" (*ZE* 47, no. 1). Cf. *E* (*DBW* 6): 449f.

NOVEL

Sunday[1]

A Hot July Day

IT WAS A HOT JULY DAY in a midsized city in northern Germany. The sun
had risen in a cloudless sky and already was burning down on the subur-
ban boulevard as Frau Karoline Brake walked home from church. A bit
exhausted, the elderly lady sat down for a rest on a bench in the city
park. She opened her gray silk parasol and allowed a slight smile to
spread around her eyes as she gazed at the rhododendrons in full
bloom. It had been forty years since[2] she had tirelessly besieged her husband—the mayor,[3] who had a say in these things—with requests to have

---

[1.] Cf. Gotthelf, *Zeitgeist und Berner Geist,* "about a Sunday when people go to the
village and how there is an outpouring of their hearts" (11). The "outpouring" is over Hans
the farmer, who has become caught up in "pseudopolitics"; cf. page 160 above, editorial
note 30. The passage continues: "Surely there is no word in any tongue that sounds more
beautiful to the ears of its ordinary people than the word Sunday. It is as if one were hearing bells ringing, as if one saw the sun in the blue sky and everything on earth in peace and
gladness." Bonhoeffer was greatly impressed by this politically engaged book; see his letter
of May 15, 1943 (*LPP* 40), and November 9, 1943 (*LPP* 125). Cf. Gotthelf's comments in
his preface to the novel: "But the main reason the author cannot get himself to leave so-
called politics alone in spite of himself is of course because today's politics . . . invades all
aspects of the life of all the classes, lays waste the sanctity of families, and undermines all
Christian elements" (8f.). [In Bonhoeffer's time, Gotthelf's writing in the context of the
pre-1848 revolutionary repression must have sounded as if it could be a description of
National Socialist propaganda.][CG]

The novel manuscript (*NL* A 70, 5) begins on standard DIN-A4 graph paper, the same
kind used in the drama beginning on page 60.

[2.] Deleted: "in the passion of youth".

[3.] Replaces: "city council delegate at the time". Bonhoeffer only later decided on
"mayor," then went back and changed most earlier occurrences of the title accordingly.

this park plaza put in. Later she had helped bring the plan to fruition by raising money among the townspeople, and by making considerable contributions from her own pocket. For years thereafter she served on the small commission[4] which considered and decided all the details concerning public landscaping. She had always had her own very definite ideas, and had a way of seeing to it that they were realized. Thus she had proposed that the elderly have a quiet place of their own in the park, where they would not be disturbed by the children's boisterousness. The children, too, should have their play area, she thought, and the joy and spontaneity[5] they experience there must not be ruined by dour faces and reprimands of older people, any more than the elderly should have to put up with the occasional[6] irreverence and mischief children often display.

Above all, though—and Frau Karoline Brake was adamant about this—noise should not be allowed in the park on Sundays. Frau Karoline was generally not fond of signs posted in public places by the police, prohibiting this or that.[7] But Sunday was different. This was a case where you had to force people to rediscover their happiness after they had so carelessly thrown it away. The thoughtlessness and folly with which most people walked right past[8] this inexhaustible wellspring of happiness that was offered to them week by week in ever new ways—indeed, the kindest of God's Ten Commandments, as Frau Brake called it—seemed just as incomprehensible to the wise, old woman now as it had in the old days. She saw this as one of the main reasons for the general dissolution of the orders of life [Lebensordnungen] that was occurring before everyone's eyes. To be sure, reestablishing peace and quiet on Sundays was not all it would take, but it was the prerequisite for everything else.[9]

[4.] Replaces: "committee".

[5.] Cf. page 65 on the spontaneity [Unbefangenheit] of secure and confident people.

[6.] Replaces: "careless" [unbedacht].

[7.] Cf. *E* 260: "One of the great naivetés, or rather follies, of the moralists is imagining that before every human action stands a sign from the divine police saying in big letters 'allowed' or 'forbidden' [verboten]" [trans. altered].

[8.] Deleted: "past this most precious gift of Christendom".

[9.] Cf. *ZE* (48, no. 1): "Organization [Aufbau] of Christian life in the world. Building up [Aufbau] of values? The *holiday* [*der Feiertag*]!?" From his own home Bonhoeffer was accustomed to Sunday being observed as a day off or "holiday." As director of the seminary at Finkenwalde from 1935–37, Bonhoeffer was determined to entice the candidates for the parish ministry away from their desks on Sundays to play games, read, and make music together. Cf. *DB-ER* 429.

This very morning, Frau Karoline had seen some youngsters heading off outdoors carrying a phonograph and had not even tried to conceal her revulsion. What kind of pleasure could thrive in the midst of such unnatural noise? Wouldn't these same young people turn homeward in the evening, beaten and sapped of their strength by counterfeit pleasure? Why were human beings so afraid of silence? Was it true, as one of her grandsons had told her recently, that silence is precisely where the pounding and ramming of machines, the noisy office machinery, and the babble of voices[10] of the metropolis rise to a deafening roar, from which the only escape is through some "gentle passage"—that had been his expression. What modern people seek after and need on Sundays, he had said, is distraction, not silence—forgetting, not collecting themselves; relaxation, not composure.[11]

Frau Karoline Brake sat upright on the park bench, her eyes lost in the red splendor of blossoms and in the dark green foliage. A few brimstone butterflies fluttered in the hushed stillness of shimmering sunlight. The birds' soft rustling in the bushes, their voices now almost silenced by the fire of the sun climbing toward noon, the chirping of crickets,[12] the mosquitoes' fine, bright hum—all these sounds reached her ear, penetrating the stillness. Feeling happy and profoundly thankful, she breathed in the fullness of the summer air.

Suddenly a shadow passed across her face. She had heard another miserable sermon.[13] She had walked out of church in a very bad mood, and only the radiant blue sky and nature's summery light had made her feel better. But now she felt her rage rising once again within her. What rubbish she had been forced to listen to again. Could one blame the children and grandchildren who, for years now, had let her go to church alone? She could still hear her oldest grandson's[14] precocious words as

[10.] Replaces: "traffic".

[11.] Cf. Bonhoeffer's comment in "After Ten Years" on "the experience of quality" as a return "from haste to leisure and silence, from diversion to concentration" (*LPP* 13 [trans. altered]).

[12.] Replaces: "the calls of the thrushes and the chirping of young birds in the nests deep in the bushes".

[13.] Cf. Bethge's description of Ruth von Kleist-Retzow, the grandmother of Dietrich Bonhoeffer's fiancée, as a person who "possessed a precise feeling for quality and substance and never hesitated to say exactly what she thought. This also led her to speak with refreshing clarity about this or that cleric's insidious lack of backbone or his glib prattle" (*DB-ER* 439) [trans. altered]. Karoline Brake also has features of Bonhoeffer's grandmother, Julie Bonhoeffer, who resolutely stood up for her convictions.

[14.] Replaces: "one of many grandsons'".

he had accompanied her to church for the last time: "You know, Grandma, we've outgrown this kind of preacher wisdom just like we've outgrown our Latin teachers rattling off Ostermann's exercises.[15] I really can't understand how you can bear to listen to it Sunday after Sunday."

At the time she had replied, "Dear boy, what's important is not that something is new, but that it's right. And we need to hear what's right again and again, because unfortunately we keep forgetting it."[16]

"I don't understand," he had replied. "I don't forget it at all. On the contrary, I can recite all these sanctimonious clichés backwards and forwards."

"Yes, you know them in your head and your lips can rattle them off, my dear, but the heart and the hand learn more slowly."

She had said this and yet did not feel right about saying it, for what they had heard in the sermon was neither new nor right. It was sanctimonious prattle, and to her mind that was the worst thing that could happen from the pulpit. Perhaps she should have admitted that openly to her grandson. Perhaps she should have said to him: "You mustn't confuse Christianity with its pathetic representatives." But he was a smart boy and would not have spared her a reply: "Anything that has such pathetic representatives can't have much power left; I'm interested in what is alive and relevant today, not in a dead faith of the past."

How could one argue with that? To distinguish between original Christianity and the church today was really a feeble attempt to justify it. After all, what mattered was simply whether the Christianity in which Frau Brake had grown up and lived her life still existed today, and whether or not it lives in its current representatives. Every bad sermon was another nail in the coffin of the Christian faith. It could no longer be denied that here, in this suburb in any event, hot air had taken the place of God's Word.[17]

Frau Karoline Brake no longer saw the bushes in full bloom; she could

77

[15.] A Latin exercise book by Christian Ostermann for sixth-graders (ten-year-olds) first appeared in 1869, with successive volumes for the rest of the secondary grades. The series was republished repeatedly in revised editions well into the twentieth century.

[16.] Cf. Bonhoeffer's comment on Acts 2:42: "It is of the essence of 'teaching' that it seeks to render itself superfluous. But in striking contrast we read here that the church 'continued' in the apostles' teaching" (*CD* 249).

[17.] The Bonhoeffer family had similar experiences when they occasionally attended church in Berlin-Grunewald, where they had moved in 1916.

no longer feel the pleasure of the warm July sun. Instead she saw her children and grandchildren before her mind's eye and uttered a quiet "Oh, well!"[18] In her voice was a little amazement about the ways of the world, a little worry about her own inability to change them, but also a good bit of that calm assurance with which older people entrust the future to hands stronger than their own. But, as if she had already let herself go too far with this little sigh, Frau Karoline straightened her body with a quick, rather indignant jerk, stood up, and strode resolutely through the park to the street that led to her home.

No, she was not the kind who gave up easily. You could tell from the way she walked that she was making decisions as she went along. She would see that this old windbag of a preacher left this pulpit, or that a second pastor, a preacher of the word of God, would be called to the parish.[19] She rejected the idea of speaking to the windbag again. She   78 had made several attempts, but had been met with nothing but vain defensiveness and hollow officiousness. In fact, she had felt the pastor avoiding her glance since these visits, and she had heard by the grapevine that he had thwarted her reelection to the parish council [Gemeindekirchenrat]. Some said he emphasized that she must be spared because of her age; others said he thought her strange. He even went so far with some as to accuse her of intolerable presumption. There

---

[18.] Deleted: "The pastor had preached on the story of plucking ears of corn on the Sabbath, and on the saying of the Lord, 'The Son of Man is lord even of the sabbath' [Mark 2:28]. Why had he left out the most important thing? Jesus had not broken the law of the Sabbath out of necessity—the disciples would not have starved to death if they had not eaten for a few more hours—nor to do a good deed. No! but in divine freedom! Jesus had simply acted and spoken, with the sovereignty [Vollmacht] of the one who was above every law—he himself, the Son of God, the free one, the Lord. But far be it from us to dare to do what Jesus was allowed to do, along with the very few who followed him. Our calling is to take seriously the commandment to keep the Sabbath holy and to learn how to do that, before we can see that 'breaking the Sabbath' could be its ultimate sanctification. It was, after all, none other than the Son of God, and he alone, who broke the Sabbath. Instead, the preacher this morning had known nothing better to say than that for Christians there is no difference between workdays and Sundays or holy days, and that Christian freedom consists in celebrating holidays in any way one sees fit. One could find God out in the fields just as well as in church." Cf. Bonhoeffer's comments in the *Ethics* on Jesus and the Sabbath, *E* 33. [See also *E* 234ff. on times when Christians may be called, acting in free responsibility, to do the will of God by breaking the law.][CG]

[19.] The Kleist family, especially Ruth von Kleist-Retzow, made every effort during the Church Struggle in the Third Reich to engage pastors from the Confessing Church to hold services in the chapel at Kiekow, which was under their patronage. [On the structure of Pomeranian "patronage" or landowner's church administration, see *DB-ER* 438f.][CG]

was no doubt about it; he was afraid of her because she saw through him. Despite these events she had continued to go to his church every Sunday, even when she had long since given up hope of ever hearing the word of God from him. She had taken this humiliation upon herself as a salutary discipline.[20] But in the end she had had enough. It wasn't so much for her own sake; she had learned through the years to ignore the talk and to focus on the few words which contained truth. She could have continued this way for the rest of her life. But more important things were at stake.[21] The congregation, the whole town, her own family was deprived of the word of God and that meant that their whole life must sooner or later lose its center. This could remain hidden for a while yet; memory and tradition could postpone[22] complete disintegration for a while yet.

But her grandchildren's generation would need to find new ways of its own, and several things these young people had said had led their grandmother to recognize the first signs of protest, even of revolt. It was not the young people's fault if things were as they were. Rather, the older people let things take their course so unperceptively, without insight or concern. That was the worst thing about it. Frau Karoline Brake had asked herself tacitly whether it could be God's will to bring judgment over this generation by withdrawing God's word from them. But even if it were so, she told herself, God would also want people to resist [widersetzen] this judgment, to take God at his word and not let him go until he blessed them.[23] But why was she so alone with her ideas and opinions? Why did hardly anyone who had been in church today, except the old sexton, notice that all they had heard were hollow phrases and cheap clichés? Why did the educated, of all people, fail so completely in their discernment? To be sure, they hardly ever went to church, but when they

---

[20.] Deleted: "Under no circumstances did she want to act out of any personal bias."

[21.] Deleted: "when the truth of God has [disappeared] from a place."

[22.] Replaces: "prevent". Cf. Bonhoeffer's remarks in the *Ethics* on the duty of Christian churches to preserve their inheritance through times of disintegration (109). One is reminded of Kamlah's *Christentum und Selbstbehauptung,* a book which Bonhoeffer had read, on the decline of Christian tradition in Germany. Kamlah comments that with the decline of Christian faith since the Enlightenment it has "turned out that the reserves of Christianity are not at all to be found in theology and not even so very much in the faith decisions of individuals, but in the faith tradition of the Christian family, including as a last stronghold the parsonages and farmhouses, where they have slowly dissipated and continue to dissipate" (3).

[23.] Cf. Gen. 32:24ff., where Jacob wrestles with God at night by the River Jabbok.

had to attend a baptism or wedding they always found the "speech" [Rede], as they called the sermon, very lovely, very artistic, very modern, very relevant. The old woman shook her head dejectedly[24] and was totally lost in her thoughts when she heard a voice behind her.

"Good morning, my dear Frau Bürgermeister,[25] hasn't the dear Lord blessed us with another beautiful day?" It was the neighbor, Direktor Warmblut's widow, who was also walking home from church. She had already greeted two or three other women[26] from the neighborhood on their way home and was now hurrying after Frau Karoline Brake to reach her before they arrived at their houses. It wasn't easy for this short, rather plump woman to catch up to her neighbor, who was ten years her senior. Now she ran breathless with a shiny, red face beside the agile and stately figure, who presented a rare picture of moderation and dignity in her gray dress, gray silk parasol, gray hair, and the dry gray skin of her intelligent face.

"Good morning," said Frau Brake with her quiet, clear voice. "Yes, the sun does us good; we need it, too."

"Oh, I do hope things are going well with you. What wonderful health   80 the dear Lord has given you! Well, of course, he loves you and why shouldn't he? Such a blessed family life, and you their beloved grand-mother, the idol of all the grandchildren. Oh, these charming children, and they're growing up now. But they're still good, cast in the same mold, and why shouldn't they be? How fortunate for you, to be sur-rounded by your family—just think, my dear Frau Bürgermeister, I have had such trouble again the last few days. Oh, I know, the heavier the cross, the closer to heaven, and why shouldn't it be so? But just think, my daughter Hilde's husband has left the church and doesn't want their child baptized. I've shed so many tears over it. What would my dear hus-band, God rest his soul, have said about it? And what will people think of us, and what will become of the poor little wretch? Yes, and I'm almost ashamed to admit it, my Hilde doesn't seem to mind at all. She says the

---

[24.] Replaces: "indignantly".

[25.] [While the novel's narrator uses Frau Brake's proper name in describing her, she is addressed by other characters in the outdated German deferential way by using her hus-band's title, i.e., "liebe Frau Bürgermeister," literally "dear Mrs. Mayor."][NL] Here and in the following instances of the original, Bonhoeffer has replaced the title "City Councillor" with "Mayor."

[26.] Replaces: "[women] churchgoers". [The form of the German noun indicates the churchgoers are female.][NL]

child can decide later on for herself what she wants. That really hurt me—and coming from my own daughter! And all this to the widow of a man of such an honorable position! I just can't understand it. I always told her about the dear Lord and prayed with her. She always had to go to church with me, and even at her wedding the pastor gave her such lovely maxims to learn, and she always had the saying over her bed, "Do right and fear no one." Believe me, dearest Frau Bürgermeister, I haven't been able to sleep for nights fretting over[27] my daughter. But during the sermon today all that blew over, and now I'm relieved and happy. Oh, and the dear Lord has given us our dear church and our dear pastor, too, who has such a beautiful way with words, so down-to-earth and close to the people. Forgive me, Frau Bürgermeister, I know you don't always agree with him, but today, don't you agree, today he outdid himself."

"Yes, today he really outdid himself, Frau Direktor."

81   "You see, you see, oh, I'm so happy that you agree. Didn't he say it beautifully? Yes—uh, what did he say, anyway? It's so lovely one could never convey it. But it really doesn't matter at all, you can just feel it and it's so uplifting and you don't even quite know why, isn't that right, dearest Frau Bürgermeister."

"Yes, you really don't quite know why."

"Well, anyway, he said everyone should live the way they see fit and then it will be the right way, and it doesn't matter that much to the dear Lord whether the little one is baptized or not, right, Frau Bürgermeister? And it really doesn't matter that much at all whether my little Hilde goes to church or not. We're all free people, after all, that's how he expressed it. Oh, what a wonderful idea! So liberating, so deep, and why shouldn't it be, right, dearest Frau Bürgermeister? In fact, he had a Bible passage. Now what was it about again?"

"Yes, indeed, what do you think it was about, Frau Direktor?"

"Yes, what was it about, anyway? Oh—you're getting me all confused, Frau Bürgermeister. But it really doesn't matter at all, does it?"

"No, it really doesn't matter at all, because it wasn't about the Bible passage at all.[28] He wanted to preach about plucking the ears of corn on the Sabbath and about the verse, 'The Son of Man is lord of the sabbath.'[29] Instead of saying that Christ may do things because he is Christ,

---

[27.] Replaces: "suffering over".
[28.] Replaces: "I'll tell you what it was about."
[29.] Mark 2:28.

but that doesn't give us the right to do them by any means, and that if Christ keeps the Sabbath by breaking it, then we first have to learn how to keep the Sabbath holy in earnest, by keeping it—instead of saying that, he babbled on about the freedom of all human beings, and that people may do whatever they think is right, and that we should spend Sunday out in nature rather than in church, and that it doesn't matter so much at all because the dear Lord is so kind and sweet and good that he isn't even capable of wrath. My dear Frau Direktor, did it escape you again that the pastor said what you wanted to hear, but didn't preach the word of God?"

Frau Karoline Brake had arrived at the garden gate of her children's house. Without hesitation, she firmly pressed the bell and, as the gate clicked open, turned once again to the woman beside her. Did it make any sense to deprive this foolish, garrulous woman of her good cheer? Do I have the right to criticize the sermon she found so lovely? Am I called upon to jolt this complacent woman out of her peace of mind? Is there even anything at all that can be done about this superficiality? Then again . . . who can see into another's heart? "For the Lord does not see as mortals see; they look on the outward appearance, but the Lord looks on the heart."[30] And yet, this pious chatter has absolutely nothing in common with Christianity; it's more dangerous than outright unbelief. These thoughts raced through Frau Karoline's mind and for a moment robbed her of the composure which she otherwise seldom lost. 82

"Farewell, dear Frau Direktor," she said, somewhat more warmly than before, "and you know, perhaps your daughter is quite right. Goodbye!"

"But dear Frau Bürgermeister, now I don't understand you at all anymore; I'm totally confused. You think my little Hilde is right? No, you can't be serious. Gracious, you're usually so very strict when it comes to matters of faith. Oh, no, you're joking. How charming of you, this priceless sense of humor. What a pity we're home already, it's always so very pleasant chatting with you. But I mustn't keep you. Your sweet family is waiting for you. Farewell. Wasn't it a wonderful morning again, though? Goodbye, and a good day to you, dear Frau Bürgermeister! Well, I really must think some more about what you just said."

Frau Brake closed the gate, and as she looked into the disappointed, good-natured face of her neighbor, a slight wave of compassion for the

---

[30.] 1 Sam. 16:7.

woman came over her. "Yes, do think about it," she said to herself. "Though it's not likely to help much," she added with a quick smile. Then her face assumed a look of great dissatisfaction with herself. "I've gone and done it wrong again; it's just too hard . . . ," she thought.

The maid appeared at the door and took Frau Brake's umbrella. "Good morning, Elfriede," said Frau Brake, "didn't I see you in church 83 today? You're speedier getting home than I am. How are you?"

"Aah, Frau Brake, ma'am, church was so nice again, so solemn. And just think of the pastor, the way he feels right at home up there in the pulpit, the way he speaks so loud and clear in his deep voice and[31] then leans over the pulpit and holds up his arms. It just touches your heart. And the way he just knows all the problems people like us have, well—being such a distinguished gentleman and all, he wouldn't need to bother with people like me. Back in our village, the pastor was really different. He always spoke in a monotone and went on and on only about the Bible and so on. No, if you compare them, you really notice we're living in a[32] suburb of the big city. You always feel uplifted when you leave church."

"Now, Elfriede, go and read this Sunday's gospel text again before dinner. It will do you good. Is the rest of the family home?"

"The professor was working in his study until a moment ago, and Madam[33] was looking over the young folks' laundry.[34] A few minutes ago they went out with their tennis racquets.[35] I was told to let Frau Brake know that they'll be back promptly at one o'clock for Sunday dinner."

"Good, my child, now go on . . .[36] Stop, wait a minute, Elfriede," Frau Brake called. "Can't you ever remember where my things belong? Again and again you hang them on the professor's hook. See, you can read, it's

---

[31.] Deleted: "moves his hands too".

[32.] Deleted: "upper-class".

[33.] The German *die gnädige Frau* is a third-person term of respect used by a domestic servant in reference to the lady of the house, just as the servant refers above to *der Herr Professor* when speaking of Frau Karoline Brake's son. [NL]

[34.] Replaces: "was checking the silver."

[35.] There was a tennis court adjacent to the house in Breslau where the Bonhoeffer family lived until 1912 (*DB-ER* 14).

[36.] Deleted: "Frau Karoline Brake walked through the spacious foyer into the living room and from there to the veranda, where she sat down in a wicker chair looking out toward the garden."

clearly written over each hook, Father, Mother, Grandmother. Now do remember!"

A little embarrassed, Elfriede quickly took Frau Brake's hat and parasol, hung them in their proper place, and disappeared. With a brief glance and a visibly satisfied expression, the grandmother surveyed the large cloak stand with its long row of hooks, which completely took up one wall of the spacious foyer.[37] The only thing found in the father's spot was his walking stick with its simple silver handle, an heirloom from his father. On the mother's hook hung the feather-light white silk shawl her husband put around her every summer evening[38] they spent in the garden. Then came the grandmother's hook, and after that the long row of those for the children.

84

On the hook of Franz, the eldest son, hung a very worn-out hat. And above it, though his mother had told him a hundred times she didn't approve, Franz had put two books, Feuerbach's lectures on religion[39] and an English work about the labor movement.[40] For weeks Franz had dragged these books around with him and would not part with them.[41] One Saturday evening, when the family had gathered to make music together and his younger brothers and sisters were playing a trio,[42]

[37.] Such coat hooks did in fact exist for the eight brothers and sisters in the big house at Wangenheimstraße 14 in Berlin-Grunewald, where the Bonhoeffer family lived until the end of 1935. The description that follows here matches this Grunewald home.

[38.] Replaces: "that she [wore] on summer evenings." At his father's request, as a birthday gift for Paula Bonhoeffer, Dietrich had brought home a Spanish shawl from Barcelona in 1928. Cf. *DBW* 10:106. The walking stick with the silver handle existed as well.

[39.] Feuerbach, *Lectures on the Essence of Religion*. On Feuerbach's view that "all theology [is] nothing but anthropology," cf. *DBW* 11:148f., 158 [*GS* 5:186f., 193]. Feuerbach had a decisive influence on the political "left" (historical materialism). In "Teilnehmen am Leiden Gottes" (446–52), Krötke calls attention to implicit positions taken by Bonhoeffer in his letters from prison on Feuerbach's *The Essence of Christianity*. Feuerbach is explicitly named in Bonhoeffer's July 16, 1944, letter to Eberhard Bethge (*LPP* 360).

[40.] Cf. Toller's 1922 stage play, *The Machine Wreckers*, subtitled *A Drama of the English Luddites*.

[41.] The eldest son in the Bonhoeffer family, Karl-Friedrich, came home from World War I at the age of nineteen with "leftist" political ideas, which led to difficulties, for example, with Karl Bonhoeffer's industrialist brother Otto Bonhoeffer. A dispute between father and son similar to the one described below took place when Karl-Friedrich refused to take part in the Advent rituals regularly celebrated in the family.

[42.] The Bonhoeffer family played a lot of trios, especially Haydn, Mozart, and Beethoven. Dietrich himself had, at the age of fifteen, composed a trio based on Schubert's art song "Gute Ruh" and performed it with his brother Klaus and sister Sabine for their parents (*DB-ER* 25). Cf. the letter of Bonhoeffer's father dated March 27, 1944, which refers to their musical Saturday evenings at home: "On Saturday we had all sorts

85 Franz pulled a book out of his pocket and began to read. His father had kindly but firmly reprimanded him. Franz had replied in a rebellious tone—previously unheard-of in this house—declaring that in times like these people should spend their time more usefully[43] than with traditional family gatherings that did nobody any good, and that they couldn't expect him to let his little brothers' and sisters' bungling attempts[44] at musical performance interrupt his work. Moreover, he said, the artificial[45] cultivation of musical achievements in people who lacked talent was an injustice and the money should be made available instead to train especially talented working-class people.

When a deathly hush had come over the room following this extraordinary exchange, their father had answered with uncharacteristic sharpness that he was still the father of the family, and he forbade his son once and for all to criticize the way he saw fit to spend his money. Besides, he added, it was utterly superfluous for Franz to pose before his father as an advocate of the poor; he knew more about the poor from his medical practice than Franz from his books. And as far as the family gatherings and musical evenings were concerned, he concluded, Franz would one day think altogether differently about them. Then, when the children, after a tender glance from their father, resumed playing their trio, Franz had quietly left the room, deathly pale and quivering with agitation.

The grandmother had worried for a long time after that about Franz's wide, fiery eyes, his pale complexion, and the fanatical streak around the mouth of the young student. Apparently he had now finally gone outdoors for a Sunday hike with his brothers and sisters, leaving his books behind for once—perhaps a hopeful sign of having regained some degree of inner calm. The grandmother, who was particularly fond of her oldest grandson, took the books from the cloak stand to put them in Franz's room and thus avoid any further irritation of the parents.

On Christoph's hook there hung an unfamiliar loden coat that 86 showed distinct signs of ample use on rainy days in the forest. "Oh yes, Ulrich's of course," Frau Brake reminded herself with a smile.

---

of musical offerings from the young people [at the home of the Wedemeyers]. . . . We were reminded very much of our own Saturday musical evenings, when you were all at home" (*LPP* 244).

    [43.] "More usefully" [nützlicher] replaces "more productively" [nutzbringender].

    [44.] "Bungling" [Gestümper] replaces "stumbling" [Gestoppel].

    [45.] "Artificial" [künstlich] replaces "laborious" [mühsam].

Then came Klara's pretty little hand-knit summer sweater, for which her grandmother had supplied the pattern, and underneath a pair of dainty little overshoes. Next was Martin's cap, which had earned him such derision in his junior year of Gymnasium.[46] "I don't see why I should always attract attention in school; no other boy wears such crazy homemade suits and silly hats as I do.[47] I don't want people on the street to stare at me and laugh as I go by." Fortunately, it had never occurred to this boy with the unusually intelligent, bright eyes and the vivacious and always cheerful[48] expression that people on the street didn't smile at him because of his somewhat unusual[49] dress, but because his whole manner gave them such deep pleasure. When people responded no differently to his appearance even now, after he had managed to convince his reluctant father[50]—over the protest of all his siblings—to let him have the school cap, Martin secretly worried for a while that there might be something ludicrous or crazy about his character or his appearance, and became embarrassed and self-conscious about it. But since he didn't want to talk about it with either his older brothers or his parents—one didn't talk about such personal things, but dealt with them on one's own—he had sounded out his grandmother on the subject one day and had then suddenly blurted out the question whether crazy people actually know they're crazy. His grandmother had answered with astonishment that he'd have to ask his father about that sometime, since he was a doctor who could tell him all about that. As far as she knew, 87

[46.] A Gymnasium is a secondary school which prepares students for the university through a humanistic curriculum with a strong foundation in the classics. In Bonhoeffer's time, one normally began at age ten and continued to eighteen. The highest class was the Prima, and the seniors of this class were called Primaner. [CG]

[47.] Renate and Eberhard Bethge have described the "more important—and even unimportant—family rules" in Dietrich Bonhoeffer's parental home (introduction to the 1978 German edition, *Fragmente aus Tegel,* and its 1981 English translation [6]): "You didn't wear an official school cap; you dressed neither to look average nor to look conspicuous—though you couldn't avoid a certain amount of attention, since the mother preferred picturesque clothes for the children" [trans. altered]. See also Eberhard Bethge, *In Zitz gab es keine Juden:* "All the relatives praised my mother whenever she had tailored another suit for me; only I suffered from this style, which violated the schoolboys' norm in Magdeburg" (54). Cf. Bethge's description of the "blue cap," a part of the conventional uniform worn by "the monastery-school boys" at the Gymnasium, Monastery of Our Dear Lady, which Eberhard Bethge had entered at the age of ten (52).

[48.] Replaces: "jovial".

[49.] Replaces: "not at all crazy, but quite simple [which in turn replaces "inconspicuous"] and practical".

[50.] Replaces: "mother".

their awareness varied a lot. The boy had beaten around the bush for a while and finally said, "I mean, Grandma, if there is something ridiculous about a person, in his face or his walk, or if he looks really dumb, does he always know that?"

Then the grandmother had known what was up and had stroked Martin's head with her hand and said, "Dear boy, what silly ideas you have."[51] And in so doing she had looked at him so kindly, almost amused, that Martin had run out of the room with a beet-red face, but overjoyed. Since then the school cap hung untouched in its place, and no one knew why but the grandmother, who knew how to hold her tongue.

The next hook, on which hung all sorts of children's things, was marked "Little Brother." His siblings, had they been asked, would scarcely have known that their youngest brother was actually named Ekkehard. And they would have been embarrassed to pronounce this name; it seemed "affected" and too "melodramatic" for them. But the mother had[52] uncharacteristically insisted on this name when he was born. Now—whether over time she herself came to feel it was too pompous, or perhaps because of its unconscious rejection by the rest of the family—at any rate, Ekkehard was never under any circumstances called anything other than "Little Brother." And as happens with such names, it clung to the little boy in school as well. For his classmates and teachers, he was "Little Brother." He was, incidentally, the only member of the Brake family who was not called by the name given him at baptism. Ordinarily it was something like a family principle that all diminutives, pet names, and nicknames were avoided. "That's a privilege of the aristocracy and film stars, to call their children Mautz and Koko and Pippy," the father had once said in passing at the table. And as sometimes happens, it had been a foregone conclusion with the children after

88 this casually dropped joke that such silly extravagances were unnecessary.[53] And, as we know, young people are often quick to turn questions of taste into moral judgments. And so they couldn't get enough of spending their time making fun of the greengrocer's children, whose names were Thekla and Armin.[54] In fact, they almost thought it was to

---

[51.] Deleted: "You are exactly right."

[52.] Deleted: "no one had ever been able to find out why—".

[53.] Replaces: "And it was as if part of their pride as members of the middle class was that they did not go along with such extravagances."

[54.] Saint Thecla, a martyr, is the main character of a late-second-century work named *The Apocryphal Acts of Paul and Thecla*. Armin [Hermann] the Cheruskian, victor in the

their own credit that their own names were neither silly nor literary nor theatrical, but sensible middle-class names, though not all that run-of-the-mill.[55] They all agreed that "Ekkehard" transcended the limits of the permissible, which were as doggedly observed as they were hard to define. "Little Brother" was definitely more natural. By the way, where was Little Brother this morning?[56] His things were all right here. The little eight-year-old latecomer often felt left out among his older siblings, so when they went out he usually preferred to stay at home in the yard.

Frau Karoline Brake cast a quick glance over the last three hooks, which were intended for guests.[57] On Sundays they were frequently occupied by the coats of the oldest daughter, married six months ago, and her husband, a high government official.

This foyer with its long coat rack would hardly give a visitor the impression of an elegant residence. One did, however, immediately see[58] that the wood and metal used in this bright space were top-quality, solid material and painstakingly polished and cared for.[59] A thick, plaited mat covered the parquet floor. There was no need for the children to run across Persian rugs before they knew how to keep their shoes clean—that was the mother's opinion. But she didn't think it was right to make the children always use the kitchen door to go in and out. On the free walls of the foyer hung several good engravings of German cities.

Frau Karoline Brake opened the door and walked through the wide, cool living room—fancy names like "parlor" were taboo in the family— and dining room, where the curtains were drawn to keep out the sun. She approached the veranda, where the window shades were down. Frau Brake felt comfortable in these large rooms. She had known the long dining table, with its simply carved but solid[60] wooden chairs, since her

89

Battle of Teutoburg Forest in the year 9, is a stage figure in Christian Grabbe's drama *Hermannsschlacht*. Viktor von Scheffel's character Ekkehard, from the novel by the same title, is named after tenth-century monks at St. Gall.

[55.] Deleted: "Frau Karoline Brake had a look in passing at . . ." This deleted sentence-fragment recurs in an altered form at the start of the next paragraph.

[56.] Deleted: "Was he out with his brothers and sisters? Actually [he] loved . . ."

[57.] Replaces: "visiting relatives."

[58.] Replaces: "Whoever looked more closely could of course recognize . . ."

[59.] Emmi Bonhoeffer, in a document of December 30, 1935, wrote of "The House on Wangenheimstraße": "The great organization of the household was also very interesting. . . . the floors were always freshly waxed" (Bonhoeffer, *Fiction from Prison,* appendix, 134 [trans. altered]).

[60.] Replaces: "well-made, stable".

childhood, when it was in her parents' home. The sideboards were old-fashioned, but of excellent design and craftsmanship. The small antique silver box from which the grandmother gave her youngest grandchildren a little piece of chocolate on special occasions had stood tightly closed in the same spot for years, and even fifteen-year-old Martin was not above being counted among the little ones in this case.

On the walls hung good portraits of all four grandparents, of whom only Frau Karoline Brake was still alive. Although both grandfathers had been respected men and held high positions, their pictures showed no sign of the public honors they had enjoyed. "I am having my portrait painted for my family, not for the town hall," Grandfather Brake had said.[61] Now, when the older children, who loved these pictures, visited other homes on occasion and saw the portraits of the patriarchs in official robes and adorned with all their medals and honors, at first they just thought it was funny. Later, in an especially dramatic instance of this kind, Christoph had boldly[62] spoken of "nouveau riche" taste. And though his father secretly agreed with him and was glad to see how certain his instincts were, he had nevertheless answered, "Dear boy, remember this. It is inappropriate for you to judge people like that at your age. If they are kind enough to invite you into their home, it is not fitting to criticize the way they live and furnish their home. That is an abuse of the law of hospitality. Listen to me and don't forget it. You still have to learn how good it is that people are different, and you must not take offense at external things. It is foolish to compare all the time and to judge everyone[63] by the same measuring stick." Since his father's word was the standard by which Christoph measured everything, a reply to this statement was out of the question.[64] But the clear sense of

90

[61.] Karl Bonhoeffer wrote to Dietrich on June 8, 1943: "Recently I've had an invitation to have a sound film made of myself for the 'Film Archive of Personalities' which has recently been instituted in the Ministry of Propaganda, to 'preserve a picture of me for later times.' I think that it will be sufficient if my picture is preserved in the family" (*LPP* 51).

[62.] Replaces: "impudently".

[63.] Deleted: "by your own standard."

[64.] On the role played by his father, Karl Bonhoeffer, see Bonhoeffer's April 22, 1944, letter to Bethge: "I don't think I have changed very much, except perhaps . . . under the first conscious influence of Papa's personality" (*LPP* 275) [trans. altered]. See also his letter of August 14, 1944: "I've found that one of the most powerful factors in our upbringing at home was the way we were given so many hurdles to overcome (having to do with sticking to the point, being clear, natural, tactful; keeping things simple, etc.), before we were ready to formulate our own ideas" (*LPP* 386) [trans. altered].

quality[65] that he and his father both possessed became more and more pronounced and conscious after this conversation. What was new to him was the idea that an integral part of judging quality was showing consideration[66] and reserve toward people who are different from oneself. It took many years and much experience to learn that.

While the grandparents' pictures were very much a part of the growing children's lives, the somewhat stiffly painted picture of Frau Brake's great-grandfather which hung over a little corner sofa had special significance.[67] An old-fashioned inscription underneath read: "This is the Reverend Josias Brake, Provost of the Cathedral, who paid the price of God's word with his life and taught it with his death." The picture showed the old provost kneeling in front of an altar with Christ on the cross and holding an hourglass that had run down.

91

This old orthodox Lutheran pastor had been driven from his pulpit during the age of rationalism, and, when he defied the orders of the authorities and refused to leave his congregation, he was thrown into prison.[68] In the end, through the efforts of his loyal congregation, he was released and reinstated in his office. But during his first service upon returning to his parish, weakened by his long imprisonment, he collapsed at the altar, his eyes on the crucified Christ, and died.[69] The

---

[65.] On the "sense of quality," see the passage with this title in "After Ten Years" and its references to "the feeling for human quality" and "a social order based on quality" (*LPP* 12f.). See also, "Thoughts on the Day of the Baptism of Dietrich Wilhelm Rüdiger Bethge," where Dietrich comments about "sensitivity [Qualitätsgefühl] for the human values of justice, achievement, and courage which is found today across all social strata" (*LPP* 299 [trans. altered]).

[66.] For "considerateness" [Nachsicht] intrinsic to sensitivity for quality, see Frau Brake's self-criticism, page 80: "I've gone and done it wrong again. . . ."

[67.] Bonhoeffer obviously alludes here to the fictional great-grandfather of Mayor Brake, Frau Karoline's husband. The Bonhoeffer children had great respect for their own maternal great-grandfather, the renowned theologian Karl August von Hase. In 1824–25, as a young fraternity man, he had been imprisoned by the authorities for over a year at the Hohenasperg fortress (*DB-ER* 5).

[68.] Bonhoeffer's reference to Lutheran confessors and protesters such as Paul Gerhardt and August F. C. Vilmar (he had quoted the latter at length in *CD* 150ff.) parallels similar incidents in the Third Reich, e.g., the arrest and imprisonment in 1936 of members of the Confessing Church who refused to comply with the Nazi state's orders to leave their churches and parsonages (*DB-ER* 540).

[69.] On November 15, 1942, Dietrich Bonhoeffer wrote to Maria von Wedemeyer: "You have probably read in the paper of Hugo Distler's sudden death. I considered him the most significant composer and church musician we've had for a long time. Now I hear that he has died by his own hand, holding the Bible and the cross, in his study in the [Berlin]

children knew this story from childhood and revered the picture of their ancestor almost like a little icon of a saint.[70] Even when as adolescents they later grew away from the church, this didn't change. They kept the old pastor quietly alive as an ideal in their hearts.

Aside from this special instance, though, ancestor worship was utterly nonexistent in this family. The Brake family tree that hung by the stairs belonged just as naturally to the household as all the objects in various rooms that had been passed down in the family. It was only with great effort that the parents were able to come to the defense of an old, wealthy uncle who had nothing to do and would show up from time to time to talk endlessly in a booming voice about the honorable achievements of the Brakes during the last four hundred years, while the children mocked him boisterously.

92

"Uncle Theodore, do you think it will be the end of the world if some day there aren't any more Brakes?" fourteen-year-old Franz had once asked, putting on a show of naiveté.

The foolish uncle had fallen for it and answered, "My, but it makes me happy to hear you say that. Just keep up this way of thinking and you'll turn into a genuine Brake."

Franz, who had nearly exploded with laughter, caught a reproachful look from his mother. Christoph, sitting next to him, whispered in his ear, "Makes you want to throw up!"

The children's favorite source of amusement was when their father would again and again gracefully evade the uncle's repeated protestations that they absolutely must establish a family club and archive.[71]

"You're a real-live family club all by yourself, Uncle Theodore!" their father would say.

"But what will happen when I'm dead?"

---

cathedral, because he couldn't take it anymore." Cf. the letter of condolence Bonhoeffer wrote the same day to Distler's widow Waltraut (*DBW* 16:368f. [*GS* 6:579f]). [*DBW* 16:369, editorial note 2, repeating the earlier note of *GS* 6:579, claims that Distler committed suicide because of the deportation of the Jews, while Larry Palmer's biography of Distler explains the suicide as the result of his depression at having been called for the third time to serve in Hitler's army (*Hugo Distler and His Church Music*, 70f.). Other sources give additional reasons.][CG]

[70.] Replaces: "the picture of their great-great-grandfather had become something almost sacred to them."

[71.] The Bonhoeffer family showed little interest in the existing von Hase family organization. See *Unsre Hauschronik*, a family history written by Karl Alfred von Hase, the son of Karl August von Hase and Pauline, née Härtel; cf. *DB-ER* 8, 7.

"Well, that will be the end of the Brakes, to be sure."

"But no, dear nephew," the uncle replied, flattered but uncertain. "You can't be serious, can you?"

At this moment their mother would come to his aid and would offer the uncle, who couldn't resist the cuisine of the Brake family, something delectable, thus changing the subject. Variations on this scene had been played repeatedly in the children's presence. So whenever the uncle came to visit, they were always waiting for this moment and kicked each other under the table when it came—though once, by mistake, the uncle himself got a good kick on the shin and looked around, utterly stunned, but without saying a word.

Thus it happened that the children in the Brake household would punish with wild mockery all attempts to "play up the family," as they called it. If one were looking for a sense of family in them, one would have found too little, rather than too much of it. They would have preferred to address distant aunts and cousins formally. "We don't even know each other," they said, "and really don't have anything to do with each other." And if their mother then said, "But children, they're Father's relatives!" they would laugh and say, "Mother's joined the family club!" 93

Nevertheless, Professor Brake's hospitable home did see an almost incessant stream of visiting relatives. Once Klara had said, "I think the relatives are taking advantage of Papa a bit. They expect him to solve all their problems; they all come with their petty complaints, even though Papa has more to do than any of them. Papa is too good-natured, and sometimes they don't even say 'thank you.'"[72] There was something to that. People all too readily took advantage of the wealth and influence of the professor[73] and his wife, who were generous in their willingness to help.[74]

Frau Maria Brake had undertaken the furnishing of the house with great confidence and independence, sparing no resources necessary to the task. Untroubled by questions of style and conventional taste, she had focused exclusively on creating a living space for her family that was beautiful and generously proportioned. It was amazing to see how this

---

[72.] Replaces: "It never really occurs to anyone to do something nice for him, too."

[73.] Replaces: "the doctor".

[74.] Deleted: "A warm smile spread over the grandmother's face as she thought about how much her grandchildren loved her son and daughter-in-law."

principle had served to bring things old and new—items of great artistic value and those whose value was only personal and sentimental—into one naturally and meaningfully coherent space.[75] This home had not been fabricated, but had grown organically. Without thinking, one could move about in it freely and without feeling anxious. One felt drawn into the warm atmosphere of a strong family life, without being oppressed by it. One sensed an unobtrusive wealth and an uninhibited taste for pleasure[76] and comfort. It wasn't so much the importance of the individual object that pleased the eye and warmed the heart as the solicitous care given to the whole.

Frau Karoline Brake had sat down on the veranda and was looking out into the large backyard. She had resigned herself to the fact that her daughter-in-law let most of the yard grow wild so that the children could move freely about and play there. The only planting was a magnificent rose arbor,[77] with blossoms of every color, by the veranda where they had breakfast on hot summer days. Beyond it the wilderness began, an unmowed meadow in full bloom, bushes with thick, overgrown foliage where you could find nice dark hiding places and robbers' dens. There was even a little bog that provided the nature-loving children endless materials for their aquarium and their microscope. Between the strong branches of an old linden tree, the children, helped by their father, had nailed together a solid and spacious treehouse[78] where they took special pleasure from eating their afternoon sandwiches. The yard

----

[75.] Paula Bonhoeffer had furnished the family home in Berlin-Grunewald in this way. Maria von Wedemeyer wrote to Dietrich Bonhoeffer in prison of her own detailed plans for furnishing the apartment they would share when they were married. On September 21, 1943, she wrote, for example: "At the moment I'm still worried about furniture. If you picture that in the most glowing colors, picture some really hideous armchairs to go with my sofa. . . . I'll definitely need some flower vases, too, to make our home pretty" (*LL* 88f.).

[76.] Replaces: "beauty".

[77.] In the yard of the house on Marienburger Allee where Bonhoeffer lived with his parents until he was put in prison, was a rose arbor with red roses; cf. *DBLP* 183. Roses of all colors growing by the house are an important motif in Adalbert Stifter's *Indian Summer*. Karl Bonhoeffer refers to this novel in a letter to his son Dietrich on July 11, 1943: "The chapter on the visit [in *Indian Summer*] reminds me very much of [Stifter's] *Mappe meines Urgroßvaters*, where he also introduces the visit to a stranger's home with a charming description of the garden" (*LPP* 75 [trans. altered]).

[78.] There was a solid treehouse for the Bonhoeffer children at their summer cottage in Wölfelsgrund—after 1945 called Miedzygórze, in the Polish district of Wroclaw—in the Glatz Mountains, where the family went from Breslau for vacations until 1912 (see *DBLP* 33).

ended at a light wood fence with a gate leading directly into the neighboring forest. Frau Brake looked out among the tall meadow grasses and the bushes and saw her youngest grandson's blue smock appear for a moment and disappear again,[79] beside him the slight figure of the   95
neighboring railway worker's ten-year-old son in his heavy gray Sunday suit. The two children's voices carried over the stillness of Sunday morning up to the open veranda. Now they sat down on a small wooden bench by the bushes. Little Brother reached into his pocket and took out a tiny piece of chocolate that had probably become rather soft in the heat, a cookie, and half an apple.

"From last night," he said, and passed these contents of his pocket to his friend.

He took them and at the same time pulled a bag[80] from his own pocket, opened it, and let Little Brother look inside. Then he gave it to him and said, "I collected these for your terrarium[81] after the rain yesterday. Look at this one!" And he pulled a fat earthworm out of the bag. Both boys studied it admiringly.

"Thanks, Erich," said Little Brother, putting the bag in his pocket.

"And I also made you a slingshot for the cat in case it tries to get up to the birds' nests here," said Erich. "You can put a pretty big stone in it." He immediately demonstrated the weapon to his friend.

Little Brother took it, and for a while the boys passed the time by taking turns aiming at a tree trunk. They didn't talk much. A little later the kitchen windows were opened and a strong aroma of roast meat found its way out into the yard.

"Mmmm, does it ever smell good at your house!" said Erich. "We're having cabbage and potatoes today. Do you always eat meat?"

"I don't know, really," answered Little Brother. "Sometimes, anyway."

[79.] The blue smock popular at the time was worn by Dietrich Bonhoeffer as a child (see *DBLP* 41), and by the next generation as well. The following continuation was deleted from the first draft: "Eight-year-old Little Brother could keep himself busy alone in the yard for hours at a time. He often sat quietly by a bush for a long time and listened to the birds singing. By now he knew almost all of them and was already very good at imitating them. That was his favorite way to amuse himself." This passage was replaced by a long insert of one double sheet.

[80.] Deleted: "made of newsprint".

[81.] Eberhard Bethge has written that the Bonhoeffer family home in Breslau included a room "in which—to the servants' alarm—all sorts of pets were kept, such as lizards, snakes, squirrels, and pigeons, as well as collections of beetles and butterflies" (*DB-ER* 14).

"We only eat meat once a week, whenever my father has a day off. Today he's at work."

"But today's Sunday, Erich," said Little Brother. "You know nobody works on Sunday."

"Yes, they do. My father works for the railway. They work Sundays too, and even at night."

"Even at night?" asked Little Brother in amazement. "Then when does he sleep?"

96 "During the day," said Erich.

"But why does he do that? Did he choose to work for the railway? And how do you celebrate Christmas, if your father happens to have to work?" asked Little Brother.

"Last time we celebrated the day after," said Erich.

"But that's no good!"

"No, it's no good, but we couldn't do anything about it."

"But what if your father just said 'I can't work today, today's Christmas'?"

"Then he'd lose his job."

"Well, that would be good, wouldn't it?"

"You're silly, Little Brother! Then we wouldn't have anything to eat."

"Oh," Little Brother said hesitantly as he thought this over. After a while he asked, "Is your family poor, Erich? Poor people are always hungry and don't have any clothes to wear and are cold in the winter."

"I don't know, Little Brother. I asked my mother once, and she said we have just enough and must be happy with what we have."[82]

"Too bad!"

"Why?"

"Because everybody should treat poor people well, just because they're poor."

"Really? I've never heard that. Is your father rich, Little Brother?"

"I don't know, Erich; I don't think so, because my mother never wants us to talk about money, and she always just says 'm' instead of 'mark',[83] and I only get ten pfennigs allowance a week and you get fifty. We're never allowed to buy ice cream on the street, and when we go on day

---

[82.] Deleted: "But sometimes when we have meat, and my mother doesn't eat any and gives it all to the others, then I think we don't have enough after all; we must be poor."

[83.] The German unit of currency, equal to 100 Pfennig. [NL]

trips we always bring everything we need from home. Do your parents say we're rich?"

"No, my parents have never said that, but other people talk that way."

"Oh, don't think anything of it, Erich; they just want to make us angry."

"By the way, what do you want to be later on, Little Brother?"

"I don't know exactly what you call it, but when I grow up I'm going to buy a big house,[84] and then I'm going to turn the veranda into a big, huge birdcage and I'll travel everywhere, even to Africa and America, and I'll collect all the birds you can find there, and then you and I will feed them and watch them all the time so we'll know how they do everything."

"That's great, but I'll have to work for the railway later, too."

"Why?"

"My father said so. But then I'll come visit you often."

"Yes, of course, all day and every Sunday, too, like now. Have you got your whistle with you? Let's go and look at the nests in the bushes for a while."

The two boys dug into their pockets and each pulled out a little reed whistle that Erich's father had made for imitating birdcalls. For months that had been their favorite form of amusement.[85] Often the two would sit quietly by the bushes for hours listening to the birdcalls, most of which they knew, and they would imitate them so skillfully that birds actually came to them.[86] They hated all cats who showed their faces in the vicinity and chased them away by throwing sand by the handful.[87] They were at it again today, as Frau Brake watched them disappear into the bushes.

She was startled by a penetrating scream. She recognized Little Brother's voice, but couldn't see him. It wasn't like him to cry, even when he

97

[84.] Deleted: "for us two".

[85.] Replaces: "favorite activity." This is the end of the insert mentioned on page 91, editorial note 79.

[86.] Karl Bonhoeffer wrote in his memoirs about his son Walter: "In our summer cottage at Friedrichsbrunn, in the Harz Mountains, he was usually in the woods by sunrise. He knew all the birds and was able to make them come with his calls" (in Zutt et al., *Karl Bonhoeffer*, 91; cf. Stifter, *Indian Summer*, 36, 279, and 473, on birdcalls).

[87.] According to Sabine Leibholz-Bonhoeffer, Dietrich's brother Walter protected the songbirds "by making cat traps baited with valerian, the horrible smell of which was attractive to the cats" (*The Bonhoeffers*, 16 [trans. altered]).

had hurt himself.[88] Besides, it sounded less like a cry for help than a cry of outrage. Frau Brake was already rushing down the stairs to the garden and toward the woods, but still couldn't spot Little Brother. Then she heard someone crying softly and found the boys kneeling on the ground in the bushes, Little Brother holding a young bird in his hand.[89]

"She knocked it out of the nest!" he said with tears streaming down his face when he saw his grandmother coming.

"Who, the cat again?"

"No, worse than that, its own mother, the mean, wicked beast!" The bird twitched once more, then died in the boy's hand. That was too much for him. Too frightened to realize what he was doing, he opened his hand and let the dead baby robin[90] fall to the ground. Then he felt sorry, reached down to pick it up, and stood up and showed it to his grandmother.

"Bury it in the earth," she said. "That's where it'll feel most comfortable."

Without a word Erich took a big spade,[91] dug it deep into the earth, and Little Brother laid the bird into its grave and covered it over. The grandmother took her young grandson by the hand and went into the house with him. Erich stayed for a moment, then ran quickly out to the street.[92]

"Why did she do that?" asked Little Brother when his grandmother took him to his room to help him to wash his face and get ready for dinner.

"Probably because the baby bird was weak and sick," answered Frau Brake quietly. She would not have approved of turning such a powerful

98

[88.] Deleted: "But his grandmother had never heard him cry like this before."

[89.] Karl Bonhoeffer wrote about Walter that he "was already an excellent [marksman] at an early age. I witnessed how he shot a circling falcon with a rifle. But when the bird fell down dead at his feet, he was so devastated that he burst into tears" (in Zutt et al., *Karl Bonhoeffer*, 91).

[90.] Stifter's *Indian Summer* (see 91f.), which Bonhoeffer read at this time, includes a description of a robin near its nest in the bushes.

[91.] Replaces: "Little Brother took a small shovel".

[92.] Deleted: "It was another half hour till dinnertime. During this time the grandson and his grandmother got into a conversation which we will describe a little later." Cf. page 28, editorial note 9, on Bonhoeffer as a catechist for children. It was presumably later, after writing the next three pages, on graph paper, that he decided to insert the conversation here after all, writing it on half of a double sheet with an Eichberger watermark.

experience into a dishonest[93] morality lesson by saying something like "because the little thing was naughty."

Frau Brake considered the truth more powerful pedagogy than clever tricks or beating around the bush.

Little Brother was taken aback at this sober answer[94] and was compelled to stop and think. His tears were drying. He was trying to understand, but he did not. "Because the baby's weak and sick, the mother throws it out of the nest? So she doesn't even take care of it?"

"No, Little Brother, in the animal world only the strong and healthy can survive. Only with humans is it different."[95]

"But that's evil[96] of the mother bird, to kill her young like that!"

"No, Little Brother, it's not fair to say that. Animals are innocent; they don't know any other way to live."

Little Brother shook his head. "I didn't know that. I think then I won't have a birdhouse later after all. Grandmother, do you think God knows all that?"   99

"Yes, of course God knows. 'Not a single sparrow falls to the ground without the will of your father,' Jesus says."[97]

"Does Jesus know that for sure?"

"Yes, he knows for sure."

"So does God know the little bird we just buried, too, and is it with God now?"[98]

"Yes, God knows it. Jesus also says, 'Before God, not a single sparrow is forgotten.'"[99]

"Well, then I guess it's all right," said Little Brother.

"Yes, God's will is always good," said his grandmother.[100]

[93.] Replaces "untrue".

[94.] Deleted: "himself quite sober".

[95.] On Bonhoeffer's decision to oppose euthanasia, see *E* 159–64. [In 1939 the Nazi regime officially began a "euthanasia" program to kill children with birth defects and institutionalized patients who were invalids, mentally impaired, or suffering from diseases like epilepsy. For a summary and an account of the churches' response see Barnett, *For the Soul of the People,* 104–21. The program was really driven by "eugenic" ideas related to the Aryan ideology and by economics, rather than by a desire to end suffering mercifully.][CG]

[96.] Replaces: "mean".

[97.] Cf. Matt. 10:29.

[98.] Replaces: "will God take it up to heaven so it can be with God there?"

[99.] Cf. Luke 12:6. Deleted: "So is the bird with God in heaven now?"

[100.] During his time as an assistant pastor in Barcelona, Bonhoeffer had counseled a ten-year-old boy about his pet German shepherd, "Herr Wolf," who had just died, and had

Little Brother thought this over. After a while he said, "But it's also right that humans do things differently from the animals.[101] Father does help people who are sick and weak, doesn't he, Grandmother?"

"Yes, child, he tries to."

"Can't he always help them?"

"Often, but not always."

"Do they have to die then?"

"Yes, child."[102]

"And what happens then?"

"Then they stand face to face with God and ask if they can come to be with God."

"Is God very strict with people?"

"Yes, God's very strict with us, but also very good."[103]

"Do people always know they're going to die before they die?"

"Not always, but sometimes."

"I want to know it before; then I'd hurry and do lots of good things so God would have to take me to heaven."

"God doesn't have to do anything, child; God does as God pleases."

"But if you ask God with all your heart?"

---

written Walter Dreß about the conversation in a letter of September 1, 1928: "Then his heart-rending crying suddenly stops completely and he says, 'Now tell me, will I see Herr Wolf again someday? He is in heaven, for sure, isn't he?' . . . And I said, rather on the spot, Well, look, God made us people and the animals too, and certainly loves the animals, too. And I think God makes sure that those who have loved each other on earth—I mean really loved—may remain together when they are with God, because loving is something which belongs to God. Of course we don't know exactly how that will come about. . . . 'So then I'll see Herr Wolf again when I'm dead too, then we can play'—in a word, he was overjoyed. I repeated several times that we can't know exactly how this happens. But he *knew*. . . . He took the whole thing as seriously as we adults do when something terribly difficult happens to us" (*DBW* 17, letter numbered 10, I, 44a).

[101.] Deleted: "Are people better than animals?"

[102.] Deleted: "Why do they have to die?"

[103.] Deleted: "Is God strict with grown-ups, too?" "Yes, with grown-ups God is especially strict."

ABOUT THIS TIME the younger generation of the Brake family was stopping for a lunchtime rest on the bank of a quiet forest pond.[1] They had started out early that morning at five o'clock, taking the train part of the way and then hiking for several hours to explore the forest somewhat farther from home.[2] Hikers rarely came to these parts,[3] and it had been an hour since they had met anyone. They had hiked along a trail through a mixed forest[4] where old, tall trees alternated with bright, open clearings and had followed the course of a fast-flowing and rapidly widening stream. With a good instinct for the terrain, they had correctly guessed that where the hills got lower, there would be a forest pond in which they could have a refreshing swim. When they actually saw the sunlit water glistening through the trees, they all shouted for joy and ran at a trot down the wooded slope to the edge of the pond.

The young men had already thrown their backpacks on the ground and pulled out their swimming suits, when Klara called out: "Stop, first we're going to collect mushrooms for lunch, and while they're cooking we'll go for a dip!"

So they each quickly grabbed the containers[5] they had brought along for that purpose. After just half an hour the group was inspecting the impressive array of specimens that lay on a platter of moss: firm, hardy edible porcini,[6] whole families of them at the edge of the forest rarely disturbed by human footsteps; bright yellow chanterelles; chestnut browncaps; tall, feathered parasol mushrooms, still closed; handsome blue tricholomae; orange agaric; and countless pungent marasmi—all presenting a colorful still-life of the fruits of the forest floor.[7]

[1.] There was a forest pond called Ranger Müller's Pond outside Friedrichsbrunn in the eastern Harz Mountains, where the Bonhoeffers owned a vacation cottage beginning in 1913 (*DB-ER* 24). Cf. Bonhoeffer's letter of February 12, 1944: "The hills of central Germany . . . represent nature to me; they are a part of me" (*LPP* 211 [trans. altered]).

[2.] Replaces: "to reach some part of the surroundings of their city they did not yet know."

[3.] Replaces: "They had reached a very secluded area by now".

[4.] Replaces: "Without talking much, they had then walked through a tall, deciduous forest."

[5.] Replaces: "net".

[6.] Deleted: "in all sizes". In a letter of July 20, 1920, Bonhoeffer wrote from Friedrichsbrunn: ". . . Just walking past, we found fifteen pounds of porcini mushrooms" (*DBW* 9:26).

[7.] The Bonhoeffer children's expertise in hunting for edible mushrooms had been passed on to them by their grandfather, Friedrich Bonhoeffer. Cf. *DB-ER* 10: "And

101   While Klara and Martin cleaned the mushrooms and peeled potatoes, the older members of the group built a safe fireplace and laid a fire. Before long the fire crackled under the pots, and in a few minutes the party of youngsters reconvened in the water amidst much splashing, spluttering, and laughing. Surprised and delighted to discover a large raft,[8] they alternated between sunning themselves briefly and tipping each other over into the water. While the boys were still swimming, Klara had gone ashore and prepared the meal, and was now calling the others to come and eat. This year's new potatoes and the aroma of fresh mushrooms outdoors under the shade trees on the shore of the cool pond made for an incomparable feast. They ate in silence, and along with the nourishing food, each of these young people took in the energy of forest, sun, water, each other's company, their family, their native land, and freedom itself. They received all this more or less consciously as one great gift in the depths of their being.

Now it was time for a midday rest. The sun's reflection shone hot and bright on the water and created a blinding glare. Dragonflies scooted back and forth above the water's surface and climbed up and down the stems of the reeds. Fifteen-year-old Martin, lying on the raft in the reeds,[9] was observing for the first time with thoughtful amazement how some of them climbed down a blade of grass into the water for a brief moment and then soon came back to the surface. What were they looking for under water? What did they have to hide there? How could they breathe down there? he wondered. Tonight he'd ask his father about it. When the sun became too hot on his back, he skillfully built a little arbor of branches on the raft and, using his hands as paddles, slowly moved along the shore of the pond. Now and then he saw a water

102   bird dive under as he approached. He enjoyed watching the small fish jump into the air and threw a fat frog back into the pond that had hopped onto the raft. One time there was a loud noise in the reeds and a large bird took off, vigorously flapping its wings directly over Martin's head.

---

grandson Dietrich was proud of his confident knowledge of mushrooms which he had inherited from his grandfather. Like the latter, Bonhoeffer experienced the forest with his nose." For the 1978 first German edition of this material, the word *blau* (blue) describing *Ritterpilze* was incorrectly deciphered as *blank* (shiny).

[8.] Sabine Leibholz-Bonhoeffer, *The Bonhoeffers,* says of Dietrich's brother, Walter: "We loved the raft he made for us to sail on the mountain pond" (16).

[9.] Replaces: "close to shore".

"A heron!" Martin cried, half terrified, half excited. Then it was quiet again.

Klara had fallen sound asleep in the shade of a mighty beech tree, her thick blonde hair[10] lying loose across her shoulders and chest. Breathing quietly and evenly, she drank in the summer woodland air.

Franz had withdrawn to the nearby clearing. He didn't want to sleep yet wished to be completely undisturbed, so he sat down on an old tree stump, a book on his knees and a well-worn rain cape around his bare neck to keep the bugs away. Now the world around him faded from his consciousness, and all he saw were the starving figures of the workers from Zola's *Germinal*.[11] "That's where real life is, where we find our real work; only there can we prove ourselves in life. Everything else is play, dreaming, and wasting time.[12] It's frivolous. In fact it's worse than that; it's irresponsible, rotten, it's thievery," Franz mumbled out loud. "Damn, why do I keep letting myself get carried away and lulled to sleep!" He knew he had to forget about his brothers and sisters if he wanted to talk this way. If he were to have seen his young sister just now, sleeping so peacefully, like a child of nature, or his little brother observing with attentive eyes and mind all that was happening at the water's edge, or if he had thought of the simple meal they had all just enjoyed together so happily and with a natural simplicity, then he would no doubt have had to see that life is richer and more diverse than it often says in books. But he didn't want to see or know that now. Like a hermit he sat there in his strange garb, and visions of a better, more just and beautiful world rose before him and made his face glow. And what was good and beautiful in the existing world so near to him disintegrated into ashes before the glowing images of the future that he beheld and whose dawning he believed had come. Anyone who had ever seen him like this, with his deep, dark eyes, his warm expression that had not yet turned fanatical, his clear features and good forehead bent over his books, would have been strongly impressed by this twenty-year-old. But he, of all people,

103

[10.] Dietrich Bonhoeffer's sister Christine (von Dohnanyi)—also known as Christel—who was especially close to her brother Walter through their shared interest in animals, was blonde (see Leibholz-Bonhoeffer, *The Bonhoeffers*, 27). Later Bonhoeffer describes Klara as having dark braids; his sister Ursula had dark hair.

[11.] A German edition of Zola's novel *Germinal*, first published in 1885, was distributed about 1930 by the German Book Club (Deutsche Buch-Gemeinschaft) in Berlin. Karl-Friedrich Bonhoeffer was the first in the family to read Zola.

[12.] Replaces: "dancing on the edge of a volcano."

who in his mind sought the company of the disadvantaged and the weak, had the reputation among his fellow students of being unapproachable, and the weak and mediocre even considered him arrogant.

On a treeless slope rising gently from the pond in full sun, Christoph and Ulrich[13] lay on their backs in the tall grass, their hands cradling their heads, their gaze directed at times to the sky, at times across the pond, each with a gray linen slouch hat on his head. Their tanned and toughened bodies were impervious to the sun. Anyone seeing the two would have thought they were brothers, as in fact often happened.

Indeed, as soon as twelve-year-old Ulrich and his mother had moved to the neighborhood and he joined Christoph's class in school, he was treated like one of the family in the Brake home and accepted as a brother among the children. It was simply taken for granted that Ulrich would be part of every project, every event, every outing, every celebration. Christoph, unlike his older brother,[14] had always felt an intense need for personal companionship and someone to talk to. But his younger brother was too young for that. Thus one could no longer imagine Christoph without Ulrich. Theirs was one of those rare, unclouded, and indestructible friendships that make youth rich and happy, and that protect one against inner dangers and losing your way. Such friendships are impetuously sealed in the midst of the awkwardness and ferment of adolescence, then become clarified as they mature,[15] until they reach the full-bodied, dry flavor of fine wine.[16]

104

In school, at home, and on countless hikes Christoph and Ulrich had come to know one another down to the most minute detail of their behavior, opinions, interests, abilities, and innate characteristics.[17] In the process they were delighted to discover a consonance between them in all the essential aspects of their lives; and now, in certain situations, the smallest hint in facial expression or phrasing sufficed to guarantee

---

[13.] Deleted: "thoroughly engrossed in conversation."

[14.] Replaces: "who was very different from his older brother and . . ."

[15.] Replaces: "which are best formed in one's youth, and by old age are still . . ."

[16.] See Sirach 9:10, a verse which is marked in the margin of Bonhoeffer's Luther Bible by an indelible pencil line: "A new friend is like new wine." Bonhoeffer wrote this verse in Otto Salomon's guest book on his Swiss trip in September of 1941; see entry of September 24, 1941 (*DBW* 16:209 [*GS* 6:542]). Gotthelf's "Hans Joggeli, die Erbvetter" deals with the friendship of two elderly men; cf. Gotthelf, *Erzählungen:* "For many years, he had lived in rare, faithful friendship with the rich farmer Hans Joggeli, who had just died" (363).

[17.] Replaces: "gifts".

that they would completely understand each other. Nevertheless, they had never become bored with one another.[18] Christoph, the vehement and lively thinker, had come to depend on the clarity and straightforwardness of Ulrich's personality. By the same token, Ulrich found in Christoph's confidence and decisiveness the support he sought.

"This sure beats the pathetic school field trips," said Ulrich, stretching his arms out wide and pulling his knees up to his chest.

"You haven't told me yet—how were your three days in S . . . ?"[19] Christoph asked, without turning around.

"Just plain ghastly, I'm telling you. I don't even want to think about it out here.[20] Beer gardens, skat,[21] bragging and filthy talk, parading around after the city lovelies all afternoon, of course in long pants, bright ties, slicked-down hair,[22] but unwashed from the neck down. I'm telling you, it was enough to make you sick. Hanging around the parks at night, etc.[23] And I don't even want to know where all the money came from that the fellows were throwing around there—and the whole thing was the brilliant idea of the senior class president of a Gymnasium."

"So why did you go along? Right away I thought it would be like that."[24]

"You know, I did too, but Mother really wanted me to go. She said we're too isolated from the others, and that isn't good. And when I told her you weren't going either, she said it was different with you; I couldn't risk going it alone like that. She just can't help worrying that by hanging around your family I might get used to a way of life that isn't appropriate to her circumstances or mine."

"And yet our so-called way of life, the way we spent today for example, is a lot less expensive than the vacation escapades of our distinguished fellow students," Christoph said, laughing.

"Of course, Christoph, and Mother knows that too, basically. It's more

[18.] Deleted: "For Christoph, Ulrich's presence was like . . ."

[19.] Ellipses in the original.

[20.] Deleted: "Our esteemed classmates, of course almost all of them wearing long trousers, in the morning already in . . ."

[21.] A three-handed card game popular in Germany. [NL]

[22.] One of the Bonhoeffers' "family rules" was that "the boys wore their hair longer than others, but they started to wear long trousers and ties later than usual" (*Fragmente aus Tegel*, 13).

[23.] Deleted: "and the whole thing of course a foretaste of academic freedom."

[24.] In the Bonhoeffer family the children did not automatically participate in class excursions and school events. If such activities didn't seem worthwhile, the parents wrote a note excusing them.

that she's afraid that I'll become isolated. 'You're one in a thousand,' she says, 'and you have to get used to dealing with them. You can't spend your whole life at the Brakes' house.' If she only knew what it is she wants me to get used to, she wouldn't have a minute of peace as long as I'm at the Gymnasium. But how can I tell her that? And maybe it's not so bad after all to have seen that, too. But ugh, it was disgusting. By the way, they aren't all like that. It's always just a few big wheels and then the rest tip right over. By the way, did you hear that Meyer got kicked out?"

"Really? That's good. He was such a swine, in every respect. I wouldn't give him the time of day."

"But that's not why he got kicked out. It's because, even before summer vacation, long before the graduation exams were held, he failed for the third time even to qualify to take them.[25] I know his mother. She's a seamstress and she's worked herself to the bone just to scrape together enough to get the boy through this school."

"Serves her right!"

"Christoph!"

"Well, Ulrich, I'm right, aren't I? What good does it do for every dimwit to get hustled and hassled through the Gymnasium and then the university? First you get what you've just seen in S . . . , then the whole thing is magnified at the university, and finally you get a completely ignorant but pompous teacher or judge or high government official, who brags to his cronies at the bar about all the Gymnasium and university escapades he's never told his wife about. It would be a hundred times better if a fellow like Meyer had learned a trade, for better or worse."

"A fellow like Meyer would be bad even at learning a trade and would never get it right."

"You're right about that, Ulrich; at least from what we knew of him, the best job for him would be mixing drinks in a sleazy bar. But the problem goes deeper. If Frau Meyer has had it drummed into her all her life that you have to be a 'councillor' or 'government official' to be anybody at all, and if this Frau Meyer, who is a diligent, independent seamstress, already gets the jitters when she has to face the bespectacled accountant in the town tax office, then something is wrong. And of course that's going to have an effect on her ambition. Her offspring, who might be quite capable, will be beaten over the head with much false ambition and anxiety until he respects all the official 'somebodies'; and Frau Meyer

---

[25.] Deleted: "[Meyer is] lazy, dumb, and insolent."

will sincerely believe that what she's doing is pleasing to the good Lord. She'll have him bow in all the wrong places.[26] And, if her child dares to make a move of his own someday, she'll pray to God to help save him from wickedness. With all that the poor fellow will be a wreck before he even begins to live. So is it any wonder if Herr Archibald Meyer, Graduating Senior, thinks the only proper thing to do is to behave like an aspiring government official by going out drinking, picking up a girl—if   107 possible one from the cabaret—etcetera, etcetera, and, last but not least, flunking his graduation exams and making his mother miserable?"

As he spoke, Christoph had sat up straight and really did not look like an aspiring official.[27] "And who's responsible for this whole calamity?" he continued. "None other than the classes that set the tone, the so-called upper class, whom everyone sees as a model for success in life. And this upper class is for the most part already a bunch of rotten, obsequious lackeys; they combine bootlicking[28] toward those above and brutality toward those below,[29] lots of rhetoric on the outside and decay on the inside. And the few decent individuals and families who could play a significant role withdraw into themselves because they're repulsed by this vacuous, conceited society. Ulrich, that's where the problem lies. We need a genuine upper class again; but where are we going to get one?[30]

[26.] Deleted: "so that the poor devil . . ."

[27.] Marginal note in pencil: "State, upper class, piety." The last two lines on this sheet of graph paper, which is numbered 11, are deleted: "Christoph, maybe my feeling about what you're saying is even stronger than yours. I see it every day from both sides, from yours as well as mine." This deleted passage is the last on the sheets of graph paper in the novel fragment. Bonhoeffer only used this lot of paper for letters from prison to his parents from June 24 to September 13, 1943. In his letter of August 17, 1943, he had asked for paper for writing drafts and outlines (*LPP* 94). The rest of the novel manuscript is written on double sheets with an Eichberger watermark; it ends on the front page of the double sheet with the number 33.

[28.] Replaces: "cowardice".

[29.] See above, page 35f., editorial note 52, on *oben* and *unten*. [CG]

[30.] On the idea of a new "upper class," cf. above, page 50f.; also see the reference in "Thoughts on the Baptism" of May 1944 to "a new elite of people . . . who will be authorized to become strong leaders" (*LPP* 299 [trans. altered]). Gerhard Ritter, whose *Machtstaat und Utopie* Bonhoeffer probably read in the spring of 1941 for his *Ethics*, says of the rulers of the utopian state in Thomas More's *Utopia*, bk. 2: "They will not be isolated as a class for they will be continuously replaced by people advancing from lower levels. But they will be distinguished from the masses as an elite of those of greatest intellectual gifts and moral maturity. They are Plato's ἄριστοι [the best, cf. 'aristocrats'], a class of people of noble qualities where you find neither ambition nor passion" (72). In the Third Reich, the National Socialists intended to breed an elite in the fascist sense; institutions that served

108   You yourself say it only takes a few to set the tone, and then the rest follow. What that means is simply that Ulrich Karstensen and Christoph
Brake have to set the tone, not Archibald Meyer. We can't get around
that, and false modesty won't improve the situation."

Ulrich had sat up as he listened, and was watching Christoph intently.
He loved to listen as Christoph developed his very definite and very passionate ideas. And although he agreed with Christoph's ideas and liked
to follow his lead, at the same time he always saw things clearly and
sometimes had a simpler but deeper view of things than Christoph.

"You're right, Christoph; it's going to depend on us. But are we really
immune to the poison of ambition [Streberei][31] and the desire to
please, which plagues people today? Look, I have to think of my mother
when we talk about this. Surely she's an ordinary woman. A village
organist and choirmaster like my father surely didn't belong to the
upper class. Yet I've never seen a trace of false ambition or anxiety in the
way my mother dealt with superiors. Though she's quite modest, she
moves with freedom and confidence wherever she goes, without wanting
to be something other than she is. Of course she knows exactly what it
means for me to be in your home, and I really don't think it troubles her
that she can't reciprocate with your parents. But I do sense her fear that
by associating with you I might come to think that I'm something more—
or want to be more—than I am, more than[32] my background and my
gifts make me. Surely she fears that someday I'd be unhappy when I realized the divide between your family background and mine. What I mean
to say is that Mother is as free from the modern plague of social climb-
109   ing as it's possible to be. When I ask myself where she gets that freedom,
there's only one clear answer—from her Christian faith. That's what
gives her such confidence and at the same time such modesty. And now
I often think the reason things are the way they are today is that most
people no longer have what Mother has. You know what I mean? And
Christoph, if things are ever to be different—if someday there should

---

this purpose included the national political academies ("Napolas"), the regional Führer
academies of the Hitler Youth, and the Reich Youth Führer Academy in Potsdam. Hermann Rauschning, in his 1938 book against National Socialism, *The Revolution of Nihilism,*
used the expression "ruling element with a historic mission" (29).

[31.] Replaces: "of false ambition".

[32.] Deleted: "the average person who". In his book *In Sitz gab es keine Juden,* Bethge
writes that his mother, the widow of a pastor, "was often troubled by the fear that her children lacked modesty and could harbor excessive ambitions" (37).

arise a new, genuine, responsible upper class—then don't you think these people will have to have what Mother has? Or else they'll go right back to their old rotten ways."

For Ulrich it was never as easy to put his ideas into words as for Christoph, and he struggled with this. But his warm and natural personality, his manner,[33] and his great modesty of character always commanded attention and won over his listeners as he spoke. While Christoph loved to present the same idea in ever new ways and from new perspectives, and enjoyed great ease of expression, Ulrich always formulated his ideas only once, leaving it to Christoph to process them, incorporate them into his thinking, and shape them into an effective message. Thus Ulrich was mostly the listener.[34] Others would get the impression that essentially he echoed Christoph's ideas, while in reality they were often Ulrich's ideas, observations, and feelings—briefly and awkwardly expressed—which Christoph delivered in brilliant form and with great conviction of his own. And Ulrich would then feel profound joy and satisfaction to find in Christoph such an understanding and convincing interpreter of his own ideas.

What Ulrich had just said had never been expressed between the two friends. This was not because Ulrich was in any way ashamed of these ideas—this was simply not the case between them. It was because it always took a long time before things that Ulrich perceived deep within himself worked themselves out, emerging in the clarity of his consciousness and his spoken word.

110

Christoph was surprised. He immediately sensed that Ulrich had just said something very new and very important for the two of them. He had experienced this with Ulrich a few times before. What Christoph had just said about the need for a new upper class had grown out of several of Ulrich's surprising ideas.[35] Christoph looked at Ulrich. "So you think we must have more religion,[36] if we want to be in responsible positions someday?"

[33.] Deleted: ". . . [he always spoke] from personal experience".

[34.] Replaces: "said much less than Christoph in conversations like these."

[35.] This division of labor is comparable to that mentioned in Bonhoeffer's letter to Bethge on November 18, 1943: "I may often have originated our ideas, but it was up to you to clarify them" (*LPP* 130 [trans. altered]).

[36.] Cf. the way this is expressed in the well-known lines of Goethe: "If you possess science and art / You also have religion; / If you possess neither, you are obliged to have religion" (*Goethes Sprüche in Reimen*, 6, no. 9, 161). The phrase "to have religion" was characteristic of Goethe.

"I think, Christoph—rather, I wonder . . . no, I think—we have to be Christians."

Christoph looked toward the pond, where Martin was paddling along on his raft, absorbed in his observations; he looked toward the forest, the broad expanse of sky. "What a damned old-fashioned idea!" he said.

Ulrich didn't answer.

"And equally uncomfortable."

Ulrich was quiet. There was a long pause.

"Ulrich, you were talking about your mother," Christoph began again, "and you know how much I like her—forgive me this stupid expression! But now I'm thinking about Papa and Mama. You can't really say they're Christians, at least not in the customary sense of the word.[37] They don't go to church. They only say grace before meals because of Little Brother. And yet they're as little infected by the spirit of false ambition, careerism, titles, and medals as your mother is. They prefer a good laborer or craftsman[38] a hundred times over some puffed-up 'Excellency.' Why is that?"

Ulrich thought for a moment. "That's because, without knowing it and certainly without talking about it, in truth they still base their lives on Christianity, an unconscious Christianity."[39]

111   Christoph became restless, stood up, and, still barefoot, paced back and forth in the tall grass. "You're a weird fellow, Ulrich, the way you say that. You're as calm and as confident as though this were self-evident— 'unconscious Christianity.'"

Ulrich sat motionless, his arms around his pulled-up knees. Suddenly he laughed out loud. "You don't need to worry, Christoph, I haven't

---

[37.] For a discussion of the role of the church and Christianity in Bonhoeffer's parents' home, cf. *DB-ER* 34ff.

[38.] Replaces: "They respect . . . a hundred times more".

[39.] See the letter of November 18, 1943, to Eberhard Bethge, which remarks that the novel set out to rehabilitate "middle-class life [Bürgertum] as we know it in our own families, and especially from a Christian [christlichen] perspective" (*LPP* 130 [trans. altered] [*DBW* 8:189]). [The reading "Christian" rather than "Christianity" reflects a revised deciphering of the original letter.][CG] At the end of the *Ethics* manuscript of November–December 1940, where Bonhoeffer explains that "being human and being good" will be treated under the rubric of the "penultimate," there is a note with the words "unconscious Christianity." See *E* 133 (*DBW* 6:151) and *DBW* 6:162, editorial note 95. Cf. also *E* 65, written in 1942: "The good—in its citizenship [bürgerlich] sense." See also *ZE*, 32, no. 71: "Christian [moral] conduct which is no longer conscious of being Christian."

knelt at the Salvation Army confessional bench, and I haven't just joined a sect."

Christoph had to laugh at this image, too. What kind of confessions would Ulrich have to deliver up on a confessional bench?[40] A grotesque idea. No, that certainly wasn't what he meant. Christoph paced back and forth some more, thinking. Then he stopped and looked at Ulrich. "Something has to be wrong here, Ulrich," he said. "As far as I know,[41] Christ made a point of making no distinction between people, good or bad, just or sinners, upright or mean. I've always thought that the so-called tax collectors were mean rascals who betrayed the people, and the prostitutes, both then and now, were people like Archibald Meyer.[42] And I still do remember[43] from confirmation class with the infamous Pastor Schönrock[44] what Paul said, that 'there is no longer Jew or Greek, there is no longer slave or free, there is no longer male or female'; and that 'God chose what is weak and despised in the world.'[45] So according to Christian teaching, all people are equal—or, I should even say, the weaker and worse, the better. That's exactly the opposite of what you and I experience every day, and what we think and want. So how in the world is Christianity supposed to help create a new upper class, an elite? That can only lead to a hopelessly superficial kind of equalization."

Ulrich was quiet again. This conversation had reminded him of the elderly Frau Karoline Brake. "And your grandmother, Christoph? She certainly takes Christianity seriously and understands it better than most pastors. Do you think she doesn't make any distinctions between people? Doesn't she think just as we do that some people must be in

112

[40.] In the letter of November 18, 1943, Bonhoeffer writes to his friend: "I know that we have shared spiritually, although not physically, in the gift of confession, absolution, and communion . . ." (*LPP* 129). [CG]

[41.] Replaces: "know about Christianity".

[42.] Cf. *E* 61–65 on the relationship of Jesus Christ to good people, in the context of Bonhoeffer's experiences in resistance against the National Socialist regime.

[43.] The manuscript shows Bonhoeffer mistakenly used the prefix *be-* rather than *ent-*, meaning "reflect about" rather than "remember." [NL]

[44.] The German contains a satirical wordplay here, for Pastor Schönrock's name literally means Pastor Finefrock. [NL]

[45.] Cf. Gal. 3:28 and 1 Cor. 1:27f. [The former reads "male and female," while Bonhoeffer writes "male or female." In the latter, verse 27 reads "God chose what is weak in the world . . ." and verse 28 "God chose what is low and despised in the world . . ." Bonhoeffer has combined the two verses. [CG]

higher and others in lower positions,[46] and that everything depends on the right people having authority?"[47]

Christoph was stunned. "I don't get it. There's some sort of contradiction here," he said.

"Right. I don't get it either, Christoph, but that's what you're here for, to figure it all out. Unfortunately, you're stuck with being the smarter[48] one here."

"Don't give me that rubbish, Ulrich."

Just then they heard diving and splashing in the pond. Shortly thereafter Klara's red bathing cap appeared. She had awakened from her midday siesta and had gone for another dip. A few seconds later Martin's voice chimed in with its joyous "Yippee!" as he jumped off the raft into the pond and surfaced next to Klara. That was a signal for Christoph and Ulrich to leave all their problems behind. They raced down the hill, and before anyone noticed, they were in the water. "Yikes, it's freezing!" they gasped, having just been roasting in the sun. Now they could see the hermitlike figure of Franz throwing down his rain cape and book on the bank and then swimming toward them. So the games and pleasures of the morning started up again.

[46.] See especially the recently discovered letter of September 20, 1941, from Bonhoeffer to Paul Lehmann. Probably reflecting the views of his co-conspirators, Bonhoeffer states that after a successful coup Germany would need "an authoritarian 'Rechtsstaat'" as a basis for justice, lawfulness, and the freedom of the church. As much as he would personally prefer in the aftermath of Nazism an Anglo-Saxon liberal democracy, Bonhoeffer believed "that sort of thing would throw Germany right into the same abyss" (*Newsletter,* International Bonhoeffer Society, English Language Section, no. 68, 10f.). See also above, page 35f., and the editorial notes to the conversation between Christoph and his father. [CG]

[47.] Cf. *E* 284–87, et passim.

[48.] Replaces: "bright".

113

SUDDENLY A SHRILL, SNARLING VOICE pierced the happy sounds of laughter in the pond. On the bank stood a slender, young man in yellow hunting boots[1] and a brand-new, green uniform, holding a riding whip[2] in his hand.

"Get out of the water, you hear, you bunch of hooligans! Can't you tramps wash off your filth somewhere else? Out of the water, one-two-three-march, on the double! Well? Move it, I say! Hurry up! Do you think I have all day, you damn riffraff?" On and on he went like this, in an impertinent voice which, lacking any sensitivity, might turn even a peaceful pond in the forest into a military drill ground. Martin, who was closest to shore, climbed out first and stood there, terrified.[3] "Are you going to get over here, you rascal!" shouted Yellowboots. Martin had collected himself in the meantime and approached the man with a defiant look.

"What, trying to get fresh with me too, are you? Well, just you wait, boy, we'll show you. The lot of you will pay dearly for your fun!" With these words the uniformed man grabbed Martin by the ears and pulled him up close.

Just that moment Franz had come ashore, and no sooner had he seen the hunter grabbing his brother than he sprang at the man in uniform with such a leap that Yellowboots stepped back in terror. "Let go of my brother this minute!" Franz cried, "or . . ."

The hunter let Martin[4] go, and turned pale at the sight of the ominous, angry expression on Franz's face. "Don't touch me, I'm warning

---

[1.] The story of "Yellowboots" is based on an incident Paula Bonhoeffer experienced around 1910 near the family's summer home in Wölfelsgrund, Silesia, in which she argued with a forester's assistant who was trying to intimidate her children and chase them out of the woods. The Bonhoeffer children coined the name "Yellowboots" [*Gelbstiefel*] at that time. Bonhoeffer's prison experience when writing this—inmates being yelled at in a demeaning way—also enters into the narrative. Cf. pages 185–88; also see Bonhoeffer's "Report on Prison Life" (*LPP* 248–52).

[2.] Replaces: "dog whip". Karl Bonhoeffer wrote in his memoirs, "My dislike and mistrust of Hitler was based [among other things] on . . . his motor trips through the countryside with his riding whip in his hand" (Zutt et al., *Karl Bonhoeffer*, 99).

[3.] Deleted: "facing the uniformed figure."

[4.] The manuscript says "Christoph" here instead of "Martin." [Writing "Christoph"—the character who represents himself—instead of "Martin" shows that Martin is in many ways also Bonhoeffer at a younger age. The character Yellowboots is inconsistently referred to by Bonhoeffer sometimes as a hunter and at other times as a forester's assistant.][CG]

you," he stammered, raising his riding whip, "any of you. How did you
114   miserable city rabble[5] find your way out here, anyway? Well, put on
your rags and scram and be glad I don't whack you one across the seat of
your trunks."

Franz, beside himself with rage, yelled, "And even if we were miserable city rabble and our clothes were made of rags, who are you, you cos-
tumed fop, you impudent brute? You're a pathetic little clown,[6] and
don't forget it!"

The man in uniform turned red. "And you've been stealing[7] to boot,
you thieves," he bellowed, kicking the pot with the leftover mushrooms
so hard it rolled down into the water. By now Christoph and Ulrich had
come over, with Klara behind them. The three tall young men with their
strong, bare bodies stood around the vainly dressed hunter, who was
barely older than they.

Christoph had just caught the word "thieves" and stepped up close to
the enemy with icy calm. "You will now take back everything you just
said, loudly and clearly," he said with frightening determination. "We are
neither riffraff nor thieves. Now you know. So there!"

The hunter became uneasy, but he tried one more time. He raised his
whip and screamed, "You [Du], little greenhorn, I won't let you scare me
by a long shot."

In the same moment, Ulrich grabbed the whip and held it tightly in
his grip, as Christoph said, "I hereby forbid you to address me that pre-
sumptuous way,[8] and I categorically demand that you take back what
you said."

"I wouldn't think of it!"

"Then you will tell me your name and under whose authority you are
here."

Klara intervened. "Let it go, Christoph. You can see the man doesn't
know how to behave and has lost[9] control of himself! There's no point
in arguing with him."

[5.] Replaces: "pack of louts".

[6.] Deleted: "Now you know! And one of these days you'll get to see what workers' fists
feel like."

[7.] Replaces: "stealing mushrooms [replaces: and violating nature]".

[8.] The German *du*, the familiar form of "you," is reserved for intimate friends, family
members, divinity, animals, and, as in this case, objects of insult. [NL]

[9.] Replaces: "the dumb man [replaces: fellow] has, after all, lost".

"No, Klara, this matter must be resolved. I can't let something like this go."[10]

By now the hunter must have noticed from the demeanor of the youths and their manner of speaking that he probably had yelled at the wrong sort of people, and he probably would have liked to back out of the situation somehow. He tried it with an artificial smile, but only met the unrelenting looks of the three young men. Klara looked at him mockingly;[11] Martin had calmed down enough almost to be able to laugh. Ulrich was still holding the whip tightly in his hand. "Take back your words," Christoph said again, with an almost frightening harshness.[12]

In this moment the hunter visibly blanched. His glance was directed past his young opponents toward the path into the woods, where he saw people approaching. "Let me go," he said suddenly in a totally different tone of voice, almost pleading. "Let's consider the matter settled.[13] You misunderstood me, gentlemen." And with that he tried to take his whip and leave.

"We have no intention of letting you go. The matter is not settled at all, and we certainly did not misunderstand you," Christoph countered calmly.

"What's going on here?" he heard a deep male voice say from behind where he stood. "Kruse, what's the matter here?"[14]

The young people turned around, surprised, and saw a gentleman of their father's generation step out of the woods, and behind him several others, apparently his family.

"Just a joke, Major, sir,[15] a little joke," the man in uniform stammered, grinning sheepishly.

"A very bad joke, in any case," said Christoph.

[10.] See Bonhoeffer's letter from prison on November 22, 1943: "Two or three times here I've given people a quite colossal dressing-down for indulging in only the slightest rudeness, and they were so disconcerted that they have behaved very correctly since then" (*LPP* 136 [*DBW* 8:198]). In 1940 in a working note for his *Ethics*, Bonhoeffer pens the expression "the power of anger [Zürnkraft]" (*ZE* 62, no. 65).

[11.] Replaces: "with pity".

[12.] Replaces: "with utmost certainty."

[13.] Deleted: "I didn't mean it like that."

[14.] Replaces: "What happened here?"

[15.] In the manuscript Bonhoeffer uses "General" here, after deleting "Colonel." Only later did he decide on "Major."

Franz, still in a rage, protested. "It wasn't a joke at all, but an outrageous impertinence!" he shouted.

Ulrich was still holding the whip.

"Now quiet down, everybody," the major called out. "Kruse, you first. Go on!"

"Major, sir," Kruse began, coming to attention facing the major, "I was—I thought it might annoy the master and mistress of the estate if strangers swam here on Sunday. So I asked the young gentlemen to leave, and as a result there was a little exchange of words.[16] Not worth mentioning, Major, really not worth mentioning. I very much regret the inconvenience."

116

Meanwhile the major's wife had approached with their three children, a young man of about twenty, a daughter of perhaps fifteen, and a twelve-year-old boy. Kruse, embarrassed, bowed deeply.

Now Christoph stepped up to the major, bowed briefly, and said with a clear and strong voice, "Please forgive us for this incident, Major. My name is Christoph Brake and these are my brothers and my sister. We went swimming here, not realizing the pond was privately owned. But we will not allow ourselves to be called a bunch of hooligans, scoundrels, or thieves, not by anyone. And to us, threatening people with a riding whip is no joke. I beg you, Major, to hold this gentleman accountable, and of course we will comply immediately if you ask us to leave. We do apologize again for our mistake."

There was an amusing contrast between the seventeen-year-old's open and honest words and spontaneity—standing there before the major wearing only his swimming trunks, his hair still wet—and the phony grin of the young man in the full-dress uniform.

Christoph was just about to take his leave after another brief bow when his glance met that of the young girl. Standing beside the major, she gazed calmly at Christoph with large, dark eyes. For a moment he felt thunderstruck.[17]

"Please stay," he heard the major say. He then heard him continue in a strikingly sharp way, "Kruse, you know very well that I do not wish to hear such behavior on my estate, in fact I abhor it. It's bad enough if you

---

[16.] Replaces: "battle of words."

[17.] Karl Bonhoeffer writes of his encounter with Paula von Hase in 1896 that "My impression of this moment when I first saw my future wife remains in my memory as an almost mystical one that determined my life" (*DB-ER* 8).

learned it on the parade ground. Even there I never tolerated it or found it necessary. I consider it disgraceful. What gives you the right to call people hooligans, scoundrels, or thieves—people you don't know at all—just because they happen to be in your power? Such insults really reflect on the person who utters them. Kruse, you will now apologize to these young people and take back your words!"

"Major, sir,"[18] stammered the young man in full-dress uniform. "Major, sir, most respectfully, sir, but that's asking too much. That's impossible, it goes against my honor!"

"Against your honor?" thundered the major. "What kind of honor is it that is too proud to admit an injustice and make amends? What a joke, how absurd, what mockery! I wouldn't give a fig for it. Kruse, where did you learn that? Who turned your head and heart inside out with these ideas? Listen to reason, Kruse, and do what you must do as a man of honor."

With a final convulsive movement Kruse snapped to attention and snarled, "Major, sir, I beg you most respectfully to relieve me of service. I cannot sacrifice my concept of honor."[19]

"Go, Kruse, go," cried the major, "I shall not keep you. But be sure not to make yourself and other people unhappy."[20]

Kruse, who had turned deathly pale, clicked his heels and saluted; the major returned the salute and Kruse left.

Shaking his head, the major looked in the direction Kruse had gone and stood still for a moment, deep in thought. Then he turned to the young people and said, "Now it is up to me to apologize to you. Please believe me when I say that I deeply regret this incident—more deeply than you can understand now. I feel sincerely ashamed, for"—he added bitterly—"I hate this kind of person from the bottom of my heart. It is

117

[18.] Bonhoeffer first called the major *Oberst* (colonel), then at page 111 he began writing *General* (general), and changed the earlier references accordingly (cf. page 111, editorial note 15). His final decision was for *Major* (major) (cf. page 143, editorial note 49).

[19.] "Loyalty is the marrow of honor" was a prized motto of the National Socialists. Lipperheide's dictionary of proverbs cites the lines, "Loyalty is the marrow of honor / That never falters when storms are roaring," from Friedrich von Schlegel's 1807 poem, "Oath." In his *Ethik der Liebe,* Lütgert wrote: "A primitive sense of honor is the opposite of love" (138). Lütgert implies that the *völkisch* milieu (privileged by National Socialism) had the effect of polarizing the two.

[20.] Deleted: "Be sure not to make yourself unhappy." [Replaces: "Believe me, you will run out of steam soon enough."]

bound to bring about great evil and suffering in our country." With these last words a look of gloom came over the gray-haired man's features.

118   "We're so sorry," said Klara, horrified. "We didn't mean to cause trouble."

"It's a blessing to be rid of him," the major's wife exclaimed. "That dandy didn't belong here in our forest. I am so happy that I do not need to see him again and, Harald, be honest now, so are you. And," she continued cheerfully, turning to the young people, "we have our young guests, whom we don't even know, to thank for this. But first, let's all make ourselves comfortable and recover from this frightful incident."

"Madam," Klara said now, "it's very kind of you to make this unpleasant situation easier for us this way. But we were just about to start home anyway, and we really don't want to impose on you any longer.[21] Besides, we promised to be home for supper so we can spend the evening with our parents. Thank you very much, but I think it's best that we go now."

"No, my dear child," said the major's wife, looking approvingly at Klara, "you can't run away from us so quickly. After all, we are very curious to know who so innocently invited themselves to be our guests today and whom I should thank for the unexpected good fortune of never having to see the stupid face of our forester's assistant again. What's more, the next train to town doesn't leave till six, and if you walk by way of our place, it will only take you half an hour to get to the station. You do want to go back into town, don't you?"

"Yes, Madam."

"Well, then come over and sit down with me for a moment and let's greet each other properly at last." The major's wife reached out to take Klara's hand.

"My name is Klara Brake and these are my brothers, Franz, Christoph, Martin, and Ulrich—or rather, Ulrich is Christoph's friend, but he counts as a brother,"[22] said Klara.

"Did I hear you correctly?" the major interrupted. "Is your name Brake? Are you in some way related to Professor Brake in town?"

"He's our father."

[21.] Replaces: "disturb you for a moment longer."
[22.] Deleted: "his name is Ulrich Karstensen."

"Is that possible?" exclaimed the major, as if transformed. "Then you are the children of my old friend from school, Hans[23] Brake? And I saw all of you ten years ago, the last time I visited your parents; but of course you don't remember that. What a strange meeting, and how delightful![24] But hasn't your father ever told you about me? Sophie,[25] children, you all know about Hans Brake, don't you? Yes, Hans Brake and Harald Bremer,[26] they were as well-known forty years ago as Castor and Pollux[27] or David and Jonathan.[28]

119

"Then you're Major von Bremer!" the young people cried in unison. "Of course we know about you, very well indeed. But we didn't know you lived here, Major."

"You could hardly know that, either. I'll explain later. But first of all let's take care of the personal matters. I will address all of you as "du"[29] of course, and you can call me Uncle Harald. This is Aunt Sophie, and—come here, children, say hello to each other—this is Johannes, our second oldest,[30] who is named after your father. This is Renate, and this is Georg."

When they came to Ulrich in this cheerful round of introductions, the major looked with kindness into his clear face and good, calm eyes and said, "And of course Ulrich, whom you call your brother, is also part of the family."

Ulrich looked at him sincerely and gratefully and shook hands.

[23.] Replaces: "Hänschen", the diminutive of Hans [replacing "Friedrich", the first name of Bonhoeffer's grandfather]. The novel continues with this usage at first. This is what Dietrich Bonhoeffer called his cousin Hans Christoph von Hase; cf. his letter of September 12, 1918 (*DBW* 9:15).

[24.] Replaces: "Yes, hasn't your father told you that I live here?" Deleted: "I've been meaning to visit him for a long time and to tell him that I took up . . ."

[25.] The manuscript has "Anna" here, and "Sophie" the next time she is mentioned.

[26.] The names, including their alliteration, resemble those of the Brigge and Brahe families in Rilke's *The Notebooks of Malte Laurids Brigge*, 35. Malte Laurids Brigge hears Count Brahe tell "about 'our little Anna Sophie,' who has lain in her grave at Roskilde for nearly a hundred and fifty years." Bonhoeffer recommended to his fiancée Maria in a letter of February 15, 1944, that she read the novel, despite his reservations about Rilke (see *DB-ER* 844, and *LL* 182).

[27.] Inseparable twins in the Greek myth of the Dioscuri, known for their devotion to each other.

[28.] Cf. 1 Sam. 18:1-5 and 1 Sam. 20.

[29.] The German familiar pronoun for "you"; see above, page 110, editorial note 8. [NL]

[30.] Replaces: "the oldest".

Prompted by this surprising turn of events,[31] Aunt Sophie suggested they take a short walk around the pond, then return to the castle[32] to 120　have afternoon tea there in the park.[33] There they could talk and get acquainted at leisure. All agreed, and after the Brake children had dressed, the whole group started out. Up front the major walked between Franz and Ulrich. Christoph and Renate and Johannes followed, then Martin and Georg. Bringing up the rear was the major's wife, walking arm in arm with Klara. Soon conversation was buzzing on all sides. Klara had to tell about their parents, their grandmother, her brothers, and herself. Georg reported how the raft had been built, and Martin told of his discoveries on the shore of the pond. Christoph had Johannes tell him about life on an estate and was especially interested in everything about how the estate owners related to the day farmhands.[34] Renate said nothing.

The major had been walking a while in silence between his two young companions and from time to time had looked closely at Franz, especially, from whom he had heard scarcely a word since the moment they met. He sensed that the young man had not yet recovered from the incident with the forester's assistant. Suddenly the major said: "Franz, we have to be able to forget, or we'll wear ourselves out."

Franz looked up, astonished, and then said, sincerely, "Yes, that's very hard for me."

"Franz, such a stupid lout can't insult you!" The major spoke with particular warmth and urgency.

"It's not the insult, Uncle Harald, it's something else."

"What is it, then, Franz?"

"I don't know how to say it so it doesn't sound like empty phrases—it's the whole situation."

[31.] Replaces: "change of scene".

[32.] Replaces: "home".

[33.] Replaces: "garden".

[34.] The early-nineteenth-century relationship between landowners of the nobility and farmhands who belonged to the estate on a hereditary basis is described in von Oertzen, *Junker*, 27–30. Rüdiger Schleicher wrote on August 14, 1941, after his visit to the East Elbian estate of Frau von Kleist: "If there is one critical, quite general observation to be made about it, it is—for the Swabian and Naumann follower, of course—the question, 'Where is the free farmer to be found, how can a small farmer advance?' Indeed, in this large agricultural region there are no real villages, I suppose" (*DBW* 16:191). [Friedrich Naumann tried to promote the advancement of industrial and agricultural workers, first as a pastor and later as a Social Democratic politician.][CG]

An ominous look came over the major's features. There was a pause before he replied: "Hmm, what do you mean by that, Franz?"

"I mean that something like this can happen at all; I'm asking myself where it comes from. There's something so destructive about it, much worse than a personal insult. It's hard for me to express myself, Uncle Harald." 121

"I understand, Franz."

"If we didn't happen to be our father's children—if we were really poor kids from town who just wanted to get outdoors on Sunday—and then, pardon me, a scoundrel like that showed up and vented his foolish arrogance and his brutality on us, then we would simply have to take it." Suddenly Franz's feelings erupted and his rage brought tears to his eyes. "I just can't bear to see someone exploiting other people's vulnerability, Uncle Harald, and trampling all over them—and on top of it all that wicked, wicked smile. The scoundrel[35] would have hit Martin if I hadn't jumped between them," said Franz, shaking with emotion. The major put his arm around the young man's shoulders.

"Franz, Franz, I know exactly how you feel, much better than you think," he added earnestly.[36] But believe me, my boy, that's not the way to deal with it. I know. You have to be stronger than these tormentors that you find everywhere today—in school, in offices, in the military.[37] One must fight them, battle them without sympathy, relentlessly; but to do that one must be stronger than they. Otherwise—" The major broke off abruptly.

Franz was startled and moved to observe a deep sadness in the eyes of the wise, old man. In this moment his glance met that of Ulrich, who appeared just as deeply affected.[38]

"Forgive me, Uncle Harald, for bringing up this stupid affair again." 122

[35.] Replaces: "fellow".

[36.] Replaces: "with a sigh."

[37.] Cf. Bonhoeffer's letter of October 10, 1942, when his nephew Hans Walter Schleicher was drafted: "It is clear, and you know yourself, that you will be facing conflicts precisely because you come from such a family. It's not only a conflict with what is meant by nature, whose power will horrify you in the coming weeks, but simply because you are different from most other people, different down to the smallest superficial details" (*DBW* 16:365 [*GS* 2:423f.]). See also above, page 64, editorial note 45, on the middle-class family. Cf. also Bonhoeffer's letter of November 22, 1943: "These petty tormentors . . ." (*LPP* 136).

[38.] Deleted: "'You're wondering about me,' said . . ."

"I started it, Franz, for it still rankles me, too."

Franz was seized by a strong, warm feeling of trust for the major. How could it be that such an old officer, of all people, seemed to understand him, even to feel what he felt? Beyond that, he was struck by the quiet kindness of the major's demeanor, yet also the strength of passion seething beneath the surface. There was an aura about this unusual man, like the atmosphere after a thunderstorm when the sun has broken through, yet in the distance there is still an occasional flash of lightning and a muffled growl of thunder.[39]

Franz got up his courage and asked, "Uncle Harald, do you really believe what you said a while ago, that one can get along at the barracks without behaving like that?"[40]

"Have you done your military service yet, Franz?"

"No, I'll be doing it in the autumn, but I've heard a lot from my friends."[41]

"Then you can begin to prepare yourself now."

"Yes."

"That's good." The major drifted again into his mysterious silence.[42] "Franz, I want to tell you something. Maybe it will be useful to you sometime. What we were talking about is more than a matter of tone, much more.[43] One mustn't be hypersensitive. When you are learning a rough job like a soldier's, you have to expect some rough language, an occasional curse, even a coarse joke now and then. Those who aren't used to all that at home find it tough. But you just have to stand firm and learn that there are other people, too, and different ways of life. You might even manage to hold your own against the majority—all the better. But it isn't necessary, and there's no need to wear yourself out over that; it's not worth it. There is a lot of brutality and filth in life; a man must know that

---

[39.] Replaces: "thunder . . . echoes."

[40.] In his letter of November 20, 1923, Bonhoeffer had reported on his brief military training as a seventeen-year-old in a student reserve company in Württemberg: "The corporal who is training us is very kindhearted and nice. I thought these people would use a quite different tone. And they're not only this way with us, but even the regular Army troops [Reichswehr] are apparently being treated very differently from before" (*DBW* 9:69). ["Before" refers to the period just after the establishment of the Weimar Republic, after World War I.][CG]

[41.] Replaces: "a lot of my friends have served already."

[42.] The following, up to "But woe to people who scorn those who sacrifice their lives in this war!" (see below, page 122), was, with a small omission, published in *GS* 3:496–99.

[43.] Replaces "a whole attitude toward life."

and come to terms with it, and still remain who he is.[44] Right, Franz?   123
We understand each other so far?"

"Yes, Uncle Harald, absolutely. For the past two years I've been helping out a former pastor who resigned from the ministry to work full-time
in the poor slums of our city.[45] I've taken on a youth club there and have
to visit my boys' parents in their homes. I've heard and seen more there
than I can tell. I know that people get involved with brutality and filth
through no fault of their own, and I've found precisely these people to
be very helpful and kind without ever wasting their breath talking
about it."

"Good," said the major quickly. "Incidentally, I doubt that work like
that makes much sense.[46] But let's leave that for now. So, anyone who
would get upset over every coarse word is a prim old maid—we don't
need that. But it's quite another thing when people exploit the power
they have been given over others to humiliate, debase, defile, and
destroy them. Then it's no longer a question of tone, it's an[47] outrage,
as much against the people concerned as against the office one holds. It
desecrates all genuine authority and[48] destroys all human community.
You can be dead sure it will lead to anarchy.   124

[44.] Deleted: "The major paused."

[45.] Replaces: "have been working for two years now with working-class youth in the
eastern part of the city." The Bonhoeffers had long-standing connections—including pro-
fessional contacts through Karl Bonhoeffer's neurological clinic in the Charité Hospital—
with Friedrich Siegmund-Schultze, who established a large-scale social work project in the
eastern part of Berlin. Cf. *DB-ER* 43: "During Anna von Gierke's social pedagogical seminar in 1922, Dietrich's eldest sister [Ursula] had already attended Siegmund-Schultze's
lectures and Klaus worked for a time in the probation service for prisoners." Franz Hildebrandt, Dietrich's friend, spent several months of 1930 with Siegmund-Schultze's social
work team in eastern Berlin. Dietrich himself worked from 1931–32 with confirmation
candidates from proletarian backgrounds at the Zion Church in Wedding, a run-down part
of Berlin (see *DB-ER* 226–29). In early 1933 he hoped to be assigned to a parish in that part
of the city (see *DB-ER* 231). [The reference to "eastern Berlin" means the poorer districts
of the city—later known as "East Berlin" in the DDR period, 1945–89. Eastern parts of
European cities are usually lower-class residential areas because of pollution carried on
westerly winds.][CG]

[46.] Replaces: "don't know whether work like that makes any sense at all." After hosting
in the family vacation home in Friedrichsbrunn some confirmands from Wedding, a working-class industrial district of Berlin, Dietrich wrote his father on March 28, 1932: "At the
end of a time like this, one of course asks oneself how much sense such a project makes in
the first place. But I guess you have to learn to wait with things like this" (*DBW* 11:77 [*GS*
6:223]).

[47.] Deleted: "most horrible".

[48.] Deleted: "thereby".

"Franz, I don't know where it comes from, but there is in all of us a dark, dangerous drive to abuse the power [Gewalt] that is given to us and thereby to destroy life—our own and that of others. Wherever we encounter this truly evil instinct—first of all in ourselves—we must counter it with the force of all the hate and passion we can muster. Don't think, Franz, that it isn't in you, too, just waiting for a chance to pounce. It's an uncanny [unheimlich] thing[49] that there must be power [Macht], indeed that power is something holy, that it is from God, and yet that it so easily turns us into devils, into great or petty tormentors of others. Look at this petty forester's assistant, a likable, harmless, good-natured fellow among his own people. Perhaps he'll be a good, loyal, ordinary family man someday. But when his ridiculous little bit of power tickles his fancy he's a devil, and with his superiors[50] he's a fawning wretch.

"There are many vices, but none that brings greater misfortune to humanity than the abuse of power, especially by powerless people.[51] Again and again history has produced great tyrants [große Gewalttäter]. They in turn have called forth great counterforces and have almost never escaped judgment.[52] They are demigods who do not bow to ordinary human judgment. They rise and fall in a few years. But the petty tyrants [kleine Gewalttäter] never die out. They depend on the favor of their masters of the moment, and bask in it, escaping all earthly judgment. It is the petty tyrants who destroy a nation from the inside. They are like the invisible tuberculosis bacteria[53] that secretly destroy a

125

[49.] Deleted: "about it".

[50.] Replaces: "where he meets greater authority". In "After Ten Years," Bonhoeffer analyzes the stupidity [Dummheit] that is created as a "human defect . . . under the overwhelming influence of an upsurge of power" (*LPP* 8 [trans. altered]). Under the spell of whatever has seized power over them, he wrote, the "stupid will be capable of any evil and at the same time incapable of seeing that it is evil. Here lies the danger of a diabolical abuse" of power [Macht] (*LPP* 9).

[51.] [In this context *kleine Leute* is translated as "powerless people," that is, those who do not have power through their own social status, profession, wealth, or rank, but who gain it through associating with the "great tyrants" like Nazi leaders.][CG] Hannah Arendt discovered to her surprise, when reporting on the trial of Adolf Eichmann in Jerusalem in 1961, that this organizer of mass genocide in the Third Reich was an ordinary middle-class man. She noted that masses of thoughtless citizens, taught to conform, could be more dependable button-pushers at the machinery of dominance and destruction than criminals would be. She gave her book about the Eichmann trial the subtitle, *A Report on the Banality of Evil*.

[52.] Replaces: "the judgment of nations."

[53.] Replaces: "microbes". [The word "microbe" here was a specific allusion to a book

young life in full bloom.[54] They are not only more dangerous, but also stronger, tougher, harder to get hold of than the great tyrants. They slip through your fingers when you want to grab them, for they are smooth and cowardly. They are like a contagious disease. As these petty tyrants suck the life force out of their victims, they infect them with their own spirit. Then, as soon as those who until now had only been victims of violent deeds get hold of the least bit of power, they take revenge for what they have suffered. But this revenge—and this is the terrible thing— is not taken against the guilty party, but against innocent, defenseless victims. And so it continues endlessly, until at last everything has been infected and poisoned and dissolution can no longer be stopped."[55]

The major paused and took a deep breath. "And yet, boys," he continued, "one mustn't be discouraged by the seeming hopelessness of the struggle. Whoever has brought down even one of these petty tormentors[56] can boast of saving many human lives. Such people are benefactors of humanity, even if no one else knows it. Many well-meaning people of our class have become accustomed to smiling about these petty tyrants[57] and regarding as fools those who have declared total war on them. Smiling about them is as foolish and irresponsible[58] as smiling about the tiny size of bacteria[59] and about the doctors who save this or that life during an epidemic and then fall victim to it themselves. To be sure, this war also needs both strategists and soldiers, as the war

126

Bonhoeffer had been reading while working on the novel, Paul de Kruif's *The Microbe Hunters,* which had been sent to him by his scientific brother, Karl-Friedrich; cf. the letter to his parents on August 24, 1943 (*LPP* 97).][CG]

[54.] Replaces: "full of hope." Deleted: "Franz, my life struggle—and not only *mine*—has been directed against these petty tyrants." This in turn replaces, "These petty tyrants are our undoing." Following this passage, not deleted, is a draft version of eleven lines. What follows here is more complete.

[55.] Cf. Bonhoeffer's words in his *Ethics* about the "void, which blows its anti-god's breath into the nostrils of all that is established and awakens it to a false semblance of new life while sucking out from it its proper essence, until at last it falls in ruin as a lifeless husk and is cast away. The void engulfs life, history, family, nation, language, faith" (*E* 106). Cf. Rauschning's 1938 book, *The Revolution of Nihilism,* referring to National Socialism as nihilistic. Cf. above, pages 103f., editorial note 30.

[56.] Replaces: "beasts".

[57.] In the earlier version this was followed by "they can afford to, for they have nothing to fear from them."

[58.] Replaces "unconscionable".

[59.] In the earlier draft this was followed by: "and in fact it is cowardly capitulation in face of a superior force [replaces: an act of violence] by the countless petty tyrants."

against an epidemic needs those who probe under the microscope for the cause of the disease, and others like doctors who attack the individual case. But woe to people who scorn those who sacrifice their lives in this war!"

The two young people listened with expressions of almost solemn gravity. They felt as if they were about to take an oath. And they sensed that the man speaking to them had himself been required to make his own great personal sacrifice for this cause,[60] even if they knew nothing about it. But how could they ask him about it if he didn't speak of it himself? The respect they felt for this extraordinary man, who was once again walking in silence between them, did not permit them to invade his privacy by asking about his personal fate.[61]

But the major himself began: "You make me happy. When we get home, I want to give you something to read.[62] Remind me about it. And now let's talk about something else."[63]

127 Ulrich now had to tell about growing up as the son of a village organist and choirmaster,[64] about his father's death, his mother's move to the city so that he could attend high school, and his life in the Brake home. In the course of their conversation, the three men had hurried far ahead of the others without noticing and now stopped on a little point of land where there was a bench. Looking out at the motionless water of the sunlit pond, each was left to his own thoughts about the conversation.

[60.] Deleted: "and had a right to . . ."

[61.] Deleted: "Then he resumed without being asked: 'You are mature enough to hear what I want to tell you now. My oldest son Harald became the victim of such a petty tyrant two years ago. He was nineteen years old.'" Also deleted: "'I lost my oldest son Harald on this battlefield. He . . .'" These allusions might refer to the suicide of the Bonhoeffer children's nineteen-year-old cousin, Wolf Kalckreuth, on October 9, 1906, during his military service in Cannstatt. A copy of a portrait of Wolf as a young boy, painted by his father, Count Leopold Kalckreuth, hung in one of the rooms of the Bonhoeffers' vacation home in Friedrichsbrunn. Cf. Johannes Kalckreuth, *Wesen und Werk meines Vaters:* "Father . . . had painted a portrait of Wolf in September [1906], and had not seen that his model was a dying man" (317). Cf. Rilke, *Requiem and Other Poems,* 137; the dedication of the second poem in the cycle, written November 4 and 5, 1908, is "For Count Wolf von Kalckreuth."

[62.] Deleted: "They are [my son's] latest diary entries."

[63.] Deleted: "With this, the major turned to Ulrich and".

[64.] Eberhard Bethge's grandfather was a village organist and choirmaster.

Christoph and Renate

SOON ONE COULD HEAR the sound of voices engaged in lively conversation, as Christoph and Renate approached. Earlier, when the group had set off for a walk, Christoph had found himself walking beside the young girl. He had looked back for a moment to see if a third would join them,[1] but the others had already formed into natural groups and the two were left together.[2] Christoph felt a strange constraint he had never experienced before. He thought a friendly glance would suffice to invite Renate to walk with him, but his eye caught hers and he could hardly look away. For the first time, he experienced the peculiar law and power of the eye, its bliss, and its danger.[3] One's whole soul, body, and blood rush into one's eye and there is no strength left for words.

"Come, Renate," he heard himself say, as if someone else were speaking. He lowered his eyes, but they had taken in an image that they wouldn't let go—the dark-blonde curly hair, the white skin of her face, the large deep-brown eyes, the slender figure in a light, raw silk dress. They walked close together on the narrow path and Christoph was aware of Renate's dress touching him from time to time.[4] "You have a beautiful place here," he finally managed to say.

"Yes, very beautiful, but so confined," Renate replied.

"Confined?" Christoph asked, astonished. "How big is your estate?"

"Oh, it's about two thousand acres, but there's no view into the distance, and there are too many people here.[5] I'm just still very

---

[1.] Cf. above, page 116; Bonhoeffer has eliminated Johannes from the trio in which Christoph and Renate had set out: ". . . the whole group started out. Up front the major walked between Franz and Ulrich. Christoph and Renate and Johannes followed . . ."

[2.] Deleted: " 'Come on, Christoph, what are you waiting for?' "

[3.] See above, page 112. Cf. also *CD* 132 on Matt. 5:29 and *CD* 173f. on Matt. 6:22f. [While the NRSV here speaks of a "healthy" eye, the German Bible uses the word *einfältig*, which Bonhoeffer in *Discipleship* interprets as "simplicity" and "singleness," that is, the eye that focuses only on Christ.][CG] Here follows the deleted phrase "the whole soul."

[4.] In Stifter, *Indian Summer*, Heinrich and Natalie take a similar first walk in the country, her arm lightly touching his: "I felt her dress moving beside me" (288). At her sister Ruth-Alice's wedding in 1939, Maria von Wedemeyer wore a dress that Bonhoeffer found "especially beautiful" (see above, page 43, editorial note 18, on Bonhoeffer's letter to his parents on July 3, 1943). Maria was fifteen years old at the time, like Renate von Bremer in the novel (see above, pages 112 and 124).

[5.] Deleted: "It might sound unthinkable [replaces: weird] to you, but . . ."

129   homesick for South Africa.[6] One year isn't long enough to acclimate
oneself."

"But this is your home, isn't it?"[7]

"That's just it, Christoph. That's not as clear for me as it is for you.[8]
You know that my mother is English. I spent the first fifteen years of my
life in South Africa, a British country, and was happy there. At home we
speak German; I have a German name; I love my father above everything[9]—and my oldest brother, bless his soul, is buried in Germany. My
home is where my parents and brothers are—that's all I know. You
mustn't think that I'm not happy to be in Germany. I walk through the
woods with my father almost every day and I'm coming to love our estate
more and more by the day. But sometimes I get the feeling again that I'm

---

[6.] In 1930 and 1939 Bonhoeffer visited descendants of his great-great uncle, Leonhard Tafel, in Philadelphia; Tafel was one of the four brothers in the Württemberg branch
of the family who had become famous. See the reference to them as "the wild, the riotous,
the handsome, and the pious Tafel" (*DB-ER* 11). The Bonhoeffers had few family connections with southern Africa; one second cousin, Hans-Jürgen von Hase, had emigrated in
1933 to German Southwest Africa, now Namibia. Helmuth James von Moltke, who along
with Bonhoeffer went to Norway and Stockholm as an emissary of the *Abwehr* resistance
group under Canaris from April 10–18, 1942 (see documentation in *DBWE* 16), felt more
at home in South Africa than in Germany. Moltke's maternal ancestors from Scotland had
immigrated to South Africa in the early nineteenth century. Eberhard Bethge remembers
that Bonhoeffer had commented after the Scandinavian trip with Moltke "how stimulating
it was to travel together, 'but our opinions differ'" (*DB-ER* 755) [trans. altered]—obviously
referring to the plans for active resistance. Bonhoeffer was convinced it was necessary to
assassinate Hitler. Moltke "believed that that would not eliminate the basic evil of the situation" (von Moltke, *Bericht aus Deutschland im Jahre 1943*, 18).

[7.] [The German *Heimat* denotes homeland or native country, as well as where one
feels at home, and is a key concept both in the following dialogue and in the larger cultural
context of the twentieth-century German reception of the romantic notion of homeland.][NL] Deleted: "'Halfway, yes,' said Renate. 'Of course you know my mother's
English. My home is where my parents are.'"

[8.] The problem of belonging to two countries and two cultures was one Bonhoeffer
had encountered daily during his pastorate in London from 1933–35. He was more immediately affected by the fate of his twin sister Sabine Leibholz and her family, who immigrated to England in 1938 and lived there until 1947. Cf. Bonhoeffer's letter of April 22,
1944: "I don't think I've ever changed very much, except perhaps at the time of my first
impressions abroad . . ." (*LPP* 275). [Other interpreters would relate this comment to experiences earlier than the London period, perhaps Rome and North Africa (1924) and
Barcelona (1929–30), and definitely New York, particularly Harlem (1930–31).][CG]

[9.] Deleted: "this estate has belonged to my father's family for centuries."

[10.] Maria von Wedemeyer wrote on October 8, 1943, remembering her father, who
had died in the Battle of Stalingrad in 1942: "From the age of eight I rode through the
fields with him every day when I was home" (*LL* 77).

choking. Then I would like to ride through the endless plantations[10] and see the scattered huts of the Africans,[11] but almost no other people, hardly any other people at all. I think it's the people here that make me feel so confined. There are too many and they are so different."

130

"Renate, you say that when your village hardly has a couple of hundred inhabitants!" cried Christoph. "Can't you stand people at all? Do you think it's terrible that you ran into us today?"[12]

"To be honest with you, at first I was terribly startled when we met you, and I thought you would ruin our Sunday. But I soon noticed that you are different from most people. You wouldn't believe how much I hated the forester[13]—so much that I was ashamed of myself. So I was happy to see you defeat him. No, it's not true that I can't stand people at all, but I always just like individuals. And then—but you mustn't be angry if I say this,[14] and I guess you can't really understand it—" Renate hesitated—"and I really don't want to hurt your feelings. . . ."

"Please, Renate, say it!"

"All right, if you wish. Do you know what an African nanny is? We had one like almost all the whites do. She lived in our house from the day I was born, took care of me, fed me, sang me my first little songs, and told

[11.] In the earlier part of this century, and when Bonhoeffer was writing, "African" was the preferred usage, as seen in the naming of the liberation movement as the "African National Congress." At the end of the century the preferred usage is "black." [CG]

[12.] Deleted: "I think it's glorious."

[13.] Replaces: "assistant".

[14.] There is an earlier draft that begins here, with the first eight words deleted (up to "Africans"), followed by these ten lines which are not crossed out: "I just like a quiet, friendly, smiling, diligent, and faithful African on our plantations better than our conceited, demanding, and surly inspector [replaces: than these . . . people here who are often so surly], or [deleted: the village schoolmaster] the tutor or the village magistrate or the gendarme [deleted: like I see them here so often]." "But these Africans are slaves, so to speak, Renate," Christoph interjected, somewhat disapprovingly [replaces: in a somewhat didactic tone]." "Slaves, oh, come on! At least everything there is done much more humanely and personally than here, where simply everybody wants to be some sort of official in order to feel really important. [Cf. Grimm, *Volk ohne Raum:* 'Back home people with official positions and honors always go to the head of the line and act overbearingly' (2:603). This comment on Germany, written before 1926, also applied to the Nazi state.] Christoph, it's just that sometimes I long for an evening on the farm when the Africans sit in front of their huts and sing—they sing beautifully and have beautiful songs—and they are friendly and say hello when you ride past them. No, they are not slaves; they have their pride too [replaces: their honor]. But it is based on something different for them."

me stories from the bush. She was always near me, always kind and friendly. She completely belonged to the household, she loved us all and served us faithfully, quietly, and with endless devotion. When she learned that we would be moving to Germany it almost broke her heart. In tears she begged my parents to take her with us. My mother was willing, but my father rejected the idea. We didn't understand why, then, but he was right. Nanny would simply have been destroyed by living here. But I can't forget her, and when I think of her now sitting in front of the hut on quiet evenings with the other Africans and singing—and they sing

131 so beautifully, so warmly[15]—and how friendly they all were as they smiled and said hello when we rode through the plantations in the evening, yes, then I'm seized by a terrible longing and I feel as if I left my soul there and can't find it here again."

They were both quiet. Christoph struggled unsuccessfully for something to say. Renate continued: "The truth is, Christoph, that sometimes I don't know whether people here really have souls. When I think of our arrogant,[16] vain, surly inspector, or the town magistrate, or even this forester, what I sense from them is nothing but formality and compulsion and officiousness—I just about freeze to death when I'm around them. Yes, everything here is so grim and cold and hard and difficult that the soul has to find some corner to crawl into and hide, where it can hardly breathe or stay alive."

Renate spoke with such simplicity [Einfachheit][17] and genuine feeling that everything Christoph could have said in reply would have seemed empty and flat to him. It had rarely or never happened that he had felt helpless in conversation. He loved discussion[18] and was a feared opponent among his own age group. But he felt flustered around this young girl. She was saying impossible things, and yet what could he offer in response?

"But your Africans are slaves, so to speak," he said, and immediately realized he had said something stupid.

Renate laughed out loud. "Slaves? Nonsense! At least they are people

---

[15.] Cf. also Bonhoeffer's experience learning spirituals during his studies at Union Theological Seminary in New York in 1930–31 (*DB-ER* 150).

[16.] Replaces: "overbearing".

[17.] Cf. above, page 123, editorial note 3, and below, page 136, editorial note 19, regarding the related word for simplicity, *Einfalt*. [NL]

[18.] Originally changed to "battles of words," then changed back.

with souls. Here all I see are dressed-up cardboard cutouts who think they're terribly important. I'd like to know where the slaves are, there or here."

Christoph shuddered.

"Forgive me, Christoph, I have just spoken with some bitterness.[19] I didn't mean to. And I know I mustn't become bitter under any circumstances, because it's Father's home and your home and perhaps my home someday, too. But believe me, it's hard to understand and love this country and these people. It takes a long time. Above all, you have to meet people who reflect the essence and the destiny of this country if you want to understand it."

Precisely because these last words were spoken with such innocence, they moved Christoph greatly. He felt as if someone were looking for help from him, and Christoph was among those people who hunger for tasks.[20] Wherever he saw a schoolmate[21] who needed his protection, his help, or even his advice and leadership, wherever he could take on responsibility for another person, he was in his element. No one dared get in his way when he stood up for someone else. Then he fought like a lion and was a terrible opponent. Christoph had a strong and healthy confidence in his ability to help others and take responsibility for them. Without such tasks his life seemed empty. It was unimportant to him whether his charges were likable. His motivation to act was less out of love for the individual than out of the need for responsibility at the core of his being. As a result, he had the reputation among some of his schoolmates of being proud and domineering. Others, however, trusted him completely, so that more than one came to him to confide his life story and ask for Christoph's help. At first Christoph was frightened by this. He had always instinctively resisted thinking about the inner life of his comrades.[22] So at first he had rejected such confessions of a personal nature when they were presented to him; he would say, "You must cope with your personal difficulties alone; I don't want to hear about them." But the other had replied with a sad smile, "That's pretty easy for

132

133

[19.] Deleted: "and hurt your feelings."

[20.] Replaces: "and wherever Christoph was confronted with a task, he . . ."; "Christoph was among those people who sought out . . ."; "he was confronted with a task"; and "and wherever he saw a task, he seized . . ."

[21.] Replaces: "[saw] somebody in class or anywhere".

[22.] Deleted: ". . . said to Ulrich" then taken up in the dialogue below.

you to say, it seems." Precisely this attitude of restraint on Christoph's part had then even strengthened the other's confidence in him. Some time later, perhaps a year ago now, Christoph had gone to Ulrich for advice.

"There must be some good reason why, by our very nature, the inner life of other people is inaccessible to us, and why no one can look into ours," he had said to Ulrich.[23] "So we are obviously meant to keep it to ourselves and not share it with anyone."[24]

After a long, thoughtful silence, Ulrich had replied, "Except with God—or with a person God sends to us who can be trusted to keep a secret like God."[25]

Christoph had not responded; he was deep in thought. Neither had said anything else at the time, but these words from Ulrich had given the friends' relationship a new foundation. Now Christoph really knew for the first time what he had in Ulrich. Since he knew that, he had greater patience to bear the confidence that other comrades had in him, even though it sometimes caused him to suffer, as if carrying a heavy weight. He still preferred to be confronted with a very specific task.[26]

And now these last words from Renate seemed to confront him with such a task. Renate needed to learn to understand and love Germany, and to do so she needed his help. He couldn't think about it without his heart starting to pound. This young girl, who was walking along next to him so freely and confidently, who had seen so much more of the world than he had, needed him. He had the privilege of doing something for her. She had asked for his help, without intending to do so. And it was an infinitely large and important task. Christoph was to become the interpreter of Germany for the young girl who was looking for a home here.

Germany? What did Christoph himself know about Germany? He and Ulrich had taken immeasurable pleasure in several long trips

---

[23.] Cf. Gotthelf, "Elsi, die seltsame Magd": "What stirs inside us God has not hidden in vain from the eyes of others" (*Erzählungen,* 124). Cf. above, pages 65f.

[24.] Cf. Lütgert, *Ethik der Liebe:* "One cannot and must not completely reveal one's inmost self to other people, and must not expect this of others either. . . . Only toward God is complete openness possible and necessary" (91f.).

[25.] Personal confession was practiced at the Finkenwalde Seminary, which Bonhoeffer directed from 1935 to 1937. Bonhoeffer in *The Cost of Discipleship* quotes Luther's *Large Catechism*: "Thus when I admonish people to confession I am simply urging them to be Christians" (*CD* 289 [trans. altered]).

[26.] Deleted: "which he knew how to handle."

[27.] Replaces: "hiking trips". In the early twentieth century this term, *Fahrt,* was preferred by the Youth Movement [Jugendbewegung].

[Fahrten][27] together, hiking through the Black Forest, East Prussia, and above all the Weser region.[28] In the forests of the Mark[29] they had swum in countless ponds, sat on their shores watching the sun setting between the trunks of the pines, and pitched their tents for the night. They had been more deeply moved by the old brick cathedrals and gates of small, north German walled cities than the high gothic style of southern churches and monasteries. In the middle of the night they had set out on the North Sea with fishermen. Then, coming in, they had watched the sun rise above the sea and the beach and had seen the men hard at work.[30]

Yes, all that was Germany—but how could it be put into words? As they viewed these sights, Christoph and Ulrich were able to understand each other with brief, suggestive cues. Otherwise their shared impressions were things which neither knew how to express. You had to see with your own eyes and experience with all your senses and take it all in. Renate would have to travel,[31] would have to see Germany in order to love it. But what would these trips have been for Christoph without Ulrich? Ulrich with his bright enthusiasm and deep sensitivity was simply part of this landscape and these cities. It was only through the mediation of the living soul of the other that the country had revealed itself to the two friends. So wasn't Germany really the people, not the things they saw? Weren't Ulrich, and Christoph's family home, the Germany he was thinking about, the Germany he knew? The musical evenings, the garden parties, his grandmother, and the images of his grandfather went through his mind.

135

[28.] Deleted: "come to know and love", which was replaced in this sentence by "taken immeasureable pleasure." In Grimm's book *Volk ohne Raum*, the region of the Weser Mountains stands for the German homeland.

[29.] The German adjective *märkisch* describes the geographical region surrounding Berlin, the *Mark* Brandenburg. [NL]

[30.] In the 1920s Bonhoeffer took hiking trips with his siblings, his cousin Hans Christoph von Hase, and university friends. For example, in 1923–24 they went to the Black Forest, setting out from his grandmother Julie Bonhoeffer's house in Tübingen; they also went to the Weser Mountains region and to Mecklenburg. Among the papers in Bonhoeffer's literary estate are numerous postcards, among other things, brought home as souvenirs from such trips; they include pictures of the city gates and churches of Mecklenburg. There are references to these trips in letters to his parents in *DBW* 9. On October 10, 1924, for example, there is a description of a nocturnal boating expedition with fishermen to the island of Sylt (*DBW* 9:148f.). Bonhoeffer only came to know East Prussia in June and July 1940 on the occasion of his visitations to parishes there.

[31.] Replaces: "join them on such a trip".

[32.] Deleted: "right away [you had to think of]".

But then there was also[32] this forester's assistant, there were these degenerate seniors at school, and there were the many surly, self-important figures Renate had talked about. They, too, were Germany; they were Germany on its way down, the endangered, decadent Germany, the Germany that needed a good, strong hand to lead it back to health.[33]

Renate had yet to experience the good, healthy Germany. Certainly, she had her father, but he could only be the one great exception for her. Now she needed to experience[34] the Germany which produced this father, which endowed him with everything, and to which he would always belong. Renate would have to enter into the Brake family home and the circle of his brothers and sisters. She would have to hike with them, and Ulrich would have to be there, but so would Klara, too. Would Renate and Klara get along? They seemed completely different. Klara knew nothing but her family's house and her brothers and sisters and didn't want to know anything else. Her native intelligence kept her from taking on problems she knew from the outset[35] could not be solved intellectually, and which, on the other hand, she found already solved by life itself. She went her way with complete calm and confidence, and seized the tasks assigned to her. She would hardly comprehend Renate's questions and difficulties and would answer them by the way she lived.
136 But maybe that was exactly what Renate needed. Yes, Klara had to help.[36]

This was how Christoph's mind worked, and he could not think without making plans. But could anything be planned in this case, really? Wouldn't anything intentional or planned have just the opposite effect with a girl like Renate? Christoph sensed all his thoughts and plans melting even as they took shape. He had never experienced that before. Suddenly he said, amazing himself at his own words, "Renate, I think that will happen all by itself." These words were like a great liberation for both.[37]

The first thing that happened all by itself was that the two began to

---

[33.] See above, page 108, editorial note 46, the letter to Lehmann. [CG]

[34.] Deleted: "behind the glowing or the cracked facades".

[35.] Replaces: "instinctively".

[36.] Deleted: "But he, Christoph, would mediate all this; only first, he would need to come to terms for himself about what Germany really was."

[37.] Cf. Stifter, *Indian Summer:* ". . . Here as everywhere it will be good: resignation, trust, patience" (255).

talk, carefree and open to each other. They did not ask questions. Whatever they wanted to tell about their lives, their views, the people they were close to, each should say without being asked.[38] In this way began one of those rare and delightful conversations in which each word is received as a gift freely given from one to the other. As it is with gifts, such a conversation begins with inconspicuous feelers signaling, as it were, questions one is too shy to ask, namely whether the other is willing to be given a gift. For unwelcome gifts denigrate the giver as well as the receiver, while the acceptance of a gift is the first and greatest gift a giver can receive in return.[39] Precisely because the most important thing is the inner freedom of both the giver and the receiver, no one who knows this gives or takes everything at once. It is a slow process of committing oneself freely. 137

It is no different with conversations like those which Christoph[40] and Renate were now beginning to have. There are conversations in which the partners challenge each other. Others resemble intrusive forays. Still others are noncommittal chats which barely veil the distance, unfamiliarity, and indifference between people. But where a conversation is a mutual giving and receiving of gifts, there is neither violence nor indifference. What remains unspoken signifies a gesture pointing toward as yet undiscovered treasures, toward riches still hidden in the other which will be disclosed when the time is right. Though Christoph[41] and Renate were very different in their ways of life, their views, and their wishes, nevertheless there was a natural harmony in the basic attitude each had toward the other.

After a half hour's walk, when they caught up with Renate's father, Franz, and Ulrich, they had learned quite a bit from one another. Above all, each knew that they had received a gift from the other. They were

---

[38.] Replaces: "Renate did not direct a single question at Christoph. Whatever he [wanted to] tell about himself and his family . . ." Deleted: "What he didn't say, she did not want to ask him about. How could she pry into his private life?" Another ten lines of deleted attempts to formulate this thought follow, including, "Words that stem from one's personal life are given freely as gifts and intended to be received as such. The slightest compulsion from within devalues them. [The] freely flowing word of one is the magic wand that calls forth the pure spring of the word in the other."

[39.] Cf. Lütgert, *Ethik der Liebe* (a passage marked by Bonhoeffer): "The person who feels devalued in receiving a gift is arrogant in giving; the person who is humble in giving can also receive with composure and dignity" (151).

[40.] The manuscript says "Ulrich" here.

[41.] Here, too, the manuscript says "Ulrich."

radiant with youthful happiness as they approached the group which was still preoccupied with the discussion of serious ideas. Renate's father reached out to draw his daughter close, looked at her kindly, stroked the hair out of her forehead and said, "My good child—well, now, isn't it beautiful here after all?"

"Very beautiful, Father dear," Renate replied. Christoph stood next to her.

"Ready, set, go!" came the command from Martin, and the two boys came shooting down the last stretch of the trail toward the finish. "One more dip in the pond until the others get here?" Martin asked. And by the time he had finished asking, the two had already thrown their clothes on the ground and were cooling their overheated bodies in the tepid pond.

FRAU VON BREMER AND KLARA had taken their time. The others saw the
two tall female figures approaching slowly along the shore some distance away and talking at leisure.[1] The older of the two still appeared
youthful and slim with her ample blonde hair,[2] as did the younger
woman in the light linen dress she had embroidered herself,[3] her long,
dark, heavy braids draping down over it.[4]

Despite the difference in their external appearance, both women's
free, calm, and confident stride expressed an inner kinship, a certain
shared feeling for life.[5] Only women from old families walk like this[6]—
women who, like their mothers before them, have always known the
assuring protection of their fathers, husbands, and brothers, and felt
safe in the domain[7] of their family. But such women walk this way even
when misfortune strikes them and leaves them bereft. Like an invisible
power that no one dares challenge, the protection that once surrounded
them still hovers over their every step, even in their hour of utmost

---

[1.] Replaces: "[The others saw] the last group [approaching] the gathering place [Sam-
melplatz]." Bonhoeffer may have chosen to avoid the latter expression because of its association in the Third Reich with the "gathering" of people at a certain place. Cf. the report
by Bonhoeffer and Christoph Perels of October 17 or 18, 1941 (*DBW* 16:212ff. [*GS*
2:640ff.]), about the beginning of mass deportations from Berlin. Jewish families were
"gathered in the previously vacated Levetzowstrasse Synagogue" and then transported off
to concentration and annihilation camps. [Apart from this particular usage, *Sammelplatz*
was a common word for gathering places that antedated the Nazi regime; there were
dozens of them throughout Berlin.][NL]

[2.] Replaces: "with her large, expressive, blue eyes". The phrase "still appeared youthful" replaces "about forty years old."

[3.] Replaces: "light blue linen dress". The Bonhoeffer children's great aunt, Countess
Helene Yorck von Wartenburg, embroidered clothing that, according to family members,
is "still treasured by the third and fourth generations."

[4.] Sabine Leibholz-Bonhoeffer describes her sister Ursula as having "long, brown
plaits. She did not play our rough games with us, but preferred to look after her dolls or do
something quiet and useful, and at fourteen she was already very skilled in household matters" (*The Bonhoeffers*, 24).

[5.] The German *Lebensgefühl*, feeling for life, replaces the expression *Lebensgrundlage*,
basic orientation to life. [Cf. above, pages 68f. on the theme "ground under one's feet,"
and below, page 206, editorial note 50, on the statement in the *Ethics* about trust as "the
foundation of historical life."][NL]

[6.] In the manuscript there is a thirteen-line draft of the passage beginning "Frau von
Bremer and Klara" up to "women from old families walk like this" which was deleted and
replaced by the preceding formulation.

[7.] Deleted: "strong domain [Reich]".

abandonment. Women of such demeanor and carriage are akin to one another, whatever their family origins.[8]

Klara was now telling about her family life, her grandmother, Little Brother, and her own household tasks. These she had taken on since she had left school in the spring.[9] Her day began at five-thirty in the morning on the dot. First she tended to her own room. By seven her parents' breakfast had to be ready. In the summertime there was a bouquet of freshly picked flowers on the table every morning. Depending on the season there was also a bowl of strawberries, currants, or raspberries, a small dish of radishes, and another with chopped herbs the way her father loved them. She did not mention to Aunt Sophie that she read a chapter of the Bible[10] every morning before she began her housework. At seven-thirty she ate breakfast with her brothers and sisters, taking her mother's place at the head of the table, since her mother liked to keep her father company for part of the way to the clinic. The children's breakfast consisted of cocoa and dry, hard rolls—on Sundays there was butter.[11]

Soon after breakfast the boys left the house, and Klara brought breakfast, served on old-fashioned silver service, to her grandmother in her little sitting room. When Klara knocked, her grandmother would put down her glasses and place a bookmark in the old Bible she had been reading. Klara would enter, kiss her grandmother's hand, and lean down

---

[8.] Deleted: "Young Klara had told her new aunt many stories of her family life." There follows a deleted ten-line earlier draft that is very similar to the next paragraph beginning "Klara . . ."

[9.] Replaces: "had taken on beginning last Easter. Every word came out with such warmth and simplicity that Frau von Bremer became very fond of Klara. [Deleted: 'and began to wish'.] She had not managed to meet many young German girls until now. Among the three kinds she had met, she had not liked any of them. She didn't like those wealthy merchants' daughters she had met abroad and in Germany; they had no inner commitment and only sought pleasure. Nor did she like the emancipated [deleted: 'open-minded'] women students, nor the unemancipated, half-educated, so-called young ladies from the 'right' kind of families. She did not want to think of Renate making friends with any of these. But here, for the first time, she was getting to know . . ." Above the word "unemancipated" in the German manuscript is the word "fearful," suggesting Bonhoeffer considered replacing the original word but did not do so.

[10.] Deleted: "as she had learned from her grandmother".

[11.] On the advice of Professor Czerny, a colleague of Karl Bonhoeffer and director of the University Pediatric Clinic in Breslau and later Berlin, this was indeed what the Bonhoeffer children had for breakfast, until Sabine as a preschooler began to show symptoms of malnourishment. Under the watchful eyes of their parents the Bonhoeffer children were allowed to spread either butter or honey on their rolls, but never both.

to receive a kiss on the forehead. She would put the Bible in its place beside the desk, then offer her grandmother her arm and lead her out where she ate breakfast all year round, the little enclosed porch with a view of the garden. Then each day Klara would spend that half hour that she could no longer imagine doing without.[12] This time sitting with her grandmother was one of the few times that Klara's hands were not busy with some sort of mending or sewing. She saw to it that her grandmother had everything she needed and had the privilege of staying for a nice, quiet chat.[13] Most of the time they talked about everyday things and events, about the little changes that every day brings even to the most orderly household.[14] They would also talk about the other children and their friends, but rarely or never about Klara's parents or about her elders in general. Without her grandmother ever giving her general advice or stating rules of conduct—or rather, precisely because she refrained from doing so—Klara learned through these simple conversations to love her everyday tasks.[15] She learned that small things must be valued neither too highly nor too little.[16] Her relationship to the organization of the household, as well as its inhabitants, took on a new inner order and an even rhythm in which she took pleasure.[17] She heard her grandmother speak openly about others without doing injustice to any natural bonds among them, and without arrogance or harshness. More than she was conscious of it, Klara sensed[18] the blessing that a kind heart like her grandmother's brings to a home.

While Klara was by her simple and straightforward nature inclined to reject—or even quick to condemn—everything different or strange, she would become thoughtful whenever her grandmother would tell stories of the differences in human circumstances, customs, and ways of life

140

[12.] Replaces: "without which her whole day would have lost its warmth and richness" ["richness" replaces "glow"].

[13.] Deleted: "interrupted only by the thoughtful little things she did to take care of her grandmother." Replaces: "necessary attention she gave her grandmother so she would have everything she needed."

[14.] Replaces: "which time [brings] here and there."

[15.] Replaces: "Klara learned . . . to see her everyday life in a new light."

[16.] Replaces: "that the trivial really is trivial, but at the same time infinitely important."

[17.] Replaces: "She took pleasure in the richness of the world that revealed itself in trivial things."

[18.] Deleted: "that light and shadow always go together and that a kind and humble heart is the best thing one can offer to people."

that she had seen during her long life.[19] There was a strange contrast
141 between her grandmother's mild, considerate, and often surprisingly
open-minded way of judging behavior and, on the other hand, her blunt
and unrelenting judgment whenever conversation turned to Christianity
and the church, which did not happen very often. "There's no room for
joking here," she said, "and only those who are tough and stick with the
truth can afford to be gentle in life and smile at people's stupidities[20]
now and then." Klara had not quite understood this yet, but she did
sense that this apparent contradiction in her grandmother had resolved
itself over time.

"I can't imagine that some day Grandmother won't exist any longer,"
said Klara to Frau Bremer, and then continued telling about her daily
routine. She told about practicing the piano several hours a day, having
free time in the afternoon; and she told about her last task of the day,
namely, playing from *The Well-Tempered Clavier* for her father when he
came home late. "We're all especially fond of Bach," she added. "There
isn't a Good Friday when we don't all listen to the *St. Matthew Passion*
together, and hardly a year passes without our hearing the Mass in B
Minor.[21] For the past few months we've been studying together the *The
Art of the Fugue* under Ulrich's direction.[22] I just can't understand why
people find this music so hard to understand; for me it's the clearest and

---

[19.] Replaces: "Her natural simplicity [Einfalt] was ennobled by goodness and humility
through her conversations with her grandmother." In Bonhoeffer's theological discourse
the word simplicity, *Einfalt*, is clearly positive, as seen in his use of the word in *The Cost of
Discipleship* and *Ethics*. See also Bonhoeffer's letter of February 12, 1944 (*LPP* 212). [The
words *Einfalt* and *einfaltig* often have a negative connotation in modern German usage,
like the English "simpleton." In the *LPP* letter Bonhoeffer defines "simplicity," *Einfachheit*,
as an ethical concept, something one can become through upbringing and education, and
"simpleness," *Einfalt*, as an innate and positive gift.][NL]

[20.] Compare the passage on stupidity, *Dummheit*, in "After Ten Years" (*LPP* 8f.).
Whereas stupidity, *Dummheit*, is an evil to be dreaded and resisted, stupidities, *Dummheiten*
(plural) is a gentle word judging childish mistakes in adult behavior. [NL]

[21.] Cf. Bonhoeffer's letter of November 17, 1943: "While I'm writing this letter on the
Day of Prayer and Repentance, the Schleichers, so Ursel told me, are all listening to the
Mass in B Minor. For years now it's been part of my observance of this particular day, just
like the *St. Matthew Passion* on Good Friday" (*LPP* 126 [trans. altered]).

[22.] In the 1930s and 1940s, Johann Sebastian Bach's *The Art of the Fugue* was played
regularly on New Year's Day in Berlin by the Hermann Diener Ensemble, and the Bonhoeffer family was regularly in attendance. Dietrich Bonhoeffer and Eberhard Bethge had
bought an arrangement of this piece for two pianos in order to study it together. On
February 23, 1944, Bonhoeffer called *The Art of the Fugue* one of those "fragments that can
only be fragments" (*LPP* 219).

most transparent music there is. But Mother doesn't think quite the same way. She prefers Brahms and Richard Strauss and sings their songs very beautifully."[23]

"Do you want to be a musician someday, Klara?" Frau von Bremer 142 asked.

"No, I've never thought of it. I have far too little talent for that; and anyway, I don't want to do something halfway. I'm going to stay home, and someday I'd like to marry and have a family."

The warmth and simplicity[24] with which Klara said this made it clear that she was not speaking of her personal happiness, but her vocation.[25] Frau von Bremer developed a deep fondness for this young girl, who was following her own path so calmly and confidently,[26] untorn by any inner dissatisfaction, and who was much too proud to pursue short-lived pleasures. This was not one of those daughters of wealthy people, so many of whom Frau von Bremer had met, who squandered their days attending cocktail parties and dancing teas and idolizing movie stars. She wasn't one of those emancipated half-men,[27] either. But neither

---

[23.] This description of respective preferences in musical performance holds true for the Bonhoeffer family. "On Saturday evenings he [the young Bonhoeffer] skillfully accompanied his mother and his sister Ursula, who had a good voice, in songs by Schubert, Schumann, Brahms, and Hugo Wolf" (*DB-ER* 25).

[24.] Cf. above, page 134, editorial note 9, and page 136, editorial note 19.

[25.] In the brief deleted passage replaced by the above, the phrase "as someone [speaks] of a vocation [Beruf]" replaces "like the young owner of a large estate [Gutsbesitzer]." Perhaps Bonhoeffer is thinking of Helmuth James von Moltke who, at the age of twenty-two, after completing his law studies, took over as administrator of the family estate of Kreisau (see Moltke, *Bericht aus Deutschland*, 7). Cf. the wedding sermon of May 1943: "It is the wife's calling [Berufung], and her happiness, to build up for her husband this world within the world and to do her life's work there" (*LPP* 44). In the letter of February 1, 1944, he speaks of the "vocation [Beruf], both as a human being and as a member of the church," of his sister Susanne, the wife of Pastor Walter Dreß (*LPP* 202)[trans. altered]. [Cf. Bonhoeffer's remarks on becoming human and Christian in *LPP* (370).][CG] Cf. Stifter, *Indian Summer,* on the home as the woman's vocation (206f.), and on the future calling of the young girl (431). In his copy of Alfred Müller's *Ethik,* in a section on the dissolution of the household economy during the Industrial Revolution, Bonhoeffer marked the passage which reads, "The home is losing its significance as the center of production. . . . 'Thus women and girls, above all, were driven out of the home.' This change of economic conditions became the driving force behind the 'woman question'" (385; 386, quoting Sombart, *Deutsche Sozialismus,* 15).

[26.] Deleted: "and who [felt satisfied] in her home".

[27.] The Weimar avant-garde ideal of the "new woman" implied dressing in men's clothing, smoking, and riding motorcycles; critics of the "emancipated" women often called them "half-men." [NL]

was she likely[28] to become an old maid, running around showing off her virtue and perfection as a living reproach to everyone else. She was born to be a mother, one who had experienced the happiness of a good family life from early childhood and now carried it within herself as an inalienable possession.

Could Klara become the companion and sister for Renate whom Frau von Bremer had sought for so long and never found? Would Klara be able to help Renate overcome her homesickness for South Africa and feel at home here? It was difficult enough for Renate's mother to see the increasing distance between her daughter and herself since their move to Germany. What Renate sought from her English mother—that she keep alive the memory and longing for the plantations of South Africa—she could not give her, much as she would have liked to, without wronging both her husband and her daughter. But she could not give her a sense of belonging in Germany, particularly since this had to mean something quite different for Renate than for her mother.

For Renate, Germany was her whole future. For her, what mattered above all else was not going through life with an open wound. Renate was young enough to start over again, to forget, or at least to remember without pain. For her mother it was different. For her, Germany was her husband and her children. But her roots were and remained English. She had learned German for her husband's sake as a young woman, and with such extraordinary mastery—since she detested broken and badly spoken speech—that no one noticed anymore that she was a foreigner. For years she had not spoken a word of English with her children. School and their general surroundings saw to it that they grew up bilingual. What they as parents had fought in the children was above all any sign of a casual mixing of languages, which happens so easily among people living bilingually, and which destroys the genuine appreciation of a language's uniqueness.

Harald von Bremer was infinitely grateful to his wife for this sacrifice, and in the evenings when the couple sat down together for some time alone, it would sometimes happen—most often spontaneously and likely an unconscious expression of his gratitude—that Harald would speak English with his wife, and his English was as good as her German. Ever since they had lived in Germany and the children had been old enough,

_____

[28.] Replaces: "born".

the family often spoke English together. At the same time they strictly observed the rule that they never speak English in the presence of others, including the domestic employees; that would have been perceived as inconsiderate.

While the boys easily switched languages without it feeling unusual, Renate came to regard as a danger the times English was spoken in the intimate family setting. Her memories became overpowering, and the return to German would evoke in her a feeling of profound inner resistance, even defiance. Sometimes she would be unapproachable for days afterward; she couldn't deal with that and suffered because of it. Whenever her mother would then try to talk with her, she had to admit she was not equal to this task.[29] Neither kind words, sensible reasons, friendly persuasion, nor serious admonitions did anything to turn the situation around. Mother had to leave daughter to deal alone with her greatest difficulty. Renate's relationship with her mother alternated between passionate love, based on the hope of rediscovering in her mother her lost homeland, and deep disappointment when she saw that her mother would not allow her to sink into the past.

Frau von Bremer was looking for help. To be sure, Renate had heartfelt affection for her father, but for fifteen years what he had been to her was the South African farmer and plantation owner. Now, when she took her morning walks in the forest with him, she could never rid herself of this memory. Her love for her father was exclusive to him, and did not transfer to his fatherland. Her brothers could not understand Renate; they attributed her behavior to moodiness and were often angry about it.

"You can also control your feelings,[30] without making everyone else suffer," the otherwise taciturn Johannes had once said. But that was unfair to Renate, for she herself considered any sort of demonstration of one's inner feelings reprehensible and already practiced the utmost self-control. But for her, homesickness had become a true illness,[31] with

144

[29.] Deleted: "And how could she be equal to it?"

[30.] Replaces: "keep your feelings to yourself".

[31.] Bonhoeffer suffered from intense homesickness, for example in June 1939 in the United States, and then even more so in Tegel prison. On homesickness and coping with longing, see his letter to Henry Smith Leiper on June 15, 1939 (*DBW* 15:187ff. [*GS* 1:298]); also see his prison letters of December 18 and 24, 1943, and April 11, 1944 (*LPP* 163, 176f., and 271 respectively). To his nephew Hans Walter Schleicher, Bonhoeffer wrote on November 7, 1942, "Homesickness . . . is truly a painful illness" (*DBW* 16:369 [*GS* 2:424f.]).

high fevers which could not be hidden from people around her no matter how hard she tried.

145 "Klara," Frau von Bremer was saying now, "wouldn't you like to spend a few weeks with us in the country sometime?"[32] Frau von Bremer kept the real reason for her question to herself. She knew that friendships that are desired and planned by parents are always rejected by emotionally independent children like Klara and Renate, and nothing ever comes of them. And it could hardly be otherwise. For in such situations the children see in the friend[33] which the parents have in mind only the model for the qualities their parents think they lack. So the friend becomes a pedagogical tool in the hands of the parents, and the children must hear countless repetitions like "look, Fritz does that differently," or "Hans would never do that," or "Grete gets up much earlier and is much neater,"[34] etc., etc., etc. Before you know it, the friends they chose for you instead scare you off, even if they don't deserve it at all. Forced friendships are worthless, and Frau von Bremer knew it. Either Klara and Renate would discover each other on their own, or not at all.

Klara was surprised—half terrified, half delighted. She had never been separated from her parents or her brothers and sisters for even a day. The invitation came too suddenly. "Thank you very much, Aunt Sophie," she said.[35] "But I don't know what to say. I think I'm needed at home. Besides, I've always gone on hikes and done everything together with my brothers, and I[36] wouldn't—forgive me for saying it so bluntly— I wouldn't like to be separated from them."

Frau von Bremer was wise enough not to be the least bit offended by this unmistakable refusal.[37] "It's better this way than if she'd gone for it right away," she thought. "Klara knows what she has at home, and she doesn't know us at all. A girl like Klara doesn't run toward uncertainty just because it's novel, an interruption of the routine. She prefers what is certain,[38] lasting, proven. She doesn't share the sort of hunger for

---

[32.] Two sentences here are deleted and inserted almost verbatim later. They begin "Klara was surprised . . ."

[33.] Deleted: "the parents' criticism at the same time".

[34.] Replaces: "helps her mother from morning till night".

[35.] Deleted: "I'm sure it would be very nice."

[36.] A long deletion of twenty-four lines begins here and is replaced by what follows.

[37.] At this point in the deleted passage this sentence was added: "On the contrary, her liking for Klara grew even stronger for this attachment to her family."

[38.] In the deleted passage this read "unchanging."

experiences, changes, the unknown, that makes life so unhappy for   146
many young girls nowadays. Why should she? She has everything she
needs; she has a very complete life."

"We must live more intensely,"[39] a worldly young woman had said to
Frau von Bremer the other day and had been quite unambiguous about
what she meant by that.[40] Klara would probably have just smiled and
shaken her head in surprise. She had no[41] need for all this; she lived
more intensely than these extravagant young women.[42]

"That's all right," Frau von Bremer said to herself, "she's hard to win
over; but when you win her she'll be steadfast. In any case, I could have
known by looking at Klara[43] that she is one of those people who would
much rather invite than be invited. In adults that is often a sign of arrogance, or of a cold, unfriendly attitude, or in any case of being tired of
people"—Frau von Bremer couldn't except herself from this last little
reproach—"but with children it's surely the most reliable sign of a happy
family life."

"Then I'll make another suggestion, Klara," said Frau von Bremer   147
kindly. "You and your brothers might come and stay with us for a few
days sometime, and before that we'll all drive to town and visit your
parents."

Soon it was arranged that Frau von Bremer would call on the Brake
family the very next day when she went to town with her husband to do

---

[39.] Bonhoeffer's twin sister Sabine recalls that her art teacher said to her, "Fräulein
Bonhoeffer, you must live more intensely." When she told the story at home the saying
became notorious and was frequently quoted thereafter. The art school, however, was
found no longer suitable and she stopped attending there.

[40.] In the deleted version, one reads here: "This girl [Klara] would only have smiled
and shaken her head in surprise about the saying 'Live intensely,' which meant, more or
less, 'Always look for new strong impressions, throw yourself into the whirlwind of life,
learn to love people and then throw them away again, don't let yourself be tied down or
fettered by anything, enjoy everything to the hilt and be independent in all things.'" Cf.
Santayana's comment that in Goethe's poem *Faust*, Mephistopheles gives Faust back his
youth "only in appearance. He remained at heart an old reprobate, with a bitter taste in the
mouth, and a diseased intellect, forcing him artificially to live hard and to try to know and
experience everything" (*The Last Puritan*, 400).

[41.] The word "no" is included in the deleted version but inadvertently omitted in the
final draft.

[42.] In the deleted version: ". . . more intensely than most. It was not change that could
bring fulfillment to a woman's life, but constancy, she had thought, or at least sensed." Cf.
the wedding sermon of May 1943: "Not novelty, but permanence; not change, but constancy . . . that is the wife's realm" (*LPP* 44 [trans. altered]).

[43.] Replaces: "I was mistaken not to know right away by looking at Klara".

some errands. And if it was all right with the parents—they could call today on the telephone and inquire right away—she would bring their children along with them. Then they could get better acquainted.[44]

"Do you agree, Johannes?" the mother now asked her grown son, who had been walking beside her without saying a word, listening quietly to the conversation with Klara. Frau von Bremer was accustomed to her son's reserve and actually would have been surprised if he had entered into the conversation without being urged.[45] But this silence had not dampened Klara's enthusiasm either, because she sensed that it revealed not intolerance, indifference, or arrogance, but simply a quiet, introverted nature. Since the sudden death of his older brother, Johannes had in fact fallen more deeply into silence than before. To be sure, his parents still were not worried about it. The other siblings were even more affectionate than before in their love for their brother. The reason was that since that difficult experience, Johannes radiated something so peaceful, so conciliatory, so clear and settled, and it did them all such good in these days and months of grief and inner turmoil.

"Certainly, Mother," Johannes replied. And there was not a hint of passive compliance to be heard in these words, but rather clear acceptance.

The big news of the plan for tomorrow was immediately presented to the rest of the family and received with delight on all sides. Amidst quite animated conversations, the party soon arrived at the meadow on the castle grounds nearby.[46] Surrounded by old trees, the meadow extended as far as the long, low castle structure, whose imposing terrace came into view in the light of the afternoon sun. The servants quickly set a large table in the shade,[47] with mountains of fresh-sliced country bread and plain yeast cake.[48] Bowls of butter and fresh honey and sturdy milk pitchers were brought out; two huge bowls, resplendent with shiny strawberries, were set on the festive, white tablecloths. The mis-

148

[44.] Deleted: "Delighted with this idea, and full of plans for the next day, Frau von Bremer and Klara arrived at the spot on the point of land where the others had already become somewhat impatient."

[45.] Deleted: "His silence was neither indifferent nor absent-minded, and certainly not arrogant."

[46.] Replaces: "the nearby castle in a few minutes." Above the word "castle" in the manuscript is the word "park?"

[47.] Replaces: "in the open", which replaces "on it [the terrace]".

[48.] Replaces: "Sunday cake."

tress of the castle invited everyone to sit down. She poured some cream into the cups in front of her place, and asked each person how many pieces of sugar they would like; then she filled the cups with dark, golden-brown tea, causing the young guests, who were not familiar with this English custom, to exchange surprised looks. In their homes tea was thin, and the children were only allowed to drink it with lots of milk. Here for the first time, they tasted this strong, full-flavored drink, whose taste and charm they had never really experienced at home.[49]

Before anyone returned to their previous conversations, the major spoke. Unfortunately, he noted, they wouldn't have time today[50] to give their dear guests a tour of their home and tell them some of its dramatic history. Most of the guests probably had heard that he and his family had only lived here a year, after spending fifteen continuous years in South Africa. The major explained that the reason he had not yet visited his old friend, the father of the young guests, during this year had to do with his and his family's wish, since the death of his eldest son two years ago, to withdraw completely and live in seclusion. The eyes of Franz and Ulrich met involuntarily as the major said this. They intended to end this seclusion and quiet, the major continued, and now this happy coinci-   149 dence had brought the children of his best childhood friend[51] as surprise visitors to their home.[52] He interpreted that as an especially good omen and would now see to it that the two families meet and have closer contact with one another. Perhaps the friendship of the fathers would be regenerated among the children. Time would tell, and only time would bring it about. But since it was his lifelong friendship with their father that had brought his young guests together here, he thought they would perhaps enjoy hearing, in the brief hour that remained today before they must part, the story of how his friendship with Hans Brake had come about. The children's father, he presumed, had had good reason to keep this particular story to himself until now.

[49.] Deleted: "'This is the only luxury in which we indulge,' said the major. 'Once you're accustomed to it . . .'" This is the point in the manuscript where Bonhoeffer finally decided to call Herr von Bremer "major" rather than "general," or "colonel" as originally. [Cf. above, page 111, editorial note 15, and page 113, editorial note 18.][CG] Hans von Wedemeyer, the father of Bonhoeffer's fiancée, was a major when he lost his life in 1942 on the Russian front.

[50.] Deleted: "to view the castle and the stables".

[51.] Replaces: "only friend".

[52.] The phrase "brought . . . to their home" replaces "sent . . . across their path."

The Major's Story

THE MAJOR'S QUIET, calm manner of speaking made the Brake children all the more eager to hear him tell his story. They knew little about their father's early years anyway, since he never spoke about himself.[1] So they asked the major to give them a special treat by doing so. There was general silence and the major began.

"I was thirteen years old when my parents, who still lived in this castle at the time, sent me to town to Gymnasium. I roomed at the home of an elderly aunt.[2] Until then I had been living at home as an only child and was tutored alone. Among my peers in the village I had enjoyed unquestioned power over the other children, and my parents doubtless considered it dangerous for me not to have any other boys of the same age around me who were my intellectual and physical equals. I had begun to take it for granted that every other schoolmate was to be my subject and obey my commands. I believe I never abused my position in relation to the weaker ones, but it also never occurred to me that I might meet my match.

"My parents' decision to send me away to Gymnasium pleased me very much, and I looked forward to my new comrades and fantasized about the games I would show them, and the war games in which they would be at my command.[3] I was so naive and inexperienced in my self-confidence that it never occurred to me that anyone could challenge, not to mention begrudge me, this position without good reason. So it was with great pride and confidence that I entered the school for the first time one day.

"The commotion on the stairs and inside the school did not faze me in the least, even though I had never seen anything like it. In fact, it pleased me exceptionally well. The principal, once my father had turned me over to him, personally showed me to my new classroom.

"'You're lucky,' he said, observing me thoughtfully from one side, 'you are joining a very special class; there's never been one like it here. I hope you'll enjoy finding your proper place in it.' He opened the door. I saw a

151

[1.] Deleted: "and they had just barely heard of their grandmother." Karl Bonhoeffer's memoirs, printed on the occasion of his hundredth birthday, are characterized by extreme economy of words (see Zutt et al., *Karl Bonhoeffer*).

[2.] Replaces: "of friends."

[3.] Replaces: "I considered it a foregone conclusion that there, too, I would soon lead the pack among my classmates, and looked forward to doing so."

group of twenty-five students crowding around a boy who was standing in the middle of the group and talking animatedly to them. All heads turned toward the door and everyone stood still as the principal entered the room with me.

"'Well, Hans, what's going on today?' the principal asked the boy in the middle of the circle. The others stepped aside and made way for the one being addressed. Only now could I see him clearly, and I will never forget that first impression. A slender, but athletic-looking boy with a striking head, whose thick, dark brown hair had no desire to submit to the will of a part,[4] intelligent brown eyes, and a rather prominent nose, stood there quite upright, facing us with self-confident demeanor, simply dressed in a light shirt and belted trousers.

"'We had to settle a bit of class business, Herr Direktor,' he said politely.

"'Something stupid happen again?' the principal asked.

"'Yes, but it's all straightened out again,' Hans answered firmly.

"'Fine, Herr Bürgermeister,' said the principal in a somewhat childish tone of admiration.

"Hans frowned.

"'Why do you have to go and sulk over that, Hans?'

"'Because I don't like being called by my father's title, sir; he's the mayor, not me.'

"'Well, Hans, I've brought you your new classmate.'

"At these words from the principal, all eyes turned toward me. I only looked at Hans.

"'His name is Harald von Bremer. You'll look out for him the first few days and orient him to life in your class. And now, Harald, good luck!' And the principal was gone.

"Hans[5] looked at me calmly, like someone accustomed to such assignments. He came up to me, shook my hand, and said, 'For the time being, Harald, your seat will be here on the front[6] bench; that's how it's always done here, until we've become acquainted with the new person.'

152

"'Where do you sit?' I asked innocently, and noticed many eyes looking at me in amazement for this question.

"'I sit way in the back,' Hans answered.

[4.] Replaces: "was somewhat tousled and messy".
[5.] The manuscript says "Harald" here.
[6.] Replaces: "back".

" 'Then I want to sit next to you,' I said. Loud giggling broke out.

" 'Quiet!' Hans ordered, and the giggling stopped. Then he turned to me, our eyes met, and we resisted one another.

" 'That's not possible, Harald,' he said, 'perhaps later on.'

"He seemed somehow astonished.

" 'And why isn't it possible, if I would like to?'[7] I said, more uncomprehending than defiant.

" 'Because Hans is the boss here, not you,' cried a child's shrill voice belonging to a short, little boy who looked eager to please and hoped to earn an approving glance from Hans.

" 'Shut your stupid mouth, Meyer!' Hans exploded, and the little boy shrank back. Then he said to me quietly, 'No, not because I give the orders here, but because that's how the class wants it. That's why it has to be this way.[8] You must understand that, Harald.'

"Our eyes met again, each probing deeply for a moment into the other. For the first time, we were silently sizing up our respective strength.

" 'So here's your seat,' Hans said and took me to a bench that I shared with a cheerful-looking older boy.

"As I sat down next to him he said to me—his voice already breaking— 'Don't be mad, Hans is a great fellow;[9] if only these damned copycats and social climbers would leave him alone. They'll spoil him yet.'

"The school bell rang, the teacher came in, and class began."

Frau von Bremer interrupted. "If you go on telling your story in such detail, Harald, the children won't be able to get around to anything else."

"It's all right, Sophie," replied the major. "It's their father's story. No one but I can tell it to them, and so I just want to do it right.[10] Eat and drink, children, and listen.[11] Your father was really a great fellow.

"It became obvious even on the first day of school," the major continued, "that Hans was solidly grounded in every subject. He was unquestionably the best in the class. His Latin conversation with the professor

---

[7.] Replaces: "want to."

[8.] Deleted: " 'Here there is only one will, that of the class. . . .' . . . 'Or rather, yours,' I would have liked to shout."

[9.] Replaces: "the greatest fellow in the whole school, but there is no contesting his will."

[10.] Replaces: "they'll never hear it again. I'm just in the middle of telling them."

[11.] Deleted: "and remember this story."

was downright delightful, and Homer, whom we had just begun to read, seemed to give him no more difficulties in the original than in Voss's translation.[12] I kept very quiet that whole day, and nobody asked me to speak, so I had time to observe in peace and quiet. I noticed that the other pupils performed especially poorly whenever independence was required in thought and judgment. Hans and his whole attitude attracted my attention all the more. He seemed to find his superiority so natural in relation to his classmates that he showed not the least trace of ambition or vanity. He was who he was, and as such he was the undisputed and absolute authority; but at the same time he was the idolized favorite of his classmates. No sooner had he appeared in the school yard at recess than he would be surrounded by a swarm of both younger and older boys. Then he would organize games or talk with others, whichever he preferred at the moment, and even students from the older grades would smile good-naturedly at him when they crossed paths.[13] They would stop and stand near him to hear his conversations, and even take part in the games he arranged. In short, they tried in every way to demonstrate to him their special preference[14] for him. Even in my later life I've never experienced anything like this. Hans was simply the school idol. And I have to say it again, the most amazing thing about it was that Hans took it all without even a trifling trace of conceit or self-importance,[15] but rather as the most natural thing in the world. He would laugh, romp, get excited just like any other boy,[16] but when he gave orders, all obeyed automatically, and no one would dare say anything mean in front of him.

154

"During the first recess I walked around the school yard by myself;[17] everything was very different from the way I had imagined it. This Hans had upset my calculation. Leaning against a tree, I tried to observe him. Suddenly someone tapped me on the shoulder; it was the boy with whom I shared my bench.

[12.] See the final sentence in Bonhoeffer's sketch on "vocation," probably written in 1932: "He gets up and translates his difficult Greek text, without a mistake, as always" (*DBW* 11:372 [*GS* 6:232]). Johann Heinrich Voss, who is mentioned here, produced the most successful German translations of Homer.

[13.] Replaces: "were not above wooing his favor."

[14.] Written in above the word "preference," *Vorliebe,* is the word "affection," *Zuneigung,* indicating a substitution was considered at this point by Bonhoeffer.

[15.] Replaces: "vanity".

[16.] Deleted: "and yet he exercised a mysterious influence on everyone he met."

[17.] Deleted: "No one seemed to notice me."

" 'I'm supposed to look after you, Harald,' he said.

" 'Who told you that?' I asked.

" 'Hans. You know, little Meyer started right in saying stupid things again, like you were a big snob because you're aristocratic, and so on, or else you'd be over with Hans too, like the others. But Hans really told him off and said you could be wherever you wanted, that wasn't any of Meyer's business, and that he could understand very well that you might want to be alone. And then he said, "Paul, you look after Harald a little." By the way, I would have come over anyway. I don't go along with everything the others do.'

"Utterly surprised, I looked into the kind, calm face of my older classmate. I was surprised as much by his assignment as by the last words he had said. I felt I could trust him.

" 'And why don't you go along with the rest?' I asked, hoping to hear something important.

" 'I'm not really sure,' Paul replied in his slow way. 'At any rate, it's a long story. We'd better save that for later. But I'll tell you one thing, it's not because of Hans. He's a great fellow.'

"My head was spinning. What's not because of Hans? And who is the problem? This was the second time he'd called Hans a great fellow. So everybody obviously agreed on that. I hadn't yet organized my confused thoughts into a question, when Paul continued.

" 'It probably won't be very easy for you here; at any rate that's how I see it. With me it's different. I'm average, so I'm not obvious. But they'll really be watching you. You'll have to find a way to deal with it. At any rate, you can count on me.'

"My head felt dizzy. I hardly understood what Paul had meant at all and looked at him questioningly.[18]

" 'Just wait,' he said, 'you'll understand all right. There's no hurry, after all.'[19]

"The bell rang for the last class. What had this quiet, somewhat awkward boy prophesied for me here? I barely had time to wake from my daydreams when the bell rang to end class and the school day. In front of the school, Hans asked me, 'Shall we walk home together?'

" 'Sure,' I answered, 'I'm going to the left, across the bridge.'

" 'I have to go to the right, through the park,' said Hans.

[18.] Replaces: "somewhat downcast."
[19.] Deleted: "We'll talk about it again for sure."

"'Too bad,' I said, 'then we can't do it.' I noticed Hans looking at me with surprise.

"'Yes, too bad,' was all he said, and already I saw the whole crowd of classmates swarming around him, wanting to walk him home. Had he expected it of me, too? I wondered. That idea hadn't even occurred to me. I had set out on my way home when Paul caught up with me. It turned out that he lived just a few houses away from me.

"'You should have gone with the others today,' said Paul.

"'But I don't live in that neighborhood at all.'"

"'Neither do the others.'

"'Well, that's their business,' I replied, 'At any rate, I'm going my own way.'

"Paul said nothing. We walked next to each other in silence.

"'They're going to spoil Hans yet,' Paul suddenly mumbled to himself, 'unless a bomb explodes soon. He must just be going crazy with all this buzzing around him. They're all just aping him. It's[20] even a wonder he's still so sensible and doesn't care about all that. It's not good for the class either, by the way. Nobody can grow there. Some of the boys who butter him up are really disgusting. Hans is way too innocent; he doesn't even notice what they're doing.'[21]

"Paul was perhaps two years older than Hans and I. I already had noticed that he was a poor student. He learned slowly and with difficulty, but—as was now apparent—he was able to think for himself and had his own way of life, which the others accepted.[22] Since he was quite without personal ambition and very kindhearted, he was the only boy in the class besides Hans who enjoyed a sort of special position. We said goodbye.

"That night I tossed and turned in my bed for a long time and could hardly go to sleep. I couldn't stop seeing Hans in my mind's eye. Then I had a dream. We were in the school yard. The other boys were playing; I was standing alone, leaning up against a tree, and watching them indifferently. Now and then a ball flew right past my head, as if on purpose,

156

[20.] Deleted: "really a shame."

[21.] Deleted: "'Are you the only one who thinks this way?' I asked."

[22.] The characterization of Paul corresponds to the "discovery" described by Bonhoeffer in "After Ten Years," 1942–43: "There are people who are mentally agile but stupid [dumm], and people who are mentally slow but very far from stupid . . ." (*LPP* 8 [trans. altered]). In Bonhoeffer's observation, "any violent display of power, whether political or religious, produces an outburst of stupidity in a large segment of the population . . ." (ibid.).

so that I was startled and ducked. I saw little Meyer snickering, his soft snicker swelling to roaring laughter, which then deafened my ears like a hurricane. At the same time, little Meyer grew visibly bigger and bigger. In his hand he held a fountain pen, which grew along with him to gigantic proportions until suddenly, laughing derisively, he squirted the ink in my face, so that it ran down my cheeks. I was raging mad and wanted to lunge at him, when I realized my hands were being tied fast to the tree from behind by several boys. In this moment, Meyer's face changed to an expression of pale horror,[23] his body shriveled up, and he assumed the figure of a dwarf. Hans had appeared and was standing in front of Meyer. He wore a splendid, full robe and a velvet beret like I had seen in pictures of mayors or high government officials. Meyer had become so tiny by now that he was hopping around our feet.[24] Hans gave him a kick, and he was dead. I cheered and was ashamed in the same moment.

157   "Meanwhile, all the other students had thrown themselves on the ground.[25] Only Paul stood a little way off, his arms crossed, shaking his head and saying over and over again, 'It's not good at all, it's not good at all.'[26] Hans smiled at him. Then he told the others to get up.

"In this moment all eyes were directed at me, and there was a piercing scream from all their mouths, as if in unison: 'The new boy didn't prostrate himself.' I was terrified, for the whole horde, in sudden metamorphosis, was attacking me in the shape of all kinds of flying vermin [Ungeziefer]—bumblebees, mosquitoes, horseflies—stinging, biting, and tormenting me horribly.[27] I lashed out, and the vermin fell to the ground in heaps all around me.[28] Then I saw Hans facing me, with his

---

[23.] Replaces: "turned deathly pale".

[24.] Replaces: "was transformed into a dog who licked his shoes."

[25.] Replaces: "all the others were on the ground." Deleted: "Hans walked past them, smiling, and . . ."

[26.] Replaces: "Later you'll understand this."

[27.] This dream scene is reminiscent of a similar one about "vermin" in Kafka's *Metamorphosis,* which uses the same word used by Bonhoeffer, *Ungeziefer,* and is interpreted by some as a dream. In Kafka's 1921 story his main character, Gregor Samsa, wakes up one day as a grotesque insect who is ostracized and eventually dies. This, and not the Nazi racist use of the term, is the likely allusion. [CG]

[28.] Cf. Friedrich Nietzsche, *Thus Spoke Zarathustra,* pt. 1, "On the Flies of the Market Place": "Flee, my friend, into your solitude: I see you stung all over by poisonous flies. . . . You have lived too close to the small and the miserable. . . . Numberless are these small and miserable creatures; and many a proud building has perished of raindrops and weeds" (164ff.).

astonished look. In one swoop I lunged at him and grabbed him, ripped his robe to shreds right off his body. A terrible wrestling began. Hans's eyes kept their astonished expression. We were gasping for breath and straining to the utmost. Neither of us could force the other to the ground. The school bell rang. We kept on wrestling. It rang louder and louder, incessantly, deafeningly. Students and teachers were now standing in a big circle around us. I heard the principal call out, 'Hans, Bürgermeister, give it to him!' A deep, calm voice responded, 'Shut up!' and someone hit the principal on the mouth with a notebook. It was Paul. Our strength was subsiding. Chest to chest, we felt each other's hot breath. I didn't think I could go on any longer. Then suddenly, the dwarf Meyer, who had come back to life in the meantime, crawled up behind me and bit deep into my leg. I felt a terrible pain, but Hans was already kicking Meyer, so that he completely disappeared into the ground. Then came the catastrophe, because Hans had lost his balance for a moment. He stumbled and fell on the ground under me. But before I was on top of him, I jumped up and released him. I felt deeply ashamed. 'Excuse me,' I stammered. All the teachers and students around us had disappeared; there was dead silence. We looked at each other for a long time in amazement.

158

"'Come,' said Hans, and as if nothing had happened, we went into our class and sat down next to each other on the last bench.[29]

"The whole next day I couldn't stop thinking about that dream. Whenever Hans walked past me, our eyes met. We hardly spoke. Paul was my only companion. In the course of the next few weeks it soon turned out that my performance in school was hardly, if at all, inferior to Hans. But I received no recognition for that. On the contrary, I thought I sensed a

[29.] After the publication of the first edition of the drama and novel in Germany in 1978, a letter was received from Dr. Hans Krause, an engineer in Jerusalem and former classmate of Dietrich Bonhoeffer at the Friedrichswerder Gymnasium in Berlin, where Dietrich was a student from the autumn of 1913 until the spring of 1919. The story of this rivalry had reminded Krause of incidents that had occurred between Dietrich and their classmate Ernst Abrahamsohn, who became a professor of classical philology after emigrating to the United States, where he died. He had been an extraordinarily gifted student and a rival to Bonhoeffer, who had been the unquestioned leader of the class. Then there had been a kind of conspiracy. A group of Abrahamsohn's fans had attacked Bonhoeffer one day to beat him up. Later, Bonhoeffer and Abrahamsohn had become friends, and Bonhoeffer's dominance came to an end. A class photograph from about 1917 shows Dietrich and Ernst sitting next to each other among the thirty-four students (including Hans Krause). In Karl Bonhoeffer's annual entry for 1915 in the family's New Year's Eve log, he wrote of Dietrich, "He likes fighting, and does a great deal of it" (*DB-ER* 24).

growing animosity toward me in the class. In physical education, too, the two of us far outperformed the others.

"As a result, when we played team sports or games, Hans and I would always be the captains of opposing teams. Thus for the first time in a long while, the team led by Hans would be defeated as often as it won. But even that didn't help me. To be sure, Hans played absolutely fairly; he would almost lose his temper over the slightest attempt by someone on his side to cheat. Then he would call his own teammates the most contemptuous names. If his team lost, he would just look at me with astonishment in his large eyes. But the others, I could sense, were plotting revenge. At recess I continued to spend my time with Paul, while the rest of the class all gathered around Hans.[30] After school we parted ways, as we had on the first day. So although everything seemed from the outside to be running smoothly and happily, on the inside all sorts of garbage was piling up. I talked with Paul about it.[31]

"'I've known from the start that something would happen between you two,' he said. When I asked why he thought so—because, after all, I really didn't have anything at all against Hans, so what could Hans possibly have against me—he replied although it really wasn't an answer, 'Perhaps a thunderstorm will clear the air in the class one of these days. It wouldn't hurt.'

"In these weeks of the gathering storm, several unsavory characters from the class attached themselves to me and tried to scheme against[32] Hans, saying he was tyrannizing the class and wouldn't tolerate anyone beside him. They claimed he was conceited, hated me, and was only waiting for a chance to humiliate me. It was time for someone to stand up to him, etc., etc. Since I knew that the only reason these boys were trying to make friends with me was because Hans had given them a hard time about some mean and indecent behavior or other, I turned my back on them immediately and said they should say all that directly to Hans, and that I didn't believe them.

"I heard from Paul that Hans was also hearing slander about me, and that he refused to go along with it just as clearly as I had. I respected him

---

[30.] Replaces: "while Hans gathered his circle around him."

[31.] Replaces: "Hans, too, who had continued to be friendly toward me for a long time, even if it never came to more than a few words exchanged between us, began to look at me suspiciously and harshly. I reported this observation to Paul."

[32.] Replaces: "harass".

159

greatly for that. As a matter of fact, during quiet moments at home I wondered what was causing this ever-growing tension. I could not find any fault with Hans, and I believed he wouldn't with me, either. I found his views sensible, his behavior always fair and kind. Indeed, I felt in myself a kind of kinship with his whole being. So it had to be our class-mates' fault. They were trying to set us against each other and were coming between us. They viewed my very presence, and especially my[33] performance and successes, as a threat and insult to their idol.

160

"One day the first of the very skillfully buried mines exploded. Hans himself came to me that morning and asked me to join his group during recess. His pale face and quivering lips betrayed an intense inner agitation that was frightening to me. I couldn't imagine what he wanted from me. When I joined the group, there was a hostile silence. Hans began speaking in a quiet, but trembling voice. Three classmates, he said, had reported that I had claimed after the last game that he, Hans, won occasionally at team sports only by cheating.[34] They also claimed that I said the only reason he had earned the sole perfect score on his last Latin exam was that the teacher was afraid of Hans's father, and so always gave Hans the exam passage beforehand. Thirdly, they had accused me of threatening to set a trap for Hans at the upcoming major competition, one that he would remember for a long time. What did I have to say of all this?

"Hans looked at me with burning eyes and waited for my reply. I felt as if the ground under my feet were shaking, and I may have turned as pale as Hans.

"I asked only who had said all these things.

"Hans, at this moment presumably thinking me capable of a terrible act of revenge, said this was immaterial.

"I had regained my composure and now said quite calmly that I would say nothing in my defense until I knew who had slandered me; I promised I would take no revenge on them except by disregard.

"Hans seemed impressed by these words. Again he shot me one of his astonished looks. A certain restlessness overcame the class.

"'Don't tell!' 'None of his business!' some of them murmured.

"When Hans didn't answer right away, I said in a loud, raging voice, 'Then I have no further reason to be here, and I won't speak another

[33.] Deleted: "good".

[34.] The single, more colloquial word for cheating used here, *Mogelei*, replaces a longer phrase using two synonyms, *Schwindelei und Mogelei*, fibbing and cheating. [NL]

161   word with anyone here until you apologize to me for this disgrace.'[35] As
       I said this, I looked sternly, straight at Hans, and turned to leave.
           "'Stay here, Harald,' Hans said. 'I now see that we have wronged you.
       It was mean slander. I apologize to you on behalf of the class. Should you
       demand to know names, I'll name them to you. But I promise you that
       nothing like this will ever happen again. I'll guarantee that.'
           "'Keep these pitiful names to yourselves,' I yelled as I was leaving,
       then turned around once more and said, 'Just the same, Hans, it's a
       shame you thought me capable of such a thing at all. You should know
       your people better.' For the first time I saw on Hans's face an expression
       of deep hurt, sadness, and shame,[36] which made me regret my words as
       soon as I had spoken them. The slanderers had stooped so low to invent
       such shrewd accusations; Hans's delicate sense of honor[37] must have
       been particularly offended. Now they had succeeded in bringing defeat
       not to me, but to Hans. That was painful to me. Impulsively, I turned
       back again, went over to Hans and offered him my hand. He took it and
       shook it without saying a word, and with no regard for the others I went
       on my way.
           "I don't want to bother you now," said the major, "with all the details
       of what came next, all of which I remember as if they had happened yes-
       terday. To be sure, my position in the class was secure and protected
       from that moment on,[38] because Hans had put his word on the line for
162   me. Still, the storm clouds had not yet broken, but rather continued to
       gather and grow ever darker. I heard from Paul that a whole group of
       boys was concentrating on nothing less than somehow getting me out of
       school.[39] Hans was changed by the unfortunate incident; he seemed to
       have lost some of his spontaneity. Often I heard him using harsh words

---

        [35.] Replaces: "until I hear the names of my slanderers."
        [36.] Replaces: "expression of pain and shame". Cf. Gotthelf, "Hans Joggeli der Erb-
    vetter": "'There may be no more bitter hour than the one when trust in humanity is bank-
    rupted, when an innocent [kindlich] mind sees those whom it has naively trusted appear
    for the first time in their naked, contemptible, and horrible selfishness.' This is what
    Bäbeli thinks because of a slander. 'Bäbeli, silly little thing,' said the old man. 'You take
    slander to be the whole truth. . . . If you want to wonder, wonder at yourself, and at why
    people can be so wrong and so silly as to prefer to believe in evil things'" (*Erzählungen*,
    341). Cf. page 149: "Hans is way too innocent [kindlich]."
        [37.] Replaces: "with his thoroughly honorable and straightforward character".
        [38.] Replaces: "after this incident".
        [39.] Replaces: "getting me to do something stupid [in turn replaces: luring me into a
    trap] which would get me removed from the school."

against classmates and saw him observing several of them suspiciously. In his behavior toward me I felt a certain degree of both distance and warmth.[40]

"The day of the big school games arrived. Preparations had been underway for a long time. Hans was very involved in organizing them. I was not, since I wasn't asked. Meanwhile, I worked through a tough daily routine of the necessary exercises, having firmly resolved to win first place.[41] For these games a point system was used to calculate two first-place positions, a best in class, and a best in school. The latter was the celebrated hero, and for the last two years Hans had won best in school. Meanwhile, we were fourteen years old and in our sixth year of Gymnasium. When we lined up on the playing field that morning, Hans made a brief speech to the class. With conspicuously harsh words he called for the highest level of good sportsmanship in the upcoming competition. He even threatened rather ominous consequences for anyone who might violate this rule. Hans looked bad; as he surveyed his classmates, there was something severe and mistrustful in his gaze and a noticeable nervousness in his movements. When he finished and was walking past me, he glanced at me briefly, as if to ask if there was anything else he could do for my protection.

"Given the generally festive atmosphere, there was something depressing about this episode. But, as it turned out, Hans was right. The first incident took place around noon. As expected, Hans's scores and my own were almost identical—in fact I had managed to pull a few points ahead. Hans didn't seem quite himself, physically or emotionally, and had done rather poorly in some events. There was nervous whispering among the classmates that Hans wouldn't pull it off today. Angry looks darted my way. Then during soccer Hans happened to receive such an unfortunate blow that he staggered and fainted for a moment. 163

" 'That was Bremer,' they were suddenly saying.

"When Hans, though still half dazed, heard the mumbling, he merely shook his head vehemently and said, 'That absolutely wasn't Harald; it was someone else.' I immediately demanded clarification from the

---

[40.] The last sentence, a marginal addition in the manuscript which was not deleted, presumably replaces: "To me he was as friendly and appropriate as ever. There were even occasions when I sensed something like warmth and affection."

[41.] Deleted: "or at least to share it with Hans." See the comment in Bethge's biography that "only when he came home from a school sports meet with the victor's laurel wreath around his shoulders, did he have to put up with the taunts of his big brothers" (*DB-ER* 15).

referee, and fortunately it could be clearly demonstrated that I had been nowhere near Hans at the decisive moment. It was obvious to me that this was no coincidence, but that one of my enemies had hatched the nastiest sort of plot to disqualify me. But since I couldn't prove it, I kept silent. Hans recovered quickly, came over to me right away and, looking sincerely troubled, expressed his regret over yet another base attempt to cast suspicion on me. I felt sorry for him. He said nothing to his school-mates. In the afternoon sessions, by exerting all the strength he could muster, he managed to catch up and tie my score. Later he told me he hadn't even cared about winning anymore, but he thought it would be better for me if I didn't win today.[42]

"Thus it happened that by evening our scores were identical, with only one last event remaining. Meanwhile, word had traveled quickly among all the classes that in a few minutes the two of us would compete in the decisive contest for best in school. So the two hundred boys[43] in the school gathered around us. I openly struggled for my victory, as Hans—for my sake—did for his.

" 'Brake and Bremer to the pole vault!'[44] shouted the referee. This event[45] was one at which I was especially good, but Hans less so. Our classmates, including Meyer, brought us a variety of poles to choose from. I saw some of the boys exchanging quick and secretive glances. Hans took the first pole offered to him, ran, and jumped.

" 'Three meters fifty!' called the referee. A murmur of disapproval rose from the crowd. Hans usually scored significantly better on the pole vault.[46] I already felt certain of victory, took the same pole from Hans, and jumped. Again the referee called 'Three meters fifty!' Disap-

164

[42.] See the passage marked by Bonhoeffer in Nohl, *Die sittlichen Grunderfahrungen:* "Christian teaching has always rejected competition because it is based on comparison and arouses all the wrong instincts. . . ." Nohl counters this observation, saying that competition "presupposes respect for one's opponent and is most successful among friends. . . . In competition, one sets the pace for the other" (68).

[43.] Deleted: "and all the teachers".

[44.] Deleted: "and the deciding event".

[45.] Deleted: "in which until now I usually [. . .] Hans" ["usually" replaces "several times"].

[46.] The pole vault champion at the 1936 Berlin Olympics (August 1–16) vaulted 4.35 meters. Bonhoeffer was among the spectators on Thursday, August 6. See his letter of August 6, 1936: "I suddenly got a ticket to the Olympics and had to go" (*DBW* 14:214f. [*GS* 6:392]). Bonhoeffer's description of the pole vault competition here suggests some lack of clarity about how this event is conducted.

pointment! We jumped again and both scored three meters seventy. Tension was building.

"'The poles are too heavy,' Meyer[47] cried. With pale face and, as I later realized, quivering hand, he handed new, lighter poles to each of us. I was just balancing mine in my hand with satisfaction when Hans moved suddenly to grab it from me, cast a terrible glance at Meyer and his crew that I did not understand, and in the same instant took off running for his vault. He planted the pole securely, pulled himself up on it with wonderful ease, and, just as I saw him pass the four-meter mark, the pole splintered at the height of his vault. Hans fell onto the lower part of the broken pole, and lay motionless.

"At that moment I understood everything as in a sudden flash of light[48]—Hans's speech, the blow he received playing soccer, the whispers among the classmates, and Hans's terrible look at Meyer before his last vault. The only other thing I remember is that I was the first to kneel at Hans's side. I ripped off my gym shirt and wrapped it around his bleeding thigh. Hans opened his eyes and looked at me,[49] I guess it is appropriate to say, as a friend looks at a friend.

165

"'I gave my word; they betrayed me. I somehow knew they would. This is the end,' he said softly.

"A deep, calm voice behind me said, 'Perhaps it's a better beginning.'[50] It was Paul.

"'Meyer and his crew are to blame; you couldn't help it,' I cried, looking around for my enemies with a threatening scowl.[51]

"Hans dismissed my words with a wave of his hand. 'No, I should have noticed what was going on and stopped it. My defense against them was too weak. But I was all alone; I didn't have a single person to help me,' he added softly, 'not a single real friend.'

"'Now you have one,' said Paul's husky voice behind me again.

"Hans put out his hand and I took it. We didn't even notice any longer that the others were standing around us.[52]

[47.] Replaces "one of the classmates".

[48.] Replaces: "a shout as if from a single mouth".

[49.] Deleted: "for the first time".

[50.] The phrase, "a better beginning," reminded the German editors of Bonhoeffer's reported last words; see *DB-ER* 1022. [CG]

[51.] Deleted: "They were standing way off somewhere."

[52.] Replaces: "hadn't sensed at all that we were not alone."

"In a flash the word spread among the students.[53] Meyer and his cronies were hauled off and now stood pale as death in a circle of older boys. Hans held onto me as he pulled himself up, and leaned on my shoulder. The athletic competition was totally forgotten. Then a loud voice rang out; it was the senior in charge of the games, calling for silence.[54] 'The school games are over. Today's winners are Hans Brake and Harald von Bremer. Three cheers for them! Meyer and all those responsible for what happened will be suspended from the games for three years.'

"Amidst thunderous cheers arising from a chorus of two hundred boys, Hans and I were then lifted onto the shoulders of several seniors, Hans with my blood-soaked gym shirt around his leg, and I beside him. I saw that Paul, who was standing beneath us, was having trouble hiding the tears in his eyes, and it was hardly different with me."

166 When the major stopped there was a profound[55] silence. Martin bit his lip.[56] Christoph and Ulrich stared into space.

"Yes, that was your father," said the major, "and that is how we became friends. I believe we both learned something that day we'll remember for the rest of our lives," he added thoughtfully, and was quiet.

After a while Christoph asked, "What do you mean by that, Uncle Harald?[57] You didn't really even have a problem getting along; your views didn't clash at all. In fact you were very similar in character. So why did something like that happen? I don't quite understand."

"You're quite right," replied the major. "We were very similar, and that was just the problem. Each of us was living in a dream, thinking that we

---

[53.] Deleted: "and teachers." Bonhoeffer's decision to omit "teachers" here and above, page 156, editorial note 43, suggested to the German editors that he may be implying that the younger generation are learning for themselves.

[54.] Deleted: "and then shouted."

[55.] Replaces: "solemn".

[56.] Deleted: "hard."

[57.] A deleted earlier version of the passage following Christoph's question reads: "Yes, that is difficult to explain in one word," the major replied. "Look, [deleted: we had both made the mistake] there are people who always want to achieve everything by themselves and think they should always succeed and everyone else should submit to their will. When two people like that meet there is friction and they can't get along, even if they don't really have anything against one another and basically accept each other. But they just can't tolerate being side by side. Then a lot of unjust things happen. There are plots, hostilities, fights, intrigues, all without any particular reason, only because neither of them wants limits put on their power. That is how it was with Hans and me, perhaps without either of us quite realizing it."

were each quite alone in the world and that everyone else existed only for our sakes.[58] This illusion had made us blind to one another.[59] To be sure, we had nothing to reproach each other about. Our views and the concepts of honor and decency that we had learned from our parents were the same. In fact, we even felt a certain attraction, and certainly we respected each other.[60] And yet neither of us could stand the other's presence. Each of us thought the other was getting in his way and should submit to his will. To put it in fancy words, you would say it was a pure power struggle. Of course neither of us was conscious of it at the time, but, given the way we were, the clash was simply inevitable. When we woke up from our dream, we understood that no one is alone in the world, but that people must live side by side with others and get along with them—and that human beings are fortunate that this is so. Certainly you must give up some[61] things; you must learn to yield without sacrificing your character. Indeed, character is only formed in the process of living with one another."

167

The young men in particular listened to the words of the major with such attentiveness that they gave a tacit invitation for him to elaborate further on this point.

"In your life," he said, turning to the young men, "you will again and again meet people who believe—and perhaps you still think this way yourselves—that it is a sign of character to use force to suppress any resistance, any contradiction, any difference. They are even proud to discover resistance and enmity because it gives them an occasion to demonstrate their power. 'Many foes, much honor,'[62] the saying goes.[63] That sounds nice, but—it's a juvenile slogan. Only a person too young to have

---

[58.] Cf. the self-centered fantasy of the Gymnasium student in the sketch on vocation, probably written in 1932: "Now he stood solemnly in the presence of his God, in the presence of his class; now he was the center of attention. . . . He stood in the center of the world, . . . Now they all had to listen to him in silence" (*DB-ER* 40; *DBW* 11:370f. [*GS* 6:230]).

[59.] Replaces: "This dream had made Hans blind to his comrades and to me, and it had kept me from recognizing, as I should have, that Hans was better than me."

[60.] The following passage, to ". . . have never forgotten since" (see below, page 161), was first published in *GS* 3:499–501.

[61.] Replaces: "many".

[62.] This is a very martial saying which goes back to the sixteenth century.

[63.] Deleted: "and 'All or nothing.' That sounds very nice—and it may be that prophets can live by such a motto. But for everyday life together—let me assure you!—it's a terrible disaster. To smash another person's skull, literally or figuratively, requires no

an eye for human relationships, lacking experience with reality[64] and a sense of inherited values speaks that way. Perennial sophomores![65] They judge their own strength only by the ruins they leave behind them. They think it smart to smash as much fine china as possible, and they cheer childishly at the clatter of broken plates.[66] They consider it a sign of strong character never to retreat a step, never to yield to another, never to compromise.

"As long as we are children, we may indulge in such dreams of our little ego's world dominion. In our naiveté we may even delight in finding that we have followers when others believe in our dreams. But what a following! Weaklings, flatterers, and, at best, dreamers themselves![67] The sooner we learn that by such dreams we sin against life itself,[68] the better. But adults who still haven't learned this are disastrous for the people who live with them—and in the end for themselves too. Smashing in another person's skull, literally or figuratively, just because they are different, has very little[69] to do with character. Indeed, it takes much more character to understand one another and to get along without losing oneself in the process. Getting along with others without smashing in one another's skulls is life's real task. How naive is the person who regards this merely as weakness and cowardly surrender. No, precisely

---

character." Marginal note: "Giving in—lack of character! etc. Make friends out of enemies!" There follows a deleted draft of the next passage. [For another use of the phrase "all or nothing," see below, page 169, editorial note 122.][NL]

[64.] Deleted: "of life".

[65.] Deleted: "One can't expect much else of sophomores [replaces: In youth this isn't surprising]; in adults, it's disastrous. To smash another person's skull, literally or figuratively, just because they're different from myself, requires no character."

[66.] This is reminiscent of the anti-Jewish pogroms of November 9, 1938, known as Kristallnacht (Crystal Night or The Night of Broken Glass) because of the broken windows of Jewish shops and synagogues, which were burned. The description here recalls the Nazi movement's radical aggression against so-called enemies of the German people.

[67.] Replaces: "and such dreamers will always turn out to have followers who reinforce them in their dream. This is how it was for me before I went to school, then for Hans in school." Grimm, in his 1926 account of the attempted Munich putsch by Hitler and his followers and their march to the *Feldherrnhalle*, the Hall of Generals [a monument to military heroes in the heart of Munich] on November 9, 1923, in protest against the Weimar Republic, describes a widespread atmosphere of self-pity. As he writes, it was a year "in which the chaos in the overpopulated German lands became so great that while word-mongers reigned all around, people of courage and hope were shot down in Munich by fellow Germans" (*Volk ohne Raum*, 2:663).

[68.] Replaces: "cannot make it through life that way".

[69.] Replaces: "nothing at all".

here is where people really struggle and wrestle, often for a long time, tenaciously, with infinite effort, before taking one step forward. And what is the point? The point is—not to leave the other person behind as a corpse on the battlefield, but to struggle to win my opponent's consent to my will or, I should say, to create a common will between the other and me, turning an enemy into a friend.

169

"Of course this will never be accomplished without both sides giving up something, and especially not without mutual respect for the other's dignity. Here alone is the field where character is formed and proved. Here the world is not destroyed but built up [aufgebaut]—not a dream or fantasy world, to be sure, but the world in which human beings really live together. Here, too, strength and power come into play, but not for their own sakes. Instead, they serve mutual understanding[70] and greater cooperation among people.

"Forgive me, I'm getting carried away, but I believe that a young man can't possibly learn this lesson too soon. We Germans so often fail to grasp real life, not out of malice, but out of dreaming, out of love for words, ideas, and feelings.[71] It is harder for us than for others to find our way to one another. We either remain individuals who will do bloody battle with one another over the slightest differences, or we sacrifice ourselves totally and surrender to the will of an individual.[72] But both of these attitudes violate life as it really is, and both must end in disaster. Life requires us to live together, and that is so hard for us. That is what Hans and I learned when we were fourteen and have never forgotten since."

The major broke off[73] and said, with a glance at the two younger boys and the empty bread and cake plates on the table, "You may be excused, boys, you aren't interested in all this."

[70.] "Mutual understanding" replaces "fruitful."

[71.] Here follows a brief deletion of four lines which are taken up in revised form at the beginning of the next paragraph.

[72.] See the passage on civil courage in "After Ten Years" where Bonhoeffer writes that Germans did not realize that their "submissiveness and self-sacrifice could be exploited for evil ends," corrupting all moral principles; civil courage, according to Bonhoeffer, "can grow only out of the free responsibility of free people" (*LPP* 6 [trans. altered]). [CG]

[73.] The four deleted lines read: "Georg had been waiting for a long time for the right moment to speak. Now, as his father finished, the boy burst out with the question, 'Father, may Martin and I be excused now?' This came as such a surprise that everyone burst out laughing, confusing Georg completely."

Protesting loudly, the two insisted that they were indeed very inter-
170   ested in what he was saying and that, anyway, it was wrong when adults
always thought boys were too young to understand their conversations.
Surely, they said, they understood much more than people realized and,
after all, how were they supposed to learn anything if all they ever heard
were their schoolmates' conversations about sports and homework.
Georg and Martin said this with such conviction and unanimity that the
major had to smile with delight.[74]

Now[75] Franz leapt into the conversation. What his uncle had said
made him think of his old history teacher from senior year, the only
teacher for whom he had great love and admiration.[76] He was very intelligent, and—unfortunately in contrast to the rest of Franz's teachers[77]—
was a truly cultured, fine, quiet man. At the same time, his whole being
expressed great magnanimity, understanding, and kindness for each
one of his students. He made an effort to do justice to anyone[78] who
was at all serious about something. Only when someone churned out
borrowed platitudes [Phrasen] did he sometimes become furious.[79]

"Still, I could never agree with him,"[80] said Franz. Then he asked if
his uncle was trying to say basically the same thing as that teacher. Some
things had reminded him of his teacher, others had not.

"I'll never forget how he presented the great historical movements to
us—the French Revolution, the Reformation, the origins of Christianity.
Even today, the memory of these classes still redeems something of my
171   school career,[81] which was otherwise a waste of time. But then, when

---

[74.] Beginning here is a deletion of one and a half pages, replaced by the section that
follows below.

[75.] The passage beginning here and continuing to page 170 below, ". . . leaned back in
his cane chair," was first published in *GS* 3:501–8.

[76.] The only teacher really respected by the Bonhoeffer children among the faculty at
the Grunewald Gymnasium in Berlin (now the Walther Rathenau School) was the
renowned classicist, Dr. Walther Kranz, for whom Dietrich voluntarily wrote an extra
paper for his graduation exams, "Catull und Horaz als Lyriker" (Catullus and Horace as
lyric poets) (*DBW* 9:201–18; cf. *DB-ER* 43). See also the Greek teacher in the sketch on
vocation in *DBW* 11:370 (*GS* 6:229, 232).

[77.] Bonhoeffer inserted the phrase, "from whom all he ever heard were terrible platitudes [Phrasen]", then he put it in brackets, meaning he intended it to be deleted.

[78.] Replaces: "even the least talented".

[79.] Cf. Bonhoeffer's letter of April 22, 1944, where he says that "[at the time of my
first impressions abroad and] under the first conscious influence of father's personality
. . . I turned from phraseology to reality" (*LPP* 275).

[80.] In the long deletion this sentence read: "Still, he often got angry with him."

[81.] Replaces: "were the greatest moments of my school career".

the teacher finished lecturing on one of these topics, he always followed up with several classes in which conclusions could be drawn from the material. In these classes it was as if our history teacher became a different person. While he lectured with fire and passion before, now there was a certain melancholy[82] about him.[83]

"He said history shows that all these great movements and ideas have brought disaster to humanity in the end. The French Revolution ended in terror and was the beginning of the rule of the masses in Europe, he told us; the Reformation destroyed the unity of the West forever and rendered it defenseless against materialism;[84] Christianity tore apart the inner life of nations and individuals and, because of that, hardly anyone was able to find inner unity again.[85] But then at the last possible moment, he explained, to prevent catastrophe, there was always a mediocre compromise between the world and the new ideas, and these compromises were exactly what buried the actual idea and the original impulse.[86] Yet you were never allowed to say that the original idea was getting lost without being branded a heretic and a misanthrope by society. But he thought perhaps this was basically right. In any case the outcome and the lesson of history and of life—and we should listen well—was that one can only live by compromise.

"Once, I answered[87] that what he called the consequences of history   172 could, with equally good reason, be called the symptoms of its decline and fall. Why, I asked him, should we sniff around amidst the stench of history's decay,[88] instead of holding fast to its high points and looking to them for the consequences and lessons of history?"

[82.] Replaces: "very unaccustomed sadness".

[83.] Deleted: "the outcome of history." At this point in the long deletion was the sentence, "The result [replaces: consequences] of history—and he said this with an ambiguous [replaces: somewhat superior] smile and, as if with a little jibe at the class—would always be that a mediocre compromise was all that remained of the great ideas and movements."

[84.] Bonhoeffer's comments about the Reformation and the French Revolution are included in "Inheritance and Decay," written in the autumn of 1940 (see *E* 89–110).

[85.] Replaces: "suffers from this disunity." Then, deleted: "But the other outcome is . . ."

[86.] The phrase "the actual" replaces "the essential." Cf. the letter of October 31, 1943 (Reformation Day): "I remember from my student days a discussion between Holl and Harnack as to whether the great intellectual and cultural movements of history made headway through their primary or their secondary motives. At the time I thought Holl was right in maintaining the former; now I think he was wrong" (*LPP* 123 [trans. altered]).

[87.] In the long deleted passage Bonhoeffer wrote: "Once I had a big argument with him because I told him . . ."

[88.] The first version of this, in the long deleted passage, reads: "I am not at all interested in the stench of the decay of history, but for the strong smell . . ."

"Well, you're a pretty skillful dialectician," the major interjected with a smile, "but it's only a conceptual game after all."

"That's just about what my teacher said, too," Franz continued. "He said he didn't care what words you use, but you have to be truthful and honest in the face of the realities of life and not deceive[89] yourself. To do this, he said, you have to have a clear picture of the so-called high points. In hindsight they look nice enough, but that's the great lie of the historians[90] who are too cowardly to take the facts to heart. Ninety-nine percent of those who[91] had to live in such great times found them to be one long story of pain and misery. My teacher called it good luck that it was only every few hundred years that a generation was unfortunate enough to live during such a 'great time.'[92] 'What right have we,' he would ask passionately, 'to view history only from the perspective of the few who succeeded, thereby forgetting the blood and tears of the millions?' 'I'm telling you, Franz,' he would say, 'it is barbarism to write history this way. It might have been all right for oriental despots two thousand years ago, but after two thousand years of Christianity it's morally a scandal.[93] It's historiography like this that produces barbarism over and over again, because it systematically makes people savage and base,'[94] he concluded.

173

"I was very impressed and unable to reply. 'The morality of the so-called great times,' my teacher continued, 'says that human life and happiness are worth nothing, indeed that human blood must be shed in order to consecrate an altar to the idol of some idea or other. Don't

---

[89.] Replaces: "talk yourself into [believing a lie]."

[90.] In the long deleted passage this section reads: "and nothing is more dangerous than when the historians want people to believe these times were luminous examples they should emulate."

[91.] Replaces: "All those who".

[92.] Cf. Spengler, "Introduction" to *The Hour of Decision*, which appeared in German in 1933: "The decades in which we live are stupendous—and accordingly terrifying and devoid of happiness. . . . As for those who seek comfort merely, they do not deserve to exist" (ix f.). [The first sentence of Spengler's introduction reads: "No one can have looked forward to the national revolution of this year with greater longing than myself."][CG] There was much talk in the Third Reich of "great times," *grosse Zeiten*, both in the language of National Socialist ideology and in that of those opposing it in bitter irony.

[93.] See "The View from Below" (*LPP* 17). [CG]

[94.] See *E* (*DBW* 6): 221, and editorial note 16, which points out that Nietzsche rejected historians' writing history as the "sneers of the victors." Bonhoeffer quotes from Jaspers's *Nietzsche* (238), which in turn quotes from Nietzsche's *Werke*, the phrase "servile attitude in the face of the facts" (10:402) and then adds "of history".

misunderstand me,' he would warn us solemnly, 'I'm not criticizing the great ideas or the great men of history. Both are semidivine beings and figures[95] who intervene in human history from time to time according to a purpose we cannot fathom. They are both marvelous and terrible, brilliant and destructive, at the same time. Whoever claims that the great ideas of history arise from hungry people, and that great men are products of the masses,[96] is childish and has no idea of their terrible, superhuman power [Gewalt]. It is both arrogant and foolish to bicker with them. No, I bow to these incomprehensible powers [Mächte] which, according to the wisdom of Holy Scripture, are born of the forbidden intercourse between sons of gods and daughters of human beings.[97] The race of giants known to the sagas of our peoples[98] is alive and can be glimpsed on our earth from time to time. But we are midgets before them. Yes, midgets![99] Remember that! And that's precisely why we, too, must not act as though we were giants. And for that same reason I won't tolerate talk about "great times." They are the arenas of mythical demigods,[100] but for the rest of us they are terrible. Indeed, even the giants are destroyed by them. Jesus, Luther, Cromwell, Robespierre, Napoleon—none of them was really concerned about human happiness, even if they talked about it. And at the end of their life's work every one of them cried out like Jesus, "My God, my God, why have you forsaken me?" ' "[101]

174

The major had listened with profound attentiveness to Franz, who spoke with ever increasing passion. Now he interrupted him briefly,

---

[95.] See the paragraph on "demonic powers," "Mächte der Dämonen," in Bonhoeffer's preparatory outline for the 1934 Fanø conference (*DBW* 13:297 [*GS* 1:214]), referring to Mark 9:29 and Eph. 6:12. Cf. *No Rusty Swords*, 291, and Henkys, *Dietrich Bonhoeffers Gefängnisgedichte*, 72, editorial note 11.

[96.] An allusion to a Marxist philosophy of history emphasizing economic factors (materialism) and the role of the proletariat. [CG]

[97.] Cf. Gen. 6:4.

[98.] Replaces: "our sagas, too, report".

[99.] Nohl, *Die sittlichen Grunderfahrungen*, quotes the sentence about midget status, *Knirpstum*, by "J. Burckhardt in the famous chapter about historical greatness in his *Reflections on History*" (66). Burckhardt's fifth chapter, which originally bore the longer title, "The Individual and the Whole (The Great Men of History)" begins: "Having considered the constant interaction of the world forces . . . we may pass on to world movements concentrated in individuals. We have now to deal with great men. . . . Our starting point is our condition as midgets. . . . Greatness is all that *we are not*" (269 [trans. altered]).

[100.] Replaces: "the site of mythical figures".

[101.] Mark 15:34 (cf. Ps. 22:1).

mumbling to himself, "A clever man, your teacher, but the last part was wrong.[102] He should have left Christ off that list; then the whole picture looks different."[103]

Franz cast an astonished and somewhat puzzled look at the major, but continued again with his story, which he had actually intended only as a question. "When I couldn't find any other answer, I asked our teacher[104] if people were created for the purpose of being happy. And he looked at me with an indescribably[105] kind and sad look, behind which was a little smile,[106] and said, almost like a child, that he really didn't know. And he even said he didn't know if anybody did,[107] but that he would talk with me about it again in twenty years;[108] maybe then we'd both know more. Well, soon after that he died. Perhaps he knows more now." As he spoke these last words there was wisdom in Franz's expression that went beyond his years. "And now, Uncle Harald, what I

175

[102.] Replaces: "that was wrong."

[103.] Cf. the *Ethics* manuscript that Bonhoeffer was working on just before his arrest in 1943, in which he wrote of "courage . . . for genuine and complete worldliness, that is to say, for allowing the world to be what it really is before God, namely, a world which in its godlessness is reconciled with God. We shall have something to say later on about the definition of the contents of 'genuine worldliness.' What is decisive at the present juncture is *that a genuine worldliness is possible solely and exclusively on the basis of the proclamation of the cross of Jesus Christ*" (*E* 293). In his prison letter of March 9, 1944, he looked to history for a worldliness that is "not 'emancipated,' but 'Christian,' even if it is anticlerical. . . . It would be so important to construct a list of good forebears" (*LPP* 229f. [trans. altered]). Bonhoeffer had found a reference to such forebears in Martin's book, *Die Religion in Jacob Burckhardts Leben und Denken*. Burckhardt, writes Martin, limits himself to "following the ways of *human beings*. And this reserve, which Burckhardt demonstrates with questions about God, is largely characteristic of the attitude of Germans at the end of the nineteenth century. It is also found in writers like Storm, Fontane, and Gottfried Keller" (148). See also Bonhoeffer's letter of February 2, 1944: "I actually wanted to become as thoroughly familiar with nineteenth-century Germany as possible" (*LPP* 204).

[104.] Deleted: "once after his lecture".

[105.] Replaces: "unspeakably".

[106.] The long deletion reads here: "looked at me sideways with an expression I could not explain, but not unkindly." In the sketch on vocation the Greek teacher who wants to keep "the secret of his study of theology, begun early and passionately and then soon given up," looks at the student in a similar way (*DBW* 11:370 [*GS* 6:229]).

[107.] The long deletion reads here: "he said he wasn't in a position to answer this question, and he also didn't know who was."

[108.] In the long deletion is the following: "Already as a young child I always became angry over such deferred promises, and saw them merely as an escape from giving real answers. 'Sometimes such a promise of an answer in the future is the only possible one, Franz,' the major interjected calmly, 'but of course, only sometimes.'"

wanted to ask you is this. When you said what you did about getting along together, did you mean that people can only live by compromising? I'd find that terrible," he added, almost boyishly.

"You have touched upon more questions than we can discuss over a cup of tea, Franz," said the uncle. "I think your teacher is right in many respects, especially in what he said about the 'great times' of history and about historiography. It's true that the history of successes has been written more or less completely, and there's probably not much of importance to be added. But now it's time—and this is a much more difficult task—to write the history of what has not succeeded, and the history of the victims of what has been called 'success.' To use your teacher's words, it's time to write the history not of the giants and demigods, but of human beings. I don't mean the history of the eternally restless and rebellious masses, gathering and building toward an explosion. They, too, are superhuman, though subterranean, mythic forces [Mächte] that are connected in some mysterious way with the great people of history who have succeeded. No, I mean the history of human beings who, tossed about between these forces, seek to live their lives in the middle of work and family, suffering and happiness.[109]

"I told you about Hans and myself. Both of us thought we were demigods, until we realized—or at least sensed—that we are human beings who must live depending on, and related to, each other, cooperating with each other side by side.[110] And that was our good fortune. We became friends. Demigods have no friends, only tools which they use or discard according to whim. I distrust anyone who has no close friend. Either they're a demigod or, much worse, imagine they are. For me, the main issue for individuals and for peoples [Völker][111] is whether or not they have learned to live with other human beings and peoples. That's[112] more important to me than all their ideas, thoughts, and convictions.

"Your history teacher probably meant something like this.[113] But I

176

[109.] Cf. "The View from Below," *LPP* 17 (*DBW* 8:38f. [*GS* 2:441]).

[110.] This brief phrase is a classic summary of key points in Bonhoeffer's theological anthropology, which stresses mutuality and the encounter of people in communal relationships, and understands freedom as "freedom for the other." See, for example, *SC* (*DBWE* 1): 4f., 49, 182ff.; *CF* (*DBWE* 3): 62ff.; and *LPP* 381 (*DBW* 8:558). [CG]

[111.] Replaces: "There is only one issue, namely . . ." [last word not deleted in manuscript].

[112.] Deleted: "much".

[113.] Replaces: "I might well agree in this respect with your history teacher."

would not agree with him that what we learn from history and life is the need for compromise. People who speak that way are still focused only on ideas[114] and therefore are continually resigning themselves to discovering that no idea prevails in life in pure form. They then call that compromise and see it as a sign of the imperfection and wickedness of the world.

"I look only at people and their task of living with other people, and I view succeeding at this very task[115] as the fulfillment of human life and history. What your teacher considers a misfortune is in my view the only good fortune and happiness human beings have. They don't need to live with ideas, principles, doctrines, and morals, but they can live with one another, providing one another with limits.[116] Precisely in so doing, they point one another toward their real task. This life alone is fruitful and human. You wouldn't believe the change in Hans and me after the games back then—and the whole class as well. For weeks I was at Hans's bedside every day; that's when we got to know each other and began to see the world differently. I would almost say that only then did we become real human beings, each thanks to the other.

"But a new life began in the class, too. The spell that Hans's personality had cast on the class, which had been further strengthened by my arrival, was broken. The talents and personalities of our classmates could develop. Whereas before there had only been blind allegiance, now strong and healthy camaraderie began to grow. Even Meyer—who was to have been expelled from school, but thanks only to Hans's intervention had been given probation instead—sought to make friends again, though he had to start all over again at the bottom. Later he was removed from school for other unpleasant reasons.

"Hans remained the leader of the class until graduation, but now as *primus inter pares* [first among equals], and he never made a decision without first discussing it with me. So, was that a compromise between Hans and me? I wouldn't call it that, because that would devalue it. But

[114.] Replaces: "the struggle of ideas".

[115.] Deleted: "working through great difficulties".

[116.] From the beginning Bonhoeffer held that in human relations the independent wills of others were limits, *Grenzen*, and barriers, *Schranken*, that challenged the limitless aspirations of the self and were essential to the formation of personal and ethical identity—indeed, the 'other' in human social existence is the analogy and form of one's encounter with God. See, for example, *SC* (*DBWE* 1): 45f., 49ff.; *AB* (*DBWE* 2): 88, 127; and *CF* (*DBWE* 3): 94ff. [CG]

the decisive thing was not what we both lost,[117] namely our claim to live alone in the world as demigods, but what we gained, namely a humane life in community with another human being.[118]

"Now I believe the same thing holds true for nations, as well, and fundamentally for all historical movements. Let me put it a little differently from your history teacher. Like nature, history also develops an extra measure of strength in order to reach a modest but necessary goal. Look at the thousands[119] of chestnuts promised us by the blossoms on the trees around us. How many of them will reach their goal of growing into new chestnut trees? Hardly one. Nature is prodigal in order to be sure.[120] Similarly, we think the end-results of the powerful movements of history, the great conflicts, revolutions, reformations, and wars, seem utterly disproportionate to the effort expended. History, too, is prodigal[121] when it is concerned to preserve the human race. It expends the most uncanny effort to bring people to a single, necessary insight. Even though we see and bemoan the unfathomable disproportion between the seemingly meaningless, fruitless sacrifices and the very modest results, we must never underrate the importance of even the most modest result. It's like the one of every thousand chestnut trees that unnoticeably takes root in the ground and in turn promises to bear fruit. Of course it's a lame comparison; history and nature are two different things. But neither is subject to the maxim, 'All or nothing.'[122] Rather,

178

[117.] Replaces: "what we both gave up".

[118.] See Bonhoeffer's relational concept of freedom as it had developed by 1932–33: "Only by being in relation with the other am I free. No one can think of freedom as a substance or as something individualistic" (*CF* [*DBWE* 3] 63). [The beginning of this development is found in *Sanctorum Communio,* especially in Bonhoeffer's discussion of the "active 'being-for-each-other' [Füreinander]" of the members of the church-community (*SC* (*DBWE* 1) 178ff. It is further developed in *AB* (*DBWE* 2): 87–89 in conversation with the work of Eberhard Grisebach, Friedrich Gogarten, and Hinrich Knittermeyer.][CG] See also the manuscript written in Geneva in early September 1941 about William Paton's book, *The Church and the New Order in Europe:* "Freedom is, after all, not primarily an *individual* right, but a *responsibility;* freedom is not primarily focused on the individual self, but directed toward the neighbor" (*DBW* 16:540 [*GS* 1:359f.]).

[119.] Replaces: "hundreds".

[120.] Klaus Bonhoeffer often expressed these ideas about the waste that occurs in nature, including his farewell letter to his parents from prison on March 31, 1945, where he wrote that "nature is of course prodigal" (Eberhard and Renate Bethge, *Last Letters of Resistance,* 40).

[121.] Deleted: "in order to [advance] even a tiny step".

[122.] See *E,* where "the miracle of the resurrection" is described as illuminating life; there "one takes of life what it offers, not all or nothing but good and evil, the important

both obey the law of the preservation, continuation, and fulfillment of life, even at the cost of great sacrifice and deprivation. If there is something to learn from history, I would not call it compromise, but love for life as it really is."

The major took a deep breath, leaned back in his cane chair, and looked out beyond the circle of good-looking, youthful figures toward the flowering chestnut trees.[123]

"Harald, Harald," Frau von Bremer now spoke up, "that's the wisdom of old age, but it's not for young people. They want to hear something else."

179 "Maybe, my dear Sophie, that may be," the major answered calmly. "What harm does it do? Old people and young people, too, must live together and get along. Is there anything more perverse and repulsive than when older people mimic the speech of the young, saying what the young want to hear? They become contemptible, not only in their own eyes, but also in those of youth. They violate the order of life.[124] Who, for example, would forbid Christoph," he added, smiling, "who I can tell has been dissatisfied with what I've been saying, from telling me just as honestly what he thinks, as I've said what I think? In fact, I very much want to hear his opinion, and I presume we do have a few minutes before we have to think of plans for the rest of the day. So, courage, Christoph!"[125]

---

and the unimportant, joy and sorrow" (80). [Cf. also the same sentiment in the important letter of July 21, 1944, in *LPP* 369f.][CG]

[123.] Schollmeyer observes that "Bonhoeffer is quite indifferent to the fact that chestnut trees, at least, cannot possibly bloom on a hot July day" (*Bonhoeffers Theologie*, 292, note 452; cf. above, page 73).

[124.] Cf. Jaspers, *Man in the Modern Age:* "The latter [the elders], instead of (as they should) keeping the young at a distance and setting them a standard, assume the airs of an invincible vitality, such as beseems youth but is unbecoming to age. Genuine youth wants to maintain its disparity, and not to be mingled without distinction among elders. Age wants form and realization and the continuity of its destiny" (50f.). National Socialism countered this "order of life" with "contempt for age and idolization of youth," as Bonhoeffer wrote (*E* 114).

[125.] Regarding the differences of opinion between the major and Christoph, cf. the theological consideration of compromise and radicalism in "The Ultimate and the Penultimate," written in late 1940: "The two solutions are equally extreme, and both alike contain elements both of truth and of untruth" (*E* 120–32, esp. 127). See also the 1942 manuscript, "History and Good," which must be understood as a reference to the conspiracy to overthrow the National Socialist regime: "There can never be a theoretical answer to the question of whether, in historical action, the ultimate is the eternal law or whether it is free responsibility over against all law but before God" (*E* 236 [trans. altered]).

CHRISTOPH HARDLY NEEDED this encouragement to express his reservations about his uncle's views. Had his upbringing been a little less refined, or had he less sense of good manners, he would have interrupted his uncle several times already. So now his pent-up protest came bursting out in full force. Christoph picked up on the major's last words, and with his unusual skill with words and his preference for clarity and simplicity of thought he presented his opposition to his uncle with candor,[1] creating one of those situations where Ulrich watched his friend with boundless admiration and a feeling of his own real limits in this respect.[2]

"With every word you said, Uncle Harald," Christoph began, "I felt as if the ground were being pulled out from under my feet, as if I had to walk on water.[3] You say that the ultimate lesson of history and of life is the love of life in its reality, living together and getting along.[4] But what

---

[1.] Replaces: "openly," which in turn replaces "fearlessly like a knight in armor with the visor open."

[2.] The section from here to page 177, "become so conspicuously serious," was first published in *GS* 3:508–12.

[3.] Discipleship may require this of a person (see *CD* 66). Cf. Bonhoeffer's reference to Matt. 14:29: "When Peter was called to walk on the rolling sea . . . only one thing was required, . . . to rely on the word of Jesus Christ, and cling to it as offering a more secure ground than all the securities in the world" (*CD* 79 [trans. altered]). On having to get along without "ground under one's feet," see "After Ten Years": "One may ask whether there have ever before in human history been people, like ourselves, with so little ground under their feet—people to whom every available alternative seemed equally intolerable, hostile to life, and futile. . . . Or perhaps one should rather ask whether people of a generation who think responsibly as they face a turning point in history ever felt differently than we do today . . . " (*LPP* 3–4 [trans. altered]). By "today" Bonhoeffer means in the circumstances of the Third Reich. Cf. Lütgert, *Ethik der Liebe*, on the "strength to do the impossible in the power of God, i.e., to be working within the kingdom of God and for the kingdom of God. It is a duty of love to will to have this power" (266). On the previous page, marked by Bonhoeffer in the margin, Lütgert writes that Paul says "of love, that it is capable of everything one believes it can be. Love is participation in God's power" (265). See Bonhoeffer's note, "Lack of power can be sinful," in *ZE* 83, no. 27.

[4.] The following replaces thirteen deleted lines and a longer marginal insert, also deleted. This deleted passage begins, "Isn't it much more important what kind of life we love, and with whom we want to live and get along? Should one sacrifice everything only in order to live and get along with one another? Only the content of life counts. You condemn the 'all or nothing' approach. But aren't there convictions and ideas for which one can only take an 'all or nothing' stand? Doesn't every religion and every moral system make this claim, and mustn't their disciples act accordingly? Don't those who do not act accordingly betray themselves? Don't truth and goodness transcend peace?"

181   if there are already forces at work that make any living together with oth-
       ers or getting along together impossible, whose very intent is to make it
       impossible? What if someone announces a struggle against us[5] in which
       there is to be no agreement, but only victory or defeat? What if a power
       [Macht] rises against us—like a beast that has slept until now—that seeks
       to destroy everything that has made our life important and worth living?
       Indeed, what if all we can see in this power is the destruction of all
       orders of life [Lebensordnungen]? What if we must recognize it as the
       incarnation of evil? Then, certainly, it can no longer be a matter of
       getting along at all costs. Then it's about the very meaning of life; it's
       about ultimate convictions, values, and standards.[6] In such times all
       that matters is the 'all or nothing' you so ardently reject. In such times,
       those who evade decision betray themselves, their past, their vocation,
       and their loved ones. I believe there is far too much easy peace from
       which we need to be roused.[7] People are looking for those who dare to
       hand them firm standards, who have the courage to live by them and
       fight for them. And we—we should be the people who go to the front of
       the line and take the lead in this confrontation. We know what we have
       to defend and what we want. And because most people are cowards and
       slow to move, there must be masters and servants, or—rather, I am even
       tempted to say—'slaves.' "[8]

182   "Christoph," cried Franz with utmost indignation. "Again what you're
       saying is simply terrible! Look, you're just getting carried away by your
       own arguments."

[5.] The German word is *Kampf*, battle or struggle, as in *Mein Kampf*, Hitler's statement
of his agenda, written during his imprisonment after the Munich putsch (the coup attempt
against the Weimar Republic) of November 9, 1923, and published in 1924.

[6.] For a discussion of the exceptional conditions under which "ultimate" convictions
may determine public discussion, cf. *E* 262–64.

[7.] Cf. Jer. 6:14 and 8:11. [CG]

[8.] Jaspers, *Nietzsche*, refers to Nietzsche's statements on the "real *new masters*" and the
future "necessary state of 'slavery'" (271). Cf. Nietzsche, *Werke*, 14:226 and 8:303f., and
Nietzsche's statement—partly quoted on the same page in Jaspers—about "an aristocracy of
intellect and body which exercises self-discipline, absorbs more and more new elements
into itself, and stands out against the democratic world of misfits and halfwits ('the
masters of the earth')" (*Werke* 14:226, no. 457). The immediately preceding piece includes
the statement, "The Christian-democratic way of thinking favors the herd beast" (*Werke* 14,
no. 456). Nietzsche also wrote that mediocrity "is itself the *first* thing that necessitates that
exceptions must be allowed. They are the condition for high culture" (*Werke* 8:303, no. 57).
See Bonhoeffer's statement above, page 36, that nothing is more terrible than when "the
rabble rules and the noble serve."

"Please let me finish, Franz," Christoph answered vehemently.[9] "I know you think differently. In fact, I agree with Aristotle's teaching that there are people who are by nature born to be slaves.[10] And I disagree with Schiller's revolutionary slogan that human beings are born free 'even if they're born in chains.'[11] But for the tiny number of masters [Herren], for the free, the elite, the leaders—for them, love of life and happiness must not be the ultimate standard.[12] An unhappy human being is better than a happy pet.[13] I just read the story of Don Quixote and Sancho Panza. . . ."[14]

183

[9.] Cf. above, page 100: Franz "in his mind sought the company of the disadvantaged and the weak." Regarding Christoph's view, cf. the strictly situational observation in "After Ten Years": "Given this state of affairs [namely the 'violent display of power' that produces an 'outburst of stupidity in a large part of humanity' (*LPP* 8), as was the case since the National Socialists took power in 1933], we have to realize why it is no use trying to find out what 'the people' really think, or why the question is so superfluous for the person who thinks and acts responsibly—but always given these particular circumstances" (*LPP* 9 [trans. altered]). The will of the people, once rendered stupid, will be "capable of any evil" (*LPP* 9).

[10.] Cf. Nohl, *Die sittlichen Grunderfahrungen*, with marginal lines marked by Bonhoeffer in his copy: "Antiquity had the concept of the 'slave by nature,' whom Aristotle defined as people who partake in reason only insofar as they perceive it in others, but who do not possess it themselves" (25). Cf. Aristotle, *Politics*, 1254 b 20.

[11.] In the deleted passage is the quotation: "'People are born free, are free. . . .'" Cf. the beginning of the second verse of Friedrich Schiller's 1797 poem, "Die Worte des Glaubens": "People are created free, are free, / Even if they're born in chains" (Schiller, *Werke*, 3:427). There are earlier passages in Bonhoeffer's writings that echo these words of Schiller, esp. *CF* (*DBWE* 3): 31 and *CD* 231.

[12.] The idea implied in the conversation between Christoph and Ulrich that "a responsible upper class" would be preserved from decay by "Christianity" is not articulated here by Christoph (see above, page 104ff.; "unconscious Christianity," as Bonhoeffer calls it in *LPP* 373). Thus his words could be misunderstood in the way National Socialism crassly distorted the meaning of mastery (*Herrentum*) and leadership (*Führertum*). Cf. the theological reflection about responsibility in "History and Good" in Bonhoeffer's *Ethics*: "People who act in the freedom of their own most personal responsibility are precisely people who see their action ultimately committed to the guidance of God" (245 [trans. altered]). [This, like other passages in the *Ethics*, is certainly to be read as referring to Bonhoeffer himself in the resistance movement.][CG]

[13.] Cf. Nohl, *Die sittlichen Grunderfahrungen*, on the "construction of a life based on pleasure": "Better an unhappy human being, or a satisfied pig?" (46). Renate Bethge recalls that the comparison with the "pet" was heard in this form in the Bonhoeffer family.

[14.] Bonhoeffer had obtained and read a complete Spanish edition of Cervantes's *Don Quixote* during his pastorate in Barcelona in 1928–29. Cf. Bonhoeffer's comments on Don Quixote in "Christ, Reality, and Good": "Good is not in itself an independent theme for life; if it were so it would be the craziest kind of quixotry" (*E* 189). Cf. "Ethics as Formation": "That is how it looks when an old world ventures to take up arms against a new one

"Oh, no!" the major cried, half laughing and half serious, covering his face with his hands. "But go on, Christoph, go on!"

Christoph blushed but pulled himself together right away and finished his sentence.[15] "I wanted to say that we must not put philosophical and moral weapons into the hands of the Sancho Panzas among us—and there are plenty of them."

"Oh no, oh no," cried the major again, "now I've been rebuffed. Don Quixote has thrown me off my horse. I'm one of the Sancho Panzas, I'm an *epicuri de grege porcus* [a pig in the herd of Epicurus],[16] an archphilistine and lowbrow. Oh Christoph, Christoph, what have you done with me? Don't get angry, I beg you! You're right, dear boy, right in many ways. But"—and the major shook his head and turned utterly serious— "what a strange generation you all are! The things that inspired us at your age, human freedom and brotherhood,[17] you clever boys throw in the garbage as childish illusions![18]

"Events cast their shadows ahead; before a harsh winter, wild animals grow thicker fur, and the beaver puts on a thicker layer of fat. What kind of times and what sort of tasks can lie ahead for a generation that must think so harshly, even at such a young age, in order to survive?[19] It's

184

---

and when a world of the past hazards an attack against present reality, and when a nobleman lost in fantasies fights the superior forces of the commonplace and mean. . . . It is all too easy to pour scorn on the weapons which we have inherited from our fathers, the weapons which served them to perform great feats but which in the present struggle can no longer be sufficient" (*E* 70). Cervantes's novel is also mentioned in "After Ten Years" (*LPP* 7) and in the prison letters of November 9, 1943, and February 21, 1944 (*LPP* 125, 217).

[15.] Deleted: "bravely."

[16.] This is a reference to the Epicureans, who were known as pleasure seekers. Cf. above, page 173, editorial note 13, the reference to the "satisfied pig" in Nohl. The Latin expression attributed to the major in the novel may have been used by Rüdiger Schleicher, Renate Bethge's father and Dietrich Bonhoeffer's brother-in-law. Earlier, Rüdiger and Dietrich had occasionally exchanged postcards written in Latin. On February 1, 1944, Bonhoeffer reports that Rüdiger had "really said some friendly things" during his visit to Tegel prison, "e.g., for the state of health of my parents only the *causa*, and not the *culpa*, lay with me—of course it was Latin!" (*LPP* 202). Rüdiger is mentioned in the prison letter of February 21, 1944, which contains the following passage: "Don Quixote is the symbol of resistance carried to the point of absurdity, even lunacy; . . . Sancho Panza is the person who complacently and cunningly accommodates himself to things as they are" (*LPP* 217 [trans. altered]).

[17.] Replaces: "the freedom and equality of all people".

[18.] Deleted: "Of course, you will be faced with greater tasks someday than we were, and you must be sober and strong to stand the test."

[19.] See Bonhoeffer's letter of October 22, 1943, after his sister, Susanne Dreß, and her eight-year-old son had left a package at the prison: "I hope the impression of the prison

enough to make you shudder. But Christoph, dear Christoph, if you must be harsh, don't glorify harshness! If you must be relentless in order to prevail, don't forget you must be able to relent and soften whenever it's at all possible![20] If you must despise life in order to gain it, then don't forget to love it once you have gained it. But, above all, beware of speaking lightly of happiness, as if it were dispensable, and flirting with unhappiness![21] That goes against nature, against life, against human nature as we are created. For we must eke out our existence as poor sinners longing for happiness as a small token of God's kindness. It's not as easy being unhappy as you might think, and those who are truly unhappy do not despise or scorn those who are happy. I beg you, Christoph, do not become accustomed to this wild and frivolous[22] talk about unhappy human beings and happy pets.

"What purpose have you in taking charge, why do you want to lead, why do you want to prepare to bear unhappiness, if not in order to be able to make others happy?[23] Unhappiness comes by itself, or better, from God. We don't need to chase after it! Becoming unhappy is a stroke of fate, but to want to be unhappy—that is blasphemy and a serious illness of the soul. People have gorged themselves on happiness; now, out of curiosity, they hanker after unhappiness for a change.[24] I can think of nothing more jaded, and—although I don't like to see the word misused—more bourgeois, if you will, than flirting with unhappiness.[25] It's

185

---

wasn't too much for the little boy. . . . But when they are eighteen, how different they will be from what we were—not too disillusioned and bitter, I hope, but actually tougher and stronger because of all that they've been through" (*LPP* 120–21 [trans. altered]).

[20.] Müller recalls in this connection Bertolt Brecht's poem, "To Those Born Later": ". . . Oh, we / Who wanted to prepare the ground for friendliness / Could not ourselves be friendly. / But you, when the time comes at last / And man is a helper to man / Think of us / With forbearance" (Brecht, *Poems, 1913–1956*, 320; cited in Müller's *Von der Kirche zur Welt*, 282f.).

[21.] Replaces: "and making heroes of unhappy people."

[22.] Replaces: "barbaric".

[23.] Deleted: "Let me say it again, quite harshly and clearly: I think it is sinful to flirt with unhappiness."

[24.] Replaces: "It seems to me as if this philosophy comes from a disturbing oversaturation with happiness. People hanker after unhappiness just to have a change, out of inner inconstancy, inability, and curiosity." Cf. the poem "Sorrow and Joy" written in June 1944 (*LPP* 334f.).

[25.] Deleted: "It's playing with fire. It's a more dangerous illusion than any other." Cf. Bonhoeffer's comment in *Ethics* that he considered it was justified to "protest against that bourgeois self-satisfaction" notwithstanding the fact that "especially during the past twenty years . . . the idealization of good citizenship has given way to the idealization of its opposite, of disorder, chaos, anarchy, and catastrophe" (*E* 64).

a dangerous product of boredom, and of profound ingratitude. Christoph, much of what you've said about our times and our tasks is true. But we must also be strong and honest enough not to make a virtue of necessity. Otherwise, you'll turn the world on its head, and it won't tolerate that."

The major sank back in his armchair and it seemed as if some image in his mind, some painful recollection, had taken complete possession of him. "You've said something very dangerous, Christoph," he said softly. "Perhaps it's necessary for Germany, but—it's playing with fire.[26] Anyone who misunderstands you can do unspeakable harm."

Only the major's family could know what he was thinking as he spoke these words. The young guests only sensed that something had been touched upon whose meaning and significance for this household[27] they didn't know.

186 Christoph had not noticed the change that had come over Renate as he spoke. Now his eyes couldn't help looking at her, and he was deeply shaken when she lowered her eyes before him as before a strange, eerie[28] creature. She sat there slumped in a heap, utterly pale, and appeared chilled even in the hot summer sun.[29] What he had said—this much he recognized at once—had created a deep chasm between her and himself. Renate had expected help from him,[30] and he had only plunged her deeper into her helplessness. By what he said, he had given his very best. That was how he saw Germany and the task of his generation. But Renate heard in those words the voice of that other Germany which made her suffer, indeed that terrified her and seemed to make it impossible for her ever to feel at home here. Had she understood him correctly? Were his words about born masters [Herren] and born slaves in some subtle way related to the appearance of the young forester, whom Christoph found just as abominable as Renate? Did Renate confuse this cruel caricature of all power and authority [Herrentum] with real sovereignty?[31] Could Christoph's real meaning be so easily misun-

---

[26.] Cf. above, page 124, editorial note 6; Helmuth James von Moltke was not convinced that Germany would be fundamentally helped if Hitler were assassinated.

[27.] Replaces: "for their hosts".

[28.] Replaces: "terrible".

[29.] Deleted: "Immediately he recalled vividly the conversation he had just had with her an hour before."

[30.] Replaces: "had indirectly asked him to help her love Germany".

[31.] From his earliest work Bonhoeffer made clear the difference between rule as dom-

derstood? Or were such caricatures perhaps even the inevitable consequence when little people applied great ideas to themselves? But why had the major too, as well as Renate, become so conspicuously serious? Christoph sensed that he had been unable to fulfill Renate's request,[32] and that tormented him.[33] His attempts to meet Renate's gaze again were unsuccessful.

---

ination and rule as service. In *Sanctorum Communio* he stated this in the theological axiom, grounded in Christology, that God rules by serving (*SC* [*DBWE* 1] 60, 63). [CG]

[32.] Replaces: "his responsibility toward Renate".

[33.] Cf. Stifter's *Indian Summer,* in which Mathilde misunderstands something said by Gustav, who reflects on the pain of "being misunderstood by you" (436). This is the most dramatic passage in the novel Bonhoeffer read in Tegel; cf. the letters of June 24, 1943, and October 22, 1943 (*LPP* 71, 121).

The Bells

FRAU VON BREMER could not allow her young guests to become depressed or uncomfortable by something that was basically incomprehensible and puzzling to them. So she now suggested in a warm, motherly voice that they leave the table and continue the conversation another time. It was time to make plans for tomorrow and the next few days and then set off for the train station together. If today weren't Sunday, they would have the horses and the coach brought out and would drive to the station.[1] But unfortunately that wasn't possible now. As she spoke she put her arm gently around Renate, who was sitting next to her.

The major jumped, as if awakening from a dream, and said he would like it very much if the young men would accompany him to his study for just a moment longer. Georg and Martin were already on their way to the stalls where the animals were resting today from their week's labors.

While Frau von Bremer took the two girls by the arm and walked toward the park, and the major together with the four young men climbed the stairs to the castle, the bells of the ancient church in the neighboring village began to ring in the evening.

"Beautiful, isn't it, children?" Frau von Bremer said, taking a deep breath. "I longed for that in Africa sometimes.[2] Listen how old Misericordia rings out its unfathomably deep, dark tones. The clear, more austere voice in the middle is Justitia. And the sweet, bright one above the other two is called Pax.[3]

[1.] Bonhoeffer once had been especially impressed when the Kleists, in spite of days of rain at harvest time, hadn't harnessed their horses to bring in the harvest on a dry, sunny Sunday at their estate at Kiekow, since the animals deserved their Sabbath rest. Cf. Stifter, *Witiko,* in which, during his long trip on horseback, young Witiko makes certain to give his horse the day off on Sundays (25, 28). Bonhoeffer read this book in November 1943; see the letter of November 9, 1943 (*LPP* 125).

[2.] Deleted: "You won't find that anywhere in the world but in Germany." On June 14, 1943, the first Pentecost after his imprisonment, Bonhoeffer wrote, "When the bells rang this morning, I longed to go to church" (*LPP* 53). On July 3, 1943, he wrote, "When the bells of the prison chapel start ringing about six o'clock on a Saturday evening, that is the best time to write home. It's remarkable what power church bells have over human beings, and how deeply they can affect us" (*LPP* 73). At the end of Grimm's *Volk ohne Raum* is a description of bells ringing in the Weser Mountains: "And then there was a kind favor: the two bells of the cloister church, the young, bright one and the huge, deep bell for the war dead [began] to ring in Sunday" (2:72). See also the beginning of the first chapter of Gotthelf's *Zeitgeist und Berner Geist* (see above, page 71, editorial note 1).

[3.] The following passage replaces a deleted earlier version of eight lines and a marginal insertion. The beginning of the earlier version reads: "As early as four hundred years

"When I arrived at this estate for the first time twenty-five years ago, the old pastor told me the story of these bells. He said that in the days of the Reformation, a Herr von Bremer, an ancestor of the major's father, had the first bell forged and donated it to the church. He gave it the name Misericordia—Mercy—in the hope that every day it would proclaim the gospel of God's mercy to the poor, fear-ridden people. For about thirty years there was only this one bell. But when it became obvious that the people were misunderstanding and abusing the good news [of mercy] by becoming careless and, although supposedly trusting in God's mercy, sinning worse than ever before, the donor of Misericordia made a provision in his will that his son should have a second bell made with a more austere tone, to be called Justitia—Justice. He also stipulated that the pastor be instructed to preach more often on the Ten Commandments—especially in weekday services—than had been customary, and to speak of God's mercy and grace only on Sundays.[4] The son, a pious man like his father, fulfilled this last wish, and in turn he left instructions in his will that in the future only Justitia would ring on weekdays, and Misericordia only on Sundays.[5] The church chronicle says that there was an improvement in the congregation for a certain amount of time, but it didn't last. Then, with the Thirty Years War, God's judgment came over the community. Several raids and serious epidemics left the village impoverished and robbed of its population. The longing for peace with God and among people became great. After the Treaty of Westphalia, another ancestor again had a new bell made, Pax [peace],[6] with its gentle, ethereal voice. The church chronicle recounts how, when this bell was rung for the first   189 time, the whole congregation cried aloud in joy and grief."

Frau von Bremer stopped and the first gust of evening wind carried the full sound of the three bells over into the park. The slanting rays fell[7] onto the mighty trees, some of which may not have been very much younger than the bells.[8]

"People here call the Sunday evening bell[9] the 'great evening

---

ago the inhabitants of this area heard these bells, and Father's forefathers and ancestors grew up with them ringing and were buried with them ringing."

[4.] Cf. "costly grace" as contrasted with "cheap grace" (*CD* 43–56).

[5.] Deleted: "Thus it went for several generations and . . ."

[6.] Deleted: "—Peace—".

[7.] Deleted: "through the leaves". Cf. above, page 26, editorial note 5.

[8.] Replaces: "which might well have been there to witness the installation of the three bells."

[9.] Replaces: "Sunday bells".

blessing,'" Frau von Bremer continued, "as opposed to the 'little evening blessing' on weekdays, when only Justitia rings. Mercy, Justice, Peace—indeed, that's a great blessing for a country.[10] Come, let's walk on up to Pine Hill."[11]

"Yes, let's, Mother," answered Renate.

They walked in silence through the park, at one end of which began a fire lane through the forest of tall pines. If one continued out along the lane, it soon turned into a peaceful, woodland meadow that belonged to the castle grounds.[12] Two deer were grazing calmly in the evening sun. They stopped for a long look at the approaching visitors[13] and slowly withdrew through the tall grass into the woods. The pines had already cast long shadows over most of the meadow; only the right side was still bright with the last rays of sun. The grassy valley was long and sloping. A short way down, there was a knoll where one could come later in the evening and watch the sun set over distant forests.[14] This little hill—with some dark, old pines, a few birches, and some heather bushes—was known among the family as Pine Hill. In the middle of the hill, which offered a view of the whole length of the wooded meadow, there stood a[15] wooden cross. A bit to the front of it on each side was a bench carved of rough birch wood. There were no traces of a grave. Instead[16] wildflowers bloomed[17] between the benches as they did everywhere.

190

[10.] At the end of the deleted earlier draft we read: "Such bells are the good spirit of a country. As long as they ring [replaces: as long as these bells ring out across the land] a country cannot be lost for good, I think."

[11.] Deleted: "walk to Harald's grave."

[12.] Above the word "continued" in the manuscript is the undeleted word "led," indicating that a replacement was considered.

[13.] On November 21, 1943, Eternity Day, Dietrich Bonhoeffer wrote to Maria von Wedemeyer, who had asked on November 12 whether he was a hunting enthusiast like his brother Walter: "I much enjoy sitting in a blind or on the edge of the forest at dusk, waiting to watch—with a pounding heart—for the animals to emerge. But I've never felt the least inclination to shoot them. Why should I, when it's not necessary" (*LL* 119).

[14.] This description fits the view from the edge of the village of Friedrichsbrunn, where Bonhoeffer's family had their summer home in his youth. Cf. his prison letter of May 15, 1943: "Stifter's woodland scenes often make me long to be back again in the quiet glades near Friedrichsbrunn" (*LPP* 40). See also the prison letter of February 12, 1944: "In my imagination I live a good deal in nature, namely the central mountains in summertime, specifically in the glades near Friedrichsbrunn" (*LPP* 211) [trans. altered].

[15.] Deleted: "simple".

[16.] Deleted: "the yellow, white, and blue".

[17.] Replaces: "especially plentifully".

An inscription on the cross read "Harald von Bremer," and beneath his name were the words, "The souls of the righteous are in the hand of God and no torment will ever touch them."[18]

"Our oldest son, whom we lost a little over a year ago, is buried here," Frau von Bremer said quietly to Klara, drawing her toward the bench to sit with her. Renate had sat down facing them. "It was his wish to have his last resting place be somewhere like this."[19] Klara said nothing; she looked at the cross and then down over the meadows. From the distance came the sound of the "great evening blessing."

Meanwhile, the major was in his study, where, except for some hunting paraphernalia and a few old pictures, all one could see was books, lining the walls from floor to ceiling. He stood leaning over an old chest with metal trim. Since leaving the table where they had sat together,[20] he had not uttered a word. The young men stood at the open windows and heard the same bells heard by the women up on the hill. With or without explanation, the bells announced their own names, so to speak, and their message. Mercy, justice, peace—anyone who had an ear for the language of bells must hear it.

191

The major stood up straight. Now he had a small, hand-bound book in his hand. He stepped over to Franz, Christoph, and Ulrich. Johannes stood a bit farther away.

"I wanted to show you this," the major said with emotion[21] in his voice. "In the few hours we've known each other today we've begun to speak of questions that will be of utmost importance for your lives. They mean more in the life of our family than you can know; perhaps you've

---

[18.] Cf. Wisd. of Sol. 3:1-3, marked in the margin of Bonhoeffer's Luther Bible with several lines: "But the souls of the righteous are in the hand of God, and no torment will ever touch them. In the eyes of the foolish they seemed to have died, and their departure was thought to be an affliction, and their going from us to be their destruction; but they are at peace." Bonhoeffer preached on this last phrase in his sermon for Eternity Sunday, November 26, 1933: "Whoever wants to ask about the dead and really get an answer, who is not content with half-hearted assurances, must dare to come to God and ask God oneself—God will answer. . . . In most certain terms, God assures the church-community that 'they are with me, they are at peace. God's world is peace'" (*DBW* 13:328 [*GS* 4:162]). [Eternity Sunday, which is different from All Saints' Day, remembering the martyrs, and All Souls' Day, remembering all the faithful departed, is celebrated in the German Protestant tradition on the last Sunday before Advent. On this day one remembers the dead, the transience of human existence, and the hope of the resurrection.][CG]

[19.] Replaces: "to be buried this way."

[20.] Replaces: "the table after tea".

[21.] Deleted: "but also with strength".

sensed it already. Since you're the sons of my best friend and—let me confess—because I have come to trust you,[22] I think I may give you these papers. Perhaps you'll read them together and give them back to me tomorrow when we come to see you. They're my oldest son Harald's diary, which continues right up to the day before his death. He died for a just cause[23]—as a victim of the abuse of power. It was very hard for us.[24] My wife and—I take the liberty of adding—Johannes helped the rest of us very much." The major looked at his son with an expression of indescribable love.

"Dear boys," he then said to the other three, "I think you would find in Johannes a good and loyal friend, and he could find a brother in each of you.[25] For one year we have lived here secluded from everyone. Now, after overcoming our bitterness, we must find our way back to other people,[26] and perhaps—perhaps—you can help our children a bit with that."

Outside, the ringing of the bells ended. Then Misericordia, Justitia, Pax—one more time. Then, silence, and it was evening.

[22.] Deleted: "and, last but not least, because my wish is for you and my children to get to know each other and make friends; that is why . . ."

[23.] For other references by Bonhoeffer to this verse from Matt. 5:10 ("Blessed are those who are persecuted for righteousness' sake"), see *CD* 113 and *E* 61–62.

[24.] Deleted: "But, praise God, it didn't break us."

[25.] The German can be read to mean that he might find in each of them the brother he had lost. [NL]

[26.] Deleted: "who hurt us so terribly".

STORY

WITH A SATISFIED and complacent smile,[1] Sergeant Major Meier accepts a rather large package and slips it into his briefcase, which he carefully locks up in his desk. Then he puts on his official face and asks, "And your heart trouble, Müller?"[2]

Müller stands at attention and stutters, "Sergeant Major, my wife—"

"I'm asking about your heart trouble, Müller! Is it no better? Is it worse?"

"Yes sir, Sergeant Major, yes sir—worse, definitely worse!" Müller insists hastily and nervously.

"But wouldn't you say, Müller, maybe in three months . . . ?"

"Yes sir, Sergeant Major, of course; certainly. I mean, perhaps. Yes, Sergeant Major, perhaps in three months. After all, three months is a long—"

"A long time, yes, of course, Müller. Who knows, by then—"[3] He cuts

---

[1.] The manuscript is written in clear blue ink on dark, porous double sheets with no watermark (NL A 70, 3). The text is untitled. The fair copy of the manuscript, written in the Latin script, begins here and continues for about half the story; see below, page 188, editorial note 20. The first draft was written in German script, this one in Latin script. [Both the German Sütterlin script (which became less popular in the 1950s) and Latin script were still commonly used for handwriting in Bonhoeffer's time; he used Latin script for texts he intended others to read.][NL] "With a satisfied and complacent smile" replaces in the first draft, "Smiling with satisfaction and with a slight [replaces: hardly noticeable] wink."

[2.] The German word *dienstlich* here replaces the more formal term *amtlich* for "official" in the first draft. [NL] [Müller is bribing Meier with food packages, in return for which Meier pretends that Müller has heart trouble, so that Müller will not be sent to the front.] [CG]

[3.] Inadvertently omitted in the fair copy is the phrase "[Deleted: Yes,] a long time . . . by then."

himself short. Müller's eyes eagerly follow the sergeant major's movements as he pulls out a list, writes something beside one name, and puts the list back into the file. Lance Corporal Müller takes a deep breath.[4] He wants to say "thank you," but he senses that he mustn't.

"All right, Müller, you may go!" says the sergeant major with dignity. As Müller puts his hand on the door handle to leave, the sergeant major adds, without looking at Müller, as if it were an afterthought, "and Müller, you won't forget now, will you!"

"Now, really, Sergeant Major!" Müller bows as if he were behind the counter of his shop waiting on a customer. Smiling obsequiously and bowing once again, he takes his leave.

194

The telephone rings. "Military Interrogation Prison, Sergeant Major Meier speaking. Who is it? I can't understand you—ah, Major!" Meier stands at attention, his face frozen into a subservient smile. "I beg your pardon sir, I hadn't—about a transfer, Major?" Meier's voice sounds hoarse. "Ah, I see. The Major intends to transfer a man here." His voice returns to normal. "Of course, Major, yes, of course we have room for him—excellent man—straight from the front—seriously wounded—totally fit for service—considerate treatment—treat him like a comrade—but of course, Major!—outstanding camaraderie here—of course! He can assume his post immediately. What did you say? Considerate treatment? Why, of course, Major, that goes without saying! Soldier from the front! Certainly, Major." Meier bows, smiles. "Thank you Major, sir. You can depend on me, completely sir—at your service, sir!"

Meier hangs up the phone quickly and somewhat nervously. New man?—no use at all for that. Frontline soldier?—these people often have such an unpleasant way of speaking. Don't fit in here[5]—see everything differently from us. Now, if a fellow like me had been out there, too. . . . Well, maybe not quite fully fit for service after all—Seriously wounded? Considerate treatment? Camaraderie? The same question twice? Meier shakes his head, puzzled. Well, after all, I'm in charge here,[6] he mumbles smugly to himself. He reaches for the key to his desk and is just opening the package he had locked up when there is a knock. The package disappears again immediately. Disgruntled, Meier calls out, "Come in!"

[4.] Deleted in the first draft: "A radiant look comes over his face."
[5.] Replaces in the first draft: "Can't adapt themselves to the group."
[6.] Replaces in the first draft: "Well, we've dealt with this kind before—."

The noncommissioned duty officer enters, shoving ahead of him a soldier with shackles on his hands and feet so that the soldier stumbles into the room. "Today's admission, Sergeant Major, sir. Desertion. Cell   195
127."

The prisoner looks around, confused. He appears to suffer from exhaustion and starvation. "Would you mind standing at attention, you scoundrel!"[7] barks the sergeant. "I guess you've never seen a parade ground?"

The prisoner pulls himself together.

"Age?"

"Eighteen, Sergeant Major."

"Occupation?"

"High school senior, Sergeant Major."

"Reason for detention?"

"Desertion, Sergeant Major."

"Deserted from where?"

"From the front line, Sergeant Major."

"From the front line, you pig? You know the consequences for that?"

"Yes sir, Sergeant Major." His whole body trembles slightly.

"From the front line?" the Sergeant Major repeats, getting himself worked up to a tantrum.[8] "From the front line, you cowardly rogue? So you leave your comrades in the lurch? You undermine manly discipline and order? You want to pursue your personal pleasure in the middle of the war? Have your fill and hang around with whores, while every decent man is sacrificing his last ounce of blood and his life for his fatherland?[9] Running after some shabby wench, eh?"

"No sir, Sergeant Major."

"No, you say? You want to lie to me on top of everything else, you filthy wretch? Why did you desert ranks?"

"I don't know, Sergeant Major. It just happened."

"You don't know? It just happened? Don't you know that the German

---

[7.] Cf. Bonhoeffer's "Report on Prison Life after One Year in Tegel": "When I had to line up with the other new arrivals, we were addressed by one of the warders as 'scoundrels,' etc., etc." (*LPP* 248 [trans. altered]). Cf. also his remark about his first twelve days in prison: "I was housed in the section for the most serious cases, prisoners who had been sentenced to death and lay shackled hand and foot" (*LPP* 249 [trans. altered]).

[8.] The sentence about the tantrum occurs only in the first draft.

[9.] In the first draft this phrase reads "offers his ultimate sacrifice, bleeding and dying for his fatherland." Then follows: "Is that so? You answer!"

man has a will so he can overcome the miserable coward in himself? It just happened!! That's a new one, the best yet!" The room shook from the superior's barking and laughter. "So you don't know why you took off? I'll tell you why. I know. Because you're a miserable scoundrel,[10] who cringes at every shot. And now you'll get the shot you deserve at close range.[11] How many hours were you on the front line before you took off, anyway, you little Mama's boy,[12] you snob, you hotshot Gymnasium graduate, you?"

"All winter, Sergeant Major."

"Where?"

"In Russia."

"All winter? When were you drafted?"

"I volunteered a year ago, Sergeant Major."

"So you could go out there and hang around! Did you ever even see a Russian?"[13]

"I have the Iron Cross First Class,[14] Sergeant Major." Instinctively the young prisoner glances at the left side of the sergeant major's chest, where the spotless, well-ironed green fabric of a new uniform is the only thing on display. Then he looks straight into the sergeant major's face and is surprised to see how strikingly young, healthy, and well-fed he looks.

The sergeant major senses this and becomes restless.[15] "The Iron Cross First Class?" he bellows. "Then why aren't you wearing it?" He looks with contempt at the prisoner's faded, tattered uniform.

"I took it off myself after my arrest."

"Iron Cross First Class—you took it off voluntarily?" says the sergeant major with a thunderous laugh. "You can try that one on someone else, but not me. I know my people."

"I am telling the truth, Sergeant Major." The prisoner's voice is very firm and determined.

[10.] The expression "miserable scoundrel" replaces in the first draft "cowardly worm," which replaces "cowardly dog."

[11.] [The German *auf dem Sandhaufen,* "at close range," implies execution.][NL] This phrase replaces in the first draft "the firing range."

[12.] The phrase "before you took off" (replaces: "ran away") appears only in the first draft, followed there by "soft little Mama's boy."

[13.] In the first draft this sentence reads: "I suppose the only action you saw there was listening to a bullet whistle past?"

[14.] The Iron Cross First Class was a medal for exceptional bravery in battle.

[15.] Deleted at the beginning of the following phrase: "Volunteered?"

The NCO who had brought him in intercedes. "Pardon me,[16] Sergeant Major, the Iron Cross is recorded in his pay-book."

"In his pay-book? You idiot!" the sergeant major yells, beside himself with rage. "Man, haven't you figured out yet that these crooks forge their pay-books too? Aggravated forgery! That, too! Well, just you wait, my boy, we'll show you a thing or two!" 197

The prisoner says nothing. He looks terribly tired and tormented, but his fiery eyes cast a piercing look into the sergeant major's bloated face.

"Where were you arrested?"

"I don't know, sir. I had fallen unconscious in the snow and they found me there."

"How long had you been walking?"

"About twelve hours, then I couldn't go on."

"Where did you want to go?"

"I don't know. Just away from the front. I just ran. I had lost my senses. The others had all[17] run away, too."

"And how did the people who found you know you had deserted?"

"Because I told them."

"And why did you admit it, you idiot? Why didn't you say your unit was retreating?"

"Because I left my assigned post without orders. Anyone who avoids the front line is a coward before the enemy and a deserter."

The sergeant major cringes. "What does your father do?"

"He's an officer."

The sergeant major looks timidly at the NCO. "Take the prisoner to his cell!" The foot shackles clatter as the prisoner stands up at attention. The door closes.

Sergeant Major Meier feels uneasy after this conversation. He wants to forget it. He quickly reaches for the package [from Müller], hastily opens it, cuts himself a thick piece of sausage, and greedily takes a bite. He instinctively feels for the left side of his uniform with his hand, as though the young prisoner's gaze were still burning there.[18] "Damn them, these frontline soldiers!" he mumbles to himself.

[16.] The sentences beginning "You can try that one" appear only in the first draft; presumably they were inadvertently omitted in the fair copy which only reads: ". . . with a thunderous laugh. The NCO intercedes, 'Sergeant Major, sir . . .'"

[17.] The first draft reads "mostly" instead of "all."

[18.] Replaces: "where he thinks he can still feel the fiery gaze of the young prisoner."

A loud knock at the door. The sergeant major is startled. He is agitated. The door opens quickly before Meier can swallow his mouthful of sausage.

"Lance Corporal Berg reporting for duty on orders from the major."[19] A calm, strong voice.

198   Meier smooths his jacket, runs his hand over his well-combed part, looks up, and is speechless for a moment. What he sees can hardly be called a human face anymore. It has been completely mutilated by burns, like those caused by flamethrowers. Pieces of other people's flesh have been grafted in. His nose is in shreds. His mouth has no lips. His ears are only half there. The sergeant major is trying to collect himself, but keeps staring, speechless, at the erect and youthful figure who stands before him. "The major sent you to us?" he finally begins.

"Yes sir, Sergeant Major."

The major's words are still racing through the sergeant major's mind: "excellent man—frontline soldier—considerate treatment—camaraderie."

"Are you fully fit for duty?"

"Yes sir, Sergeant Major."

"Are you still in treatment at the military hospital?"

"No sir, I was discharged as recovered."

Meier struggles for words. "And so you think—" He stops short.

"Yes sir, Sergeant Major, I think I will do my duty here just as I did on the front line."[20]

The sergeant major flinches. "Of course, of course, my friend. The major—" Suddenly he asks, "Are you married?"

"No, not yet, Sergeant Major."

Not yet?[21] What does this man still have left to hope for? "How old are you?"

"Twenty-eight."

Exactly the same as I am, thinks the sergeant major. It gives him the shivers. "What is your occupation?"

"Elementary-school teacher, Sergeant Major."

[19.] Replaces: "on orders of major." The first draft reads: "Major W."

[20.] The fair copy, written in Latin script and copied from the first draft in German script, ends here. The remainder of this edition is based on the first draft written in German script.

[21.] Replaces: "This 'Not yet' haunts the sergeant major through and through."

That's the end of his career.[22] Wouldn't it have been better for someone like this if—? The sergeant major cuts this thought short. "All right,"
he says. "You can go. The duty NCO will give you your instructions."

Meier paces back and forth in his office, oblivious to what he is really
thinking. He feels a clutching pressure on his heart and stomach like that
of approaching nausea. He opens the window and takes a deep breath.
Again he paces back and forth. Suddenly he stops in front of the mirror
and takes a long look.[23] This reassures him. He finds himself handsome
and well-groomed. His new high boots and tight-fitting uniform,
acquired recently,[24] give his figure a dashing, officerlike quality which
gives him extreme satisfaction.[25] He is suddenly reminded of the last
soirée with his comrades and the ladies, where he made quite an impression on several young women. He imagines himself at the head of the
table, but when he tries to look into the face of an especially charming
woman, he sees instead the ghastly visage of the wounded soldier from
the front. Then several adventures of recent weeks come to mind. He
had secured a supply of champagne and a rather respectable buffet of
cold-cuts,[26] thereby scoring the highest regard from his female companion. Then the face again. The face—the lady—the platter of cold-
cuts—everything races confusedly through his mind. He walks to the
telephone and asks for the kitchen: "Send Müller to my office immediately!"[27]

After more than an hour[28] Müller leaves the sergeant major's office.
His last words were, "You can count on me, Sergeant Major; I completely
understand. It's really quite impossible!"[29]

Just outside the door he runs into Lance Corporal Berg, who is returning from his first round through the cells. Müller quickly collects himself[30] and, with a polite smile, just to say something, asks, "Well, how do
you like our scoundrels?"

199

[22.] Replaces: "'He'll have to start all over,' thinks the sergeant major."
[23.] The three short sentences beginning "He opens the window . . ." replace "He
opens the door of the wardrobe and looks in the mirror for a long time."
[24.] Replaces: "His personal [uniform] . . ." [This refers to a uniform Meier had purchased himself.][CG]
[25.] Replaces: "Meier is pleased with himself."
[26.] Deleted: "This makes him think of Lance Corporal Müller."
[27.] Replaces: "Employees' kitchen: Müller is to report to me immediately!"
[28.] Replaces: "After some time" [replaces: "After a few minutes Müller leaves again"].
[29.] Deleted: "in our circles."
[30.] Replaces: "pulls himself together".

"Scoundrels?" Berg asks. "I just saw a boy in Cell 127—I'd be happy if all the soldiers were like him. Except—it's a terrible pity about his case— desertion. Not a thing you can do about it. If they'd give him a chance for once, he would blot out the disgrace.[31] A pity."

200

"No, certainly there's nothing to be done," says Müller with a crude sneer, gesturing[32] to suggest the impending fate of the young soldier.

Berg shakes his head. "Comrade, have you ever been out there on the Russian front?"

Müller is embarrassed. "No, unfortunately—I have heart trouble, a nervous condition. But after all, you make your sacrifices here, too,[33] the bombing attacks, the stressful work with these louts—"[34]

"Hmm . . .," Berg shakes his head again, "from what I've seen today, most of the comrades doing time here have done something stupid once,[35] but louts or scoundrels—I don't know. I'm afraid they're to be found elsewhere. I don't want to hold you up, I guess you're on your way to the kitchen. So, see you later! And cook the prisoners something decent. We'll need them[36] out on the front again. Skeletons will do us no good there. See you later!"

Berg turns around and leaves Müller standing there.[37] Müller hesitates, wanting to say something but not knowing what. He thinks for a moment and then mumbles to himself, "So, my boy, so you're one of those."[38] Instead of going to the kitchen, he immediately goes to the infirmary. There he casually mentions Berg, "excellent man—frontline soldier—considerate treatment—to be sure—but a man like that can't be expected to do too much. It's certainly not responsible from a medical point of view to assign him to this difficult post, etc., etc."

[31.] Replaces: "he would become a frontline soldier like few others."

[32.] Deleted: "appropriately".

[33.] Marginal deletion: "twice a week".

[34.] Replaces: "scoundrels".

[35.] "Comrades" replaces "boys." Cf. Latmiral, "Einige Erinnerungen der Haft in dem Wehrmachtsuntersuchungsgefängnis Berlin-Tegel": "Most of the prisoners were accused of 'undermining military authority' [Zersetzung der Wehrkraft]; they were soldiers and NCOs most of whom, in the company of several people, had spoken against the war and the government while home on leave. Many of them . . . faced the death sentence for this reason. Some were deserters. . . . On Friday evening the death-row inmates (forty days after their sentencing, when it had been confirmed) were transferred to Plötzensee and beheaded. . . . The sign on their cell doors was painted red. There were red signs everywhere" (3f., 7f.). Cf. also Latmiral, "Erinnerungen eines Mithäftlings in Tegel."

[36.] Deleted: "healthy".

[37.] Deleted: "dumbfounded".

[38.] Replaces: "We'll deal with you all right."

He is rebuffed point-blank with the assurance that Berg is completely capable of serving. Besides, the other adds, it's difficult to understand why Müller is so interested in the matter.[39] Does he have some personal interest at stake?[40]

201

Müller stammers that he only wanted to help. After all, it was a comrade from the front line, and the sergeant major had some doubts himself. He is told he can assure the sergeant major that such doubts are unfounded.

Lunch.[41] Müller sits down next to Berg and begins to entertain him with a saccharine smile. He asks about the front and Berg's injury. Berg is monosyllabic.[42] The sergeant major is seated opposite them. Berg must use a tube in order to drink, since he has no sensation in his lips. He drinks as inconspicuously as possible. The sergeant major stares in horror at this process. Müller turns away.[43] Both turn their thoughts to the next soldiers' soirée with the ladies. This is simply impossible. During the meal Berg comments that the food is unusually good, and adds that now he should try the prisoners' food, too. After all, while they themselves were just on home assignment, most of the prisoners would have to return to the front. This comment is met with icy silence.

After lunch, when everyone has left the dining room, the sergeant major pauses to exchange a few words with Müller.

The next day Müller greets Lance Corporal Berg with special friendliness and shoves a small package into his hand. "You'll need this after everything you've been through."

Berg opens it. "Why do I get a pound of butter?!" he says loudly, just as another NCO walks by. "If you can spare it, which would surprise me, I'll pass it around among the prisoners on my wing. By the way, the grub they got yesterday was lousy.[44] Well, thanks!" Müller bites his lips and leaves. So Berg can't be bribed that way.[45]

[39.] Replaces: "what Müller has to do with the matter."

[40.] Replaces: "Does someone have a personal interest in this?"

[41.] Deleted: "The sergeant major requests."

[42.] Replaces: "reticent."

[43.] Deleted: "repulsed."

[44.] Cf. Bonhoeffer's "Report on Prison Life": "An occasional comparison between the food served the prisoners and the employees is simply amazing" (*LPP* 250).

[45.] A pencil note on the upper margin of the page following this passage reads: "long imprisonments? [The following handwriting is uncertain:] "Found them too long. What would happen to us?" Cf. later in the story, the phrase "these months—long imprisonments."

202   But Müller is persistent. He knows how important it is for him to satisfy the sergeant major. The next day, in express violation of the non-fraternization rule (but he has the sergeant major on his side!), he engages in conversation with individual prisoners from Berg's wing about how they like Berg, casually asking[46] whether the terrible mutilation of his face isn't depressing for the prisoners in their already difficult situation. The reply comes in the form of astonished shakes of their heads and uncomprehending or even overtly hostile answers in the negative. Müller hastens to babble on about nothing in particular in order to erase the poor impression created by his question.

At lunch Berg, whose mouth muscles do not function properly, happens to drop his drinking tube while sipping his drink, and spills the drink on the table. Indignant head-shaking by the sergeant major and a mean smile of mock pity on the part of Müller.[47]

The next day Berg is assigned to process visitation permits for the prisoners and their families. The sergeant major receives some of the lady visitors in his office afterward. Later he has Müller circulate the information that one female visitor had asked him if it was possible to find a different NCO to process her visitation permit the next time; she found it unbearable to utter a single word[48] when faced with such hideous mutilation.

Berg senses that people are talking about him. He begins to suspect[49] the reason.

Again Müller sits with him at lunch. "These months-long imprisonments in the cases of people who pulled stupid boys' pranks are nonsense; it only spoils them," Berg says. "A quick, brief, and strict punishment would be much better."[50]

[46.] Replaces: "stating."

[47.] Replaces: "[and] a mean laugh . . . on the part of Müller is the response."

[48.] Replaces: "to speak with her husband" [replaces: "son"].

[49.] Replaces: "is realistic enough to know".

[50.] Cf. Bonhoeffer's prison letter of November 20, 1943: "One sees a great deal in seven and a half months, especially how serious the consequences can be for petty acts of stupidity. It is my view that deprivation of liberty for longer periods is demoralizing in *every* respect. I have figured out an alternative penal system on the principle of making the punishment fit the crime; e.g., for absence without leave, cancellation of leave, etc.; for unauthorized wearing of medals, more dangerous assignment on the front; for robbing one's comrades, temporary identification as a thief; for black marketeering, a reduction of rations, etc." (*LPP* 134). See also his prison letter of April 26, 1944: "I think a long imprisonment of very young people is very dangerous for their inner development" (*LPP* 277).

"Yeah, and what would become of us, then?" Müller blurts out.[51] "I mean"—he now tries in vain to soften[52] his words—"I mean, after all, these people must have committed some crime or other, or they wouldn't be here, would they. And it doesn't hurt them at all to stew for a few months—"

"On the contrary, I think that's wrong in every respect!" Berg cries, with emotion.

"Be careful, Berg, be careful," warns Müller, playing his trump card. "You're being critical here, and if the sergeant major hears about it . . . !"

"I assure you, what is going on here will be heard and judged by quite another sort of people than the sergeant major!" shouts Berg. Müller pales.

The next day, Berg is ordered to report to the sergeant major. "Regretfully, Berg, I must tell you that you have been ordered to leave your post, effective immediately. I'm truly sorry. I would have especially liked to keep a frontline soldier like you here."

"May I ask the reason for my dismissal, Sergeant Major?"

"You have no right to a[53] reply to that question."

"But I insist on a reply, sir," says Berg defiantly.[54]

"Well, all right, my friend, I will make an exception and tell you. There is an official order."[55] Berg turns pale. He does not believe what the sergeant major is saying; in fact, he is convinced the sergeant major is lying to him, but he has no opportunity to test this conviction. Berg salutes and leaves the room.

After taking care of the formalities, Berg unlocks the eighteen-year-old's cell once more and sees traces of tears in the prisoner's eyes. But when the young deserter glimpses Berg, his face lights up.[56] "What's the matter, my boy?" Berg asks.

"I want to go back to the front," he says, his eyes brimming with tears.

"Me, too," says Berg, clenching his teeth. "Keep your head up, my boy, I'm going to speak to the general on your behalf. You'll be able to go back. But—I have to say goodbye to you now. I'm leaving."

203

204

[51.] An earlier replacement with "bursts out" is crossed out.
[52.] Deleted: "the impression of".
[53.] Deleted: "medical".
[54.] Replaces: "with determination" [replaces: "with emotion"].
[55.] Replaces: "doctor's order" [replaces: "instruction"].
[56.] Replaces: "At the same moment [his face, despite the tears,] lights up."

"You're leaving?" cries the boy in horror and desperation. "Why? But why? You were the only one here—"

"I'll tell you why. The sergeant major doesn't like my face."

They are both silent with emotion.[57] Berg walks to the door. "Farewell, comrade!"

"Farewell, comrade!"

[57.] Deleted: "Farewell, my boy. Farewell, comrade."

EDITOR'S AFTERWORD
TO THE GERMAN EDITION

AFTER FORTY DAYS in prison, in May 1943, Dietrich Bonhoeffer wrote to his parents:

> I'm now trying my hand at a little study on "The Feeling of Time," an experience that is presumably quite familiar to anyone undergoing pre-trial custody. One of my predecessors in the cell scribbled over the door, "In a hundred years it will all be over." That was his attempt to cope with this experience of empty time. I don't think I could fully agree, but there's a lot one could say on that subject. . . .[1]

He made notes for the study, including phrases like "Insight into the past.—Fulfillment, gratitude. Regret."—"*The significance of illusion.*"—"Past: why write 'Everything will be over in a hundred years' instead of 'Until recently everything was all right'? No *possession* (that will outlast time) no *task*"—"Emptiness of time in spite of all the ways to fill it—'*Fulfilled*' time very different."—"Time as help—as torment, as enemy."—"Continuity with the past and the future interrupted."[2] On June 4, he reported: "I've just written a little more about 'The feeling of time'; I'm very much enjoying it, and what I write from immediate experience comes out more fluently and freely."[3] In his letter of the Monday after Pentecost, 1943, he reports that "my study on 'The feeling of time' is practically finished; now I'm going to leave it alone for a while and see whether it will survive that test."[4]

[1.] Letter to Eberhard Bethge, May 15, 1943 (*LPP* 39 [trans. altered]).
[2.] See *NL* A 86, 1, and *NL* A 86, 2; cf. *LPP* 33–35.
[3.] Letter of June 4, 1943 (*LPP* 50 [trans. altered]).
[4.] Letter of June 14, 1943 (*LPP* 54 [trans. altered]). The study has not survived. An

206   It was probably July when Bonhoeffer began his larger literary undertaking, which required significantly more energy and momentum than
the study about "The Feeling of Time." In mid-August he described it to
his parents: "During the past weeks I sketched the outlines of a play, but
meanwhile I've realized that the material is not suitable for drama; and
so I shall now try to rewrite it as a story."[5]

Bonhoeffer had no intention of writing a memoir of his youth or of
his life. He would have thought that too direct. The literary form—drama
or novel—enabled him to represent people and situations without claiming to base his writing on fact. Persons and experiences appeared in a
form created by Bonhoeffer's productive imagination. Certain characteristics, modes of action, and attitudes of people in his immediate surroundings could be merged into a single fictitious character or be
distributed among various figures.

This also applies to the author and his main character in the drama
and the novel. Anyone who wanted to find autobiographical references
in these texts and knew Bonhoeffer's biography, found them despite the
fictional distancing of himself. As late as his second year in prison, Bonhoeffer wrote, "For me, this struggle with the past, this attempt to catch
hold of it and recapture it and, above all, the fear of losing it, is like a
daily musical accompaniment to my life here."[6] Throughout all this personal reflection the political dimension was always present. Again and
again in his literary writings it shows through, sometimes more obviously and sometimes less so, since it had to be crafted to remain unrec-
ognizable to Nazi eyes.

In the drama, the main character, Christoph, is twenty-four years
old,[7] his father a respected physician like Bonhoeffer's father.

---

undated letter of late April 1944 to his fiancée, Maria von Wedemeyer, shows how helpful
it was for Bonhoeffer to reflect on this theme: "You recently wrote that the good things of
the past avail us little once they're over. I myself have often wrestled with that idea, during
the past year in particular and especially in the beginning, but I've discovered that it's very
dangerous and wrong, and that one mustn't yield to it. . . . It is the past, granted, but it is *my*
past, and as such it will retain its immediacy if we are profoundly, unselfishly grateful for
God's gifts and regretful for the perverse way in which we so often vitiate them. That is
how, without tormenting ourselves, we can look back on the past and draw all our strength
from it. God's grace and God's forgiveness preside over all that is past" (*LL* 229–30 [trans.
altered]). Cf. Bonhoeffer's poem "The Past," written in the summer of 1944 after a visit in
prison from his fiancée (*LPP* 320–23).

[5.] Letter of August 17, 1943 (*LPP* 93–94 [trans. altered]).

[6.] Letter to Bethge, June 5, 1944 (*LPP* 319 [trans. altered]).

[7.] See above, page 39. Also see below, page 239, the indication of age in the "Drama
Working Notes": "25 years" [*NL* A 70, 4 (2)].

Christoph also appears in the novel, likewise his friend Ulrich, Little   207
Brother, the grandmother, and Renate. Despite the recurrence of some
of the same central characters in the drama and the novel, the two are
distinct in atmosphere and content.

The drama is fraught with a high degree of tension—understandably,
given the stressful situation of the writer's early weeks and months of imprisonment and hearings. The theme of the drama is death. It is introduced by the grandmother, who tells Little Brother a fairy tale of a
wondrous beast and its mysterious death. Christoph, just returned from
the war with a serious injury, though apparently recovered, has only a
short time to live. He knows it, and the grandmother and the mother
suspect it; the mother's suspicion is confirmed by the father, who, as a
physician, has definite knowledge. Renate and above all Ulrich only
learn the news later, when they discover something Christoph had written to himself. Each person believes the other knows nothing of the fateful situation. None of them wants to burden the others by telling what
they know. On the other hand, Christoph's silence had led to miscom-
munication between himself and Ulrich.

Among Christoph and Ulrich's circle of friends is a new person, a
"stranger," Heinrich.[8] Ulrich had heard from him that he had grown up
amidst terrible proletarian circumstances. There he lived under the
influence of the figure of Christ among the poorest of the poor. He was
badly wounded in the war and had been brought back to life against his
will. He now no longer feels any strength to create a meaningful life:
" . . . now I belong to the devil."[9]

Heinrich is visited in his room by another "stranger" who claims that
Heinrich had summoned him.[10] He comes as a business representative
of death. When God is mentioned, he cringes.[11] In order to help Heinrich understand why he has come he tells him, "I was condemned to
death. . . . For four weeks I stared at Death, at first gaping . . . then terrified . . . then again with burning desire . . . then with admiration as for a   208
powerful superior. When I was released it was too late, I couldn't return
to life. I had already come to an agreement with Death." He has acquired
an infallible sense for others' approaching death, but it leaves him

---

[8.] The text implies that one must be cautious toward strangers, as was necessary under
the Nazi regime: "He could be an informer" (see above, page 39).

[9.] See above, page 43.

[10.] See above, pages 52f.

[11.] See above, page 54.

"cold." "Nothing could excite me any more, nothing could upset me. On the contrary, I felt as calm, as empty, as solemn, and as indifferent as if I were in a strange cemetery."[12] He appeals to Heinrich to work with him in the service of Death.[13]

When Christoph comes to Heinrich's place to talk with him, the "stranger" is just leaving. In a deleted section of the drama Bonhoeffer has Christoph tell Heinrich of this uncanny visitor that he has "seen him often before."[14] The drama breaks off during the conversation between Christoph and Heinrich about "ground under your feet—in order to be able to live and be able to die."[15]

In the novel, Bonhoeffer begins the narrative earlier than in the drama; Christoph is seventeen years old. Death is again a theme, but it plays a much more peripheral role. Themes now moving to the foreground include the individual and history, power, rivalry and cooperation, and the question of the responsibility of a new elite.

After about three months of working on the novel, which was planned to cover a long period of time, Bonhoeffer reported in mid-November 1943 in his first letter from prison to Eberhard Bethge:

209 I began to write the history of a middle-class family of our time. . . . It tells of two families on terms of friendship. Their children grow up and, as they gradually enter into the responsibilities of official positions in a small town, they try to work together to build up the community as mayor, teacher, pastor, doctor, engineer.[16]

The novel fragment that Bonhoeffer left us contains nothing of what is alluded to here, except the two families and their children.

[12.] See above, pages 54–57. In "After Ten Years," a text written in 1942–43, the fourth year of the war, Bonhoeffer had said: "We are surprised how calmly we receive the news of the death of people our own age" (*LPP* 16 [trans. altered]).

[13.] See above, page 62.

[14.] See above, page 61, editorial note 33. Bonhoeffer's experiences of the first few weeks of prison may have informed this writing. In a letter of May 15, 1943, he speaks of "existential threat" or *Anfechtung* (*LPP* 39 [trans. altered]); on November 18, 1943, he writes to Bethge that the "'*accidie, tristitia*' (depression, melancholy) with its menacing consequences" had often put him to the test (*LPP* 129). Cf. *Ethics* 170 [*DBW* 6:199]: "temptation to [commit] suicide." *NL* A 86, 2, pertaining to the study on the feeling of time, contains the sentence: "Suicide, not out of guilt, but because I'm basically already dead, full stop, finish."

[15.] See above, page 70.

[16.] Letter of November 18, 1943 (*LPP* 128–30 [trans. altered]). There was very little contact with people from the fields of economics and finance in the Bonhoeffer home.

The basic mood in the novel is more relaxed than that of the drama. Bonhoeffer's situation seemed more hopeful. Would he be released and be able to marry his fiancée, Maria von Wedemeyer? He thought a lot about the connection between his family and hers. In his descriptions he reproduced characteristics of his family home and the people with whom he had grown up, what was done or not done, what was approved or disapproved. This family, to whom he gives the name Brake, is joined in the narrative by the von Bremer family, who represent the von Wedemeyers. There is a basic kinship between the von Bremers' lifestyle and that of the Brakes.[17]

The opening chapter comprising the novel fragment is entitled "Sunday." Like the drama it begins with the grandmother, who in this case is returning from church. Her teenage grandchildren are hiking to a forest lake for a picnic. The forester's assistant "Yellowboots" appears there and brutally attempts to remove them. During this scene the von Bremer family, who own the land in this area, arrives at the lake. Major von Bremer reprimands the forester's assistant, then discovers that the young people are the children of his childhood friend. He invites them to walk back with him and his family to their house.

The von Bremer family has recently returned to Germany from South Africa. The oldest son, Harald, had become a victim of the kind of people typified by "Yellowboots"; no further detail is given of the circumstances of Harald's death. During the walk to the von Bremers' home, Christoph and Renate von Bremer become attracted to one another. Back at the house, as they drink tea on the patio, Herr von Bremer tells the guests about how he first came to know Hans Brake, the father of the visiting children, how they became rivals, and then finally friends. In response to the conclusions the major draws from these events, Christoph offers his frank opinions. His statements—for reasons that are not clear to the Brakes—elicit a strong but unspoken negative reaction from Renate. It is connected to the death of the oldest von Bremer son. The novel fragment ends as Herr von Bremer presents the young men with his son's diary. Frau von Bremer, meanwhile, has

210

[17.] There is no class division separating the two families. In Bonhoeffer's perspective, the nobility is included with the middle class, as was largely the case in the educated German middle class. There were numerous aristocrats among the Bonhoeffer relatives. Cf. the "Introduction" to *Fiction from Prison*, 7.

walked through the park to Harald's grave. The church bells announce the arrival of evening: Misericordia, Justitia, Pax—Mercy, Justice, Peace.

Bourgeois Life

Bonhoeffer's intention with his attempts at fiction was "to rehabilitate middle-class life as we know it in our families, specifically from the Christian perspective."[18] The National Socialists set about to defame and repress the middle class, not to mention to corrupt it, and not without success. Bonhoeffer counters this reality in the drama as Christoph asserts, "I come from what people call a good family, that is, from an old, distinguished, educated middle-class family, and I am not one of those people who are ashamed to admit it. On the contrary, I know what quiet strength you find in a good middle-class home."[19]

211 The pervasively oppressive atmosphere of Nazism was especially palpable in prison. Bonhoeffer was quite aware that in this situation some of his descriptions were very emotional. In June 1943 he wrote, "In general, prisoners are no doubt inclined to indulge in exaggerated emotion to make up for the lack of warmth and comfort in their surroundings."[20] Thus the characters Bonhoeffer created in his mind's eye, after the image of his sorely missed loved ones, were drawn too much to perfection,[21] while the forester's assistant, "Yellowboots," appears as the embodiment of the cruel banality of evil.[22]

Bonhoeffer's interest in the middle class has to do with both their personal and private attitudes and their function in public, political-social life. To be sure, he makes occasional negative observations, but he emphasizes the positive. Here we will begin by elaborating on two elements of the personal domain—simplicity and reserve—and then we will proceed to the public domain.

[18.] Letter of November 18, 1943, to Bethge (*LPP* 130 [trans. altered]). The reading "Christian" rather than "Christianity" reflects a revised deciphering of the manuscript; cf. *E* (*DBW* 6) 365 on "das 'Christliche.'"

[19.] See above, page 64.

[20.] Letter of June 24, 1943, *LPP* 71 [trans. altered].

[21.] Cf. the letter of June 4, 1943, regarding Stifter's drawing only likable characters. "The intimate life of his characters—of course, it is very old-fashioned of him to describe only likable people—is very pleasant in this atmosphere here, and makes one think of the things that really matter in life" (*LPP* 50).

[22.] Zerner pointed to Arendt's phrase, "the banality of evil," in her essay in *Fiction from Prison*, 159.

Simplicity

Again and again Bonhoeffer emphasizes simplicity. At the beginning of the novel, in describing the Brake's home, he points to the functional and unconventional furnishings, the pictures of the grandfathers who would not have their portraits painted wearing official robes and medals, and their refusing the "privilege of the aristocracy and film stars, to call their children Mautz and Koko and Pippy."[23] For the Brake children it was "as if part of their pride as members of the middle class was that they did not go along with such extravagances."[24] Even the name Ekkehard "seemed 'affected' and 'too melodramatic' for them,"[25] not sufficiently simple.

In the letters written from prison, too, it becomes clear that Bonhoeffer considers simplicity an essential attribute of middle-class life. In February 1944 he characterizes Adalbert Stifter, who became especially important to him in prison, as follows: "Stifter is . . . simple (just as 'middle-class' life is simple). . . . You can train and teach people 'simplicity'—indeed, it is one of the essential goals of training [Erziehung] and education [Bildung]."[26]   212

Simplicity is by no means oversimplification or primitiveness. Quite the contrary: "Simplicity is an intellectual [geistig] achievement, one of the greatest."[27] Bonhoeffer was taught this at home. "I've found it one of the strongest elements of our intellectual training at home that we were given so many obstacles to overcome (having to do with relevance, clarity, naturalness, tact, simplicity, etc.), before we could come to the point of formulating our own statements."[28] The novel speaks of Christoph's "unusual skill with words and his preference for clarity and simplicity of expression."[29]

Bonhoeffer sees "his" mountains—those of moderate elevation in central Germany, the "Mittelgebirge"—as a kind of landmark of middle-class life. "Childhood impressions" such as vacation in Friedrichsbrunn in the Harz Mountains obviously have what he calls a

---

[23.] See above, pages 89f., 86, 84.
[24.] From a deleted passage; see above, page 84, editorial note 53.
[25.] See above, page 84.
[26.] Letter of February 12, 1944 (*LPP* 212) [trans. altered].
[27.] Letter of August 1, 1944 (*LPP* 384–85).
[28.] Letter of August 14, 1944 (*LPP* 386–87).
[29.] See above, page 171.

formative effect on the whole personality, so that it would appear nearly impossible and contradictory to my nature for us to have had a house, say, in the Alps or even on the ocean. The hills of central Germany are the nature that is part of myself . . . or rather the nature that formed part of me. . . . So perhaps "my" *Mittelgebirge* are "bourgeois" in the sense of what is natural, not exalted, modest, and self-sufficient (?), non-ideological, satisfied with concrete realities, and above all "not-given-to-self-advertisement."[30]

213

Reserve [Schweigen]

The notion of "not-given-to-self-advertisement" brings us to the second point about the personal domain: reserve and keeping silent in certain situations and, above all, about things that affect one most deeply. In these fragments reserve as a quality of educated people is characteristic of both bourgeois and aristocratic circles. The Brake family rules provided that "one didn't talk about such personal things, but dealt with them on one's own."[31] Renate von Bremer "considered any sort of demonstration of one's inner feelings reprehensible and already practiced the utmost self-control."[32] In the drama we read: "Openness is something wonderful, but being open for the other, even for the other's silence, is more important." "There are things that sometimes one must keep silent about for a while before one can talk about them, even between friends, even between husband and wife. One must give the other time." The secret that some special people carry within themselves "shines through their every word, every glance. But if you tried to put it into words, the best part of it would be destroyed."[33]

In a 1942 *Ethics* manuscript Bonhoeffer had quoted Nietzsche's dictum, "Every profound mind [Geist] requires a mask," explaining that it could be "felt to be a violation of the sense of shame to express in words what one feels in relation to another, for in doing so the self would be revealed and laid bare before itself. Nor will the most profound and intimate joy or grief allow itself to be disclosed in words."[34] Bonhoeffer

---

[30.] Letter of February 12, 1944 (*LPP* 211–12 [trans. altered]).

[31.] See above, page 83.

[32.] See above, page 139.

[33.] See above, pages 48f. Also see below, "Drama Working Notes," page 237, *NL* A 86, 10.

[34.] *E* 26 and 27 [trans. altered]. The Nietzsche quote is from Jaspers, *Nietzsche,* 406.

does not see this mask as a disguise intended to deceive the other, but as something necessary to being human. When fellow prisoners in Tegel talked uninhibitedly about their immense fear during the bombings of November 1943, Bonhoeffer wrote, "I don't quite know what to make of it, for after all, fear is actually something people are ashamed of. I have the feeling that it shouldn't be talked about except in making one's confession. Otherwise it can so easily involve a certain lack of shame."[35] A week later he wrote about the same phenomenon, "God himself made clothes for Adam and Eve. . . . Exposure is cynical, and although cynics pride themselves on their exceptional honesty, or their fanatical desire for truth, they miss the crucial fact that since the fall into sin, human beings must cloak and conceal things."[36] Similarly, Bonhoeffer has Christoph in the drama say that "people don't exist to look into the abyss of each other's hearts—nor can they"; and in the novel he says, "There must be some good reason why, by our very nature, the inner life of other people is inaccessible to us, and why no one can look into ours. . . . So we are obviously meant to keep it to ourselves and not share it with anyone."[37]

   214

In the drama everyone tries to cope with the burden of knowing about Christoph's terminal illness without speaking about it. "I have to get through this by myself," says Christoph.[38] If one succeeds in keeping silence, this can help others. Bonhoeffer himself experienced this in prison amidst the threat of an ominous outcome in his own case. In November 1943 he wrote his parents after he had been permitted a visit by his sister Ursula Schleicher:

> Ursel's visit this morning was a great delight. I'm most grateful to her for it. It's always so comforting to find all of you so calm and cheerful despite all the obnoxious things you have to deal with because of my imprisonment. You, dear Mama, wrote recently that you were proud of your children for behaving "decently" in horrendous situations like this. In fact, we've learned that from you two. . . .[39]

[35.] Letter of November 27, 1943 (*LPP* 146 [trans. altered]).

[36.] Letter of December 5, 1943 (*LPP* 158 [trans. altered]). The passage continues: "For me, the great thing about Stifter is that he . . . contemplates people only very cautiously, from the outside so to speak, not from the inside." Cf. *CF* (*DBWE* 3) 139f. on Gen. 3:21.

[37.] See above, pages 65f. and 128.

[38.] See above, page 46.

[39.] Letter of November 17, 1943 (*LPP* 127) [trans. altered].

Without this attitude it would have been impossible to participate in the conspiracy.

215　　At the same time Bonhoeffer also questions the attitude of reserve and self-control. In the drama, when Christoph has become an enigma to others because of his silence and he stands utterly alone, saying, "and now . . . I feel like a madman. That's what I get for wanting to lord it over people without being cut out for the job. Theatrical heroics!"[40] Bonhoeffer writes of himself in December 1943, "I often wonder who I really am—the man who squirms and squirms over these ghastly things here and breaks down bawling miserably, or the man who lashes himself with the whip and pretends to others (and even to himself) that he's calm, cheerful, composed, and in control, and expects to be admired for it (that is, for this theatrical accomplishment—or isn't it theatrical?). What is self-control [Haltung], anyway?"[41]

Bonhoeffer could not bear to see words used which had become banal and hollow from fraudulent misuse. Thus Christoph's notes in the drama read:

> I speak to you to protect from abuse the great words that have been given to humanity. . . . What well-meaning person today can still utter the besmirched words "freedom," "brotherhood," or even the word "Germany"? . . . Let us honor the highest values by silence for a while. Let us learn to do right without words for a while.[42]

Similarly, we read in Bonhoeffer's baptismal letter from Tegel about the utterances of the church, which had failed in the face of National Socialism: "Our earlier words are therefore bound to lose their force and fall into oblivion, and our life as Christians today will consist of only two things: prayer and righteous action among people."[43] Bonhoeffer had realized even before 1933 that "qualified reticence could be more appropriate for the church today than a kind of speech that is possibly very unqualified."[44]

[40.] See above, page 46.

[41.] Letter of December 15, 1943 (*LPP* 162 [trans. altered]). Bonhoeffer expressed these ideas in the poem "Who Am I?" which was written in the summer of 1944 (*LPP* 347–48).

[42.] See above, page 50.

[43.] "Thoughts on the Day of the Baptism of Dietrich Wilhelm Rüdiger Bethge," May 1944 (*LPP* 300 [trans. altered]).

[44.] July 1932 (*DBW* 11:330 [*GS* 1:143]).

Bonhoeffer also did not want to offer answers where there were in 216 reality no answers. In the beginning of 1944, after one of the heavy bomb attacks on Berlin, he wrote:

> Those who had been bombed out here came to me in the morning looking for a bit of comfort. . . . I can listen all right, but I can hardly ever find anything to say. But perhaps the way one asks about certain things and not about others helps to suggest what really matters.[45]

This is reminiscent of Dietrich's father, about whom his former assistant, Professor Jürg Zutt, said: "There was no one from whom one could better learn that silence, too, is an important form of speech."[46]

In the following sections, we will elaborate on bourgeois attitudes and values in social and public life that interested Bonhoeffer.

The Middle Class and the "Little Guy"

Decent people who did not let themselves be duped by the National Socialist rulers and who were also willing to take risks to help those being persecuted were represented in all social classes. The same was true of opportunists who sacrificed their conscience to the Hitler regime. Too few tried to stand fast. There were corrupt people in the upper class, and there were those in the lower class who looked to the corrupt upper class for their formulas for success.[47] The well-intentioned hoped that after Hitler the decent people would comprise the new upper class. Even before his imprisonment Bonhoeffer wrote in his essay, "After Ten Years: A Reckoning Made at New Year 1943": "We are witnessing . . . the birth of a new nobility of attitude which is connecting people from all former social classes."[48] In the 1944 baptismal letter from Tegel he explains that "the sensitivity for quality [Qualitätsgefühl] in all ranks of society with regard to the human values of justice, achievement, and courage could create a new elite of people who will be allowed the right 217 to provide strong leadership."[49]

It becomes especially clear in the conversation in the drama between Christoph and Heinrich that difference of social class can be something

---

[45.] February 1, 1944 (*LPP* 203 [trans. altered]).
[46.] *DB-ER* 564.
[47.] Cf. page 103.
[48.] *LPP* 12–13 [trans. altered].
[49.] *LPP* 299.

very divisive. Christoph approaches Heinrich with carefree self-confidence. Heinrich, however, makes it clear to Christoph that such candor is much more difficult for him, coming as he does from the proletariat. "But that's precisely our plight, that we can't afford to trust. Our experiences are too bitter."[50] "People like you have a foundation, you have ground under your feet, you have a place in the world. . . . If you want to live, you need ground under your feet—and we don't have this ground."[51]

The theme of social difference is articulated in the novel in the conversation between Little Brother and his friend Erich. Erich, the son of a railway worker, only has meat once a week at home, when his father "happens to have his day off." Because of his job, the father often has to work on Sundays and even on Christmas. Little Brother asks whether Erich's family is poor. Erich asks whether Little Brother's family is rich. Neither knows how to answer, but they sense the disconcerting difference between them.[52]

After the Brake children have been harassed by the forester's assistant "Yellowboots," Franz, the oldest brother, complains heatedly that "if we really were poor kids from town who just wanted to get outdoors on Sunday—and then, pardon me, a scoundrel like that showed up and vented his foolish arrogance and his brutality on us, then we would simply have to take it."[53] Bonhoeffer became painfully aware, precisely because he was in prison, how different were the situations of those who were privileged and those who were not. In his report about the way warders treated the prisoners, he wrote: "Private means, cigarettes, promises for later on, play a significant role. The 'little guy' with no connections, etc., has to submit to everything."[54]

Petty Tyrants

Bonhoeffer put great emphasis on an observation he had made under National Socialism: It was above all the petty tyrants who caused great

---

[50.] See above, page 66. In the 1941 *Ethics* manuscript "Inheritance and Decay," Bonhoeffer called "confidence" the "basis of historical life" (*E* 108). See also the letter of July 8, 1944: "In my contacts with the 'outcasts' of society, its 'pariahs,' I've noticed repeatedly that suspicion is the definitive factor in their judgment of other people. . . . By the way, these 'outcasts' are found in all classes of society" (*LPP* 345 [trans. altered]).

[51.] See above, pages 68f.

[52.] See above, pages 91–93

[53.] See above, page 117.

[54.] "Report on Prison Life after One Year in Tegel" (*LPP* 250 [trans. altered]).

evil. It wasn't one "great evil," but the mean, base evil that was ever-present to tyrannize people—and not only in prison, though there it was unconcealed. In his prison report of April 1944 he wrote:

> The tone is set by those warders who address the prisoners in the most evil and brutal way. The whole building resounds with vile and insulting abuse, so that the quieter and more fair-minded warders, too, are nauseated by it, but they can hardly exercise any influence.[55]

He sounded less matter-of-fact in a letter of late 1943: "It makes me furious to see quite defenseless people being unjustly shouted at and insulted. These petty tormentors of people who let off steam by yelling at others, and who are simply everywhere, can still upset me for hours on end."[56]

Bonhoeffer presumably wrote his short story about Lance Corporal Berg about the same time as the prison report. Berg has been ordered back from the front to serve as a prison guard after suffering a disfiguring injury. He sincerely cares about the prisoners' welfare. This infuriates the other guards who are set in their ways; they feel that their abuse of power is being hemmed in, so they immediately arrange for Berg to be transferred again.[57]

The way those who set the tone in the prison interact with Berg, the injured war veteran, corresponds to the insults reported to have been hurled at a wounded veteran on crutches in the drama.[58] In the novel, the vocabulary of "Yellowboots"—"louts," and so forth—resembles the "vile and insulting abuse" that Bonhoeffer mentions in the prison report.[59] In writing it as a scene from a novel, Bonhoeffer could both get the detested cascades of insults off his chest and articulate his rage about such behavior. He did so directly in the voice of Franz, and indirectly—as he himself did occasionally with the warders in Tegel Prison—with Christoph's "icy calm" and "frightening determination."[60]

During the time of National Socialism especially, the petty tyrants could assert themselves to the full. They exercised their power as regional group leaders [Ortsgruppenleiter], block wardens of the

219

[55.] *LPP* 249 [trans. altered].

[56.] Smuggled letter, November 22, 1943 (*LPP* 136 [trans. altered]).

[57.] See above, pages 184, 187–93.

[58.] See above, page 31.

[59.] See above, page 109; see *LPP* 249.

[60.] See above, page 110.

National Socialist Party, or even, if they had no official authority, by denouncing others or threatening to do so. Whenever opportunity presented itself they did even worse things. Thus developed the terrible climate of constant spying and anxious indecision about taking action when it became necessary. "It is the petty tyrants who destroy a nation from the inside," says Major von Bremer in the novel.[61] "You have to be stronger than these tormentors. . . . One must fight them, battle them without sympathy, relentlessly."[62] In a deleted passage the major explains that "my oldest son Harald became the victim of such a petty tyrant two years ago. He was nineteen years old."[63]

Under Hitler's regime people were surprised at the downright respectability of rabid Nazis. This quality, too, Bonhoeffer includes in the figure of "Yellowboots." "Look at this petty forester's assistant, a likable, harmless, good-natured fellow among his own people. Perhaps he'll be a good, loyal, ordinary family man someday. But when his ridiculous little bit of power tickles his fancy he's a devil, and with his employers he's a fawning wretch."[64]

220

The danger of power being abused "especially by powerless people [kleine Leute]" Bonhoeffer compares with the danger of bacteria despite their minute size. He has the major say:

> Again and again history has produced great tyrants. They in turn have called forth great counterforces and have almost never escaped judgment. . . . But the petty tyrants never die out. They depend on the favor of their masters of the moment, and bask in it, escaping all earthly judgment.[65]

The author has him impress upon his listeners his warning that "there is in all of us a dark, dangerous drive to abuse the power that is given to us. . . . Wherever we encounter this truly evil instinct—first of all in ourselves—we must counter it with the force of all the hate and passion we can muster."[66]

[61.] See above, page 120.
[62.] See above, page 117.
[63.] See above, page 122, editorial note 161.
[64.] See above, page 120.
[65.] See above, page 120; cf. pages 121f.
[66.] See above, page 120.

Power

A significant portion of the novel consists of the story Major von Bremer tells about the beginning of his teenage friendship with Hans Brake, the father of the visiting children to whom he tells it. Hans Brake was the best student in his class and the best athlete in his school, the "undisputed and absolute authority [Herr], but at the same time the idolized favorite of his classmates."[67] Harald von Bremer, who, as the son of a wealthy landowner, was accustomed to being first in everything, joined the class as a new student and performed no worse than Hans. He was rejected by his fellow students, who immediately sensed that he threatened their idol's status. Hans and Harald were consistently fair toward one another. Yet intrigues plotted by others led to complications. A plot to inflict a serious injury on Harald during a day of athletic competition was deliberately diverted by Hans, who took the injury upon himself. This escalation of ill will not only resulted in Hans and Harald becoming friends, but also cleared the air in the whole class. "The talents and personalities of our classmates could develop. Whereas before there had only been blind allegiance, now strong and healthy camaraderie began to grow."[68]

The excesses of the leader-cult [Führerkult] of Nazi Germany are easily recognized in Bonhoeffer's description of the climate among the class whose allegiance was sworn to their idol Hans—their fawning behavior, their suspicions, their slander, and ultimately their criminal attempt to eliminate their opponent.[69] One is prompted to think of the words of Bonhoeffer's essay, "After Ten Years,"

> that any violent display of power . . . produces an outburst of stupidity among a large segment of the population. It's not that certain human capacities, intellectual capacities, for instance, suddenly become stunted or destroyed, but rather that under the overwhelming influence of the display of power, people are robbed of their independent judgment.[70]

In this vein Harald von Bremer had observed as a newcomer to the class "that the other pupils [besides Hans] performed especially poorly

221

[67.] See above, page 147.

[68.] See above, page 168.

[69.] See above, page 147, describing Hans as the "the school idol."

[70.] *LPP* 8–9 [trans. altered]. See above, page 120, editorial note 50.

whenever independence was required in thought and judgment."[71] Paul, older than the other boys and an outsider, had said of his class-mates at the time, "They're going to spoil Hans yet. . . . They're all just aping him. . . . It's not good for the class either, by the way. Nobody can grow there." Of Paul it is said that he "learned slowly and with diffi-culty," but was "able to think for himself."[72]

For Harald von Bremer, the friendship with Hans Brake that had de-veloped after the terrible incident at the school games had broken a spell. Before that, the only thing each of them had was his sole authority over his own group. The dream of unlimited power

222

> had made us blind to one another. To be sure, we . . . even felt a certain attraction, and certainly we respected each other. And yet neither of us could stand the other's presence. . . . To put it in fancy words, you would say it was a pure power struggle. . . . When we woke up from our dream, we understood that no one is alone in the world, but that people must live side by side with others and get along with them—and that human beings are fortunate that this is so. . . . You must learn to yield without sacrificing your character.[73]

Thinking of this experience from his high school years, the major emphasizes that "getting along with others without smashing in one another's skulls" will never be possible without both sides giving up something, and especially not without mutual respect for the other's dig-nity.[74] "For me the main issue for individuals and for peoples [Völker] is whether or not they have learned to live with other human beings and peoples. That's more important to me than all their ideas, thoughts, and convictions."[75]

This ran counter to National Socialist principles. They wanted men "as hard as Krupp steel," and rejected compromises just as thoroughly as they rejected the idea of respecting the other. They fought for ideas which meant "more than death" to them, as symbolized in their flag.[76]

[71.] See above, page 147.
[72.] See above, page 149.
[73.] See above, page 159.
[74.] See above, page 160.
[75.] See above, page 167.
[76.] Cf. the final rhymed couplet in the youth hymn written by Schirach in 1933: "For-ward! Forward! . . . Our flag is the new times, and the flag will lead us into eternity. Hooray, the flag is more than death!" ("Die Fahne der Verfolgten," as cited from *Uns geht die Sonne nicht unter: Lieder der Hitler-Jugend,* a Hitler Youth songbook published in 1934).

Christoph rebels against the major's thesis that getting along with one another is the main issue.

> But what if there are already forces at work that make any living together with others or getting along together impossible, whose very intent is to make it impossible? What if someone announces a struggle against us in which there is to be no agreement, but only victory or defeat? . . . Then it's about the very meaning of life; it's about ultimate convictions, values, and standards. . . . And we—we should be the people who go to the front of the line and take the lead in this confrontation. We know what we have to defend and what we want. And because most people are cowards and slow to move, there must be masters and servants, or—rather, I am even tempted to say—"slaves."[77]

223

There are plenty of objections to Christoph's argument, but there is also agreement, along with the admonition "not to make a virtue of necessity."[78] Nevertheless, the major's argument is still valid. The fundamental distinction being made here is between what the major describes as a predictable order of life that *always* applies, and Christoph's necessary resolve to act *now*, in an extraordinary situation.[79]

The conversation between the major and Christoph highlights the inner tension experienced by those who conspired to overthrow Hitler. In "After Ten Years" Bonhoeffer had already written, on the one hand, "The only fruitful way to relate to other people—especially weaker people—is with love, and that implies the will to share common ground with them." On the other hand we read in the same essay, "Today it is Christianity that must passionately advocate a wholesome reserve between people and respect for their distinctive qualities as human beings." Faced with the stranglehold of National Socialism's totalizing claims, "It is precisely we Christians who must be willing to risk being misunderstood as acting in our own interest; we must risk the facile accusation that our attitude is anti-social."[80]

In 1940 Bonhoeffer had already warned against the oversimplification of an either-or: "People who are willing to sacrifice an unproductive principle to the more productive compromise, or a less productive

---

[77.] See above, pages 172f.
[78.] See above, page 176.
[79.] Cf. *E* 236: "extraordinary necessity," and yet "validity of the law."
[80.] *LPP* 10, 12 [trans. altered].

insight of moderation to a productive radicalism, should be careful not to let the very freedom they possess bring them to their ruin."[81]

At the end of the novel, Christoph, with all his righteous zeal, nevertheless appears the loser, especially in relation to Renate, who turns away from him after his radical statement. The reactions of others to his extreme view make him aware that it is easily misunderstood and open to challenge, despite the fact that "by what he said, he had given his very best."[82]

The major recognizes the pressure Christoph's generation faces to take radical action:

> Events cast their shadows ahead; before a harsh winter, wild animals grow thicker fur and the beaver puts on a thicker layer of fat. What kind of times and what sort of tasks can lie ahead for a generation that must think so harshly, even at such a young age, in order to survive? It's enough to make you shudder. . . . Christoph, much of what you've said about our times and our tasks is true. . . .[83]

Bonhoeffer includes both values—the willingness to compromise and the willingness to engage in resistance—in his notion of "the middle class as we know it in our families."[84] Forces were at work in National Socialism which "make any living together with others or getting along together impossible."[85] Unyielding resistance had become necessary because terrible crimes were going unpunished. Indeed, they were ordered and committed by the government itself.

[81.] *E* 69 [trans. altered]. This passage is incorporated into the essay "After Ten Years" with slight changes in wording (*LPP* 5).

[82.] See above, page 176.

[83.] See above, pages 174f., 176. One must have power to engage in active resistance, and because of the necessity of using power, resistance includes the risk of abusing power. Also see above, page 120: Every human being is tempted to abuse power.

[84.] Letter of November 18, 1943 (*LPP* 130). In his book *Grond onder de Voeten*, 33, a study of bourgeois values in Dietrich Bonhoeffer's works, de Lange considers whether Bonhoeffer began to doubt the value of the political conspiracy which some middle-class Germans, after far too much soul-searching, finally decided to join. He finds that it is "no longer clear to Christoph whether the case he makes for the sacrifice by the middle-class 'elite' is consistent with loving life as it really is." In de Lange's view, the conclusion of the novel contradicts the drama fragment in this respect: "Instead of the notion of 'above' [oben], here we see the notion of 'side by side.' Here we see not resistance at any cost, but rather the willingness to compromise. The 'I' is 'formed' not without the other and detached from the other, but together with and thanks to the other" (ibid.).

[85.] See above, page 172.

Responsibility

In Christoph's conversation with the major, the arguments of both are based on a conscious sense of responsibility. The major is thinking about the conditions for sustainable life in human community. Christoph, by contrast, is thinking about what must be freely wagered in the face of extreme necessity. In everyday life at school, too, Christoph had "a strong and healthy confidence in his ability to help others and take responsibility for them."[86] The result of his acting "out of the need . . . at the core of his being" for taking responsibility was that he "had the reputation among some of his schoolmates of being proud and domineering [herrisch]. Others, however, trusted him completely. . . ." Striving to take on responsibility appears in an ambivalent light; while it is essential to muster the courage and strength to act, one also risks being judged as "domineering."

As the major describes the school in his story, the students and teachers at first allow Hans Brake to take responsibility for the class. This is an unhealthy situation, because the other students do not recognize or assume any responsibility of their own, and so they do not learn how to do so. In a 1942 *Ethics* manuscript Bonhoeffer had explained that part of

> the limitedness of responsible life and action is that it assumes those whom one encounters are responsible as well. This is precisely the difference between responsible behavior and violent exploitation [Vergewaltigung] of others. Responsibility recognizes others as responsible agents and also encourages them to become aware of their own responsibility.[87]

In any given situation, the responsible people must decide what particular action or behavior is called for, according to their best information and as conscience dictates, without any assurance that it will be the right decision. If in doing so one brings sacrifices and suffering upon oneself and others, it is especially hard to take responsibility for freely choosing such a path. In "After Ten Years" Bonhoeffer writes: "It is infinitely easier to suffer in obedience to a human command than in the freedom of one's own responsible act." It is also "much easier to pursue a cause through to the end based upon principles than based upon

---

[86.] See above, page 127, for this and the two following quotations.
[87.] *E* 231 [trans. altered].

225

concrete, responsible decision."[88] In the baptismal letter he wrote from Tegel, Bonhoeffer recalls:

226

> We lived too much in the realm of abstraction and thought it was possible, by thinking through every possible outcome beforehand, to be so sure of the chosen course that action would follow quite automatically. We did not learn until it was too late that what engenders action is not abstract thought, but the willingness to assume responsibility.

In view of the child being baptized, who will grow up knowing that responsible action implies dealing with the "enemy," Bonhoeffer cites Old Testament passages with a martial tone: "Is it not so that human beings must always struggle on earth?" "Praise the Lord, my refuge, who trains my hands for combat, and my fists for battle."[89]

The baptismal letter demonstrates clearly how closely Bonhoeffer associated responsibility with the middle class.

> The urban culture embodied in the home of your mother's parents stems from a long-standing tradition of bourgeois values. The bearers of this tradition have been given a conscious pride in being called to assume great responsibility in public service, intellectual achievement, and leadership. They also have been given a deep-rooted sense of duty to nurture a great historical heritage and cultural tradition. This will give you, even before you can grasp it, a way of thinking and acting which you can never lose without betraying yourself.[90]

In 1943–44, when, on the advice of friends inside the Nazi legal system who were not Nazis themselves, the Bonhoeffer family sought a way to have Bonhoeffer's trial postponed so that it would come to naught—for they knew of cases in which even an acquittal could result in transfer to a concentration camp—Bonhoeffer wrote with both impatience and self-criticism: "I wonder whether excessive brooding about things . . . isn't a negative corollary to the bourgeois life? . . ."[91]

On the one hand, he saw that the long-standing consciousness of the middle class of being called to assume responsibility in public service was still alive and well. On the other hand, he recognized their fateful lack of willingness to risk free responsible action without safeguards in

---

[88.] *LPP* 7, 14 [trans. altered].
[89.] *LPP* 298 [trans. altered].
[90.] *LPP* 294–95 [trans. altered].
[91.] Letter of February 21, 1944 (*LPP* 217) [trans. altered].

confusing and threatening circumstances. To be sure, other social classes shared this fault, but Bonhoeffer saw it as a specific failure of the middle class. In July 1944, Bonhoeffer reckoned the middle class's "aversion to free responsibility" among their "sins of strength [starke Sünden]."[92] He had written of the "man of duty" that "in this confinement within the limits of duty there can never come the bold stroke of the deed which is done on one's own free responsibility, the only kind of deed which can strike at the heart of evil and overcome it."[93]

227

Authority

Soon after Hitler's "seizure of power" on January 30, 1933, Bonhoeffer stated in his lecture "The Führer and the Individual in the Younger Generation," "True leaders . . . must lead their followers away from the authority of their person . . . into personal responsibility for the orders of life [Ordnungen des Lebens]."[94] Bonhoeffer's standard of genuine authority was his own father.[95]

Christoph's father does not play a dominant role in the drama or the novel. In the novel fragment the father's friend, the major, is an authority in the sense that, without being authoritarian, he challenges his listeners to test all points of view. Nevertheless it does sound like an authoritative command when he demands that the forester's assistant, "Yellowboots," apologize to the young Brakes. Kruse replies, "That's impossible, it goes against my honor!" causing the major to burst out, "What kind of honor is it that is too proud to admit an injustice and make amends? . . . Listen to reason, Kruse, and do what you must do as a man of honor." But Kruse retorts, "I cannot sacrifice my concept of honor," and takes his leave.[96]

[92.] Letter of July 8, 1944 (*LPP* 345) [trans. altered].

[93.] *E* 68–69. This was written in 1940 and taken over almost word for word in "After Ten Years" at Christmas-New Year 1942–43 (*LPP* 5).

[94.] *No Rusty Swords*, 202 [trans. altered].

[95.] Schollmeyer writes that Bonhoeffer was raised in the "critical, liberal school of thought rooted in the natural sciences," and thus "trained to test every dogmatic authority" (*Bonhoeffers Theologie*, 149). Schollmeyer summarizes by saying that "Bonhoeffer speaks the intellectual language of his father. It is the language of an authority that insists that all authority be *put to the test* in order that it might itself become genuine authority" (152).

[96.] See above, page 113.

228   The different conceptions of honor in the major and "Yellowboots" illustrate the world of difference between pseudo-authority which can never admit to a mistake, and genuine authority, which can question itself. The major says, "[W]hen people exploit the power they have been given over others to humiliate, debase, defile, and destroy them . . . it's an outrage, as much against the people concerned as against the office one holds. It desecrates all genuine authority. . . ."[97]

    In the following we will address four more themes from the Tegel literary fragments: Bonhoeffer's perspective on women at the time, his ideas about friendship, his quest for a nonreligious Christianity and, finally, his probing attempt to come to terms with death.

Women

Women had a significant function in Dietrich Bonhoeffer's family. They played no less important a role in discussions at home than the men. Although Paula Bonhoeffer, née von Hase, was certified to become a teacher in a girl's high school, which was still unusual in her circles, she was later so busy with her large family that this qualification became quite unimportant to her. For her daughters, too, it did not seem important to her that they complete vocational training, although they all began a training program. But they married so early—at twenty or twenty-one—that they never got around to finishing. At that time it was not common practice for women to continue pursuing career goals after marriage. Family life was ruled primarily by the mother.[98] Important

229 decisions regarding family matters were unthinkable without her. Outside the family, too, she knew how to assert her influence with energy and intelligence, for example when it came to helping victims of persecution. Grandmother Julie Bonhoeffer enjoyed great respect in the family for her uncompromising clearheadedness.

[97.] See above, page 119.

[98.] This was duly documented in an amusing "Constitution" of the Bonhoeffer household written in 1926 (see *Fiction from Prison*, 131ff.): "*Preamble: The Constitution is Patriarchal.* . . . Owner: Privy Councillor [Karl] Bonhoeffer [Professor of Medicine]. Sole Business Manager: Frau Paula Bonhoeffer. . . . The Sole Business Manager will decide by herself on medical problems. The male descendants of the Owner receive half a vote after they have passed the age of thirty [none of the Bonhoeffer children was thirty in 1926]. . . . The female descendants are expected, before completion of their twenty-first year, to find an opportunity to found a branch company."

During his university studies Bonhoeffer met a number of fellow students, women on whom he often made a great impression. He formed a close friendship with a woman student who was a distant cousin of his; this ended in 1936. For a long time he thought he would have to forego marriage in order to devote all his energy to the urgent problems facing the church and the state.[99] Only much later did he find in Maria von Wedemeyer the girl he wanted to marry. The women he has appear in his literary fragments represent only a limited selection of the reality he had experienced.

The drama and the novel are both introduced by the grandmother. She is the only woman who emerges as an essential character with a critical mind. In the drama she tells the young grandson a mysterious fairy tale which leads them into a conversation about God and death. At the beginning of the novel she is pensively critical as she reflects on the Sunday sermon. As her neighbor indulges in foolish clichés praising the preacher, the grandmother barely manages to keep her irritation to herself. Later in the novel other characters refer to the grandmother. Ulrich asks, "And your grandmother, Christoph? She certainly takes Christianity seriously and understands it better than most pastors."[100] Klara's description of her daily routine also revolves to a great extent around the grandmother.[101]

By contrast, the mother in the drama remains somewhat in the background, though she shows exemplary behavior when she learns of Christoph's impending death. Rather than complaining, she only wants to make sure that the time he has left to live will be "one year of indescribable happiness" for him and the family.[102] She is cautious in her disapproving response to Christoph's thesis that "the rabble only know how to live, but the noble also know how to die."[103] The mother appears in the novel only indirectly. 230

Christoph does not have a sister in the drama,[104] and in the novel he has only one, Klara.[105] In the novel the Brake family has four brothers,

---

[99.] Letter of May 29, 1944 (*LL* 246).

[100.] See above, page 107.

[101.] See above, pages 134–36.

[102.] See above, page 33.

[103.] See above, page 36.

[104.] A sister is mentioned in the "Drama Working Notes" (see below, page 240, *NL* A 70, 4[2]). Also see above, page 32: "Little Annie died."

[105.] The beginning of the novel alludes to a recently married sister (see above, page 85).

including Christoph, like Bonhoeffer's own family. But Bonhoeffer had four sisters as well. They were domestically inclined and close to their family, as was the custom in those days. At the same time, they possessed vitality and absolutely uncompromising judgment, and two of the four enjoyed fighting. In the prison fiction there are no female characters in Christoph's generation who behave aggressively.[106]

Christoph's girlfriend Renate in the drama is an unselfish woman. She understands Christoph's situation and tries unobtrusively to make things easier for him. In the novel Renate herself feels oppressed. She is homesick for South Africa and is grieving the death of her brother.[107] Renate von Bremer's English mother in the novel is also described as unselfish. In South Africa she had not spoken a word of English with her children for years in order to assure they had firm roots in German. Her husband "was infinitely grateful to his wife for this sacrifice."[108]

Klara, when asked if she wants to become a musician, replies, "No, I've never thought of it. I have far too little talent for that; and anyway. . . . I'm going to stay home, and someday I'd like to marry and have a family."

> The warmth and simplicity with which Klara said this made it clear that she was not speaking of her personal happiness, but her vocation. . . . She was born to be a mother, one who had experienced the happiness of a good family life from early childhood and now carried it within herself as an inalienable possession.[109]

231   In his attempts at writing literature in prison, Bonhoeffer creates an almost sentimental image of unselfish women with domestic virtues. They are completely fulfilled by their family life, but exist there under the protection of men. They are "women from old families . . . , women who, like their mothers before them, have always known the assuring protection of their fathers, husbands, and brothers, and felt safe in the domain of their family." As a prisoner who is anticipating that he and other men in his family will be murdered, Bonhoeffer knows that the women will continue to be protected, "even when misfortune strikes

---

[106.] In prison, where he needed quiet empathy and nurturing, Bonhoeffer may have resisted thinking of demanding women.

[107.] Bonhoeffer's fiancée, Maria von Wedemeyer, a lively and energetic young woman, had also lost a brother in battle in October 1942, on the eastern front.

[108.] See above, page 138.

[109.] See above, page 137f.

them and leaves them bereft. Like an invisible power that no one dares challenge, the protection that once surrounded them still hovers over their every step, even in their hour of utmost abandonment."[110] He sees women in their relation to men. This is consistent with the view reflected in his wedding sermon from prison: "The place where God has put the wife is the husband's home."[111] In general, the image of women Bonhoeffer creates can be said to reflect what was customary in the church in his generation.

The women in the prison fragments are not dumb. They are also capable of self-criticism. Klara judges her own musical ability as insufficient. The women are more empathetic than the men. Renate in the drama understands Christoph's situation better than his best friend Ulrich. In family life, others look to the women to organize and set the pace. "Stop, first we're going to collect mushrooms for lunch," Klara calls out, and her brothers follow her direction.[112] Frau von Bremer plans the family visit for the next day and all agree with her plan. In the Brake home it was the mother who accomplished the generous and well-appointed furnishing and decorating of the home and planned the garden. This was consistent with the way things were done in the Bonhoeffer family.

The women Bonhoeffer describes remain limited to the domestic   232
horizon. Other gifts or desires they might have do not come into view. Because these writings were never finished, it is scarcely appropriate to draw conclusions from the image of women in the fragments. In prison, Bonhoeffer lived in a world populated by men, and women possibly symbolized for him the ideal, opposite world. The "domestic" women in his family—including his fiancée—who knew when and how they could make a difference, became especially important to him at this time. They obtained for him whatever they possibly could and went on his behalf to the Gestapo officials. They even provided him with a certain feeling of comfort and protection while in prison. Thinking of the households

---

[110.] See above, pages 133f.

[111.] May 1943 (*LPP* 44). In several instances in which Bonhoeffer makes changes to his original fiction draft, it appears that he first spontaneously thinks of the mother, but then changes the references to "father" (see above, page 83, editorial note 50). Bonhoeffer had written at first that Martin's school cap had been wrested away from "his mother," but changed it to "his father." On page 27, editorial note 8, Bonhoeffer changed "you know that you have a good mother" to "that you have good parents."

[112.] See above, page 100.

they were managing, he wrote, "Most people today have forgotten what a home can mean, but it has become clear to the rest of us especially in these times. The home is a realm of its own in the midst of the world, a stronghold in the storm of time, a refuge, even a sacred place."[113]

Friendship

Besides the main character's family and his girlfriend, the drama also features Christoph's best friend and confidant, Ulrich. These two share everything with one another. In the drama, Ulrich explains to Renate, "There's really nothing in this room that doesn't belong as much to me as to Christoph. There are no secrets here."[114] But despite their common interests and unqualified friendship for each other, it takes Ulrich a long time to understand his friend, who is anticipating his own approaching death. Ulrich overlooks Heinrich's allusions to Christoph's compromised health and Christoph's interest in Heinrich, the man bonded with death. Neither can he understand the change in Christoph's behavior toward Renate.[115]

233   In the novel Ulrich and Christoph have a relaxed conversation during their Sunday excursion to the forest pond. The friends "were delighted to discover a consonance between them in all the essential aspects of their lives. . . ."[116] They talk about the origins of sycophancy and showing-off behavior among those classmates who set the tone. This brings them to see the necessity of a responsible elite, which seems to contradict the apostle Paul's "There is no longer slave or free."[117] In the course of this conversation Ulrich introduces the theme of "unconscious Christianity."[118] After this he only plays a secondary role in the action of the novel. Now the brothers Franz and Christoph have a turn to speak. They present Major von Bremer with their burning questions and ideas about the social and political situation. The major, for his part, tells the story of his friendship with the Brake children's father in their school days.

[113.] May 1943 (*LPP* 44) [trans. altered].
[114.] See above, page 49.
[115.] See above, pages 40, 43–45.
[116.] See above, page 100.
[117.] Gal. 3:28; cf. page 107.
[118.] See above, page 106.

The first friendship described in the novel is that between Little Brother, the youngest Brake son, and his neighborhood companion Erich, the son of the railway worker.[119] The two boys play in the garden, observe animals, and make cautious attempts to imagine what each other's lives are like.

In the case of Dietrich Bonhoeffer, there was always a friend in his life. Even when he was a young child his parents saw to it that his cousin Hans Christoph von Hase, who was roughly the same age, was around. Otherwise, the only children surrounding Dietrich who were his age were his sisters—his own twin, the youngest sister who came after them, and the two older sisters. He was considerably younger than his three older brothers, the oldest children in the family. Dietrich's close friendship with Hans Christoph continued well past their university years.[120]

In his university years a close friend was Walter Dreß, who married Dietrich's youngest sister. As Bonhoeffer completed his studies and entered the pastorate and university teaching, his friendship with Franz Hildebrandt was especially important. From the very beginning of the Third Reich, Franz and Dietrich planned strategies in the Church Struggle [Kirchenkampf] and translated them into action. Hildebrandt had to emigrate in 1937 because of the "Aryan Paragraph." As early as the end of 1933 he had wanted to emigrate, and at that time had stayed in Dietrich's parsonage in London. But when Pastor Martin Niemöller called upon Hildebrandt in 1934 to be his assistant in his Dahlem parish, he returned to Germany. The theological discussions between Bonhoeffer and his friend Hildebrandt were passionate and often humorous at the same time. They also enjoyed making music in the homes of Bonhoeffer's brothers and sisters, and Hildebrandt became a beloved "uncle" to Dietrich's nieces and nephews.

Then came Eberhard Bethge who, in April 1935, entered the theological seminary of which Bonhoeffer was the director. The many letters Bonhoeffer wrote to Bethge, which were smuggled out of prison and later published as *Letters and Papers from Prison*,[121] offer tangible evidence of the many dimensions and the intensity of this friendship.

Not until his prison years did Bonhoeffer focus on the subject of

234

[119.] See above, page 92.

[120.] A childhood letter from Dietrich to Hans Christoph, dated July 15, 1918, is reproduced in *DBW* 9:13f.

[121.] See *LPP* (*DBW* 8).

friendship. This began with his descriptions of friendship in the drama and novel fragments. In his letter of December 25, 1943, he mentions that Eberhard Bethge's first visit to him in prison on December 23 "gave [him] the idea for a little piece" he planned to send him. And on January 29, 1944, he writes that "in the last few days I've been working again on the little literary piece I mentioned before. It's about two longtime friends meeting again after a long separation during wartime."[122] After this, illness sapped his creative energy. In July 1944 he confesses that "the novel got stuck, and the little piece I was writing for you didn't quite get done, either. I had such an unproductive time from January to March."[123]

Although friendship, "in contrast to marriage and kinship, has no generally recognized rights," Bonhoeffer held in January 1944 that

235

it must be confidently defended . . . not claiming for it the *necessitas* of a divine decree, but certainly claiming the *necessitas* of freedom! I believe that within the sphere of this freedom friendship is by far the rarest and most priceless good. Where else can you still find friendship in our world, which is defined predominantly by the *first three* mandates? It cannot be compared with the goods of the mandates. It is in a class by itself, *sui generis*, though it belongs with them in the way that the cornflower belongs in the cornfield.[124]

The epitome of Bonhoeffer's thoughts on friendship is the poem "The Friend," which he sent to Eberhard Bethge for his birthday in August 1944: Of the cornflower, he writes, "defenseless, it grows in freedom, . . . / Beside necessities of life, things fashioned from heavy, earthly stuff, / alongside marriage, labor, and sword, / the free also strive / to live and grow and face the sun."[125]

[122.] *LPP* 178 and 199f. [trans. altered].

[123.] July 8, 1944 (*LPP* 346). Cf. February 23, 1944 (*LPP* 222). See below, the "Fragment of a Story," page 236.

[124.] Cf. letter of January 23, 1944, to Renate and Eberhard Bethge (*LPP* 192 and 193 [trans. altered]). The "first three mandates" are marriage, work, and the state. The word *necessitas* here echoes a January 2, 1944, letter from Bethge in Lissa, Poland, which described the difficulties he had encountered obtaining permission to speak to Bonhoeffer in prison: "Friendship, no matter how exclusive and how all-embracing it may be, is accorded no 'necessitas' by authorities in the way they would accord it to family members" (*LPP* 181) [trans. altered].

[125.] *LPP* 388 [trans. altered].

Christianity

In the drama and the novel fragments, Bonhoeffer very seldom speaks directly of faith, Christianity, or theology. Yet there is a pervasive sense of how important he holds Christian faith and theology to be.

The subject of "the Christian"[126] is mentioned at the beginning of both the drama and the novel. It is the grandmother's theme. The story of the "wondrous beast" which she tells Little Brother at bedtime in the first scene of the drama ends with a shot.[127] The hunter kills the animal because he loves it so much that he can't bear to part from it. When Little Brother asks his grandmother why the animal didn't run away, she answers, "Maybe it sensed its hunter's great love, and that made it love its hunter a little, too, and look at him with such calm, fearless eyes. Maybe it knew death was near and yet wasn't afraid."[128]

236

Bonhoeffer gives the novel fragment the title "Sunday." Sunday is a special day, a day for going to church, for reflection and rest. Even the domestic animals are allowed to rest. It is a day on which all three church bells, Misericordia, Justitia, and Pax, ring out, whereas during the week only the austere voice of Justitia is heard.[129]

Frau Karoline Brake, the grandmother, goes to church as a matter of course, even though this minister offers her nothing but "sanctimonious prattle." It pains her that her grandchildren have stopped going to church, but she understands. One of them would explain reproachfully,

"Anything that has such pathetic representatives can't have much power left; I'm interested in what is alive and relevant today, not in a dead faith of the past." How could one argue with that? . . . After all, what mattered was simply whether the Christianity in which Frau Brake had grown up and

---

[126.] Cf. the title of the *Ethics* manuscript written in early 1943, "The 'Ethical' and the 'Christian' as a Subject" *(E* 259–97).

[127.] Schollmeyer connects this story with Bonhoeffer's experience as a thirteen-year-old, writing his grandmother a letter thanking her for a book of fairy tales about animals from which the family was reading aloud each night. See his letter of February 11, 1919 *(DBW* 9:20), and Schollmeyer, "The 'Wondrous Beast.' "

[128.] See above, page 27. Bonhoeffer first used the image of the hunted wild animal in a London sermon of January 21, 1934, on Jer. 20:7. He has the prophet Jeremiah say to God, when God's love becomes palpable to him: "You hounded me, you did not want to let me go . . . and now I can no longer part from you, now you drag me off as your prey" *(DBW* 13:348f. [*GS* 5:507]). It is possible that Bonhoeffer had read Zweig's drama *Jeremiah* by this time (see scene one, "The Awakening of the Prophet," where Jeremiah cries out to God: "Seize thy quarry, Lord, or hunt me yet farther to the goal!" [8]).

[129.] See above, pages 178–80.

lived her life still existed today, and whether or not it lives in its current representatives.[130]

This is a central problem for Bonhoeffer. At the end of April 1944 he writes:

> The question that is constantly on my mind is the question what Christianity really is, or indeed, who Christ really is, for us today. The time when you could convey this to people with words—whether in theological language or the language of piety—is over. Likewise the time for inwardness and conscience; and that means the time of religion in general is over. We are moving toward a completely religionless age; people as they are simply cannot be religious anymore.
>
> . . . How do we speak (or perhaps we just cannot even "speak" anymore as we used to) in a "worldly" way about "God"? In what way are we "religionless-worldly" Christians, in what way are we the ἐκ-κλησία [church], those who are called forth, not considering ourselves as religiously privileged, but rather as belonging completely in the world?[131]

237

A neighbor of the Brakes who attends church faithfully speaks highly of the pastor in a conversation with Frau Karoline Brake. He is "so human, so down to earth, and can speak so beautifully. . . . Didn't he say it beautifully? Yes—uh, what did he say, anyway? It's so lovely one could never convey it. But it really doesn't matter at all, you can just feel it and it's so uplifting, and you don't even quite know why. . . ." Frau Brake tells her what she thinks of the pastor, that he said what he thought the congregation wanted to hear, but did not preach God's word, and decides quietly for herself that "this pious chatter has absolutely nothing in common with Christianity; it's more dangerous than outright unbelief."[132]

This neighbor lady embodies the "religious" people Bonhoeffer writes about on April 30, 1944:

> I frequently wonder why a "Christian instinct" draws me more often to the religionless people than to the religious. And I don't in the least mean with any evangelizing intention, but I would almost say in a "brotherly" way. I'm often reluctant to mention God by name to religious people—because that name sounds inauthentic to me in that context, and I feel a bit dishonest. It's particularly bad when others start talking in religious jargon, then I shut up almost completely in this hothouse atmosphere and feel uneasy. By con-

---

[130.] See above, page 74.
[131.] Letter of April 30, 1944 (*LPP* 279 and 280f.) [trans. altered].
[132.] See above, pages 77–79.

trast, when speaking with religionless people, I can sometimes quite calmly and matter-of-factly mention God by name.[133]

The "brotherly" feeling Bonhoeffer describes having toward religion-   238
less people can be understood quite literally. Some of his brothers and sisters can be regarded as "religionless," but certainly as Christians. The Brake children, who do not go to church, are easily recognizable as characters based on Bonhoeffer's brothers and sisters.

Later in the novel, as Christoph speaks with Ulrich, he thinks about his parents' attitude: "They don't go to church. They only say grace before meals because of Little Brother. And yet they're as little infected by the spirit of false ambition, careerism, titles, and medals as your mother is. . . . Why is that?" Ulrich thinks for a moment and responds, "That's because, without knowing it and certainly without talking about it, in truth they still base their lives on Christianity, an unconscious Christianity."[134] Bonhoeffer clearly articulates here that patterns of behavior that   239

[133.] April 30, 1944 (*LPP* 281) [trans. altered]. What is important to Bonhoeffer is an unconditional honesty which precludes making any statement of which one is not sure. For his *Ethics* he had written in 1940: "Intellectual honesty in all things, including questions of faith, . . . [is] one of the indispensable moral demands of Western culture" (*E* 98) [trans. altered]. Cf. Bonhoeffer's reflections entitled "What Do We Really Believe?" and "Honesty with Ourselves" in his "Outline for a Book" from the summer of 1944 (*LPP* 382).

[134.] See above, page 106. Bonhoeffer had already used the expression "unconscious Christianity" in late 1940 in a marginal note on an *Ethics* manuscript, saying that what is humane and good "should be, and may be, claimed for Jesus Christ, especially in cases where [humanity and goodness] persist as the unconscious residue of a former attachment to the ultimate. Addressing people in this situation simply as non-Christians and pushing them to confess their unbelief may look like a more serious attitude. It will be more Christian, however, to claim as Christian precisely those people who would no longer call themselves Christian . . ." (*E* 142 [trans. altered]). Under this passage in the manuscript is written in the margin "unconscious Christianity" (*DBW* 6:162, editorial note 95). Cf. the note from summer 1944, "Unconscious Christianity: left does not know what the right is doing. Matt. 25" (*NL* A 86, 20); see *LPP* 380 [trans. altered]. Cf. Matt. 6:3: "Do not let your left hand know what your right hand is doing, so that your alms may be done in secret." See *CD* 155–62, especially 159f. On Matt. 25:31-46, see *CD* 297: "While we knew it not, we gave him food, drink, and clothing, and visited him." On July 27, 1944, Bonhoeffer wrote to Eberhard Bethge: "The question how there can be a 'natural' piety is at the same time the question of 'unconscious Christianity,' with which I'm more and more concerned" (*LPP* 373). Even before his imprisonment Bonhoeffer had talked about this with his brother-in-law Rüdiger Schleicher, who would then speak about the *anima naturaliter christiana*. Tertullian's saying, "Anima humana naturaliter est christiana" (the human soul is naturally Christian), is the motto of Martin's book, *Die Religion in Jacob Burckhardts Leben und Denken*, a study on the subject of humanism and Christianity, which Bonhoeffer read for his *Ethics*.

have otherwise become rare are still alive in the middle class "as we know it in our families . . . precisely because of their Christian origins."[135]

In the Brake family Christianity is not exactly unconscious. Rather there is a reserve about speaking of it. Klara Brake tells Frau von Bremer about her everyday routine, but "did not mention . . . that she read a chapter of the Bible every morning before she began her house-work."[136]

A letter from Bonhoeffer's sister Christine reveals how widespread was the reticence in Bonhoeffer's family when it came to speaking about matters of faith. She as well as her husband Hans von Dohnanyi and her brother Dietrich had been arrested on April 5, 1943. On Easter Sunday, April 25, she wrote to her children from prison:

> We have, you know, never spoken much with each other about religious things. Not everyone can speak about these things. But I want to say to you that I am so convinced that all things work together for good to those who love God—and our entire life has proved it again and again—that, in all the loneliness and worry about all of you, I was never really in despair even for a moment. You will probably be surprised to hear this from me, a person whom you no doubt have thought stood quite removed from all these matters of faith. Well, that's just how I am—I must actually be in prison to express such things.[137]

It became increasingly clear to Bonhoeffer that Jesus' example of "existing for others"[138] could hardly be experienced in the church of his time. By contrast, members of his family who had only a loose relationship to the church—like others who fought in the resistance—took courageous risks for victims of persecution. This observation is certainly among the motivations that led Bonhoeffer in Tegel to focus on the 240 bourgeois tradition of his family and "religionless" and "unconscious" Christianity.[139]

Of course there were also people outside the educated middle class

---

[135.] Cf. letter of November 18, 1943 (*LPP* 130) [trans. altered].

[136.] See above, page 134. This keeping things to oneself is reminiscent of the "discipline of the secret . . . whereby the mysteries of the Christian faith are protected against profanation" (letter of May 5, 1944 [*LPP* 286] [trans. altered]).

[137.] Eberhard and Renate Bethge, *Last Letters of Resistance*, 56 [trans. altered]. The Bible passage alluded to by Christine von Dohnanyi in writing her children is Rom. 8:28.

[138.] See "Outline for a Book" from the summer of 1944 (*LPP* 381).

[139.] Cf. the letters of April 30 and July 27, 1944 (*LPP* 279f., 373).

who were not cowed by National Socialism. There was a carpenter, for example, who frequently worked in the Bonhoeffer's home, whose opinion was eagerly sought out by the whole family. He would inform them what was going on in his working-class circles, since otherwise the family's relationships there were not sufficiently intimate to allow open political discussion. Among laborers, in the prisons, and even in the slums [Elendsquartiere] there were those of whom Franz Brake says in the novel that precisely among them he found people who, living in miserable conditions through no fault of their own, were "very helpful and kind without ever wasting their breath talking about it."[140]

In the drama we read the account of the dock worker Heinrich who, seeing a Rembrandt painting of Christ healing the poor, "suddenly, there in the middle of hell, . . . met—God." He began to read at night, particularly the Bible. "I simply couldn't forget God anymore, and I wanted to live in my hell with God, out of pity." He was never religious while living through all this, and he never went to church.[141] Heinrich's character was important to Bonhoeffer. He resembles a prison warden in Tegel whom Bonhoeffer described in a letter of January 1944 after one of the heavy bombings of Berlin. Bonhoeffer was "very much distressed" at the loss of this "man who was, to my mind, by far the most intelligent and humanly likable in this place," who "was killed downtown by a direct hit. . . . We had many interesting conversations. . . . He was a man of working-class origin who was truly educated."[142]

In the story, Lance Corporal Berg, in his good-natured kindness toward other people, is not led astray by the hostile behavior of his co-workers and superiors. This man, too, with his unbearably disfigured face, is tacitly "claimed as Christian."

Death and Resurrection   241

Death became a reality for Bonhoeffer early in his life. His sister Sabine Leibholz writes:

> Dietrich and I slept in the same room when we [twins] were eight to ten years old, and had very serious conversations in bed at night about death and eternal life. World War I had broken out in 1914, and we heard about

---

[140.] See above, page 119.
[141.] See above, pages 41f.
[142.] Letters of January 29 and 30, 1944 (*LPP* 199) [trans. altered].

the deaths of our older cousins and our classmates' fathers. . . . We tried to
come closer to eternity every night by trying to focus only on the word
"eternity" and not to let any other thought enter our minds. Eternity
seemed vast and eerie. After a long time of intense concentration we would
often feel dizzy. We kept up this self-appointed discipline for a long
time.[143]

The family was hit especially hard by the death of eighteen-year-old
Walter, who died of wounds in France in 1918.

If this experience brought the horror of death home to Dietrich for
the first time, it also began the formation of a notion of dying a heroic
death. It is significant that he wrote an early school essay about Julian the
Apostate, who died young in battle like Dietrich's own brother Walter.[144] In Bonhoeffer's preoccupation with death there is also the recur-
rent theme of early fulfillment through death for a high purpose.

Another early influence on Bonhoeffer was certainly the longing for
death as it is expressed in art. At fourteen he bought a reproduction of
the Klinger lithograph "Of Death."[145] He knew many lieder and poems
by heart in which death is represented as a place of peace and is even
sought for various reasons. Even as a young boy, he accompanied on the
piano the family's singing of lieder.[146]

242   The Bonhoeffer children knew about the vital hope of eternity from
the hymns of the Moravian Brethren.[147] The degree to which this

---

[143.] "Childhood and Home," in Zimmermann and Smith, *I Knew Dietrich Bonhoeffer,*
23f. [trans. altered].

[144.] Hans Pfeifer, editor of *DBW* 9, points out such connections in *DBW* 9:622.

[145.] Schollmeyer attributes great significance to this fact in his *Bonhoeffers Theologie,*
211.

[146.] One of the German lieder Bonhoeffer loved was Brahms's "Feldeinsamkeit": "I
calmly rest amid the high green grass. . . . I feel as if I died in olden days / and through
eternal spaces glide along." Another was Schumann's "Die beiden Grenadiere," based on
the poem by Heine, which Dietrich's mother sang frequently and with great feeling. In it
one of the grenadiers kills himself because his country has been conquered and the
emperor has been taken prisoner. The song ends accompanied by the tune of the revolutionary anthem, the "Marseillaise," on a note of hope for later victory. An example of the
many chorales in which death is promised as redemption is the verse from Paul Gerhardt's
hymn from 1666–67, "Gib dich zufrieden" (*Evangelisches Gesangbuch,* 371). Bonhoeffer and
Franz Hildebrandt had introduced this to the family of his sister and brother-in-law, Ursula
and Rüdiger Schleicher, and sung with them often: "A day of rest awaits the weary / when
the good Lord will acquit us; / God will snatch us from the fetters / of this body and all
evil. / Then at once death will leap in / and all from agony release. / Therefore find peace
here!"

[147.] Their mother, Paula Bonhoeffer, who had attended a boarding school in Gnadau

influence was at work in Bonhoeffer's early life is evidenced in his children's sermon for Eternity Day, 1926: "Death is God coming to us, calling us, knocking at our door; now we are closer than ever to the realm of glory. The kingdom of God is at the door, indeed, the kingdom of God is near at hand."[148]

A bizarre little piece of writing by Bonhoeffer, probably written about 1932, describes a young boy who imagines himself on his deathbed and speaking his dying words to his family. He wants to die "a beautiful, pious death," and show the others "that dying is not terrible, but glorious for those who believe in God." But then one day the boy is struck with panic at the idea of really dying. "So he was a coward after all; he was disgusted by his theatrical fantasy. And yet he often prayed in moments of strength that God would please finally redeem him." His fear won out, however, literally turning into a sickness, and in the end he realized in horror that "his sickness was that he saw reality as real; his sickness was incurable. . . . From this day on, he buried something inside himself that he neither spoke nor thought about for a long time."[149] This text offers an important corrective to the childish fantasy of glorious death.

In his winter semester lectures of 1932–33 on "Creation and Sin," a theological exegesis on the first three chapters of Genesis, Bonhoeffer reflected on the reality of death. Fallen Adam, who has broken the fruit off the tree of knowledge, is prevented by God from also eating from the tree of life and living eternally. Adam after the fall is *sicut deus*, "like God." Adam

> has indeed become Adam's own God, the creator of Adam's own life. When Adam seeks God, when Adam seeks life, Adam seeks only Adam. . . . Pining away as Adam is without life, Adam wants death; perhaps death may give Adam life. . . . Yet in this very act of dying Adam hopes to rescue his life from the bondservice and drudgery [Frohn] of having to live without life. Thus Adam flees from life and seeks to grasp life at the same time. . . . Adam is sicut deus, but as such in a state of death.[150]

243

---

run by the Moravian Brethren, and their tutor, Fräulein Maria Horn, who was a Moravian, taught them these hymns.

[148.] *DBW* 9:556. Later, Bonhoeffer contrasted the longing for eternity, which he recognized as one-sided, with "the profound this-worldliness of Christianity" (letter of July 21, 1944, *LPP* 369).

[149.] See the sketch on "Death," *DBW* 11:373f. [*GS* 6:232–33].

[150.] See *CF* (*DBWE* 3) 143 on Gen. 3:22-24.

This is how death looks for humanity after the fall. Bonhoeffer was able to stand looking death in the face in this way because of his knowledge of the resurrection: "But Christ lives." "The world exists from the beginning in the sign of the resurrection of Christ from the dead."[151]

In the Tegel drama fragment, what Bonhoeffer had written in 1932–33 about Adam's "being in death" is embodied in the uncanny figure of the "Stranger." For him, death is at once grizzly and fascinating—like the impenetrable blackness of a starless night, like the "falling blade of a guillotine," "a bride on the eve of the wedding." Death is an admired, powerful boss [Chef] and a "gentleman." Bonhoeffer thought about these formulations very carefully.[152] He well knew what it was to stare death in the face, transfixed—he knew it as a temptation [Anfechtung]. He represents the "Stranger" as having fallen into servitude to Death. He has him sing the praises of life in the service of Death as the only lord, claiming to be quoting the Bible: " 'They struggle to find death' . . . is a wise saying. That is how people are nowadays. They do not fear Death, they don't flee from him, but seek him out, love him. 'They struggle to find death.' "[153]

244   The other aspect of death alluded to in *Creation and Fall*, namely death viewed from the perspective of the death and resurrection of Christ, occupied Bonhoeffer between 1935 and 1937 in Finkenwalde at the Preacher's Seminary of the Confessing Church. In his book *Discipleship*, which was the fruit of his New Testament lectures at Finkenwalde, one hears the echo again and again of the verse "I die daily" from the first letter of Paul to the Corinthians. The suffering of the church-community [Gemeinde] of Jesus Christ "is first the suffering of death on the cross through baptism, and after that the 'daily dying' of Christians (1 Cor. 15:31) in the power of their baptism."[154]

In the fall of 1939, when death had come within close reach with the beginning of the war on September 1, Bonhoeffer wrote a letter to his former Finkenwalde students in which he reminded them of this death through baptism. On September 3 the first member of the Finkenwalde community was killed in battle during the invasion of Poland. The news

---

[151.] *CF* 146 (on Gen. 4:1) and *CF* 34–35 (on Gen. 1:1f.).

[152.] Cf. below, page 243, *NL* A 86, 8, and above, page 55.

[153.] See above, page 58; cf. Matt. 6:24 and Wisd. of Sol. 1:16.

[154.] *CD* 244 [trans. altered]. In the subject index to *Nachfolge*, for the subject "death," Bonhoeffer created subheadings referring the reader to "cross" and "baptism"; cf. *DBW* 4:387.

of this led Bonhoeffer to write in the newsletter of the distinction between death from external forces [von außen] and one's personal death from the inside [in uns]. Death from external forces is the unpredictable, chance, sudden, senseless, premature death which comes like an attack and is almost impossible to cope with. By contrast, one's personal death as a Christian is experienced daily through total surrender of oneself in repentance and love for Christ and others. Such everyday practice and experience of death and life then lessens the dread of external death that lurks at every turn in wartime. "We are privileged to pray that external death may strike only after we have been prepared for it through this personal death. Then our death is really only the passage through to the perfect love of God."[155]

Bonhoeffer took this pastoral distinction one step further at the end of 1942 in "After Ten Years," when he contrasted the threat of death from external forces with the death one willingly risks as an act of free responsibility—including the consequences of conspiracy against the regime.[156] "It is not outward circumstances but we ourselves who will make our death what it can be, death freely and willingly accepted."[157]

245

Three months later Bonhoeffer was arrested, and from that moment on necessarily lived anticipating that his imminent death was likely. When Christoph in the drama, facing his own imminent death, speaks of a better future for Germany, his words foreshadow those written by Bonhoeffer in a letter of May 1944: "We are anxious . . . about our life, but at the same time we must think about things much more important to us than our own life."[158] In Bonhoeffer's poem "Night Voices in Tegel," the writer addresses the prisoner who has been condemned to death, saying "I hear you stride bravely and with proud step. / It's no longer the present moment you see, you look into the future. / I go with you, brother, / to that place, and I hear your last words: / 'Brother, when the sun has faded for me, / Live then in my place.'"[159] In the drama

---

[155.] "The First Circular Letter of the War," September 20, 1939 (*The Way to Freedom,* 255 [trans. altered]; cf. also 251).

[156.] In 1940–41, when writing the *Ethics,* Bonhoeffer had already weighed the issues raised by the possibility that "prisoners take their own lives for fear that under torture they might betray their people, their country, their families or friends" and thus endanger the conspiracy (*E* 169) [trans. altered].

[157.] *LPP* 16 [trans. altered].

[158.] Letter of May 29, 1944, to Bethge (*LPP* 311) [trans. altered]; cf. above, pages 50f.

[159.] "Night Voices in Tegel," summer 1944 (*LPP* 355) [trans. altered].

fragment Christoph tells Little Brother very gently about the task his brother will face, to live on after his own death on the "mountain-top."[160]

Toward the end of the drama fragment, Heinrich says to Christoph:

> People like you have a foundation, you have ground under your feet, you have a place in the world. There are things you take for granted, that you stand up for, and for which you are willing to put your head on the line, because you know your roots go so deep that they'll sprout new growth again.

After thinking this over for some time, Christoph replies: "Ground under your feet—I've never understood it like that—I think you're right—I understand—Ground under your feet—in order to be able to live and in order to be able to die. . . ."[161] Here the dockworker Heinrich's words suddenly make sense to Christoph, the son of educated middle-class parents, who now understands how powerful are the forces of his family background. This background can motivate one to undertake necessary or even dangerous action; it can also provide certainty, even comfort and safety despite physical, geographical, and temporal separation. The basis of this family tradition, though barely ever mentioned, is Christianity. Heinrich, too, had lived in the Christian faith; but without the support of a family tradition like that, such a life was more difficult to sustain.

"Dying is interesting, not being dead," asserts the Stranger in the drama, the agent of Death.[162] In a letter Bonhoeffer wrote before Easter 1944, we read: "We're more concerned to get over the act of dying than to overcome death. Socrates overcame the act of dying; Christ overcame death as the ἔσχατος ἐχθρός [last enemy] (1 Cor. 15:26)."[163] Looking at Christ, Bonhoeffer realized that the "art of dying" is not the ultimate thing, not what counts in reality. The letter continues, "It's not from the ars moriendi [art of dying], but from the resurrection of Christ, that a new and purifying wind can blow through the present world. Here is the answer to δὸς μοὶ ποῦ στῶ καὶ κινήσω τὴν γῆν, 'Give me somewhere to stand, and I will move the earth.'[164] If a few people really believed

246

[160.] See above, page 37.

[161.] See above, page 70.

[162.] See above, page 57.

[163.] Letter of March 27, 1944, to Bethge (*LPP* 240) [trans. altered].

[164.] Cf. above, page 69, editorial note 66, concerning the question of the "Archimedean point on which I can stand."

this and allowed their earthly actions to be motivated by it, a lot of things would change."[165]

The same theme of "ground under your feet—in order to be able to live and be able to die"[166] is heard again clearly and calmly in Bonhoeffer's birthday letter to Bethge in August 1944:

> It is certain . . . that no earthly power can touch us without God's will, . . . it is certain that our joy is hidden in suffering, our life in death; it is certain that in all this we stand in a community [Gemeinschaft] that sustains us. God has said "Yes" and "Amen" to all this in Jesus. This Yes and Amen is the firm ground on which we stand.[167]

The certainty "that no earthly power can touch us without God's will" denies Adolf Hitler the power to be lord over the life and death of his political prisoners. In late July 1944, one week after the attempted coup, Bonhoeffer had written,

247

> not only action, but also suffering is a way to freedom. In suffering, liberation consists in being allowed to let go of the matter and lay it in the hands of God. In this sense, death is the epitome of human freedom. Whether human action stems from faith or not depends on whether or not we see our suffering as an extension of our action, as a fulfillment of our freedom. I think that is very important and very comforting.[168]

During this time Bonhoeffer wrote the poem "Stations on the Way to Freedom." The fourth and last verse bears the heading "Death": "Come now, highest feast on the journey to freedom eternal, / Death. . . / Freedom, long have we sought you in discipline, action, and suffering. / Dying, we now may behold your face in the countenance of God."[169]

[165.] Letter of March 27, 1944 (*LPP* 240) [trans. altered].

[166.] See above, page 70.

[167.] Letter of August 21, 1944 (*LPP* 391) [trans. altered].

[168.] Letter of July 28, 1944, to Bethge (*LPP* 375) [trans. altered].

[169.] *LPP* 371 [trans. altered]. The Reich Security Headquarters saw to it that on April 9, 1945, Hans von Dohnanyi and Dietrich Bonhoeffer were killed, and likewise Rüdiger Schleicher and Klaus Bonhoeffer on April 30. With Hitler's suicide on April 30, 1945, the National Socialist regime collapsed.

CHRONOLOGY OF
FICTION FROM TEGEL PRISON

1938
Bonhoeffer makes initial contacts with leaders in the resistance movement

1940–43
Bonhoeffer writes his *Ethics* manuscripts while working for the resistance movement

April 5, 1943
Bonhoeffer imprisoned in Tegel military interrogation prison, Berlin

1943–44
Writes manuscripts of drama, novel, and short story

April 9, 1945
Bonhoeffer executed at Flossenbürg

1948
First publication of an excerpt from Scene 3 of the drama in *Die Schöpfung*

1949
Publication of first edition of Bonhoeffer's *Ethik*

1954
Excerpt of dialogue from the novel is published in *Unterwegs*

1955
A second excerpt from Scene 3 of the drama is published in *Die Kirche in Hamburg*

First English publication of an excerpt from the novel—the piece published in *Unterwegs*—as "Happiness and Power" in *The Bridge*

1960
Gesammelte Schriften 3 is published with two excerpts from Scenes 1 and 2 of the drama, the whole of Scene 3, and two long dialogues with the major from the novel

1965
"From a Fragment of a Drama," an excerpt from Scene 2 is published in *Gesammelte Schriften* 3, translated in the Bonhoeffer selections entitled *I Loved This People*

1970
The short story is published as "Gefreiter Berg" in *Widerstand und Ergebung: Neuausgabe*

1971
"Lance-Corporal Berg: A Narrative" is published in *Letters and Papers from Prison*, The Enlarged Edition.

1973
The drama and novel excerpts which had been published in *Gesammelte Schriften* 3 are published in English in *True Patriotism*, volume 3 of selections from Bonhoeffer's collected writings

1978
First complete publication of the drama and novel fragments as *Fragmente aus Tegel*, edited by Renate and Eberhard Bethge

1981
English translation is published by Fortress Press as *Fiction from Prison: Gathering Up the Past*

1994
German critical edition of *Fragmente aus Tegel* is published as volume 7 of the *Dietrich Bonhoeffer Werke*

APPENDIX[1]

Fragment of a Story[2]

AND FOR WHAT PURPOSE do you think the two of us are friends today if it's not to start from the ground up again, beginning with ourselves?

<In any case, it wouldn't have occurred to him to hold it against Martin if he lost his temper.>[3]

Then he was quiet for a moment, as if to collect his thoughts, and said, "I think we're walking on two different paths toward the same goal, Martin."[4]

[1.] In this fragment and the drama working notes that follow it, these symbols are used to print the contents of these handwritten note papers *(Zettel):* angle brackets < . . . > enclose words that were deleted, and carets ^ . . . ^ enclose words that were added later. As much as possible, printed lines correspond to lines on the working notes. When necessary, the symbol | is used to indicate a line break, but word order in the translation often does not correspond exactly to the German, and therefore the line break will not always appear after the corresponding English word. The use of pencil and ink is indicated by the editors in brackets in the text. Horizontal lines appearing in some passages are reproduced as they appeared in the original notes.

[2.] [This does not belong to the story above (183–94) about Lance Corporal Berg, but to the lost story about the meeting of two friends after a long wartime separation.][CG] This is a working note for the story fragment, *NL* A 86, 12, on a sheet of DIN-A4 paper, written in ink. Bonhoeffer used this size paper for all his *Ethics* manuscripts and the literary pieces he wrote in Tegel. Deleted after the question mark at the end of the first sentence: "I". At the bottom of this page is a penciled outline about finding a way.

[3.] This is the first sentence on the back of the same sheet of paper, deleted.

[4.] Replaces: "The paths we are each following are two different paths, I think." This material obviously represents three rejected beginnings of a manuscript page for the short literary work Bonhoeffer mentions in his letters to Eberhard Bethge of December 25, 1943, and January 29–30, February 23, and July 8, 1944, saying it is about the reunion of two friends after a long separation during the war. The July letter refers to the piece as "not completely finished" (cf. *LPP* 178, 199f., 220, and 346).

Drama Working Notes 252

NL A 86, 7[1]

Death of a middle-class person [Bürger]. Death of a soldier.
    act as if everything were beginning anew, as if
    there weren't. . . .
    Assuming another's motives.
    [Pencil] Love for people, "rabble"
    Kindness is part of refinement [Vornehmheit]
    [Ink]
^Wordless^ ^Reverence^ for what has developed over time, what is given
    Words are not important; one under-
    stands glances, gestures
    one gives the other the freedom to
    trust. Each has their place.
    Slowly building
    Safety.
    [Pencil] _____
^The^ *big shots* discredited.

NL A 86, 10[2]

‹Trust does not mean knowing everything about one another, but

^Still^ more important than openness is being open for the other, in-
cluding for | their silence, and trust is based not on[3] knowing[4] every-
thing | about one another, but on believing the | other›[5] 253

[1.] This is written on small pieces of paper of DIN-A6 format, like that Bonhoeffer used for the *Ethics* working notes in the last period before his arrest in 1943 (cf. *ZE* 120–26). There is water damage at the bottom; it is written in ink and pencil. The reverse sides show traces of pencil marks including the word "police" (?), possibly erased. For passages in the text which correspond to these notes, cf. above, pages 65–70.

[2.] Penciled notes on a piece of paper used for carbon copies; it is somewhat wider than DIN-A4 format, like *NL* A 70, 4(2), folded once to conform with the DIN-A5-size double sheets. On the back of the DIN-A5 half-sheet are the four lines and one word reproduced at the beginning. The sheet is covered with writing in its DIN-A4 format, in the lower part next to the four lines written along the side.

[3.] Replaces: "does not mean".

[4.] Replaces: "having to know".

[5.] These four lines were the first written on a page of a working note [Zettel]. They were incorporated into page 48 above and then presumably deleted.

Germany—much abused, it is hard for me to utter it. *Words.* What we
once took for granted has been turned into an empty cliché. We do not
do something because it is preached to us ^in newspapers and at rallies^
but because it is a matter of course for us. We love to keep silent about
^the highest good^.[6] | ^about work or honor^[7] freedom, love of one's
people [Volk], camaraderie—were not as easy for us to utter as for the
journalists, because we have lived with them day by day, because we have
experienced their value and their limit. But neither will we let ourselves
be intimidated by the cynics. You know where the word cynic comes
from, from the dogs who do their dirty business shamelessly in public
view. We smile about our deliberate reserve.[8]

The difference is that [these words] can cost us our heads, while for
them they are[9] profitable. | It is not a good sign when[10] that which
^from time immemorial^ has been held quietly and firmly ^in the
hearts^ of all people of goodwill in the land ^as a[11] matter of course^ is
barked out as the latest wisdom in the marketplace.[12] Those who with
their lives, their work, their home[13] are[14] the protectors of genuine values [Güter] will always turn away in repulsion from the clanging words
people use to flatter[15] those who are eternally restless and lacking in
deeds.

[6.] Replaces a phrase that was probably not deleted: "our great ideals."

[7.] Marginal addition, illegible.

[8.] Replaces: "We don't need [to do] this." This paragraph has normal margins; the
next paragraph, heavily corrected, has almost no left margin. Not all changes to the
manuscript are noted here.

[9.] Replaces: "to them they are".

[10.] Replaces: "The times are petty-minded [replaces: sick] when . . ."

[11.] Replaces: "calm and firm possession"; the word "firm" was at first replaced by
"unspoken," which was then deleted.

[12.] Replaces: "becomes the language of market barkers." The following beginnings of
drafts are deleted in the manuscript: "the zealots' and revolutionaries' supposedly new
ideas, and" | "the slogans of revolution have never been new; those who guard the value of
words turn away in | disgust."

[13.] Added, then deleted: "through a long sequence of generations".

[14.] Replaces: "were".

[15.] Replaces: "incite". Then, deleted: "Those who have put their lives | on the line for
the highest values consider these people;" then, deleted: "One does the great things
^because one cannot do otherwise^, or one does not | do them, | but | There are two
kinds of people: one." The word "but" and everything that follows is written on the bottom
half of the sheet to the right of the deleted four lines described at the beginning.

Freedom—who may ^learn to^ pronounce that word?[16]

only the majesty of the law and of discipline

The great words of humanity are sanctuaries, where only the humble and faithful may approach. They do not belong in the street.

Let us honor the highest values by silence. Let us learn | to act justly without words for a long[17]

^Teach^ people[18] first to do justice again without a lot of words, to avoid abusing our sacred possessions.

Not birth, not success, but only humility has the right to approach the highest values. The nobility of humility and of faith and of sacrifice | the nobility of dying.

I speak to you to protect the great words from abuse. They do not belong on the lips of the masses, but in the hearts of the few, who guard and protect them with their lives.[19]

NL A 70, 4(2)[20]

Father

Mother

<War> Christoph—Took part in war—Student, 25 years.[21]

^Sister^   255

Little Brother

Grandmother

Fiancée[22]

Friend

^old^ Gypsy

Doctor

[16.] The word "learn" is directly above the word "pronounce," with no clear indication where it belongs. Then, deleted: "without [replaces: except only]"; after the question "Freedom—who may pronounce that word?", deleted: "no one as."

[17.] Probably meant to be added: "time." Then, deleted: "with".

[18.] Replaces: "People must first [be taught] . . ."

[19.] Replaces: "who watch over them."

[20.] This working note is written on a sheet of paper for carbon copies, somewhat wider than DIN-A4, like *NL* A 86, 10, folded once to a DIN-A5 double sheet. The writing, in pencil, is only on the front page.

[21.] This line was written first, then moved to the third line.

[22.] In the drama Renate is not identified as Christoph's fiancée, nor do the characters of the Gypsy or the Pastor appear there.

Pastor
Students

---

1. Living room of Grandmother and Little Brother (sister?)
then mother; then father; last, Christoph—conversation about
   students, fiancée, and friend.—
^from: "I'm going to write a little more"—"what?"—"as yet unborn, forgive me for not wanting to talk about it"^
2. Christoph's study
   Books, harpsichord. Lute. Pictures?
   Friend and fiancée. Little Brother.
   Alone
3. Evening with students ^fiancée^—at home in early morning.
   Grandmother. Awake already? Watching the sun | rise
4. On a trip with a friend (and Little Brother?) Gypsy.
   Stranger | who tells the truth. Pastor, whether one must always tell
   the truth?—
5. Little Brother's bedroom—Grandmother and Little Brother;
   later Christoph
6. Christoph's study. Alone. At the end, ^only^ Little Brother, are you
   thinking about | God? Yes, I think how he [. . .] a happier Ger-
   many—

256 *NL* A 86, 11[23]

I speak to you to protect from abuse the great words that have been given
to humanity.[24] They do not belong on the lips of the masses, but in the
hearts of the few, who guard and protect them with their lives. It is never
a good sign when what has always been the calm and firm possession
and the self-evident attitude of all well-meaning people in the land is

---

[23.] This passage is incorporated almost word for word in the drama; see above, pages
49–51. It is written on a DIN-A4-size sheet of graph paper cut in half (as used in the manuscript, beginning with page 61 above, and for letters and notes written between April and
September 1943). It is written in ink, showing through on the reverse side, and is corrected
from notes *NL* A 86, 10. It is a fair copy on the basis of working note *NL* A 86, 10, and further work.
[24.] Replaces: "to them." The next word, "freedom," is deleted.

barked out as the latest wisdom on the street.[25] Those who with their lives, their ^work^, and their homes are the protectors of genuine[26] values turn away in disgust from the clanging words intoned to turn the masses into prophets. What well-meaning person today can still utter the besmirched words "freedom," "brotherhood"—or even the word "Germany"?[27] They seek genuine values in the silence of the sanctuary where only the humble and faithful may approach. Each of us has put our life on the line for these values. Those who mouth them today find them profitable. | Let us honor the highest values by silence for a while. | Let us learn to do right without words for a while. Around the silent sanctuary of lofty words a new nobility will develop, must develop, in our time. Neither birth nor success ^will be the foundation of this nobility^, but humility, faith, and sacrifice. There is an infallible standard for what is great and small, what is valid and what is immaterial, for what is genuine and what is fraudulent; that standard is death. Whoever is close to death is resolute,

[continued on the reverse side]

but the person near death is also reticent. Wordless, even misunderstood if need be, | one does what is necessary and right—"

it stops here. I hadn't seen this paragraph. Strange—here's an addition ^in pencil^: "Are these, too, not merely great words? Would I not do better to keep silent about them? How[28] difficult—to | do it. How difficult [it] is | ^simply^ to do what is ^necessary^ right[29] really without words, misunderstood | —Renate, Ulrich—why can't I tell you?—

    Renate, do you understand that?

    I believe so.

    Forgive me, Renate, I didn't know. You were right.—^God, it's impossible.^

     Stop it, Ulrich, it was meant to[30] happen. Let's go.

     Let's take time to leave Christoph a note.[31]

     (both write, leave notes on the table.)

257

[25.] Replaces: "the marketplace."

[26.] At first changed to "ultimate" [letzte], then changed back to "genuine."

[27.] Replaces: "dares . . . to utter [replaces: to pronounce]".

[28.] Deleted: "it's easy ^to^ write this and [how]"; the "how" is not deleted. In the next line the names "—Renate, Ulrich—" are also not deleted.

[29.] The word "necessary" is written above the word "right," which is not deleted.

[30.] Replaces: "had to".

[31.] Two similar versions of "Let's write Christoph a quick note" were replaced.

Come on, Ulrich! (They leave quietly. After some time Little Brother[32] enters. Looks around, notices the notes, | reads. Christoph, we were here. Forgive me. Renate | Christoph, I'm going along ^with you^ to the mountains.[33] Ulrich.

To the mountains!

NL 86, 9[34]

                    the doctor, vicar,[35] housekeeper | teacher
1.   Communication
1a   Answer doubt, superficial calming down. Maybe everything I write [is] wrong?
            ^Mountains, Spring, here you | had your health. Without you^
2.   everything easy, joy reading, music, time.
      feel uplifted, ecstasy. Always known
      am in a daze; no pain. My own death.
2.[36] happy. Hope to hold out.
3.   Getting tedious. Work. Be useful.
3.[37]
      Death announcement | of soldiers killed in battle | Phrasing?[38]
4.   All the things I haven't had, Unfulfilled
      Celebrate marriage. The nights.
4.
5.   <Bad disposition> Fiancée's letter / Bad disposition.
      Mistrust, rejecting. doesn't want to write. doing nothing
                  ^but complains | about receiving | no letter^[39]
6.   Fiancée's letter; soft, miserable, cried
7.   Anxious state
8.   <Guilt> Suicide
9.   Guilt. Extinguish? Does it do any good?

[32.] Replaces: "Christoph".
[33.] Replaces: "coming with you to the mountains."
[34.] Written in ink on a light, porous DIN-A5 sheet.
[35.] Replaces: "pastor". Deleted in the next line: "[illegible] pastor."
[36.] Apparently changed from "3" to "2."
[37.] Changed from "4" to "3."
[38.] Three-line addition in the left margin.
[39.] Three-line addition in the right margin.

NL A 86, 8[40]

[Ink]
Now all at once ambition, burning. Fame.
    Possessions, Wealth.
    ^Health^
    Sensual pleasure. In a fog.
    Suicide.
Have not found *my* death that I sought; it has avoided me.
The Death who seeks me is not *mine,* but enemy I am fighting against.
    Envy, Contempt for misery.
Future, Prophecy: I see . . .
[Pencil]_____
Second sight. Terrible! Used to it. The world looks completely | differ-
ent. Insurance agent, marriage counselor—^good business^ now nothing
has | *one* limit, if ^something^ is not ^in^ the power of death—the believ-
ers | *talk* with Death, Death not *an event,* but a *power,* | a being; he has
preferences,[41] some he loves, | others he scorns, to some he shows him-
self, some he tosses | on the garbage heap, gently, wildly, some he avoids,
they desperately seek him | and do not find him. With some he even
carries on afterwards | with his magic tricks.—a distinguished gentle-
man, pays[42] | good wages—but cold-blooded, no sympathy, ^no heart^
no friendship, | no love, no faith.
    Sentenced ^to^ Death.
[Reverse side, in ink]
^<Prison term>^ too long[43]
    At first like walking into a dark night,[44] ^when it^ faces one like an
impenetrable black wall, then ^full of terror^ as if facing a falling guillotine, <then> ^again with burning desire^ like a bride on the eve of the wedding, then again full of admiration as if for a powerful[45] master.[46]
[Pencil]

259

[40.] Written in ink and pencil on a page of DIN-A5 paper, light, porous. The outline is
used in the text on pages 42 and 54–60.
[41.] Deleted: "partly".
[42.] Replaces: "gives".
[43.] The added word for "prison term," which itself was first inserted and then later
deleted, is illegible; the entire passage from "too long" to "powerful master" is deleted.
[44.] Replaces: "as one stares into the ^starless^ night".
[45.] At first replaced with "divine," then changed back.
[46.] This passage, which is written in ink on the back of the sheet, appears almost ver-

I've just heard . . . is said to be a very diligent <and> ^warm-hearted and^ decent man and I assume a calm ^distinguished^ negotiator. That[47] is very important ^to me^ in view | of the nature of the negotiations up to now which took place in this tone | of voice. So I thank you very much for your efforts.[48]

---

batim on page 55 above, as an addition on the edge of the manuscript; it was presumably deleted afterward.

[47.] Deleted: "would be" [replaces: "the human forms in which"].

[48.] This penciled note is an early draft of Bonhoeffer's prison letter to his parents of August 3, 1943: "my request for a lawyer to defend me . . . Dr. Roeder expressed the opinion that it is a case that any decent lawyer can take on, and if he's a competent, warm-hearted, respectable man, and a quiet and distinguished negotiator who can keep the tone that has been maintained so far in the proceedings . . . " (*LPP* 87).

BIBLIOGRAPHY

1. Literature Used by Bonhoeffer

Barth, Karl. *Die kirchliche Dogmatik*. Vol. 2/2, *Die Lehre von Gott*. Zurich: Evangelischer Verlag, 1942. English translation: *Church Dogmatics*. Vol. 2/2, *The Doctrine of God*. Translated by G. W. Bromiley et al. Edinburgh: T. & T. Clark, 1957.

Bernanos, Georges. *Tagebuch eines Landpfarrers*. Vienna, 1936. *NL* 8 C 5. Translation of *Journal d'un curé de campagne*. Paris: Plon, 1936. English translation: *Diary of a Country Priest*. Translated by Pamela Morris. New York: Carroll & Graf, 1983.

Die Bibel oder die ganze Heilige Schrift des Alten und Neuen Testaments nach der deutschen Übersetzung D. Martin Luthers (The Bible or all of the Holy Scriptures of the Old and New Testaments in the German translation of Dr. Martin Luther). Supervised by the Commission of the Deutsche Evangelische Kirchenkonferenz. Stuttgart, 1911; Munich, 1937. *NL* 1 A 6.

Cervantes Saavedra, Miguel de. *Obras Completas* (Complete works). Madrid, n.d. *NL* 8 C 9; purchased in Barcelona 1928–29. English translation of *Don Quixote* (not based on this edition): Translated by P. A. Motteux. Introduction by A. J. Close. New York: Knopf, 1991.

Gotthelf, Jeremias. *Wie Uli der Knecht glücklich wird: Eine Gabe für Dienstboten und Meisterleute*. 2 pts. Pt. 1, *Uli der Knecht* (Uli the farmhand). Bielefeld, 1841, 1941. *NL* 8 C 18 English translation: *Ulric, the Farm Servant*. Edited by Ernest Rhys. London: J. M. Dent; New York: E. P. Dutton, 1907.

———. *Zeitgeist und Berner Geist* (The spirit of the time and the spirit of Bern). Zurich and Stuttgart: Erlenbach, 1849, 1966.

Grabbe, Christian Dietrich. *Hermannsschlacht.* Detmold: Grabbe-Gesellschaft, 1977.

Guardini, Romano. *Religiöse Gestalten in Dostojewskijs Werk* (Religious characters in Dostoyevsky's works). 2d ed. Leipzig, 1939. *NL* 8–2.

Jaspers, Karl. *Die geistige Situation der Zeit.* Eighth printing of the 1932 revised fifth edition. Berlin and New York: Walter de Gruyter, 1979. *NL* 7 A 32. English translation: *Man in the Modern Age.* Translated by Eden Paul and Cedar Paul. London: Routledge & Kegan Paul, 1951.

———. *Nietzsche: Einführung in das Verständnis seines Philosophierens.* Berlin and Leipzig, 1936. *NL* 7 A 34. English translation: *Nietzsche: An Introduction to the Understanding of His Philosophical Activity.* Translated by Charles F. Wallraff and Frederick J. Schmitz. Lanham, Md.: University Press of America, 1985.

Kamlah, Wilhelm. *Christentum und Selbstbehauptung: Historisch-philosophische Untersuchung* (Christianity and self-assertion: A historical and philosophical examination). Frankfurt am Main, 1940. *NL* 2 C 1.13.

Lütgert, Wilhelm. *Ethik der Liebe* (The ethics of love). Gütersloh: C. Bertelsmann, 1938. *NL* 4.24.

Luther, Martin. *Werke: Kritische Gesamtausgabe* Weimar: H. Böhlau, 1883–. English translation: *Luther's Works,* 55 vols. Vols. 1–30 edited by Jaroslav Pelikan. St. Louis: Concordia, 1958–67. Vols. 31–55 edited by Helmut Lehmann. Philadelphia: Muhlenberg Press and Fortress Press, 1957–67.

Martin, Alfred von. *Die Religion in Jacob Burckhardts Leben und Denken: Eine Studie zum Thema Humanismus und Christentum* (Religion in the life and thought of Jacob Burckhardt: A study on the subject of humanism and Christianity). Munich, 1942.

Müller, Alfred Dedo. *Ethik: Der evangelische Weg der Verwirklichung des Guten* (Ethics: The Protestant way of realization of the good). Berlin, 1937. *NL* 4.32.

Nietzsche, Friedrich. *Also sprach Zarathustra: Ein Buch für alle und keinen.* In *Werke,* Pt. 1:6. Leipzig, 1899. *NL* 7 A 61. English translation: *Thus Spoke Zarathustra.* In *The Portable Nietzsche,* translated and edited by Walter Kaufmann, 103–439. New York: Viking Press, 1968.

Nohl, Herman. *Die sittlichen Grunderfahrungen: Eine Einführung in die Ethik* (Fundamental moral experiences: An introduction to ethics). Frankfurt am Main, 1939. *NL* 4.24.

Novum Testamentum Graece et Germanice: Das Neue Testament griechisch und deutsch (The New Testament in Greek and German). Edited by Eberhard Nestle and revised by Erwin Nestle. 13th ed. Stuttgart, 1929. *NL* 1 A 4.

Oertzen, Friedrich Wilhelm von. *Junker: Preussischer Adel im Jahrhundert des Liberalismus* (The Junkers: Prussian nobility in the century of liberalism). Oldenburg and Berlin, 1939.

Pieper, Josef. *Über die Hoffnung.* 1935. 2d ed., Leipzig, 1938. *NL* 3–55. English translation: *On Hope.* San Francisco: Ignatius Press, 1986.

Ritter, Josef. *Machtstaat und Utopie: Vom Streit um die Dämonie der Macht seit Machiavelli und Morus* (Despotism and utopia: The debate about demonic power since Machiavelli and Thomas More). Munich and Berlin, 1940.

Santayana, George. *Der letzte Puritaner: Die Geschichte eines tragischen Lebens.* Munich: Beck, [1936]. English original: *The Last Puritan: A Memoir in the Form of a Novel.* Vol. 4 of *The Works of George Santayana.* Critical edition. Cambridge, Mass.: MIT Press, 1994.

Spengler, Oswald. *Jahre der Entscheidung.* Pt. 1, *Deutschland und die weltgeschichtliche Entwicklung.* Munich: C. H. Beck, 1933. *NL* 2 B 22. English translation: *The Hour of Decision.* Pt. 1, *Germany and World-Historical Evolution.* Translated by Charles Francis Atkinson. New York: Alfred A. Knopf, 1934, 1942.

Stifter, Adalbert. *Die Mappe meines Urgrossvaters: Letzte Fassung* (My great-grandfather's briefcase: Final version). Edited by Franz Hüller. Freiburg: K. Alber, 1949.

———. *Der Nachsommer.* Munich, 1857, 1987. English translation: *Indian Summer.* Translated by Wendell Frye. New York: Peter Lang, 1985.

———. *Witiko.* Munich, 1865–67, 1986.

Toller, Ernst. *Die Maschinenstürmer: Ein Drama aus der Zeit der Ludditenbewegung in England.* Leipzig, Vienna, and Zurich: E. P. Tal, 1922. Also appears in vol. 2 of *Gesammelte Werke,* 113–90. Munich, 1978. English translation: *The Machine Wreckers.* New York: Knopf, 1923. [See also *The Machine Wreckers.* English version by Ashley Dukes. London: Royal National Theatre, Nick Hern Books, 1995.]

———. *Masse Mensch: Ein Stück aus der sozialen Revolution des 20. Jahrhunderts.* Potsdam, 1920. Also published in *Gesammelte Werke,* 5 vols. Vol. 2, *Dramen und Gedichte aus dem Gefängnis (1918–1924)* (Plays and poems from prison), 63–112. Munich: Hanser, 1978. English translation: *Masses and Man.* In *Seven Plays,* by Ernst Toller and Hermann

Kesten, together with Mary Baker Eddy, 3–54. With a new introduction by the author. New York: Liveright, 1936.

Zola, Émile. *Germinal.* Berlin, 1885, 1930. English translation: *Germinal.* Baltimore: Penguin Books, 1969.

2. Literature Consulted by the Editors

The Apocryphal Acts of Paul and Thecla. Edited by Jan N. Bremmer. Kampen, The Netherlands: Kok Pharos, 1996.

Arendt, Hannah. *Eichmann in Jerusalem: Ein Bericht von der Banalität des Bösen.* Munich, 1964. [A translation of the original English: *Eichmann in Jerusalem: A Report on the Banality of Evil.* Revised and enlarged edition. New York: Penguin Books, 1963, 1994.]

Aristotle. "Politics." In *The Basic Works of Aristotle,* 1127–316. Edited by Richard McKeon. New York: Random House, 1941.

Barnett, Victoria. *For the Soul of the People: Protestant Protest against Hitler.* New York: Oxford University Press, 1992.

Baumann, Hans. *Lieder: Eine Auswahl* (Songs: A selection). Potsdam, n.d.

Bethge, Eberhard. *Dietrich Bonhoeffer: Theologe, Christ, Zeitgenosse. Eine Biographie.* Munich: Chr. Kaiser, 1967; 7th. ed., 1989. English translation: *Dietrich Bonhoeffer: A Biography.* Revised edition. Edited and revised by Victoria Barnett. Minneapolis: Fortress Press, 1999.

———. *In Zitz gab es keine Juden: Erinnerungen aus meinen ersten vierzig Jahren* (In Zitz, there were no Jews: Recollections from my first forty years). Munich: Chr. Kaiser, 1989.

Bethge, Eberhard, and Renate Bethge, eds. *Letzte Briefe im Widerstand: Aus dem Kreis der Familie Bonhoeffer.* 2d ed. Munich, 1984, 1988. English translation: *Last Letters of Resistance: Farewells from the Bonhoeffer Family.* Philadelphia: Fortress Press, 1986.

Bethge, Eberhard, Renate Bethge, and Christian Gremmels, eds. *Dietrich Bonhoeffer: Sein Leben in Bildern und Texten.* 2d ed. Munich: Chr. Kaiser, 1989. English translation: *Dietrich Bonhoeffer: A Life in Pictures.* London: SCM Press; Philadelphia: Fortress Press, 1986.

Bethge, Renate. "Bonhoeffer and the Role of Women." *Church and Society* 85, no. 6 (July–August 1995): 78–92.

———. "Bonhoeffer's Family and Its Significance for His Theology." In *Dietrich Bonhoeffer–His Significance for North Americans,* by Larry Rasmussen. Minneapolis: Fortress Press, 1989.

———. "Bonhoeffer's Picture of Women." In *Bonhoeffer's Ethics: Old Europe and New Frontiers,* edited by Guy C. Carter et al., 194–99. Kampen: Kok Pharos, 1991.

———. "'Elite' and 'Silence' in Bonhoeffer's Person and Thoughts." In *Ethical Responsibility: Bonhoeffer's Legacy to the Churches,* edited by John D. Godsey and Geffrey B. Kelly, 293–305. New York and Toronto: Edwin Mellen Press, 1981.

Bethge, Renate, and Eberhard Bethge. "Einleitung." In *Fragmente aus Tegel: Drama und Roman,* by Dietrich Bonhoeffer, 7–20. Munich: Chr. Kaiser, 1978. English translation: "Introduction." In *Fiction from Prison: Gathering Up the Past,* by Dietrich Bonhoeffer. Philadelphia: Fortress Press, 1981.

Bonhoeffer, Dietrich. "Boden unter den Füßen" (Ground under our feet). *Die Kirche in Hamburg* 2 (1955): 4.

———. *Christ the Center.* A new translation [from the *GS*] by Edwin H. Robertson. London: Collins; San Francisco: Harper & Row, 1978. [U.K. title: *Christology.*]

———. "Der Nachbar" (The neighbor). *Die Schöpfung* (Berlin), 2d issue (1948): 43–47. English translation: In *True Patriotism* (see below), 199–215.

———. *Dietrich Bonhoeffer Werke.* 17 vols. Edited by Eberhard Bethge et al. Gütersloh: Chr. Kaiser/Gütersloher Verlagshaus, 1986–99. English translation: *Dietrich Bonhoeffer Works.* 17 vols. Wayne Whitson Floyd, Jr., General Editor. Minneapolis: Fortress Press, 1996–.

2: *Akt und Sein: Transzendentalphilosophie und Ontologie in der systematischen Theologie.* Edited by Hans-Richard Reuter. Munich: Chr. Kaiser Verlag, 1988. English translation: *Act and Being: Transcendental Philosophy and Ontology in Systematic Theology.* Edited by Wayne Whitson Floyd, Jr. Translated by H. Martin Rumscheidt. Minneapolis: Fortress Press, 1996.

3: *Schöpfung und Fall: Theologische Auslegung von Genesis 1–3.* Edited by Martin Rüter and Ilse Tödt. Munich: Chr. Kaiser Verlag, 1989. English translation: *Creation and Fall: A Theological Exposition of Genesis 1–3.* Edited by John W. de Gruchy. Translated by Douglas Stephen Bax. Minneapolis: Fortress Press, 1997.

4: *Nachfolge.* Edited by Martin Kuske and Ilse Tödt. Munich: Chr. Kaiser, 1989; 2d ed., Gütersloh, 1994.

6: *Ethik.* Edited by Ilse Tödt et al. Munich: Chr. Kaiser, 1992; 2d ed., Gütersloh, 1998.

9: *Jugend und Studium, 1918–1927*. Edited by Hans Pfeifer with Clifford Green and Carl-Jürgen Kaltenborn. Munich: Chr. Kaiser, 1986.

10: *Barcelona, Berlin, Amerika, 1928–1931*. Edited by Reinhard Staats and Hans Christoph von Hase with Holger Roggelin and Matthias Wünsche. Munich: Chr. Kaiser, 1991.

——. *Fragmente aus Tegel: Drama und Roman*. Edited by Renate Bethge and Eberhard Bethge. Munich: Chr. Kaiser, 1978. English translation: *Fiction from Prison: Gathering Up the Past*. Edited by Renate Bethge and Eberhard Bethge with Clifford Green. Translated by Ursula Hoffmann. Commentary by Ruth Zerner. Philadelphia: Fortress Press, 1981.

——. *Gesammelte Schriften* (Collected works). 6 vols. Edited by Eberhard Bethge. Munich: Chr. Kaiser, 1958–74.

——. "Glück und Macht." *Unterwegs* 4 (1954): 196–205. Also in *Dietrich Bonhoeffer: Einführung in seine Botschaft* (Dietrich Bonhoeffer: Introduction to his message). Wuppertal: Evangelische Kirche im Rheinland, 1955. English translation: "Happiness and Power." Translated by Hilda M. Bishop. *The Bridge* (April 1945): 4–15.

——. *I Loved This People*. Translated by Keith Crim. London: SPCK; Richmond: John Knox Press, 1965.

——. "Letter to Paul Lehmann (September 20, 1941)." *Newsletter,* International Bonhoeffer Society, English Language Section, no. 68 (October 1998): 10–11.

——. "Letters: Dietrich Bonhoeffer, Paul Lehmann, and Others, 1932–1949." In Green, *Bonhoeffer: A Theology of Sociality*.

——. *No Rusty Swords: Letters, Lectures and Notes. 1928–1936*. From the Collected Works of Dietrich Bonhoeffer, vol. 1. Edited and with an introduction by Edwin H. Robertson. Translated by Edwin H. Robertson and John Bowden. London: Collins; New York: Harper and Row, 1965.

——. *True Patriotism: Letters and Notes, 1939–1945*. Edited by Edwin H. Robertson. Translated by Edwin H. Robertson, and John Bowden. New York: Harper and Row, 1973.

——. *The Way to Freedom: Letters, Lectures and Notes, 1935–1939*. Edited by Edwin H. Robertson. Translated by Edwin H. Robertson and John Bowden. New York: Harper and Row, 1966.

——. *Widerstand und Ergebung: Briefe und Aufzeichnungen aus der Haft*. Edited by Eberhard Bethge with an afterword by Christian Gremmels. Munich: Chr. Kaiser, 1951; 14th ed., 1990.

———. *Widerstand und Ergebung: Briefe und Aufzeichnungen aus der Haft.* Neuausgabe. Edited by Eberhard Bethge. Munich, 1985. English translation: *Letters and Papers from Prison.* Edited by Eberhard Bethge. Enlarged edition. London: SCM Press, 1971; New York: Simon & Schuster, 1997.

———. *Zettelnotizen fur eine "Ethik"* (*Ethics* working notes). Supplementary volume to *DBW* 6: *Ethik.* Edited by Ilse Tödt. Gütersloh: Chr. Kaiser/Güterloher Verlagshaus, 1993.

Bonhoeffer, Dietrich, and Maria von Wedemeyer. *Brautbriefe Zelle 92: Dietrich Bonhoeffer-Maria von Wedemeyer, 1943–1945.* Edited by Ruth-Alice von Bismarck and Ulrich Kabitz. Munich: Beck, 1992. English translation: *Love Letters from Cell 92: The Correspondence between Dietrich Bonhoeffer and Maria von Wedemeyer, 1943–45.* Translated by John Brownjohn. Nashville: Abingdon Press, 1995.

Bonhoeffer, Emmi. "Das Haus in der Wangenheimstraße: Mama zum ersten Geburtstag im neuen Haus, [December 30,] 1935." In *Fragmente aus Tegel: Drama und Roman,* by Dietrich Bonhoeffer, 174–80. English translation: "The House on Wangenheimstrasse: For Mother on Her First Birthday in the New House, [December 30,] 1935." In *Fiction from Prison,* by Dietrich Bonhoeffer, 133–38.

Bonhoeffer, Karl. "Lebenserinnerungen: Geschrieben für die Familie" (Memoir: Written for the family). In *Karl Bonhoeffer zum Hundertsten Geburtstag am 31. Marz 1968* (Karl Bonhoeffer on his hundredth birthday, March 31, 1968), edited by Jürg Zutt, E. Straus, and H. Scheller, 8–107. Berlin, Heidelberg, and New York, 1969.

Bonhoeffer, Klaus. "Verfassung [des Hauses Bonhoeffer, Dezember 1926]" (A constitution [of the Bonhoeffer house as of December 1926]). In *Fiction from Prison,* by Dietrich Bonhoeffer, 131–33.

Borchert, Wolfgang. *The Man Outside: Selected Works.* London and New York: Marion Boyars, 1996.

Brecht, Bertolt. "An die Nachgeborenen." In *Hundert Gedichte.* Berlin, 1951. English translation: "To Those Born Later." In *Poems, 1913–1956,* edited by John Willett and Ralph Mannheim with Erich Fried, translated by John Willet. New York: Methuen, 1976.

Burckhardt, Jacob. *Weltgeschichtliche Betrachtungen.* Bern: Verlag Hallwag, 1941. English translation: *Reflections on History.* Translated by M. D. Hottinger. Introduction by Gottfried Dietze. Indianapolis: Liberty Classics, 1943, 1979.

de Lange, Frits. "Grond onder de voeten: Burgerlijkheid bij Dietrich

Bonhoeffer" (Ground under one's feet: Civic responsibility according to Dietrich Bonhoeffer). Theology diss., Kampen, 1985.

Eliot, Thomas Stearns. *The Rock: A Pageant Play.* London: Faber & Faber; New York: Harcourt Brace, 1934.

Evangelisches Gesangbuch erarbeitet im Auftrag der Evangelischen Kirche in Deutschland seit 1992 (Protestant hymnbook compiled under commission by the Evangelical Church in Germany, since 1992). Hannover: Lutherisches Verlagshaus, 1994.

Evangelisches Kirchengesangbuch in den Gliedkirchen der Evangelischen Kirche in Deutschland, seit 1951 (Protestant church hymnal for the member churches of the Protestant Church of Germany, in use since 1951).

Feuerbach, Ludwig. *Vorlesungen über das Wesen der Religion.* Vol. 8 of *Sämtliche Werke.* Nebst Zusätzen und Anmerkungen. Leipzig, 1851. English translation: *Lectures on the Essence of Religion.* New York: Harper & Row, 1967.

———. *Das Wesen des Christentums.* Vol. 7 of *Sämtliche Werke.* Leipzig, 1841; 3d ed., 1849. English translation: *The Essence of Christianity.* New York: Harper, 1957.

Freyer, Hans. *Antäus: Grundlegung einer Ethik des bewussten Lebens* (Antaeus: Foundation for an ethic of conscious life). Jena, Germany: E. Diederichs, 1918.

George, Stefan. *Der Stern des Bundes.* Berlin, 1913, 1928. Also appears as vol. 8 of *Gesamtausgabe der Werke* (Complete edition of works). 18 vols. Critical ed. Berlin, 1927–34. English translation: *Poems.* Translated by Carol North Valhope and Ernest Morwitz. New York: Schocken, 1943.

Godsey, John. *Preface to Bonhoeffer: The Man and Two of His Shorter Writings.* Philadelphia: Fortress Press, 1965.

Goethe, Johann Wolfgang von. *Goethes Sprüche in Reimen: Zahme Xenien und Invektiven* (Goethe's aphorisms in rhyme: Tame epigrams and invectives). Edited by Max Hecker. Leipzig: Insel-Verlag, 1908.

Gotthelf, Jeremias. "Elsi, die seltsame Magd" (Elsie, the quaint maiden). In *Erzählungen* (Stories). Leipzig: Dieterich, 1965.

———. "Hans Joggeli der Erbvetter" (Hans Joggeli, the rich cousin). In his *Erzählungen* (Stories). Leipzig: Dieterich, 1965.

Grabbe, Christian Dietrich. *Die Hermannsschlacht.* Berlin: Volkschaft–verlagt für buch, bühne und film, 1934.

Green, Clifford. *Bonhoeffer: A Theology of Sociality.* Grand Rapids, Mich.: Eerdmans, 1999.

——, ed. "Letters: Dietrich Bonhoeffer, Paul Lehmann, and Others, 1932–1949." In Green, *Bonhoeffer: A Theology of Sociality.*

Grimm, Hans. *Volk ohne Raum* (Nation without room). 2 vols. Munich: A. Langen, 1926. English translation: "A Nation without Room." Translated by Henry Safford King. The Bancroft Library, Berkeley, Calif. Typescript.

Hase, Karl Alfred von. *Unsre Hauschronik: Geschichte der Familie Hase in vier Jahrhunderten* (Our house chronicles: A history of the Hase family over four centuries). Leipzig: Breitkopf & Härtel, 1898.

Henkys, Jürgen. *Dietrich Bonhoeffers Gefängnisgedichte: Beiträge zu ihrer Interpretation* (Dietrich Bonhoeffer's prison poems: Toward an interpretation). Munich: Chr. Kaiser, 1986.

Jost, Adolf. *Das Recht auf den Tod: Soziale Studie* (The right to die: A social study). Göttingen: Dieterich, 1895.

Kafka, Franz. *The Metamorphosis: Translation, Backgrounds and Contexts, Criticism.* Translated and edited by Stanley Corngold. New York: W. W. Norton, 1996.

——. *Der Prozeß.* 1925. English translation: *The Trial.* A new translation, based on the restored text. Translated and with a preface by Breon Mitchell. New York: Schocken, 1998.

Kalckreuth, Johannes. *Wesen und Werk meines Vaters: Lebensbild des Malers Graf Leopold von Kalckreuth* (The life and work of my father: A life portrait of the painter Graf Leopold von Kalckreuth). Hamburg: Christians, 1967.

Kelly, Geffrey B., and F. Burton Nelson, eds. *A Testament to Freedom: The Essential Writings of Dietrich Bonhoeffer.* Rev. ed. San Francisco: HarperSanFrancisco, 1995.

Krötke, Wolf. "Teilnehmen am Leiden Gottes: Zu Dietrich Bonhoeffers Verstandnis eines 'religionsloses Christentums' " (Participation in the suffering of God: On Dietrich Bonhoeffer's understanding of a "nonreligious Christianity"). In *450 Jahre Evangelische Theologie in Berlin* (450 years of Protestant theology in Berlin), edited by Gerhard Besier and Christof Gestrich, 39–457. Göttingen: Vandenhoeck & Ruprecht, 1989.

Latmiral, Gaetano. "Einige Erinnerungen der Haft in dem Wehrmachtsuntersuchungsgefängnis Berlin-Tegel [Anfang Oktober 1943 bis Ende

Dezember 1944] von einigen italienischen Offizieren" (Recollections of imprisonment in the Berlin-Tegel army interrogation prison [from the beginning of October 1943 to the end of December 1944] by some Italian officers). Unpublished manuscript, 1972.

——. "Erinnerungen eines Mithäftlings in Tegel" (Recollections of a fellow prisoner in Tegel). In *Wie eine Flaschenpost: Ökumenische Briefe und Beiträge für Eberhard Bethge* (Like a message in a bottle: Ecumenical letters and essays for Eberhard Bethge), edited by Heinz Eduard Tödt et al., 92–94. Munich: Chr. Kaiser, 1979.

Leibholz-Bonhoeffer, Sabine. *Vergangen, erlebt, überwunden: Schicksal der Familie Bonhoeffer.* 4th ed. Gütersloh: Gütersloher Verlagshaus, 1983. English translation: *The Bonhoeffers: Portrait of a Family.* 2d ed. Chicago: Covenant Publications, 1994.

Lipperheide, Franz Freiherr von. *Spruchwörterbuch* (Dictionary of phrases). 2d ed. Munich: Bruckmann, 1907, 1909.

Luther, Martin. *Vorlesung über den Römerbrief 1515/1516. Werke: Kritische Gesamtausgabe,* vol. 56. English translation: *Lectures on Romans. Luther's Works,* vol. 25. Edited by Hilton C. Oswald. "Glosses": chaps. 1-2, trans. Walter G. Tillmanns; chaps. 3-16, trans. Jacob A. O. Preus. "Scholia": chaps. 1-2, trans. Walter G. Tillmanns; chaps. 3-15, trans. Jacob A. O. Preus.

Moltke, Helmuth James von. *Bericht aus Deutschland im Jahre 1943: Letzte Briefe aus dem Gefängnis Tegel 1945* (Report from Germany in 1943: Last letters from Tegel Prison 1945.)

More, Sir Thomas. *Utopia.* Latin text and an English translation. Cambridge and New York: Cambridge University Press, 1995.

Müller, Hanfried. *Von der Kirche zur Welt: Ein Beitrag zu der Beziehung des Wortes Gottes auf die societas in Dietrich Bonhoeffers theologischer Entwicklung* (From the church to the world: A study of the relationship of the word of God to society in Dietrich Bonhoeffer's theological development). Leipzig, 1961; 2d ed., Hamburg-Bergstedt, 1966.

Nachlaß Dietrich Bonhoeffer: Ein Verzeichnis. Archiv–Sammlung–Bibliothek (Dietrich Bonhoeffer's literary estate: An inventory. Archive, collection, and library). Edited by Dietrich Meyer with Eberhard Bethge. Munich: Chr. Kaiser, 1987.

Nietzsche, Friedrich. *Samtliche Werke: Kritische Gesamtausgabe* (Collected works: Critical edition). Edited by Giorgio Colli and Mazzino Montinari. Berlin: W. de Gruyter, 1967–77.

Ostermann, Christian. *Lateinisches Übungsbuch* (Latin exercise book). Leipzig, 1869–75; 13th ed., 1937.

Palmer, Larry. *Hugo Distler and His Church Music.* St. Louis and London: Concordia, 1967.

Paton, William. *The Church and the New Order in Europe.* New York: Macmillan, 1941.

Peck, William J., ed. *New Studies in Bonhoeffer's Ethics.* Lewiston, New York, and Queenston, Ontario: Edwin Mellen Press, 1987.

Polack, William Gustave. *The Handbook to the "Lutheran Hymnal."* St. Louis: Concordia, 1942.

Rauschning, Hermann. *Die Revolution des Nihilismus: Kulisse und Wirklichkeit im dritten Reich.* Zürich: Europa Verlag, 1938; rev. ed. by Golo Mann, 1964. English translation: *The Revolution of Nihilism: Warning to the West.* New York: Longmans, Green, 1939.

Rilke, Rainer Maria. *Die Aufzeichnungen des Malte Laurids Brigge.* Vol. 5 of *Gesammelte Werke.* Leipzig, 1930. English translation: *The Notebooks of Malte Laurids Brigge.* Translated by M. D. Herter Norton. New York: W. W. Norton, 1964.

———. *Das Stundenbuch: Drittes Buch. Das Buch von der Armut und vom Tode.* Vol. 2 of *Gesammelte Werke.* Leipzig, 1930. English translation: *Rilke's Book of Hours: Love Poems to God.* Translated by Anita Barrows and Joanna Macy. New York: Riverhead Books, 1996.

———. *Requiem.* Leipzig, 1923. Also published as vol. 2 of *Gesammelte Werke.* Leipzig, 1930. English translation: *Requiem and Other Poems.* Translated by J. B. Leishman. London: Hogarth Press, 1957.

Robertson, Edwin. *The Prison Poems of Dietrich Bonhoeffer.* Guildford: Inter Publishing Service, 1998.

Scheffel, Viktor von. *Ekkehard.* Edited by Friedrich Panzer. Leipzig: Bibliographisches Institut, 1920.

Schiller, Friedrich. *Werke.* 4 vols. Potsdam and Berlin, n.d. English translation: *The Works of Frederick Schiller.* London: Bell & Daldy, 1872.

Schirach, Baldur von. *Die Fahne der Verfolgten* (The banner of the persecuted). Berlin, 1933.

Schollmeyer, Matthias. "Bonhoeffers Theologie zwischen Geheimnis und Rationalität: Untersuchungen zur Struktur eines Fragments" (Bonhoeffer's theology between secrecy and rationality: A study of the structure of a fragment). Theology diss., Halle an der Saale, 1986.

———. "Das 'wunderbare Tier': Der Mythos in der späten 'belletristischen' Theologie Bonhoeffers und der Einfluß Nietzsches im Tegeler Dramenfragment" (The "wondrous beast": Myth in the late "literary" theology of Bonhoeffer and the influence of Nietzsche on the Tegel drama fragment). Unpublished manuscript, 1989.

Die Schöpfung: Schriften der Besinnung (The creation: Contemplative writings). 2d ser. Berlin, 1948.

Sombart, Werner. *Deutsche Sozialismus* (German socialism). Berlin-Charlottenburg: Buchholz & Weisswange, 1934.

Sperna Weiland, Jan. *Het einde van de religie: Verder op het spoor van Bonhoeffer* (The end of religion: Following in Bonhoeffer's path). Baarn, The Netherlands, 1970.

Tödt, Heinz Eduard. *Theologische Perspektiven nach Dietrich Bonhoeffer* (Theological perspectives according to Dietrich Bonhoeffer). Edited by Ernst Albert Scharffenorth. Gütersloh: Gütersloher Verlagshaus, 1993.

Tödt, Heinz Eduard et al., eds. *Wie eine Flaschenpost: Ökumenische Briefe und Beiträge für Eberhard Bethge* (Like a message in a bottle: Ecumenical letters and essays for Eberhard Bethge). Munich: Chr. Kaiser, 1979.

Uns geht die Sonne nicht unter: Lieder der Hitler Jugend (Our sun never sets: Songs of the Hitler Youth). Edited by the upper-west region of the Hitler Youth. July 1934.

Wendel, Ernst Georg. *Studien zur Homiletik Dietrich Bonhoeffers: Predigt–Hermeneutik–Sprache* (Studies in Dietrich Bonhoeffer's homiletics: Preaching, hermeneutics, language). Vol. 21 of *Hermeneutische Untersuchungen zur Theologie* (Hermeneutical investigations into theology). Tübingen: Mohr, 1985.

West, Charles C. "Ground under Our Feet: A Reflection on the Worldliness of Dietrich Bonhoeffer's Life and Thought." In *New Studies in Bonhoeffer's Ethics,* edited by William J. Peck, 235–73. Lewiston, N.Y.: Edwin Mellen Press, 1987.

Wotquennne, Alfred. *Thematisches Verzeichnis der Werke von Carl Philipp Emanuel Bach, 1714–1788* (A thematic inventory of the works of Carl Philipp Emanuel Bach, 1714–1788). Wiesbaden: Breitkopf & Härtel, 1904, 1964.

Zerner, Ruth. "Regression und Kreativität: Ein Nachwort." In *Fragmente aus Tegel: Drama und Roman,* by Dietrich Bonhoeffer, translated by Renate and Eberhard Bethge, 181–216, 237–42. Munich: Chr. Kaiser,

1978. English original: "Dietrich Bonhoeffer's Prison Fiction: A Commentary." In *Fiction from Prison: Gathering Up the Past,* by Dietrich Bonhoeffer, 139–67, 200–206. Philadelphia: Fortress Press, 1981.

Zimmermann, Wolf-Dieter, ed. *Begegnungen mit Dietrich Bonhoeffer.* Munich: Chr. Kaiser, 1964; 4th ed., 1969. English translation: *I Knew Dietrich Bonhoeffer: Reminiscences by His Friends.* Edited by Wolf-Dieter Zimmermann and Ronald Gregor Smith. Translated by Käthe Gregor Smith. London: Collins; New York: Harper & Row, 1966.

Zutt, Jürg, Erwin Strauss, and Heinrich Scheller, eds. *Karl Bonhoeffer: Zum Hundertsten Geburtstag am 31. März 1968* (Karl Bonhoeffer: On the one-hundredth anniversary of his birth, March 31, 1968). Berlin, Heidelberg, and New York, 1969.

Zweig, Stefan. *Jeremias: Eine dramatische Dichtung in neun Bildern.* Leipzig, 1917, 1928. English translation: *Jeremiah: A Drama in Nine Scenes.* Translated by Eden Paul and Cedar Paul from the revised German edition. With a new preface by the author. New York: Viking Press, 1939.

Index of
Scriptural References

INDEX OF NAMES

THIS INDEX LISTS people mentioned in this book and particularly authors of literature cited. It provides profiles of these people, and differs from the German edition by also including information about those whose work began after 1945. The characters in Bonhoeffer's drama, novel, and story are listed as well. The index does not, however, include translators of works cited who are listed in the bibliography. The index includes significant references to Dietrich Bonhoeffer and Eberhard Bethge, but it does not itemize routine references as in "Bonhoeffer wrote . . ." and "letter to Bethge."

1981, professor of Protestant theology at the University of Kassel; from 1985 on, chair of West German Section of the International Bonhoeffer Society; following German unification, after 1992, chair of the International Bonhoeffer Society, German Section—21

Grimm, Hans (1875–1959): German author; salesman in South Africa for many years—125, 129, 160, 178

Guardini, Romano (1885–1968): German-speaking religious philosopher; 1923–39, professor in Breslau with a teaching position in Berlin; 1939, forced to take a pension; 1945, professor in Tübingen; 1948, in Munich—26, 52, 55f.

Gypsy: proposed character in drama—239f.

Hans: character in the drama, father and doctor; see also Brake, Hans—25, 28ff., 34, 36

Harnack, Adolf von (1851–1930): German theologian; after 1888, professor of church history in Berlin; 1911, cofounder and first president of the Kaiser Wilhelm Society for the Advancement of Science; 1914, knighted—163

Hase, Hans Christoph von (b. 1907): cousin of Dietrich Bonhoeffer and German theologian—115, 129, 221

Hase, Hans-Jürgen von: second cousin of Dietrich Bonhoeffer; mid-January 1933, emigrated to Southwest Africa where he was at first a civil servant; 1940–46, interned in camps in South Africa; 1947–75, farmer in Namibia—124

Hase, Karl Alfred von (1842–1914): grandfather of Dietrich Bonhoeffer and German theologian; 1889, court preacher in Potsdam; 1894, high consistory counselor and professor of theology; wrote a history of the von Hase family titled *Unsre Hauschronik*—88

Hase, Karl August (1800–1890): German theologian and church historian; 1824–25, in custody for eleven months in Hohenasperg as a student fraternity member; after 1830, professor in Jena; 1831, married Paula, née Härtel; 1833, knighted, but never used his title—87f.

Hase, Pauline Härtel von—112

Haydn, Joseph: Austrian composer—81

Heidegger, Martin (1889–1976): German philosopher; 1928–45, professor in Freiburg im Breisgau; in 1933 he was the first National Socialist rector of the university; 1945, forbidden to teach by the occupation forces until 1951—60

Heine, Heinrich (1797–1856): German poet; 1825, converted from Judaism to Christianity; 1831, left Germany for Paris—228

Heinrich: character in the drama—25, 39, 46f., 52–70, 197f., 205f., 220, 227

Henkys, Jürgen: studied Protestant theology in Wuppertal, Göttingen, Heidelberg, and Bonn; 1954, assistant pastor in Gross Mehssow, Niederlausitz; 1956–65, assistant pastor, director of studies and instructor at the preachers' seminary in Havel, Brandenburg, and also pastor at the cathedral there; 1965, doctorate in practical theology; and professor of practical theology at the Protestant theological institute in Berlin-Brandenburg; 1991, professor at Humboldt University; publications in practical theology, Bible study, hymnody, and Bonhoeffer's prison poetry—165

Hercules: Greek mythic hero, son of Zeus—68

Hilde: character in the novel—77, 79

Hildebrandt, Franz (1909–85): German theologian; after 1927, a close friend of Dietrich Bonhoeffer; 1930, spent several months in Friedrich Siegmund-Schultze's Social Welfare Working Group, East Berlin; 1931, doctoral graduation; 1933, ordained; after the "Brown Synod" in September 1933, which demanded that the clergy act wholeheartedly for the National Socialist state and be of Aryan descent, Hildebrandt, who had some Jewish ancestry, resigned his ordination; until 1934, with Bonhoeffer in his London parsonage; 1934, assistant to Martin Niemöller in Berlin; 1935–37, instructor at the theological seminary in Berlin; 1937, after a short period in custody from July to August, emigrated to England; 1939–46, pastor of the German Lutheran refugees in Cambridge; 1946, Methodist minister and professor of theology in England, at Drew University in the United States, and in Scotland; 1968, resigned from the Methodist Conference—7, 119, 221, 228

Hitler, Adolf (1889–1945): German dictator, founder of the National Socialist German Workers' Party (NSDAP) in 1920; 1933, became Reich Chancellor; 1934, called "Führer and Reich Chancellor" of the "Third Reich"; April 30, 1945, committed suicide—31, 57, 88, 109, 124, 160, 172, 205, 208, 211, 215, 233

Holl, Karl (1866–1926): German theologian and Luther scholar; after 1906, professor in Berlin; 1915, became a member of the Prussian Academy of Sciences—163

Homer: Greek poet; the epics, the *Odyssey* and the *Iliad,* are attributed to him—147

Horn, Maria (1884–1967): German educator, came from the Herrnhut community of Moravian Brethren; from 1908 until her marriage to Dr. Richard Czeppan in 1923 she was in the Bonhoeffer house, serving as governess when the children were young—229

Hoskin, Marilyn—23

Howard, Molly—23

Jacob: biblical character, renamed Israel in Gen. 32:28—76

Jaspers, Karl (1883–1969): German philosopher—50, 67, 164, 170, 172, 202

Jeremiah: biblical character and prophet—27, 223

Jonathan: biblical character—115

Jost, Adolf—35

Julianus, Flavius Claudius (332–63): Roman emperor from 361–63; known as Julian the Apostate—228

Kafka, Franz (1883–1924): German novelist and short-story writer—21f., 39

Kalckreuth, Johannes Graf (1893–1956): German musician and writer on music—122

Tafel, Leonhard (1800–1880): Great-great uncle of Dietrich Bonhoeffer; one of the four Würtemburg Tafel brothers; a philologist and preceptor at the Latin school in Schorndorf; emigrated to the United States where he was pastor of the Swedenborgian "New Church"—124

Tertullian (c. 160–220): Roman Christian theologian—225

Thecla: martyr and saint—84

Tödt, Heinz Eduard (1918–91): after school graduation, military service from 1937–39; 1939–45, action at the front; 1945–50, Soviet prisoner of war; 1951–57, studied theology in Bethel, Basel, Göttingen, and Heidelberg, earning doctorate in theology; 1947–61, theological director of Protestant student work in Villigst near Schwerte an der Ruhr; after 1963, professor of systematic theology, ethics, and social ethics at the University of Heidelberg; 1983, emeritus, then directed research seminar on contemporary church history; 1978–1985, chair of the International Bonhoeffer Society, West German Section; from 1985 until his death, chair of the editorial board of the *Dietrich Bonhoeffer Werke*—8

Tödt, Ilse (b. 1930): studied anthropology and indigenous religion at the Technical University, Hanover, at the universities of Göttingen, Hamburg, Frankfurt, and at Ohio State University; 1957, Ph.D, Göttingen; since 1961, at the Protestant Research Institute (FEST) in Heidelberg, concentrating on editing and translating, above all in many volumes of the *Dietrich Bonhoeffer Werke;* since 1992, member of the *DBW* editorial board; 1995, honorary doctorate in theology, University of Basel—8, 13, 16, 22f., 62

Toller, Ernst (1893–1939): German author; in 1918 participated in the Bavarian communist revolt in Munich; 1919–24, in prison, where he wrote revolutionary expressionist plays which gained much attention in the 1920s; in 1933, citizenship revoked by the National Socialist regime because of his Jewish ancestry; 1939, committed suicide in a New York hotel—52, 64, 67, 81

Trott, Adam von (1909–44): 1931, completed law degree; 1931–33, Rhodes Scholar at Oxford; 1933–36, magistrate posts in Kassel and Hamburg; turned down political job at I. G. Farben chemical corporation; 1937–38, study year in China; 1939–44, used position in Foreign Office to travel to the U.S., France, Britain, Scandinavia, Switzerland and Italy on behalf of Jews and anti-Nazi conspiracy; arrested July 25, 1944 in Berlin after failed coup; executed August 26, 1944—22

Ulrich: character in the drama and the novel—25, 30, 33, 36, 38–51, 82, 100–108, 110–12, 114–17, 123, 127–31, 136, 143, 158, 171, 173, 181, 197, 217, 219f., 225, 239f., 241f.

Vick, Valerie—23

Vilmar, August Friedrich Christian (1800–1868): German theologian, literary historian, and member of the state parliament; after 1855, professor in Marburg; fought for a specifically Hessian Lutheranism against the foreign control of Hesse by Prussia—87

Voss, Johann Heinrich (1751–1826): German poet and translator of Homer, among others; 1781, translated the *Odyssey* and, in 1793, the *Iliad*—147

Warmblut, Frau (Frau Warmblood): character in the novel—17, 77–79

Wedemeyer, Hans von (1888–1942): estate owner in Pätzig and Klein Reetz/Neumark; married Ruth, née von Kleist-Retzow; was a member of the Berneuchen circle; on August 22, 1942, he fell near Stalingrad as a major and a battalion leader of an infantry regiment—124, 143

Wedemeyer, Ruth von, née von Kleist–Retzow (1897–1983): 1918, married Hans von Wedemeyer in Pätzig/Neumark; 1945, fled to Westphalia, and later to Hannover—82

Wedemeyer-Weller, Maria von (1924–77): daughter of Hans and Ruth von Wedemeyer and niece of Ruth von Kleist-Retzow, née Zedlitz-Trützschler; 1942, school graduation; January 1943 engaged to Dietrich Bonhoeffer; worked as a Red Cross nurse in Hannover; 1944, teacher in Altenburg; after 1946, studied mathematics in Göttingen and at Bryn Mawr College; 1949, married Paul–Werner Schniewind; emigrated to the United States; worked in computer firms; 1959, married Barton Weller; eventually head of the development department at Honeywell Corporation, Boston—5, 7, 26, 43f., 87, 90, 115, 123f., 143, 180, 196, 199, 217f.

Wedemeyer, Ruth-Alice von: see Bismarck

Wendel, Ernst Georg—69

West, Charles C. (b. 1921): 1947–50, mission service in China; 1950–53, ecumenical service in Mainz and Berlin; 1955, Ph.D. Yale, in ethics; 1956–61, associate director, Ecumenical Institute, Bossey, World Council of Churches, Celigny, Switzerland; 1961–91, professor of Christian ethics, Princeton Theological Seminary; 1991, emeritus—69

Wolf, Hugo (1860–1903): Austrian composer; master of the art song; composed over three hundred lieder—137

Wotquenne, Alfred (1867–1939): German musicologist—38

"Yellowboots": see Kruse

York von Wartenburg, Duchess Helene, née Kalckreuth (1852–1925): great-aunt of Dietrich Bonhoeffer—133

Zerner, Ruth (b. 1935): 1957–58, Fulbright Fellowship, Free University of Berlin; 1962, Ph.D., University of California, Berkeley, in modern German history; 1962–68, professor of history, Hunter College, City University of New York; after 1968, Associate Professor of History, Lehman College, City University of New York—8, 16, 200

Zimmermann, Wolf-Dieter (b. 1911): German pastor; one of Bonhoeffer's students of theology in Berlin in 1932; during the 1936 summer term he was at the Finkenwalde Preachers' Seminary of the Confessing Church led

INDEX OF SUBJECTS

EDITORS AND TRANSLATOR

WAYNE WHITSON FLOYD, JR. (Ph.D., Emory University), is visiting professor and director of the Dietrich Bonhoeffer Center at the Lutheran Theological Seminary at Philadelphia, a Dean's Fellow in the Religion Department of Dickinson College, and serves as Canon Theologian for the Episcopal Cathedral of St. Stephen in Harrisburg, Pennsylvania. He is General Editor and Project Director of the *Dietrich Bonhoeffer Works* English edition. He is the author of *Theology and the Dialectics of Otherness: On Reading Bonhoeffer and Adorno* (University Press of America, 1988); he co-authored with Clifford Green the *Bonhoeffer Bibliography: Primary Sources and Secondary Literature in English* (American Theological Library Association, 1992); and he co-edited with Charles Marsh *Theology and the Practice of Responsibility: Essays on Dietrich Bonhoeffer* (Trinity Press International, 1995). Dr. Floyd's articles on Bonhoeffer have appeared in *Union Seminary Quarterly Review, The Lutheran, Modern Theology, Religious Studies Review, Dialog, Modern Theology,* and *Christian Century.*

CLIFFORD GREEN (Ph.D., Union Theological Seminary, New York) is Professor of Theology at Hartford Seminary. A native of Australia, his early education was at Sydney University and Melbourne College of Divinity. Founding president of the International Bonhoeffer Society, English Language Section, he now serves as Executive Director of the *Dietrich Bonhoeffer Works* English edition. He is the author of *Bonhoeffer: A Theology of Sociality* (Eerdmans, 1999); co-editor of *Ethik* and *Jugend und Studium* in the German *Dietrich Bonhoeffer Werke;* editor of the previous English translation of Bonhoeffer's *Fiction from Prison* (Fortress Press, 1981); and author of numerous articles and bibliographical works on Bonhoeffer. His other publications include *Karl Barth: Theologian of Freedom* (Collins, 1989; Augsburg Fortress, 1991); *Churches, Cities, and Human Community* (Eerdmans, 1996); and chapters on Tillich, Marx, Cone, and Gutiérrez in *Critical Issues in Modern Religion* (Prentice-Hall, 1973, 1990).

NANCY LUKENS (Ph.D., University of Chicago) is Professor of German and Women's Studies at the University of New Hampshire, Durham, N.H., and a certified freelance translator. Her scholarly interests include German drama and the theatrical fool tradition, German Holocaust and resistance literature, GDR studies, feminist criticism and theory, literary translation, and translation theory. She encountered Bonhoeffer's work as an undergraduate and has been a member of the International Bonhoeffer Society since 1980. As a Humboldt Foundation fellow in Berlin her research focused on the literary and intellectual history of anti-Nazi conspirators including Adam von Trott and Dietrich Bonhoeffer. Her translations of Bonhoeffer's prison poems appeared in *A Testament to Freedom: The Essential Writings of Dietrich Bonhoeffer* and in *Sojourners Magazine;* she also created subtitles for the film *Dietrich Bonhoeffer: Memories and Perspectives.* A member of the editorial board of the *Dietrich Bonhoeffer Works,* she is co-translator of volume 1 of the English edition, *Sanctorum Communio: A Theological Study of the Sociology of the Church.* She is also co-editor and co-translator of *Daughters of Eve: Women Writers of the German Democratic Republic* (1993).